'THANK YOU FOR YOUR BUSINESS':
THE JEWISH CONTRIBUTION TO THE BRITISH ECONOMY

pears
foundation

The publication of this book would not have been
possible without the generous support of
Graham Edwards and the Pears Foundation.

'THANK YOU FOR YOUR BUSINESS':

The Jewish Contribution to the British Economy

DEREK TAYLOR

VALLENTINE MITCHELL

LONDON • PORTLAND, OR

First published in 2013 by Vallentine Mitchell

Middlesex House,	920 NE 58th Avenue, Suite 300
29/45 High Street, Edgware,	Portland, Oregon,
Middlesex HA8 7UU, UK	97213-3786, USA

www.vmbooks.com

British Library Cataloguing in Publication Data

Taylor, Derek, 1932 Aug. 5-
'Thank you for your business' : the Jewish contribution to
the British economy, 1655-2012.
1. Jewish businesspeople--Great Britain--History.
2. Jews--Commerce--Great Britain--History. 3. Jews--
Great Britain--Economic conditions.
I. Title
338'.04'089924'041-dc23

ISBN 978 0 85303 853 5 (cloth)
ISBN 978 0 85303 916 7 (paper)
ISBN 978 0 85303 985 3 (ebook)

Library of Congress Cataloging in Publication Data
Catalogue record has been applied for

Printed by CPI Group (UK) Ltd, Croydon, CR0 4YY

Contents

For Diane

Plates

1. Airfix – the Tiger Moth construction kit was just one best seller.
2. Amstrad's CPC464 – great marketing builds on great inventions. Photograph by Bill Bertram.
3. Archie Shine furniture, designed by Robert Heritage, is in the V&A. Photograph by courtesy of Michelle Hanlon: made-good.com.
4. El Horria (Mahroussa) yacht built on the Isle of Dogs by Samuda Brothers. Photograph by Lawrence Dalli.
5. Forman's Smoked Salmon, the best of British haute cuisine.
6. The Gestetner Cyclostyle copying machine, 1910. The ultimate accolade, a generic term: To Gestetner.
7. Glaxo's 'Builds Bonnie Babies' campaign – from impoverished beginnings to international fame.
8. The original Marks & Spencer Penny Bazaar, where it all started.
9. The Multitone VPM Vacuum Tube Hearing Aid, 1937. Multitone provided Winston Churchill with his hearing aids. Photograph courtesy of hearingaidmuseum.com
10. The Pantherella factory in Britain where Pantherella's long socks are still made.
11. Tucks - the populariser of Christmas cards, postcards and jigsaw puzzles. Courtesy of tuckdb.org.
12. Moss Bros store fascia, circa 1920. Moss Bros provided court dress for the first Labour cabinet. Courtesy of Moss Bros Group PLC.
13. First World War Decca portable gramophone – to while away the terrible hours in the trenches. Courtesy of John Sleep Gramophones.
14. Interior of the Kilburn State Cinema showing stairs to circle, wall, Wurlitzer and screen. The Palaces of the People – and the State Kilburn chandeliers had more bulbs than those at Buckingham Palace. Photograph by Malcolm Barres-Baker. Courtesy of Brent archives.

15. The Triumph 1919 Type H for the motorcycle Formula 1 races of its day. Courtesy of Triumph Motorcycles Ltd.
16. Ford Zodiac MK2 Corgi Car. Corgi produced so many cars, it was like General Motors. Courtesy of Sir David Michels.

HM Treasury, 1 Horse Guards Road, London, SW1A 2HQ

When in 2010 I addressed the 250th Anniversary Dinner of the Board of Deputies of British Jews I said that the Anglo-Jewish community had not only 'become a vibrant, generous and fully integrated part of our society today' but that it also 'encapsulated the spirit of enterprise and innovation' in our economy.

It is clear to see why. As Derek sets out in this book, Jewish people were the innovators behind postcards and jigsaw puzzles. They were the business brains behind Lyons and Burtons. Marks and Spencer, Tesco, General Electric and Shell all have Jewish roots. In finance, some of the most influential figures in the history of the City, such as Siegmund Warburg and Marcus Samuel, were Jewish.

That is why I think this is a story worth telling. And I cannot think of anyone better to do so than Derek Taylor. Few people are able to bring together such ample experience in business and deep knowledge of history. This book is an important contribution to our society's understanding of the great service the Jewish community has made to the British economy over the centuries. It is a contribution which we should all celebrate. I am, for one, very grateful for their business.

Rt Hon. George Osborne, MP

Introduction

Jewish Success in British Business

In recent years it has become a commonplace among academics and commentators to assert that the descendants of the Jewish mass migration have successfully integrated into western societies. The evidence to support these claims of a particularly successful outcome for the Jewish path to integration was undeniable by the latter quarter of the twentieth century. It is worth reflecting on the impact these successive surveys and historical studies on Jewish upward social mobility in the West have had in order to better understand the significance of Derek Taylor's, *The Jewish Contribution to the British Economy*, which compiles case upon case of successful Jewish businessmen (and the occasional women) in British business.

The destruction of European Jewry in the Holocaust changed forever the character of that Diaspora, with the world Jewish population's centre of gravity shifting from Yiddish Eastern Europe to the Anglo-dominated cultures of the United States, Britain and the Dominions. In 1880 almost 80 per cent of world Jewry lived in Eastern Europe, less than 5 per cent in the Anglophone world. By 1914 mass migration meant that around one-in-three Jews lived in Anglo-cultures, although still in Yiddish-dominated enclaves. But by 1948 outside Britain and the Soviet Union, European Jewry was almost annihilated, and half of the much-reduced world Jewish population lived in Anglophone countries; most of the remnant in non-Soviet Europe left for the new State of Israel. The world's Jewish Diaspora had become irrevocably Anglophone. And in this Anglophone world, Diaspora Jewry were doing rather well.[1]

In the United States a 1984 survey concluded that Jewish incomes were higher than any other religious group.[2] In Canada the 1970 census confirmed that Canadian Jews enjoyed a higher income than average.[3] The *Jewish Chronicle* reported that the median Jewish household income in Britain was sufficiently high to be included in the top decile of all British households. Among smaller Diaspora communities elsewhere the story was similar. In South Africa, Australia and New Zealand, Jewish families by the final quarter of the twentieth century enjoyed prosperous, middle-class lifestyles. If income growth like this had occurred across a nation, we would have to rewrite twentieth century economic history text books. Among this population, all from a common cultural background, something quite exceptional had happened over the course of three generations of settlement in Anglophone nations. But it is difficult to really know what.

Evidence for earlier in the twentieth century is scarcer. But it remains the case that, where the evidence exists, Jewish incomes had already attained relatively high levels; indeed, higher than could be expected. In his path-breaking article 'The Earnings and Human Capital of America's Jews', Barry Chiswick reported that second-generation Jewish immigrants in the United States were enjoying exceptionally high-income levels by the 1950s, not only compared with any other comparable non-Jewish second-generation immigrants, but also with native-born Americans.[4] At first the common explanation of such relatively high incomes was thought to rest on the Jewish community's famed concentration in the high-earning professions, especially law and medicine. The exceptional ability of the Jews to move into the professions was, it was claimed, an outcome from earlier over-representation in higher education. As 'the Jewish presence on campuses swelled …, [c]ontact probabilities shifted, producing greater exposure to gentiles, which in turn accelerated the Jewish "structural assimilation" into the American mainstream', and especially into the professions.[5]

The argument is an elegant and simple algorithm, relating over-representation in university attendance to subsequent professional status and income levels. The key to progress among the Jews therefore was their specific thirst for learning, a cultural attribute that provided the motivation for pursuing student qualifications. The difficulty, however, is that the basic data don't support such a logical flow. When the longer time frame of the entire twentieth-century assimilation experience is considered, and when the experience of other Diaspora communities elsewhere is taken into account, the actual explanation of the disproportionate Jewish presence in the professions by 1980 seems more to be a consequence of previous income gains rather than their cause.[6]

Somewhere between 40 to 50 per cent of second generation East European Jewish immigrants in the United States went to college by the 1930s. But this didn't translate into mass professional status.[7] In 1940 around 15 per cent of native-born Jews were professionals, a share that was static in 1950, and increased only to 20 per cent by 1960. The long-held belief that the era of Roosevelt and the Second World War heralded the mass entry of second generation Jews into the professions simply does not materialize from the data.[8]

The level of professionalization among the Jewish community in Britain was similar by the end of the period, over 50 per cent by 2000. But the British Jewish experience of higher education has been wholly different. One careful study of a representative Jewish population in 1977 found that university graduates comprised 3 per cent of those aged 60 or more (and so born before 1917), 6 per cent of those aged 30 to 59 (and so born between 1918 and 1947), rising to 9 per cent of those aged 25 to 29, and 12 per cent of those aged 20 to 24. Assuming the normal age profile among the student body, this translates broadly into Jewish *under*-representation at British universities among those gaining their degrees in the 1930s, rising to parity among those gaining their degrees in the 1940s, with only slight over-representation emerging in the postwar era.[9] Compared to the American experience (where the *bon mot* was that a Jewish drop-out was an MA), British Jews avoided the university cloisters.[10]

In fact middle-class status was overwhelmingly dependent on self-employment among the Jewish immigrants in Britain and America, as well as Canada and, as much as the data can tell us, in South Africa, Australia and in New Zealand too. Not the professions.

Jewish over-representation among the self-employed should hardly come as any surprise. But as many studies have shown, self-employment itself may be more a status of refuge than of attainment, reflecting the barriers to progression in the wider labour market.[11] And the Jews were no strangers to discrimination. Indeed much of their historic propensity to entrepreneurship may well owe its origins to legal prohibitions against Jewish land ownership. In Eastern Europe, for example, the Jewish population was subject to an increasing number of discriminatory laws that pushed them to the very margins of economic subsistence.

There is no systematic source of evidence on Jewish income levels in Eastern Europe, but in the Pale of Settlement in the late-1890s income levels were so low that one-in-five families received charitable relief. Underemployment was pervasive. Perhaps as many as one-in-three men was described by contemporaries as '*Luftmensch'n*', or those who lived off air, because they had no way of earning sufficient funds to pay for food.[12] Unemployment among the Jews in the Pale was at levels not seen elsewhere until the worst of the Great Depression of the 1930s. Within this dysfunctional labour market, Kahan estimated that almost 60 per cent of the Jewish workforce was self-employed.[13] In the depressed Lithuanian region, Jewish self-employment was even higher, despite Jewish wages being only half to a third of those in the Southwestern and Southern regions of the Pale.[14] In Germany in 1882, 70 per cent of Jews in Munich were self-employed, despite very high Jewish poverty rates then.[15] From the perspective of contemporaries, the high rates of self-employment were far from being strong indicators of labour market success; they were thought to be part of the problem. Entrepreneurship levels alone cannot be equated with successful labour market integration. Income must be the arbiter of that.

It is the history of upward mobility and higher income attainment *en masse* that sets the Jewish experience in Anglophone nations apart from other immigrant populations. This is the evidence that has provided such a powerful model advocated as a path for more recent ethnic minorities to follow; the classic example of integration into western societies through ethnic entrepreneurship. Yet this remains a strikingly underemphasized feature of Jewish historiography. Perhaps when compared with the other remarkable events of the twentieth century, Jewish historians attach less drama to the simple activities of earning a living. Perhaps, as we shall see, the weight of successive generations of hostility from Jewish intellectuals toward entrepreneurship has robbed the account of successful integration of the significance it ought to carry. Perhaps simply because it was so common for second generation Jews in Anglophone countries to acquire middle-class status and high incomes, nobody thought that it was anything out of the ordinary. But when compared with either contemporary or current immigrant populations, the Jewish route was clearly exceptional.

Derek Taylor's contribution to this research agenda, identifying and compiling a far greater volume of case studies of successful Jewish entrepreneurs in Britain than anyone before, is therefore timely and highly valued. But important questions remain. First, if what was truly exceptional about Jewish immigrant entrepreneurship in the West was that it was so widespread, powering the upward social mobility of the mass, then even the three hundred examples that follow represents only a tiny minority of the true number of Jewish entrepreneurs in Britain. In which case we need to understand more clearly how these examples of successful entrepreneurs differ from the still hidden majority.

Moreover, we are still no closer to explaining Jewish immigrant entrepreneurial success. Perhaps the most popular set of explanations, repeated here by Derek Taylor, emphasize that there is no single element of Jewish culture that is the key determinant of Jewish success. Barry Chiswick was able to demonstrate that American Jewish occupational attainment could not be explained by investment in education, or residential location, nor discrimination in favour of Jews among the mainstream labour market. But rather 'from cultural characteristics that enable Jews to acquire more units of human capital per dollar of investment ... or there are cultural characteristics that enable Jews to be more productive in the labour market with the human capital embodied in them'.[16] But what cultural characteristics might these be?

A common theme has been to emphasize how Jewish culture has developed in response to generations of persecution, responses that have led to a particular set of attitudes helpful to economic activity. Nathan Glazer commenting in 1950, for instance, suggested that the link might be between the propensity towards 'middle class' occupations in the Pale of Settlement and subsequent upward mobility among second-generation immigrants in the United States.[17] Simon Kuznets articulated one possible mechanism especially clearly, suggesting that the most important elements of the transfer of East European Jewish human capital into the United States were a 'fundamental capacity for social organization and for adjustment to the challenges of a new environment. [Arising from] the long-standing scale of priorities inherited from the past and likely to shape the goals of immigrants and their descendants for several generations after their arrival in the country of destination.' Persecution led to better entrepreneurship. Similar echoes can be found in the work of Thomas Sowell.[18]

These all may very well be true. And while it is very difficult to think of how a pertinent hypothesis could be constructed, never mind refuted, the greatest hurdle to overcome before stressing the advantages of East European Yiddish culture to Jewish integration in the West is that it flies in the face of what contemporaries believed. Opinions of the likely effect of East European Jewish culture on the likely progress of East European Jews in the American and British immigrant milieus of the day were in fact unequivocal, but in an entirely opposite direction than that presumed by the later commentators. East European Orthodox Jewish culture was criticized, often from within, for its obscurantism, for its concern with matters of ritual, its backwardness and its tribalism, for its unsuitability for modern living, and for its adherence to characteristics considered by some to be incompatible with normal business life. Even those criticisms that came from beyond the Jewish community cannot simply be dismissed as views from crackpots and racists.

In part this was a result of a vigorous Jewish intellectual movement in the nineteenth century that saw the atypical occupational structure in Europe as a barrier to assimilation. Change the occupational structure to reflect the norm of the surrounding societies, the argument went, and much of the justification for anti-Semitism would disappear.[19] Turn-of-the-century Jewish intellectuals, therefore, did their utmost to emphasize elements within the Jewish economy that appeared to be 'modern', and to denounce those, like a disproportionate level of self-employment and the attitudes that sustained it, that they saw as backward.[20]

There is in other words, with contributions like Derek Taylor's building on the works of others, increasing evidence about the characteristics of the Jewish immigrant population and its successful entrepreneurship.

Andrew Godley
Henley Business School, University of Reading

NOTES

1. Lloyd Gartner, *History of the Jews in Modern Times* (Oxford: Oxford University Press, 2001), chs 7, 8 and 9 for an overview. East European immigration to Australia and New Zealand was far smaller and so represents a much smaller proportion of the Jewish communities there than for the US, British, Canadian and South African Jewish populations. Australia and New Zealand are strictly speaking not comparable cases, therefore. See Hilary Rubinstein, *The Jews in Victoria, 1835–1985* (London and Sydney: George Allen and Unwin, 1986), especially the Appendix by Bill Rubinstein; Michael King, *History of New Zealand* (Auckland: Penguin, 2003), pp.370–1; Jacob Lestschinsky, 'Jewish Migrations, 1840–1946', in L. Finkelstein (ed.), *The Jews: their History, Culture and Religion* (New York: Jewish Encyclopedic Handbooks, 1946), Vol.1, pp.407–30.
2. Hilary Rubinstein, Dan Cohn-Sherbok, Abraham Edelheit and William Rubinstein, *The Jews in the Modern World: A History since 1750* (London: Arnold, 2002), p.420.
3. Reported in Barry Chiswick, 'The Earnings and Human Capital of American Jews', *Journal of Human Resources* 18, no.3 (1983), p.330, n.23.
4. Ibid. Jews outstripped native-born American earnings if they had completed elementary education.
5. Joel Perlman and Roger Waldinger, 'Immigrants Past and Present: A Reconsideration', in Charles Hirschman, Philip Kasinitz and Josh DeWind (eds), *The Handbook of International Migration: The American Experience* (New York: Russell Sage Foundation, 1999), p.233.
6. There were also formal religious barriers on university entrance in the UK, covered by Bill Rubinstein, *History of the Jews in the English-Speaking World: Great Britain* (Basingstoke: Macmillan, 1996). Nevertheless there are several examples of first generation immigrants becoming professionals in Andrew Godley, *Jewish Immigrant Entrepreneurship in New York and London, 1880–1914* (Basingstoke: Macmillan, 2001); and Thomas Kessner, *The Golden Door: Italian and Jewish Immigrant Mobility in New York City, 1880–1915* (New York: Oxford University Press, 1977).
7. Andrew Greeley, *Ethnicity, Denomination and Inequality* (Beverly Hills, CA: Sage, 1976), p.32.
8. Gary Gerstle, *American Crucible: Race and Nation in the Twentieth Century* (Princeton, NJ and Oxford: Princeton University Press, 2002); Barry Chiswick, 'The Occupational Attainment and Earnings of American Jewry, 1890–1990', *Contemporary Jewry* 20 (1999), chart 1.
9. Rubinstein, *History of the Jews in the English-Speaking World*, p.401.
10. Rubinstein's *History of the Jews in the English-Speaking World* is the source of the witticism. See Harold Pollins, *An Economic History of the Jews in Britain* (Madison, NJ: Fairleigh Dickson University Press, 1982); and Vivien Lipman, *A Social History of the Jews in England* (London: Watts, 1954), more generally.
11. David Storey, *Understanding the Small Business Sector* (London: Routledge, 1994); Graham Bannock and John Stanworth, *The Making of Entrepreneurs* (London: Small Business Research Trust, 1990).
12. Lucien Wolf, *The Legal Sufferings of the Jews in Russia* (London: T.F. Unwin, 1912); Beatrice Baskerville, *The Polish Jew: His Social and Economic Value* (London: Macmillan, 1906); Simon Dubnow, *History of the Jews in Russia and Poland*, three volumes (New York: Jewish Publication Society of America, 1916).
13. Arcadius Kahan, 'The Impact of Industrialization in Tsarist Russia on the Socioeconomic Conditions of the Jewish Population', in Arcadius Kahan, *Essays in Jewish Social and Economic History*, ed. Roger Weiss (Chicago, IL and London: University of Chicago Press, 1986), p.7 for self-employment, and pp.44–5 for poverty.
14. Kahan, 'Impact of Industrialization', p.22, Table 8 gives comparative values of output per workers, and it is reasonable to assume wages were in a roughly constant proportion to this.
15. Derek Penslar, *Shylock's Children: Economics and Jewish Identity in Modern Europe* (Berkeley and Los Angeles, CA: University of California Press, 2001), p.129, and on poverty levels in Germany and Austria, pp.179–82.
16. Chiswick, 'Earnings and Human Capital', p.334.
17. Nathan Glazer, 'The Economic Structure of Jewry', in L. Finkelstein (ed.), *The Jews: their History, Culture and Religion* (New York: Jewish Encyclopedic Handbooks, 1946).

18. Simon Kuznets, *Immigration of Russian Jews to the United States* (Cambridge, MA: Charles Warren Center for Studies in American History, 1975), p.124. See also Simon Kuznets, 'Economic Structure and Life of the Jews', in L. Finkelstein (ed.), *The Jews: their History, Culture and Religion* (New York: Jewish Encyclopedic Handbooks, 1946); Thomas Sowell, *Markets and Minorities* (New York: Basic Books, 1981); and Thomas Sowell, *Migrations And Cultures: A World View* (New York: Basic Books, 1996). An excellent survey is in Harold Pollins, 'Immigrants and Minorities – The Outsiders in Business', *Immigrants and Minorities* 8 (1989); also see N. Gross, 'Entrepreneurship of Religious and Ethnic Minorities', *Zietschrift für Unternehmensgeschichte* 64 (1992); and Stephen Aris, *The Jews in Business* (London: Jonathan Cape, 1970), esp. pp.228–34.

19. Rubinstein et al., *Jews in the Modern World*, pp.418–19.

20. A good example is Isaac M. Rubinov, *Economic Conditions of the Jews in Russia* (Bulletin #15, United States Bureau of Labor, Washington DC, 1907).

Chapter one

The Story So Far

Britain in 2012 is a multi-cultural nation with a large number of ethnic communities. One of the oldest is the Jewish community, and they have retained their separate existence for over 300 years, while still playing a full part in the life of the country. How has this been achieved? Why didn't they disappear? How were so many of them able to climb out of terrible poverty, with no education, in a country whose language the immigrants couldn't even speak? What lessons might there be for other ethnic communities or, indeed, for the nation at large? It will surely be worthwhile to look into their stories more deeply.

The Jews were officially allowed back into England by Charles II in 1661. Oliver Cromwell had told the authorities that if they wanted to return, they were not to be harassed, but no law on the subject was ever passed. Which was just as well for them, because almost every law that Cromwell promulgated, Charles abrogated. From the point of view of the king, when he finally got back on the throne, he was well aware that the Jews had been helpful to him financially when he was in exile in Amsterdam.[1] At the time, he had promised to aid them in return, if he regained the throne. When he turned down a request from a City of London delegation to have them expelled again in 1661, he probably regarded the return of the Jewish community as a sensible precaution, for he might well have needed their support once more if he had to set out on his travels again.

Over the next 200 years the number of Jews in Britain increased, but only very slowly. In 1851, the population of Great Britain and Ireland was 20 million, of whom about 35,000 were Jews. That's about 0.175 per cent of the population. In 2012, the population will be about 60 million in the UK and Northern Ireland, and approximately 300,000 of them will be Jews, about 0.5 per cent of the population. This increase is largely due to the number of immigrants who were taken in by Britain in two waves; the results of pogroms and the Russian May Laws in Eastern Europe between 1880 and 1914, and refugees from Nazism during the 1930s.

There were, however, other smaller waves. One was the influx of Jews from Gibraltar, who came to London when the Rock was shelled by the Spanish between 1779 and 1782. The whole population had to be evacuated and a considerable number of Gibraltarian Jews stayed in Britain. The newcomers played an important role in strengthening the Sephardi community, Mediterranean in origin, which had been diminishing over the years through intermarriage.

There was also a considerable intake from Europe after the revolutions of 1848 had been put down by autocratic continental monarchies. Britain and Russia were the only major European countries not to be seriously affected by revolution, and Queen Victoria looked a much safer bet to the migrants than the czars.

Again, after 1948, the Middle Eastern Jewish communities in Arab countries came under severe pressure and largely migrated. The same applied after the fall of the Shah of Iran in 1979. From the 1960s onwards, there was a considerable influx from South Africa, where the excesses of apartheid were anathema to many of those brought up with a very different cultural background.

The successive waves came from different business backgrounds. While most immigrants lived and died without becoming in any way prominent in the business world, those who did make their mark very often had their roots in the economies of the countries from which they came. So the Sephardim arriving in the late seventeenth century were brokers and merchants, as they had been in Amsterdam, from where many of them had come. The Gibraltarians were international traders. The Germans, who came around 1848, had often had a good scientific training, which was more difficult to obtain in Britain. On the other hand, the refugees from Russian pogroms were impoverished, and it was normally their children who developed major businesses in the late nineteenth and twentieth centuries.

The refugees from Nazism had very varied backgrounds, but were more likely to come from middle-class families. The Middle East communities had provided the sophistication in business which was much needed in tribal Arab societies. Some of those refugees came from rich and powerful families, but if they were from among the rank and file, they were more likely to go to Israel. There are always exceptions, of course, but this is the overall picture.

The growth in the size of the Jewish community in Britain always depended on immigrants, as there was a constant decline in the existing population through the loss of those who gave up the religion. It is only in recent years that there has been a degree of stabilization, due to the growth of the very Orthodox section of the community who believe in having large families. Indeed, after the Holocaust, there was a dedication in their community to replace those slaughtered in order totally to negate the Nazi 'Final Solution'.

When examining the Jewish contribution to the British economy over 350 years, the temptation is to reject the facts as totally outlandish. As Lord Chris Patten, the former EU Commissioner for External Affairs, said: 'How do we pass over the extraordinary Jewish contribution – out of all proportion to their beleaguered numbers – to what we call European civilization?'[2] The extent of the list of major British companies founded by Jews bears no relation to the size of their tiny community: British Land, Clayton Aniline, Compass, GEC, Granada, Grand Metropolitan, GUS, Hammersons, Harland and Wolff, ICI, Ladbrokes, Lyons, Mocatta and Goldsmid, Rothschilds, H. Samuel, Samuel Montagu, Shell, Tesco, Warburgs and WPP are just a score of them. The book, in fact, covers well over 300 more.

How could such a tiny group, whose only common factor was the religion of its members, manage to make such an impact when, at various times, they were excluded from serving in the armed forces, attending university, being elected to Parliament, joining a guild, or occupying municipal office? To answer the question obviously involves generalizations. And there are always exceptions to generalizations. Nevertheless, a number of conclusions suggest themselves from a study of the Jewish contribution, and these are worth setting down at the outset. When examining the individuals and the companies they created, these same themes will emerge time and time again.

To begin with, it would stick in the Jewish craw a little to give unintended credit where credit is due, but they do owe a great deal to their enemies. Expulsion and discrimination in some senses worked very much in their favour in the long run. Under pressure, it forced Jewish entrepreneurs to think 'outside the box', in a commercial world largely ruled by tradition. To find the gap. To always be ready to see the positive possibilities of a situation, no matter how unpromising.

For example, the five-day working week emerged in the 1960s. For the British hotel industry, there were two ways of looking at this development. One was to lament the elimination of the Friday-night businessmen market, because they wouldn't stay in hotels if they weren't working on Saturday. The other was to recognize that a vastly increased number of people would now have a two-day weekend and could go away more easily. It was the Jewish Max Joseph's Grand Metropolitan Hotels which developed what is now called the Short Break holiday market, to take advantage of the additional leisure time, and the company made a fortune in additional profits from it. The idea was, of course, copied and the total market is now estimated to be worth some £6 billion to the British hotel industry.

A civilized society, as against anarchy, depends on the mass of the citizenry accepting the laws and traditions of the country. These have usually been established for many years and have become part of the nation's way of life. It was different for the Jews. Certainly the Talmud, their law book, instructed them to obey the law of the country in which they lived and they fully accepted this. It was a third-century dictate – *dina de-malchuta dina*. The community was always, very largely, law-abiding.

The Talmud did not, however, insist that they should accept traditional practices which were *not* laws. On occasions they were even forbidden from participating in activities which were perfectly legal. A simple example is hunting; a traditional pursuit in Britain, but forbidden in the Talmud because it involves cruelty to animals. The Talmud permits killing an animal for food, but not hunting them for sport.

This principle extends a long way. When they were massacred by mobs, the murderers were often drunk. There came to be a saying '*shikker* is a *goy*', which translates as 'a drunk is a non-Jew'. The Jews didn't follow the national drinking tradition of many countries. The salutation in Britain is 'Cheers'. In Judaism it is '*Le Chaim*', which means 'To life'; it's part of thanking the Almighty for providing food and drink.

So the community always knew they were not automatically tied to fashionable attitudes. Phrases like 'There is nothing you can do about it', 'it has never been any different', 'the problem is much more complex than you think', 'you are focusing on the wrong issue' and 'everyone is doing it, so how can you object?' are not compelling arguments and explanations for Jews who have a centuries-old tradition that they are not expected to accept lame excuses for doing the wrong thing.[3]

The situation also applied to business. It might be accepted at the end of the nineteenth century that only rich people could afford made-to-measure suits. This was a recognized tradition – but it was not a law. So Montague Burton could ignore the precept and decide to produce made-to-measure suits at a price which less affluent people could pay. He thereby made a fortune, but was just one Jewish entrepreneur who looked for the hole in the market; the possibility of making a product which would appeal to the public but which it was believed was out of their reach.

This fellow feeling for the wishes of the general public came, in part, from the fact that the Jews were themselves from that class of society. Apart from a very small percentage of established families, the majority of Jews started their business lives in Britain by trying to claw their way out of poverty. When they did so, they were motivated to try even harder by the difficulty they had in being accepted by society; even the winners could be disqualified from membership by being labelled 'nouveau riche', and there were few social stigmas worse than that.

It wasn't just the fact that the immigrants might well have spoken grammatical Yiddish better than grammatical English. It wasn't just the foreign accents and the decision not to become Christians. It was the fact that they were condemned as common because they didn't know many of the rules and customs of polite British society. In a Britain which is today a far less class-ridden world, it is difficult to appreciate just how important those trifles were: that a proper suit had four sleeve buttons, that gentlemen wore waistcoats and that good manners included eating peas from the top of the fork and not scooping them up. In Britain, well after the Second World War, there was a mass of no-no's; camel hair coats, clip-on bow ties, ostentatious jewellery worn at the wrong time, suede shoes, cutting a bread roll with a knife, brightly coloured cars – particularly American models – metal watch straps, unfurled umbrellas – the list was a very long one.

Until comparatively recently Britain had a very strongly based class structure. Until the early part of the twentieth century, members of parliament weren't paid, and so only came from wealthy families. One third of the women who worked were in service. The officer corps was recruited mostly from the public schools. There was a saying about those who didn't conform: 'He doesn't know his place.' Most of the working classes were brought up to believe that their place was on the terraces of football clubs and in the public bars of pubs. A considerable number of Jews didn't know their place. They came from an ancient people and their Talmud was a body of law far in advance of those applying in monarchies and dictatorships all over the world. They would conform but, in private, they wouldn't kow-tow. If they were born into poverty, they believed there was no reason to stay there.

Even well after the Second World War, once labelled common – and 'common' was often the anti-Semite's rationale for discrimination – children would be turned down by public schools, applicants black-balled for membership of London clubs, golf and tennis clubs, good tables in restaurants were not available, many luxury hotels were full if your name was Cohen, and you would certainly not be selected as the Conservative candidate for a winnable seat. Before the Race Relations Acts, in the latter half of the twentieth century, it was perfectly legal for the *British Medical Journal* to advertise posts with the proviso that they were not available to 'Jews or men of colour'.

The reaction of Jewish entrepreneurs was often to retire into their shells when it came to their social lives, but to redouble their efforts in business to prove they were as good as anybody else. After all, these were almost all perfectly respectable citizens, good parents, honest tax payers and patriotic to boot. There was absolutely no justification for discrimination, and a lot of the victims fought back. It is true that the enemies of the Jews in other countries also subjected them to massacre and pogroms, special taxes and the ghetto system, but in Britain, none of that applied after the Restoration.

Their enemies provided them with another advantage. When the Jews were expelled from the Holy Land by the Romans, they moved to many different countries. When those countries oppressed them, they moved to others. For many, many centuries, however, moving was not the norm for other people. If you were born in an English village in the eighteenth century, the likelihood was that you would die in the same place and might never have ventured outside the locality.

For the majority of the inhabitants, travelling was difficult and dangerous, there was no economic need for it and the great majority of the citizenry certainly only spoke one language. Of course there were considerable exceptions; there was Latin in the Church, soldiers learned foreign languages fighting abroad, and there was sizeable emigration to escape economic hardship. Most people, however, stayed put.

This was not always an option for the Jews outside Britain. They were often expelled, or threatened with death or forced conversion if they didn't leave with despatch. They adapted to the situation. They had the language of the country they were born in, eventually the language of the country they fled to and their own polyglot language – Yiddish for the Ashkenazim (East European Jews) and Ladino for the Sephardim.

This was one reason why so many finished up in ports. Cargoes would arrive from other countries and there would be a local Jew who spoke the language of the crew. International trade was also always a possibility because they knew the ropes; in Morocco, for hundreds of years the Jews ran overseas trade for the sultan because nobody else knew how to manage it.[4] In Britain, they could also contribute, because the growth of the British Empire depended a great deal on its performance in international trade.

When countries protected their home industries by heavy import tariffs, British exports were adversely affected; it was always in Britain's interests to support free trade between nations. The crucial point came when the Corn Laws were repealed in 1846, adversely affecting British farmers but setting the country's posture firmly in favour of reducing import taxes on foreign goods internationally. This was very much the position of the Jews, who were far more comfortable trading around the world, because that is what they had been doing for so many centuries.

One unique advantage that they had in international trade came from their own resources – the Talmud again – in which could be found, in a large section called *Nezikin*, all the rules for conducting business. A Frenchman might feel unhappy about doing business with India where he didn't know if he would be paid or whether he would receive the goods he had ordered. The French Jew negotiating with the Indian Jew had no such worries; the conditions for conducting business were laid down in the Talmud in great detail.

Furthermore, there are Jewish courts available (called Beth Din) where qualified judges settle disputes between plaintiff and defender strictly according to these laws. Such judges have studied the Talmud and their certificates (*semicha*) specify that they are fit to make (*posken*) these judgements. These courts can be found wherever there is a sizeable Jewish community, but any traders who have a disagreement can put forward their evidence to Jewish courts thousands of miles away from either of them. The decisions are known as *responsa*. The more famous the court and its *rabbonim*, the more likely it is to receive requests to adjudicate from around the world.

Naturally, other religions have business laws as well but, for instance, between a Christian merchant and a Moslem merchant there could be differences in the laws of their respective countries. When only Jews are involved, national boundaries are not a factor.

The relevance of the laws of Judaism in conducting business remains intact after thousands of years. In disputes between themselves, the Jewish religious court can still hand down judgements based on the laws in the Talmud. That is if both parties agree to abide by their rulings. If they don't, of course, the British courts are always available.

The laws of Judaism are very extensive; there are over 600 commandments – *mitzvot*. Now if you have 600 commandments, you obviously need a word for 'obey' and in Hebrew – there isn't one! Judaism isn't about doing what you're told. The equivalent word for 'obey' is *shema*, which means 'listen'. That a Jew should listen, understand, evaluate and then come to the conclusion on his or her own volition that they should carry out the laws. The culture is about thinking for yourself, not taking orders. The laws of dictatorships demand that you do what the law lays down or suffer the consequences; it is noticeable in such societies that the ordinary citizen mostly looks for instruction from the authorities. This makes it much more difficult to concentrate on coming up with one's own new ideas. The Talmud gives the Jews that other advantage.

There is a corollary to this. The Jews knew from bitter experience on the Continent that they could not rely on the governments of many countries in which they lived to look after them; the government could well be the enemy. They were on their own, and that made self-reliance an essential perquisite to survival. It was a quality that became ingrained in their culture and it stood them in very good stead when they tried to build up businesses. It was another gift from their enemies.

In Judaism the importance of giving to charity has a very high priority. Every autumn, on the day of the festival of Yom Kippur, Orthodox Jews believe that the Almighty decides who will live and who will die in the coming year. The only chance of getting the Almighty to change His mind is to practise penitence, prayer and charity. It is partly this taking out of insurance that has led to them earning a well-deserved reputation for being among the best fund raisers in the country. In recent years, that task has been given to Jews by both the Conservative and Labour Parties. This book is peppered with examples of the massive contributions they have made to a host of good causes, both Jewish and non-Jewish.

A considerable number of towns throughout the country have benefited; Arnold Ziff of Stylo was a great Leeds benefactor. The Djanogly family did a lot for Nottingham. The businesses Jews built in provincial cities sustained the local economy and provided much-needed jobs; Lord Schon in Whitehaven, Fred Worms in Swansea, Gustav Wolff in Belfast, Siegfried Bettmann in Coventry and Mac Goldsmith in Leicester, to name just a few.

This attitude to doing good deeds, however, extends beyond Yom Kippur. It is part of the effort needed to merit the greatest compliment one Jew can give another – that he is a *mensch*. A *mensch* is not just a kind man or woman. It is someone who positively searches for ways to do good. As a consequence, the sheer size of the charitable donations of members of the community is also remarkable: an Oxford and a Cambridge college financed by Sir Isaac Wolfson; Lord Fink's £13.75 million to found the Oxford-Man Institution of Quantitative Finance; Lloyd Dorfman's £10 million to the National Theatre. There are many equally generous examples.

It is also significant that few major Jewish companies have had bad relations between management and unions. It isn't just that some Jewish companies became yardsticks for how staff should be looked after, Marks and Spencer being the prime, though by no means only, example. It was also that the Jewish founders usually came from similar backgrounds to their work force; they weren't from the upper echelons of a class-conscious society. They knew the struggles of poverty and couldn't so easily be labelled as bosses grinding the faces of the poor, though sweat-shop owners were hard taskmasters.

Even discrimination in business could be turned into a positive benefit. The rulers of countries that were willing to accept Jews were often anxious to protect their own local trade-guild members from competition. They not only stopped Jews from becoming members of guilds; they would refuse to let them work in the industries represented by guilds, even on their own behalf. The only industries in which, in many countries, they were allowed to participate were ones that hadn't been exploited thus far; industries that were the result of new inventions and new discoveries. It was, therefore, not surprising that a Jew, Luis de Terres, who sailed with Columbus in 1492, is credited with introducing tobacco to Europe.[5] The Jews grew to seek out the opportunities created by new industries, and they still do.

As a community, they have a tendency to be self-employed. This, of course, leads to more Jews becoming entrepreneurs, and the historic reason is again down to their enemies. Orthodox Jews need time off to worship on the Sabbath and the festivals: when employed by non-Jews, these needs are often difficult to satisfy. They involve giving Jewish staff privileges which are not requested by the rest of the employees. Many Jews in the late nineteenth century, who had come from very Orthodox communities in Eastern Europe, could only find work in sweat shops, and would need new jobs every Monday morning. They would leave work on Friday afternoon, without the permission of their employer, to observe the Sabbath. The employer would dismiss them for taking the time off, and so they would need to start again. If they were self-employed, there was no similar problem.

As British society grew more secular, the embarrassment of asking for special treatment from non-Jewish employers remained, to a greater or lesser extent. It was not surprising that the results of a *Jewish Chronicle* survey in 1952 illustrated a popular solution. Research in one area of the country showed that out of 1,250 Jews earning their living in business, 69 per cent were self-employed, compared to a national average of 6 per cent.[6] This replicated a survey conducted in 1948 where, of 72,000 businesses in London, Manchester, Cardiff and Newcastle, 14 per cent were Jewish, even though the community was less than 1 per cent of the population.

Wherever a new industry emerged, there were often Jews who were keen to be involved from the outset. For example, many of the early American cinema moguls were Jewish, and in Britain they played their full part as well. Names like Lew Grade, Alexander Korda, Michael Balcon, the Boulting brothers, Essoldo cinemas – Esther, Solly and Dorothy Sheckman – and Oscar Deutsch with Odeon Cinemas. It is equally true that, when the industry declined, they would often look for alternative opportunities rather than go down with the ship. As is also normal, many sons and daughters would often not want to follow in the footsteps of their parents.

Many Jews succeeded because they were prepared to gamble. The downside, of course, is that gambling is the Jewish disease, just as alcoholism has blighted the lives of millions all over the world. The upside, however, is that Jews would be inclined to take risks where others lacked the courage. One reason was obvious; life was far more of a risk for Jews than for most other people. A change of government, a word from the pope, and there could be an expulsion or a crusade; everything from the plague, to a slump, to a lost war could be blamed on them, and often was. Many Arab propagandists today try to blame a Zionist plot for 9/11. Life was a risk, staying Jewish was a risk, putting your head above the parapet was a risk. They knew all about the need to gamble.

So gambling was in the blood and it stayed in the blood of many of them even after they were baptised. The founder of Hambros may have become a Christian when he was 15 years old, but in London he gambled wildly on the success of Cavour in Italy in the nineteenth century, where other merchant bankers wouldn't stick their necks out for what could easily have been a lost cause.[7]

In the post-war property boom in blitzed Britain, 70 per cent of the major property developers were Jewish, and success in that world was very much a gamble.[8] Max Joseph, whose Grand Metropolitan was the tenth-largest company in the UK in his time, was originally a property man and was well known to have, on many occasions, put the largest amount allowable on a single number at the roulette tables in Monte Carlo.[9] The ultimate fallback position for the Orthodox Jew was, 'G-d will provide'. If the future looked hopeless, there was always that possibility.

The prominence of Jews in the property world also illustrates two other factors: the longing for status and the need for inexpensive overheads. For centuries Jews were not allowed to own land. The churchwardens of St Katherine Creechurch had to rent the house in Creechurch Lane in the City to the Sephardim, when the community wanted to establish its first synagogue in Cromwell's time. When eventually they were allowed to own property, they could use it as concrete proof that they were as good as anybody else. It was also a major attraction if you only needed an office and a phone to begin trading, cutting out so many start-up exenses. Many a successful future entrepreneur started in his bedroom in the family home.

Over the centuries, the Jews were also spurred on by their enemies. Success was not just a desirable option, as it was for the average citizen; it could easily be a matter of life and death. Failure could not only lead to ruin for the individual, but privation for his family as well. Worse, in the centuries of the Inquisition, practising Judaism in secret could lead to being burnt at the stake for those who had been forcibly converted and were found out. Money might be desperately needed to buy off the executioners or flee the country. The habit of going the extra mile to achieve success was common. As Dr Johnson said, 'Depend upon it, sir, when a man knows he is to be hanged in a fortnight, it concentrates his mind wonderfully.'

The genuine threat of personal danger was a great incentive to sustain a strong work ethic as part of the culture. Jewish founders not only put in the hours, but made it clear to their management from the start that this was the way the company would be run. When the Indian head of Tata closed factories in Britain in 2011, he complained about what he perceived as the laziness of his British management. Whether true or not, this was not a modus operandi that would be tolerated in the successful Jewish companies.

If a willingness to gamble was often found in Jewish businessmen, there was another motive spurring on the founder of Hambros, Carl Joachim Hambro, and which was an equally common attribute. He wanted to prove he was as good as the pre-eminent international banking house of the time, Rothschilds.[10] If Rothschilds wouldn't take on a risk, often Hambro would, just to prove them wrong.

This is an attitude that will come up many times in studying the men and women who made the Jewish contribution to the economy. The approach is partly a resentment of discrimination and partly a well-developed competitive instinct, often grounded in fear. Then again, if a government tried to make them accept a subservient role, for no better reason than that they were Jews, then some of them would try to prove to the state that they were at least their equals. Being excluded, from Parliament, golf clubs, universities and hotels just strengthened their desire to find ways to fight back.

Where there is contempt for Jews, there has often been no recognition by the oppressors that those who are discriminated against might indeed fight back. Like Goliath, the critics see their opponents as cowed and craven before their overwhelming might. A lot of Jews, however, continue in the traditions of David; if you can out-think the opposition, it is still possible to win. One part of the strategy, however, is to lull that opposition into a false sense of superiority, and the entrepreneurs learned to be good negotiators.

To succeed in business, it is often necessary to accept abuse, patronizing attitudes and unfair treatment of all kinds; this can happen to anyone, but the ways of dealing with it differ. As Jews are a minority who stick to their own religion, they need their self-esteem to come from within, because it often doesn't come from without. If a Jew is denied the status he deserves, he must just shrug and get on with it – unless, of course, he wants to leave the religion and join the majority. This, however, doesn't always bring acceptance either – as Disraeli's career amply illustrates – but it gives him a better chance. Those who stay on board, though, might well crumble less easily when the going gets rough. So, if high-powered members of the business Establishment said it couldn't be done, this was a challenge to the Jews involved to prove them wrong. The subsequent profit from being right was nice, but the pleasure of proving the Establishment wrong was particularly enjoyable.

In some ways, the Jews wanted to conform. They certainly wanted to be accepted in society, allowed the same privileges as any other citizen, permitted to join the same clubs and occupy the same offices of state, even if these opportunities were denied them. At the same time, they had defended their right to be different for millennia. They knew they were seen as different and that nothing was going to change that fundamental fact; Judaism was not the mainstream religion, so they were different. Of course, as the years went by, the discrimination they had to put up with from the state – even in Britain on a minor scale – gradually decreased. But the pleasure of proving conventional opinion wrong remained a powerful stimulus.

So, within the Jewish communities, there would normally be a few who made a difference. They would do so because, by pulling themselves out of the gutter, they were not only able to prosper, but would also be able to take revenge on their oppressors. The conclusion must still be that the benefits they acquired from their foes were essential to their long-term success.

They had one additional advantage that didn't come from their enemies.

Go and visit a Jewish cemetery. The most important part of it is the chapel where the services are held before the bodies are buried. The most prestigious graves in the cemetery are those which are nearest the chapel. They are traditionally reserved for the wisest members of the community, not for the richest.

Judaism teaches that wisdom, not wealth, is to be admired. For a religious Jew, one of the main reasons why lending money was a popular career choice was that it didn't take much time. There would, therefore, be ample hours left over to study the Talmud, and this many of them did every day. Studying the Talmud, however, also developed the brain well beyond that of the average uneducated person. It may sound far-fetched in a secular society, but it is absolutely true that, for religious Jews, hours of studying the Talmud remained – and still remains – by far the most enjoyable and productive way to spend their days.

This emphasis on study focused them more on mental, rather than physical, activity. The jokes which a comedian like Jackie Mason makes, about how useless Jews are with their hands, produces roars of laughter from Jewish audiences, who recognize the truth within the humour. Given the choice, most would be more inclined to office work than to manual labour. This option wasn't available to refugee immigrants who worked as pedlars in the valleys, or in trades like tailoring, but as the community struggled out of poverty, the number of businessmen, lawyers, doctors and accountants increased.

One reason why the success of so many Jewish entrepreneurs was surprising is that they usually lacked the connections, which smoothed the paths of so many of their competitors. They didn't belong to the old-boy networks. They hadn't family connections to great enterprises, they didn't belong to public school coteries and university societies. There were only infrequently well-placed relatives to put them in a favoured position in a large organization which would, almost inevitably, lead to a seat on the Board of Directors later in life.

There were exceptions to this too, of course. When the community was looking for a successor to Chief Rabbi Solomon Herschell in 1842, one of the options was the chief rabbi of Hanover, Nathan Marcus Adler. It did his candidature no harm that he had made a good friend at

Hanover University back in Germany – Prince Albert! When he was appointed and Albert was preparing the Great Exhibition of 1851, he recruited Adler for the organizing committee.

That was the common way of making one's way in the world in Victorian Britain and, to some extent, it still is. Membership of the Bullingdon Club in Oxford and the senior offices of the Oxford and Cambridge Union Societies are useful stepping stones to fame and fortune. Future Jewish entrepreneurs seldom had such advantages until the twentieth century.

It would be expected that the immigrant Jews would make their mark in those industries they knew well. As we've seen, international trading, banking and broking were typical activities of the Sephardim. The broker Solomon Dormido was among the first to offer insurance on cargoes in 1655: the regulations for this business were also in the Talmud from post-biblical times. Jewish merchants also developed such essential instruments of international trade as letters of credit and bearer bonds.

Clothing and furniture were the industries of choice for those who came from Eastern Europe. What neither group in England specialized in, was anything scientific. The Jews in Britain only obtained full access to Oxford and Cambridge in 1871, so science was difficult to study. Where German immigrants after 1848 had that training, a number created industrial firms which were very beneficial to the UK economy.

One group of immigrants – the refugees from Europe before the Second World War – brought another attitude with them, which was to be particularly beneficial in the years to come: they were Europeans. They were not originally British, focused on the Commonwealth and Empire, steeped in British perspectives, as the Empire started to disintegrate a few years later. Indeed, when the German refugees first arrived in the 1930s, they aroused a good deal of adverse comment because of their continuing loyalty to German culture and mores. They criticized what they found in Britain, in the way of order and efficiency. The British belief in the effectiveness of 'muddling through' ran counter to the more Prussian attitudes in Germany.

Moreover, the refugees were genuine German patriots, long resident in the country and brought up to be patriotic to the fatherland; within many of the families there were men who had fought on the German side in the First World War. Nazism, they hoped against hope, was simply a passing phase.

Even though they were comprehensively disabused, it was men of this kind after the war who still looked at Europe with a very different attitude to much of British industry. They were just as comfortable trading in Europe as they were in English-speaking lands; Jacob Speiringen of Kangol and Bela Horwitz of Phaidon are typical examples. As a consequence, when they looked at exports, it was at least as likely that they would open branches in Europe as in the Commonwealth. When General de Gaulle sabotaged Britain's effort to join the Common Market in the 1960s, he dismissed Britain as not being European. That couldn't be said of those who had found refuge from Europe in the UK.

A number of the Jews who made a difference were unpopular in their companies, and were ditched as soon as the rest of the board could pluck up sufficient courage to drop the pilot. Many a company has foundered in the struggle to move from the regime of the entrepreneurial – and often very autocratic – founder, to the subsequent committee of men in grey-flannel suits, directors more anxious to look after their pensions, share options and company cars.

Fortunately, there is no need to judge which side was in the right. What is true is that the founders were often tough men, fighting against the odds in a world that did not intend to do them any favours. Matthew 5:3 says, 'Blessed are the meek: for they shall inherit the earth.' As the Jewish meek had done nothing of the sort for over a thousand years, the successful entrepreneurs regularly adopted a more forceful attitude.

The need to be strong and resolute can have a downside. It can lead to a view that you have to do whatever is necessary to succeed, because the odds are stacked against you. You can make a fallacious case that all's fair in love and business, because it isn't a level playing field. This can take you to another step in the argument that, as you consider the laws are unfair, it is, therefore, ethical to try to evade them. There are examples of Jewish businessmen who have been extremely successful and lost their companies, their freedom and even their lives by disobeying a law quite unnecessarily.

It was a non-Jew, Ivor Kreuger, the 'Swedish Match King', who for many years held the record for the highest level of embezzlement. Yet he didn't start to embezzle money between the wars until he was already a millionaire. Why bother? Because a few personalities can rationalize that there are laws which shouldn't apply to them. The Jewish business community, over the years, has had rotten apples like any other group. Grant, Kagan, Maxwell, Miller and Rachman are examples the Jewish community would rather forget.

It is, of course, ludicrous that the success of so many Jewish businessmen is explained away by anti-Semites as part of a dastardly international conspiracy, involving all Jews. It is true that Jews do stick together. So do Old Etonians, Freemasons, old soldiers' association comrades and members of Women's Institutes.

Happily, there is seldom anything threatening about people with common values, similar cultures and traditional practices remaining friends. To extrapolate this relationship into a major international conspiracy is, however, to assume a degree of organization, a level of discipline and an acceptance of a common purpose that is well beyond the capabilities of almost all organizations below – and often including – national governments. It is certainly beyond the Jews. Even fascism and communism had short lifespans; the Jews have survived for 5,000 years because they are members of a religion, not a movement for world domination.

There is one final theme which emerges. The regimes which create conditions that lead to the expulsion of their Jewish communities never seem to consider what they, themselves, might lose as a result. To give just a few typical examples, it was Sigmund Warburg who was forced out of Nazi Germany and, after the war, ensured that the Eurobond market was centred in the City of London. The Nazis also lost Eric Weiss, whose Foseco company today services the foundry industry worldwide. It was the Egyptian, Sir Ronald Cohen, who did so much to create venture capitalism. The Huguenots are a seventeenth-century example of another refugee community which benefited Britain; tolerance pays very large dividends.

The question arises, of course, as to whether culture and traditions can really still retain an influence over so many centuries. Can a people truly be inspired by what happened to them in mediaeval times, or by what was laid down in the Talmud? With the Jews, the traditions are built into their lives from birth. It goes down from generation to generation. The Holocaust ended seventy years ago, but it still influences the thinking of the vast majority of Jews. When they are described as 'the People of the Book', it is factually accurate. The new generations may not know the details of the past, but they are still influenced by them. There is a saying, *'selicht in der beiner'*, which means 'it's in the blood'.

In writing this book, I would first like to acknowledge the support I have received from the Pears Foundation and Graham Edwards. Many members of families of Jewish company founders have filled in gaps in the available information and I am grateful to them for their time and interest. I would also like to thank the *Jewish Chronicle* and the descendents of the Jewish founders for helping provide the illustrations. I am also indebted to my academic adviser, Oliver Westall of the University of Lancaster, Professor Aubrey Goodman of the University of Leicester, Richard Burton of the *Jewish Chronicle*, to my editor, Heather Marchant, to Nigel Wheale who markedly improved the manuscript, to Adam Gillard who helped with the illustrations, to Stanley Kalms, John Ritblat and Alex Brummer for their kind remarks, and to my wife, Diane, as always. The mistakes are mine, of course, and in a book which attempts to cover such a wide range of people, events and organizations, there will be some. I apologize now when they emerge, but it wasn't from a want of trying to avoid them.

NOTES

1. Derek Taylor, *British Chief Rabbis: 1664–2006* (London and Portland, OR: Vallentine Mitchell, 2007), p.16.
2. Chris Patten, *Not Quite the Diplomat. Home Truths about World Affairs* (Harmondsworth: Penguin, 2005), p.198.
3. David Selbourne, *Moral Evasion* (London: Centre for Policy Studies, 1998).
4. Derek Taylor, *Don Pacifico: The Acceptable Face of Gunboat Diplomacy* (London and Portland, OR: Vallentine Mitchell, 2008), p.13.
5. http://www.jewishencyclopedia.com/articles/14416-tobacco.
6. Stephen Aris, *The Jews in Business* (Harmondsworth: Pelican, 1970), p.69.

7. Joseph Wechsberg, *The Merchant Bankers* (London: Weidenfeld and Nicolson, 1966).
8. Oliver Marriott, *The Property Boom* (London: Hamish Hamilton, 1967).
9. In conversation with the author.
10. Wechsberg, *The Merchant Bankers*.

Chapter two

Slow Growth

Oliver Cromwell wanted the Jews to be allowed to live in England again for many reasons. One of them was that they had enemies in common; the English had beaten the Armada in 1588, but Spain remained a threat. The Jews hated Spain for its cruelty in expelling the community in 1492 and murdering so many of their co-religionists. They could also be helpful allies because they provided Cromwell with a spy network, which had already warned him of Charles II's plans to try to reconquer England for the crown.

There was however another major reason why the Jews could be useful. They were seriously involved in international trade and Cromwell needed them to oppose the Dutch, who were worthy opponents in the marketplaces of the world at the time. When the Jews started to set up a community in London, they were granted twelve positions as brokers in the City. When you consider that the number of all the other foreign brokers in London was also restricted to twelve, the treatment of the Jews powerfully acknowledged their economic nous.

From the beginning, therefore, they were recognized as being able to help the country's economy. Cromwell might well have known of Sir Francis Drake's voyage round the world which started from Plymouth in 1577. The navigator on board was recorded as Moses the Jew. Over the years the Jews competed in the Brazilian wood trade, the Indian diamond trade, and in many other overseas markets. They also proved their worth in times of war because they were experts in international finance.

To pay for William III's expedition, the Glorious Revolution, in 1688, the king was given an interest-free loan of two million crowns by Francisco Lopez Suasso in Amsterdam. Sir Solomon de Medina (c.1650–1730) also supplied William III with provisions for his army in the 1698 campaign against France. He was consequently owed over £40,000 and the king himself agreed a moratorium on the debt until it was repaid in 1702. It was not likely to have been a coincidence that de Medina was knighted in 1700, the first and last Jew to be so honoured for well over a hundred years thereafter. His importance can be calculated by the fact that his firm's turnover in 1702 was £83,000 – £129 million today if measured by average earnings.

Providing the king with money involved a major problem. From the late 1680s to the mid 1690s, the sheer volume of silver currency in the country constantly diminished. It was being sent overseas to centres like Amsterdam where it was melted down. The resulting blocks of silver could then be sold for more gold than the same amount of coinage would be worth in London. Bring the gold back to London, sell it for more silver and repeat the process. This was perfectly legal, but it started to cripple commercial activity in the country.[1] The ability of Jewish merchants, with their contacts in Amsterdam, to come up with the necessary funds was, therefore, vital to the successful operation of William's campaigns.

Solomon de Medina was also awarded the bread contract for the protracted campaigns in the War of the Spanish Succession. Between 1707 and 1711, he paid the British general, Marlborough, over £63,000 in bribes to keep the business. When this came out in a parliamentary enquiry, Marlborough was disgraced and de Medina's bills were not settled. He was nearly bankrupt when he died. Another Jewish contractor, Joseph Carizos, died in utter poverty when the government reneged on similar debts to him.

When William III needed finance, it was decided to launch a new company, to be called the Bank of England. The community invested in its launch and Moses da Costa (c.1670–1747), known as Anthony da Costa outside the synagogue, was a prominent shareholder. In 1694, the list of subscribers included many Jews. If you invested £500 you could vote, for £2,000 you were eligible to become a director, for £3,000 you could even try for deputy governor, and for £4,000, for governor. In 1701, almost 10 per cent of the £4,000 subscribers were Jewish.[2] This percentage increased in the latter half of the eighteenth century.

What the Sephardim were not interested in was the Royal Africa Company, which had the monopoly in the slave trade.[3] Neither did they fancy investing in what became known as the South Sea Bubble, a scheme which suckered in a large number of unfortunates who believed, unlike the Jews, that there was such a thing as a free lunch. The lists of shareholders of both companies had very few Jewish names on them.

The next occasion when the Jews were needed in time of war was 1715, when the Old Pretender, James Stuart, invaded the country. By this time, as Cromwell had hoped, the Jews had been successful in competing for foreign markets for England: 'they had engrossed the Portugal and Barbary (North African) trade to themselves ... that they were running a close race for that of Spain ... that they had got into their hands Barbados and Jamaica; and that by their foreign relations they regulated the course of the Exchanges.'[4]

That first crisis in 1715 found the community initially schizophrenic about whether to support the claims of King George of Hanover or the Stuart pretender to the throne. The problem was that James Stuart was in direct line of succession from his father, James II, and George was about fiftieth on the list. He was the first Protestant, though, and that was good enough for the government. The Sephardi ruling body, the Mahamad, voted 19–2 to support the government and George of Hanover. Jewish brokers, like Menassah Lopez, steadied the pound when the Stuarts invaded. The reputation of the community, as loyal to the crown, was even more firmly established.

Jews also imported gold at the time to improve the country's bullion reserves and they bought gilt-edged stock to stop its value declining. Where foreign bankers and investors had difficulty in knowing whom to trust if asked for money, the use of local Jewish intermediaries was a reassurance. They could offer that service because, in general, Jews trusted Jews wherever they lived. When James was defeated, the market recovered and the investors did very well, but it hadn't looked that likely when James first invaded. Fortunately for the government, the Jewish brokers were prepared to gamble on a massive scale.

In 1745, with the invasion of the Young Pretender, Bonnie Prince Charlie, the initial successes of the prince led to another shaky period for sterling. This time it was Samson Gideon (1699–1762) who came to the rescue. Gideon was one of the twelve Jewish brokers, and 'he advanced every guinea he possessed, he staked his credit and he held as much stock as all the remaining speculators together'.[5] When bank notes started to be sold at a discount if the payment for them was in gold, Gideon said he would buy them without any discount at all.

He 'proposed the subscription for circulating the bank notes and restoring their credit, and was one of the four persons that carried that Association, and there is now in Mr Gideon's hands the original papers and the signatures of above 1,300 merchants and others who signed in little more than one day which had that good effect that should be remembered'.[6] When, this time, Bonnie Prince Charlie was finally defeated, the brokers who had backed the government were again able to harvest very large profits as sterling recovered. As an additional benefit, they had also proved their loyalty to the crown up to the hilt once more. Gideon had invested a million pounds. He later quarreled with the community, had his children baptised, but left a will in which he asked to be buried in a Jewish cemetery.[7]

When Samson Gideon first began business as a 'jobber' in 1719, he estimated his capital worth that year at £1,500; in 1750 he estimated the sum as £180,000, some indication of his success. Gideon was a tough operator: 'His correspondence bears the imprint of an almost savage vigour and contempt of weakness or cowardice. He was uncouth in dress and sardonic in his humour.'[8] Nevertheless, the government very often looked to him for advice in the years up to his death in 1762. Horace Walpole wrote thereafter, 'Gideon, who is worth more than the whole land of Canaan, has left the reversion of his milk and honey, after his son and daughter and their children, to the Duke of Devonshire, without insisting on his taking the name, or even being circumcised.'[9]

Another Sephardi broker who supported the government was Joseph Salvador (1716–86) of Francis and Joseph Salvador. He was said to have raised a million pounds for the government in 1745 at two hours' notice.[10] After the death of the Gideons, the government referred to Salvador on many occasions to raise funds for them. He was an expert on public finance and advised the Treasury when the Duke of Newcastle was prime minister.

There are differing opinions about whether Salvador was the only Jew ever to have been made a director of the East India Company, but he was certainly made a Fellow of the Royal Society in 1759. He was also the leader of the seven Sephardi Deputados who called on George III in 1760 to offer the felicitations of the community on his accession. The Ashkenazi objected to not being invited to come along as well and, after some discussion, the Board of Deputies of British Jews was formed to represent both communities in their relations with the government. It still does. Salvador served as president of the Board until 1783.

His latter years were difficult as he lost a great deal of money in the Lisbon earthquake and in supporting a British government loan designed to pay for the Seven Years' War with France. Salvador took £250,000 of the stock and suffered when their value fell heavily in 1763. He had, however, also bought 100,000 acres in South Carolina for £2,000 in the same year, 1755. He kept afloat by selling parcels of the land until he died in 1786. Abraham Prado and David Mendes Da Costa supplied the British troops in the Seven Years War, as did David Franks in America and Aaron Hart in Canada.[11]

For most of the eighteenth century, the Jews were prominent in the Indian diamond trade. One of the most popular books in Victorian times was Jules Verne's *Around the World in 80 Days*, but the task of doing so seemed impossible at that time. It puts into perspective the astonishing scope of the logistics involved in the Indian diamond business 100 years before. First, you needed a base in India to buy and ship the diamonds. That was helpfully provided by, among others, the Jewish community in Goa in the west of India. It was a small Portuguese colony and the Jews were able to set up shop there, because the kings of Portugal wanted their help in developing the market; this was in spite of the fact that Jews were not allowed to live in Portugal itself. Only converts, known as New Christians, could do that.

In Portugal, the Inquisition was always likely to be seeking out those who clung to the faith and, if they were discovered they were all too often burnt at the stake. During the time of the Inquisition 1,500 Portuguese Jews were put to death in this inhuman way. Yet the Portuguese and the Jews still worked together in India.

Next you needed a method of payment, and the Indians favoured coral, which necessitated a town where it could be purchased. The kind of red coral the Indians wanted had been harvested from the Mediterranean for thousands of years. The preferred harbour was Leghorn, where the Medicis, to bolster its economy, had uniquely offered freedom of religion if Jews and other non-Catholics would come to live there. There was, as a result, a strong colony of Jews. 'Of the £1,600,000 worth of licences granted between 1750 and 1774 [in England] for the export of coral, as much as £1,200,000 (75 per cent) was issued to Jews.'[12] In general terms, the Sephardi merchants paid with coral and the Ashkenazi with silver.

Then you had to move the diamonds to the marketplace, which was Amsterdam but later became, to a considerable extent, the City of London. When Cromwell decided he could use some Jews back in England, one of the markets he hoped to gain from the Dutch was the trade in Indian diamonds, and they managed that for the country.

All this was in the days when, before you set out on a journey of a lot less than a thousand miles, it was customary for Jews to go into mourning for the departing traveller in case he didn't return. The small wooden ships could sink in storms, their navigation could be faulty and they might never be heard from again. They could be seized by pirates, decimated by disease or captured by whoever was the enemy that year. International trading was very dangerous indeed, but the market was still developed to the benefit of the British balance of trade. Buying and selling Indian diamonds benefited the country's economy until late into the eighteenth century. 'In the fifty years between 1717 and 1766 the importation of diamonds by Jews was greater than by non-Jews in all but four years.'[13] Salvador was a major exporter of coral to India and an importer of diamonds.

It is difficult to assess correctly the total Jewish contribution to Britain's overseas trade in the eighteenth century, because they often operated under English names. The Inquisition employed spies in London to try to identify Jews who had been converted in Spain or Portugal but had reverted to their former faith in London. If they found them, the families of those men could be persecuted back home. To avoid this, the Jews would use their own names in the synagogue but trade under English names in the outside world.

There is some evidence of Jewish involvement in the Brazilian wood trade, in American tobacco and in a number of other fields, but it is sparse overall, which reflects the fact that there was still only a small Jewish community in Britain.

The Industrial Revolution transformed the means of manufacture, introducing mass production. The problem then was to move all the goods around the country and through the ports. One solution was to improve the roads. This was absolutely essential. In the early part of the eighteenth century, there had been reports of horses drowning in potholes on the Great North Road. The government, therefore, started to create a system of turnpike roads, which were paid for by charging tolls at various points. The right to levy the charges was auctioned and one of the most successful of the entrepreneurs investing in this way was Lewis (Turnpike) Levy (1785–1856).

In 1832, when Levy was still under 50 years old, *The Times* labelled him 'Master of nearly all the toll gates within 15 miles of London'.[14] The tolls were also meant to maintain and illuminate the roads, but when Levy was taking between £400,000 and £500,000 a year, there was a large profit left over after such expenses. Even so, it was only those who were prepared to take the risk who enabled one of the key factors in British industrial growth to be satisfactorily developed before the invention of the railways.

Although the number of Jews in Britain increased considerably during the eighteenth century, there were still so few of them that they tended to concentrate in just a few economic areas. Most were poor, many were pedlars or used the few skills they had to scrape a living. A few branched out.

Lemon Hart (1768–1845) made rum for the navy in Penzance and the product is still to be found in pubs and off-licences today. Mayer Oppenheim produced such fine red (ruby) glass that he was granted the royal warrant from George II. Isaac Jacob Lazarus produced such excellent Bristol blue glass that he earned the royal warrant from George III, but the firm went bankrupt in 1820. Isaac Alexander in Colchester ran stage coaches to London, and from London to Brighton, but the railways eventually killed off his trade.

The 1715 and 1745 rebellions were, of course, small change compared to the Napoleonic Wars. These stretched, with a short break, over twenty years, and the national debt increased from £238 million in 1793 to £567 million in 1802, £735 million in 1810 and a staggering £1,004 million in 1816. Effectively, the government paid for the wars by introducing income tax, it issued a tremendous amount of gilt-edged stock, and Britain was also taken off the gold standard.

The invasion of the Old Pretender in 1715 and Bonnie Prince Charlie in 1745 had been short-lived affairs. They had also not turned out to be anything like as dangerous as had initially been thought. The Napoleonic Wars were very different. When Wellington described the victory at Waterloo as a 'damn close-run thing', it was only the climax of a conflict which had been going on between Britain and France, with a short interlude after the Peace of Amiens in 1801, for over two decades.

To pay for the conflict, government funds were offered to investors, but the First War Loan only attracted one offer. Although government stock had been $97\frac{1}{8}$ in 1792, it was down to 72 for the 1793 offer. Government stock was in £100 denominations and paid $3\frac{1}{2}$ per cent interest. So if you could buy £100's worth for £72, you were going to earn 5.2 per cent on your money. If the stock rose in value, say to 85, the interest rate would still be $3\frac{1}{2}$ per cent, but if you sold your holding, you'd make the difference between 72 and 85.

Of course, the stock could also go down and, if the war was lost, it would slump disastrously. So what was needed was investors who not only believed in a British victory, but were also patriotic enough to support the government with hard cash. In 1795, the offers for the £18 million the government wanted to raise came from a number of syndicates, including the Jewish brothers B. and A. Goldsmid.

Benjamin (1755–1808) and Abraham (1756–1810) Goldsmid were originally bill brokers; for a commission, they would take a note issued by a country bank and raise money for it in London. So, if a country bank lent £100, it would need the money to lend. It issued an IOU and a London investor would buy it at a discount. As the country bank would lend the money at a high rate of interest, everybody made a profit if the original borrower eventually paid off the debt.

At this point, however, the Goldsmids were moving into a much bigger league. They were already dealing in foreign exchange and raising loans, but now they were also trying to help the government pay for a major war.

Where the backing for all government funds had previously been in gold, now in 1797 the Bank of England's reserves had fallen from £10.5 million to £1.5 million and the offer to honour bills in specie had to be abandoned until 1821.

Not surprisingly, the parlous state of the currency led to a run on the pound and government bonds fell to 47¼. Even so, the general public started to buy the stock as a patriotic gesture. The decision as to who the government should select to raise the money was the responsibility of the chief cashier of the Bank of England and that executive, Abraham Newland, came to rely more and more on the Goldsmids and the Establishment's favourite, Baring Brothers. *The Times* referred to Abraham Goldsmid and Sir Francis Baring as 'the pillars of the City'. One reason why Newland favoured Goldsmid was that the City brokers would gang up on the government and demand high discounts on the bonds they sold. Goldsmid wouldn't join such a cartel and the government benefited accordingly. If some clubs wouldn't accept Jews, some Jews wouldn't join cartels.

It wasn't even that Britain just needed to pay for its own outgoings. The government gave subsidies to other countries who were prepared to fight the French: Russia, Prussia, Austria, Hanover and many others received financial help. By 1805, Britain needed £100 million a year just to pay the interest on all the loans.

The strain of raising the money bore heavily on the Goldsmids and, in 1808, Benjamin committed suicide. Abraham continued his efforts but, in 1810, Baring died in the middle of a military crisis. Abraham had kept £800,000 of the current issue in his own hands and, when the bonds dropped heavily in value, he committed suicide as well.

At this crucial moment, there stepped into the breach Nathan Mayer Rothschild (1777–1836). The story of the Rothschilds begins in the ghetto in Frankfurt, the *Judengasse*. They lived in a house with a red shield on the outside wall – *Zum Roter Schild*. So they changed their original name of Bauer to Rothschild. The founding father of the firm was Mayer Amschel Rothschild (1744–1812) who was a dealer in rare coins, and among his customers was Prince William, the elector of Hesse-Cassell.

When the king was forced into exile after Napoleon conquered his country in 1806, he gave his assets – some £550,000 – to Amschel Rothschild to invest in British government securities. It was the best way of ensuring that the money was safe. Amschel's son, Nathan Mayer, had gone to Manchester in 1798 to set up as a textile merchant, but when he was sent the money, he soon switched to being a banker.

The elector's money was not, in fact, invested in gilts by Rothschild. Nathaniel thought he had better uses for it and did, indeed, make a fortune out of investing it in the many opportunities for profit there were during the Napoleonic Wars. For example, brother James had gone to Paris in 1812 to set up a French branch of the family firm. When Wellington's army needed paying, James and Nathaniel between them got the money raised in Europe and transferred, through France, to Wellington in Spain.

There was much bribery involved, but it was patriotic as far as Nathaniel was concerned and there was also a substantial commission to be earned. Between 1811 and 1813, it was paid on a total of at least £21 million sent to pay the army. This successful operation made the Rothschild's name. If they had been unsuccessful, the population of Hesse-Cassell would have been facing higher taxes and the Rothschild story might have come to a premature end.

When the war was over, Rothschilds gave the elector his money back with all the interest it would have earned if it had been invested in British government securities. The surplus, which came from not doing so, they kept. The other Rothschild sons went to Vienna (Salomon in 1820), and Naples (Carl in 1821), while Amschel's oldest son, Amschel, stayed in Frankfurt.

After the war, the British economy needed London to be the key financial centre of the world. The prospects were good. Britain had won the war against Napoleon and most of the other major European nations were indebted to it for their freedom. So the nation began the post-war period in a favourable position. One market of particular importance was sovereign debt, the raising of money for governments worldwide. Unlike today, there were no international bodies at the time to rate a country's credit. If you were going to invest in a sovereign debt bond, the name of the company acting on behalf of the foreign government was the most important factor in judging your level of risk. Being a British firm helped.

Being the Rothschilds helped too, as the firm had a fine reputation internationally and were chosen to handle about 35 per cent of the loans launched between 1820 and 1830. Some loans were always going to be safe, because countries like Prussia and France were not going to default. Others were highly speculative. As James Rothschild wrote to Nathaniel on one occasion, 'We have a great many asses who have been buying this shit.'[15]

The Rothschilds were enormously charitable, with both Jewish and non-Jewish good causes benefiting. The family does not brag about their generosity. The Jews' Free School in London was founded to educate the children of the Jewish poor. Its house colours are blue and yellow, the colours of the Rothschilds, reflecting the support the school has always had from the family.

Equally quietly, the modern Rothschilds ensured the future of the Brady Street cemetery in the East End of London. Nathan Mayer Rothschild was buried there, but the cemetery was full by about 1880. Now the law is that, if no burials take place in a cemetery for 100 years, the bodies can be reinterred elsewhere and the cemetery used for other purposes. So in the 1980s the local council wanted to apply for permission to do just that on the Brady Street site. The Rothschilds, however, had no wish for their ancestors' remains to be so treated. When the third Lord Rothschild (1910–90) died, he was duly buried in Brady Street next to Nathan Mayer, and the cemetery will continue to be open now until at least 2090.

The companies promoting the bonds could make fortunes. B.A. Goldschmidt and Co., who promoted about 15 per cent of the loans before 1826, made a profit of £500,000 in 1825 and were valued at £1.5 million. They specialized, however, in Central and South America. Here the possibility of default was much greater. As a consequence, interest rates were higher and the stock could rise or fall in value to a much greater extent than for countries with sounder finances.

In 1826, there came a banking crisis and buyers for sovereign debt dried up. Too much of the stock was left with the issuing companies and Goldschmidts was only one of the greats in the City to go bankrupt. It happened on a Thursday, and on the following Saturday, Louis

Goldschmidt (1769–1826), the senior partner, suffered a fatal heart attack as a result of the shock. Goldschmidt's death was sincerely regretted and its cause considered avoidable. As a correspondent wrote in *The Times*, 'Support of this nature his own former acts of kindness in assisting others would have assured him, for no man could be more liberal than he was where the object was to assist a friend who had fallen into embarrassment.'[16]

The Rothschilds struggled through the 1826 crisis but were never in danger of going under. The core reason was that they were far better capitalized. They had over £4 million in their reserves and they simply hung on to the loan stock they were promoting until things improved. The power of the Rothschilds in international banking was immense for most of the nineteenth century. Between the end of the Napoleonic Wars and the start of the Great War they arranged eighteen government loans and raised £1,600,000,000 (about £135 billion today, using the Retail Price Index.). One other reason for the popularity of their loans was that the interest was always paid in sterling where, before, it had often been disbursed in more volatile foreign currencies.

The solidity of Rothschild loans was, however, ammunition for those who wanted to spread the fiction of a Jewish conspiracy to rule the world through the influence of their bankers, a story which is given credence in anti-Semitic circles to this day. Certainly, it was true that no country could fight a war without the necessary funds to finance the enormous expenditure involved. In Britain during the Glorious Revolution of 1689, the 1715 and 1745 crises and the Napoleonic Wars, the support which the government received from Jewish financiers was crucial, and their efforts were considered entirely beneficial and, therefore, welcomed. If you were a Stuart or a supporter of Napoleon, they would have been condemned. Similarly, the Jewish bankers during the nineteenth century more than pulled their weight in helping the country.

Opinion on Jewish participation depended on whose side you took, and anti-Semitic attacks on Jewish businessmen focused on their importance in the financial world. When William Cobbett attacked the Jews in Parliament in the 1830s, he said, 'usury is the only pursuit for which they are fit'. Thomas Macauley, the great historian, responded scathingly: 'Such, sir, has been in every age the reasoning of bigots. They never fail to plead in justification of persecution the vices which persecution has engendered.'[17] If you could call supporting the government a vice. The fact remained that offering tolerance brought any government, in return, substantial dividends from the Jewish community.

The Rothschilds were certainly involved in a great deal more than promoting war loans. Nathan Rothschild also raised $75 million to recompense the slave owners, dispossessed by the abolition of slavery. This loan 'was bigger, as a percentage of government spending, than the bailout of the banks' in recent years.[18]

By the middle of the nineteenth century, London was firmly entrenched as the major issuer of sovereign debt. The problem remained the number of countries that defaulted, so that investors lost their capital. Their protection was improved considerably by Isidor Gerstenberg (1821–76).

Gerstenberg was born in Breslau, where his family was comfortably off. His father was a teacher who also sold lottery tickets. In 1841, when he was 20, Gerstenberg went to Manchester to work for his uncle, but finding the town too dull for his taste, he moved on to London. He had a banking relative who probably lent him the money to set up in business as an exchange broker and, by 1852, he was sufficiently successful to launch his company on the stock exchange. He had many friends in the German émigré community and he served as a governor of the German Hospital from 1852 to 1875.

As a broker, Gerstenberg was keenly aware of the dangers of sovereign debt and, in 1866, he started to put together a sufficiently influential body of backers to create a new organization, the Council of Foreign Bond Holders. The idea was to negotiate with the governments of countries that defaulted to see what could be done for the victims. As he pointed out, the absence of such a body could lead to many good opportunities being missed. The orderly handling of sovereign debt was unavailable in many countries.

When, for example, Mexico couldn't pay its debts in 1859, the best it could offer the London bond holders was California as compensation! Nobody was willing to take up the offer, probably because the Mexicans had lost California in the Mexican–American War of 1846. The American title was, however, very questionable, even if California had become a State of the Union soon afterwards. Gerstenberg was very annoyed, though he would never have known that, by such a narrow margin, did Hollywood fail to become British![19]

Not surprisingly, there was a good deal of support for the idea of the Council, particularly from the London, Paris and Berlin stock exchanges. The first meeting of the backers passed a resolution explaining that the kind of organization they proposed 'for the purpose of watching over and protecting the interests of holders of foreign loans is extremely necessary and desirable'. The new body was accordingly founded in 1868 and licensed by the Board of Trade in 1873. It was non-profit making and it would be further guaranteed by an Act of Parliament in 1898. Gerstenberg was elected the first president.

It was agreed that the Council would endeavour to achieve its objective purely by moral persuasion and, in its long history, it was involved in settling dividends of over £1 billion. Countries such as France, the United States, Belgium and the Netherlands went on to set up similar organizations. The image of London as a centre for raising foreign loans was much improved by its existence. In Neville Chamberlain's day, he said that the government recognized the Council as its representative, but in later times the Council became increasingly associated with the Bank of England, and it was finally wound up in 1988. Whether the EC could have learned from it during the present financial crisis is an interesting possibility. Unfortunately, Gerstenberg died in an accident on board ship in 1875 but, in his memory, there is a Gerstenberg prize at London University for the promotion of political sciences.

The Council of Foreign Bond Holders could help a lot with sovereign debt defaults, but companies promoted by con artists were a different problem. There were many of these charlatans, but one who was particularly notorious was Abraham Rotheimer (1831–99) or, as he was known in public, Albert Grant. He was born in Dublin, the son of a Jewish pedlar. As a youngster he worked as a wine salesman but, in 1859, he promoted his first company, Mercantile Discount, which went bankrupt in 1861. In 1864 he tried again with Crédit Foncier et Mobilier. That also only lasted a couple of years, and there were several other highly dubious companies that he promoted between 1864 and 1872.

During those years, he was elected MP for Kidderminster from 1865 to

1868, in spite of his opponents denouncing him as a fraudulent adventurer. In 1872, he promoted the North Wales Narrow Gauge railways between Dinas and Brygwyd and Rhyd Ddu. That went bankrupt in 1877. In 1868, he was made a baron by King Victor Emmanuel of Italy for help with the Victor Emmanuel Gallery in Milan, and he gained a Portuguese honour as well. It was said he had bought them.

Grant always did things in a big way and there was talk that his 'splendid marble palace' in the West End of London had cost £750,000. This was a figure likely to have been much exaggerated, but there is no doubt that when he was in funds in 1874, he spent £30,000 of his own money on a gift to the Metropolitan Board of Works in London. The gift was – Leicester Square! There is a plaque on the statue of Shakespeare on the South Side commemorating the present. He also gave Landseer's portrait of Sir Walter Scott to the National Gallery and was thanked for that in Parliament.

As the years went by, the scandals continued. Grant was elected again in 1874, but disbarred for spending more than he declared on election expenses. He was also said to have been given $500,000 to promote a worthless silver mine in Utah. The idea was to sell a million shares with a nominal face value of $100. What was certain was that the American ambassador in London was given a bribe of $50,000 to promote it as well. The public were promised an 80 per cent annual dividend! Many took the bait, and as is rightly said, 'a fool and his money are soon parted'. The ambassador was recalled when the scandal broke and the company went under in 1877. Grant went bankrupt twice more, including just before his death in 1899. Nothing can be said in defence of such a career, but visitors can still enjoy Leicester Square.

In the first half of the nineteenth century, the majority of Jews in Britain were usually trained within the family. They were not allowed to attend university until 1828, when University College, London was founded with the financial help of Sir Isaac Lyon Goldsmid (1778–1859). If they wanted to study for a science degree of any kind, they had a much better chance of doing so on the Continent, and some of the most successful Victorian businessmen were Jews who had migrated to Britain after obtaining their degrees abroad.

The conditions under which Jews lived in Germany differed from state to state. The country actually consisted of about 300 individual kingdoms in 1815 and it was only after the Zollverein economic alliance was started in 1834 that Germany moved towards becoming a single nation. Napoleon had abolished the ghettos but, after 1815, some were reinstated. Amschel Rothschild voluntarily went back to the reconstituted ghetto in Frankfurt. At the same time, it became much easier for Jews to attend university and many barriers against their participation in civil life were abolished.

The relations between Britain and Germany were very warm. George IV and William IV were also kings of Hanover, and the Battle of Waterloo had turned on the arrival of the army of the Prussian Marshal Blücher. The accepted natural enemy of Britain throughout the eighteenth century had been France.

Many German Jews built major companies in their country or, on occasions, migrated because they felt that their chances were better with nations like Britain. If they were continental Liberals and involved in the uprisings of 1848, it was also often much wiser to emigrate. On arrival in Britain, they transferred their loyalty to their new homeland, but this did not prevent them retaining links with the country in which they were born, and where they often had relatives.

When you look at the origins of the major firms in Britain, you won't find many of them predating 1856. It was in that year that Parliament passed the Joint Stock Companies Act which allowed seven founders to set up a limited company with an unlimited number of shareholders. This had not been permitted since 1720, as a result of the South Sea Bubble, the major stock-market scam at the time. The South Sea Company had made wildly exaggerated promises that it couldn't fulfil, notably that it could take over a lot of the national debt. Its shares rose from 128 in January 1720 to 1,000 in August and then collapsed to about the original figure. A very large number of people lost a great deal of money, but not the chancellor of the Exchequer, John Aislabie, who was paid £20,000 in shares to promote the idea in Parliament (that's £32 million in today's money, in terms of average earnings!).

In the middle of the summer of that year, Aislabie got Parliament to pass the Royal Exchange and London Assurance Corporation Act, which effectively laid down that you would need a Royal Charter to launch any other company in future. It became known as the Bubble Act, but it wasn't the result of the fiasco. It was to help those two companies who already had such a charter and they remained the beneficiaries until the bill was finally abolished in 1824.

In the meantime, there were rare occasions when the national interest made it sensible for bills to be passed in Parliament which would allow companies to be formed to develop particular opportunities, building the canals and the railways being the most important. Otherwise, firms were small partnerships or family concerns.

In those circumstances, while Jews could help the economy in terms of foreign trade, the value of the pound, foreign loans and currency exchange, the development of major limited companies was not possible. The Joint Stock Companies Act made it legal to form such companies and the Limited Liability Act 1855 made sure the shareholders could only lose their investment and not be responsible for the debts of a bankrupt company, if they had, originally, specified limited liability. The way was now clear for such companies to be formed and there was a rush to do so, particularly after the passing of the Companies Act in 1862, which made life even easier for company promoters.

Britain was not only attractive because it was tolerant and democratic. It was also the major hub of the world's commerce. If a company was based in Britain, the markets of the British Empire were automatically open to it, and about one quarter of the globe would eventually be coloured red on the map. Britain was 'where it was at' and this, in itself, would attract a lot of Jewish entrepreneurs.

German origins, however, would give rise to many problems during the First World War, when many prominent German immigrants, with no matter how good a record of helping to build the British economy, were still subject to attacks on their patriotism in the press. Where their British companies had retained links with German industry, their position was even easier to criticize.

A very large number of new inventions were created in the nineteenth century all over the world. Where they were successful, there was a great opportunity for the entrepreneur who negotiated the export rights. The pure water of Apolinnaris was sourced in Germany, but a larger fortune than could be obtained from the domestic market was to be made by exporting it to the extensive colonies of the British Empire. With all their experience of international trade, many of these special situations were exploited by Jewish entrepreneurs.

Of course, trade had to be financed and this was only partially achieved by government loans. Another aspect was providing countries with bullion. Here, Samuel Montagu (1832–1911) was a major player. He came from a Liverpool family which had arrived from Germany in the eighteenth century. With a loan from his father, he set up a business in London in 1852 to deal in international bullion and money exchange. It also offered a bill collection service and became deeply involved in dealing with the circulation of the gold that was discovered in the Australian gold rush. Samuel Montagu and Co. became extremely influential. Among other coups, it raised £1 million in silver for the German government, and managed the launch of a loan to finance Belgium's budget. Within twenty years of starting in business, Montagu was the undisputed leader of the London silver market. He was at least partially responsible for London becoming the centre of the international money market. His success was partly based on working within very fine margins. The quarter pfennig and the half centime were his kind of profits; it's another version of the street market trader's philosophy of 'pile 'em high and sell 'em cheap'.

The argument which raged between competing camps was over 'bimetallism': if a currency was measured against gold, should it also be possible to measure it against silver? Montagu was a bimetallist; Rothschild wanted only gold to be the criterion. Rothschild was deeply involved in government loans. Montagu was more interested in trade. If India, for example, used silver, then he believed London should accept silver as a standard.

This idea was part of free trade and, therefore, part of the political philosophy of the Liberal Party and Gladstone. When the party split over Home Rule for Ireland, the Rothschilds went over to the Unionists and Montagu was one of the few who stayed loyal to Gladstone. He helped finance the Liberals for many years and was made Lord Swaythling in 1907.

As far as the Jewish community was concerned, their leadership in Montagu's time was firmly with the Rothschilds. Montagu was far more devout than the average man and was meticulous in carrying out all the *mitzvot* of the religion. He had much in common with the very Orthodox immigrants in the East End. He also needed a power base to compete with Rothschild's new United Synagogue after it was established in 1870. So he collected the small immigrant synagogues together into the Federation of Synagogues, though he also saw to the building of one of the finest United Synagogues, the New West End in Bayswater. Extremely charitable, Montagu supported humanitarian legislation of all kinds in the House of Commons, where he sat for the East End of London constituency of Whitechapel for many years.

With the success of the bank, Montagu's numerous relatives applied to him for jobs. Eventually there were too many of them to absorb and they weren't all of a very high quality. So Montagu started A. Keyser and Co. for the junior members of the family. It came to specialize in placing American railway bonds in the City and eventually became the merchant bank of Keyser Ullmann in 1956. In 1962 it became a public company with a £3 million share issue, but still abided by the original practice of not conducting business on Saturdays, the Jewish Sabbath.[20]

In 1969, Samuel Montagu, the parent firm, had assets which had grown to £300 million. In 1973, however, a director of Keyser Ullmann authorized a multi-million pound loan to a charlatan and, when the fraudster left the country, the bank was crippled and had to be rescued by the Bank of England. Samuel Montagu was eventually bought by the Midland Bank which, in its turn, was bought by HSBC. The beautiful New West End Synagogue is still there though.

If Jews had little to do with creating the major high-street banking companies, they had a considerable influence on the value of the currency. In 1670, a Jewish diamond merchant, Antonio de Marchena, came to London from Holland and, in 1671, started a bullion business. He changed his name to Moses Mocatta and today, as Scotia Mocatta, it is the oldest bank in continuous existence in the world. In the records of the East India Company in 1676 there is a note, 'By cash of Moses Mocatta for freight on 75 ounces of gold on their ships *Nathaniel* and *Society-6*'. The gold was to pay for the diamonds. Moses Mocatta became a bullion broker to the Bank of England, and the figures involved were very large indeed.

In 1783, the latest in a long line of Mocattas took in a relative, Asher

Goldsmid, and the firm became Mocatta and Goldsmid. Nine generations of the family would lead the company into the late twentieth century. It was only comparatively recently that the firm was sold to the Bank of Nova Scotia.

As the twentieth century dawned, the Rothschilds were still a powerful house and would remain so as the years went by. They were one of the few Jewish entrepreneurial families who were able to produce younger generations capable of taking over the helm. The family would split into two merchant-banking firms in the 1980s and both would continue to perform well. It was the fourth baron, Jacob Rothschild (1936–), who left the family firm and started his own. Both financially and philanthropically he would continue the great traditions of the past.

NOTES

1. Thomas Levenson, *Newton and the Counterfeiter* (London: Faber and Faber, 2009).
2. Sir John Clapham, *History of the Bank of England* (Cambridge: Cambridge University Press, 1944).
3. Eli Faber, *Jews, Slaves and the Slave Trade* (New York: New York University Press, 1998).
4. Derek Taylor, *British Chief Rabbis, 1664–2006* (London and Portland, OR: Vallentine Mitchell, 2007), p.204.
5. *Jewish Chronicle*, 15 August 1873.
6. Taylor, *British Chief Rabbis*, p.125.
7. Chaim Bermant, *The Cousinhood: The Anglo-Jewish Gentry* (London: Eyre and Spottiswoode, 1971).
8. Lucy Stuart Sutherland, 'Samson Gideon; 18th Century Jewish Financier', *Jewish Historical Society of England*, vol. 17 (1951/52), p.79.
9. Stephen Aris, *The Jews in Business* (Harmondsworth: Pelican, 1970), p.48.
10. Rabbi Dr Barnett Elzas, 'Joseph Salvador', *Boston News and Courier*, 1903, http://archive.org/details/josephsalvadorje00elza.
11. Bermant, *The Cousinhood*.
12. Harold Pollins, *Economic History of the Jews of England* (London and Toronto: Fairleigh Dickinson University Press, 1982), p.49.
13. Ibid.
14. *The Times*, Business Section, 29 August 1832.
15. Niall Ferguson, *The World's Banker: The House of Rothschild* (London: Weidenfeld and Nicolson, 1998).
16. *The Times*, 20 February 1826.
17. Taylor, *British Chief Rabbis*.
18. Tim Rayment, *Sunday Times*, 1 May 2011.
19 Alexander Behr, 'Isidor Gerstenberg (1821–1876). Founder of the Council of Foreign Bondholders', *Jewish Historical Society of England*, vol.17, p.207, http:/www.jhse.org/book/export/article/16075.
20. Aris, *The Jews in Business*.

Chapter three

Grown-up Moneylending

One of the major reasons for expelling the Jews in the time of Edward I was that far too many important people owed them a great deal of money. The Jews acted as merchant bankers to some of the greatest families in the kingdom, and expelling them was an all too effective way of cancelling the debts. When they came back to Britain, many of them were still involved in finance on their own behalf, or putting together consortia, to deal in government stock, to buy diamonds or in international trade.

As we've seen, soon after the end of the Napoleonic Wars, by far the most important merchant bankers internationally were the Rothschilds. For the next 100 years, they financed everything from railways in South America to Rockefeller's Standard Oil, while Lionel Rothschild raised the money for Disraeli to buy control of the Suez Canal in 1875. The five branches of the family company in Frankfurt, London, Paris, Vienna and Rome became a tremendous power in the international banking world, which benefited the British economy enormously.

They raised loans for any number of foreign governments and, as the money was always raised in sterling, it can fairly be said that they created the international bond market. In addition, in 1840, Rothschilds became bullion brokers for the Bank of England and from 1852, for 100 years, they operated the Royal Mint Refinery, refining and casting for the Bank.

Besides the Rothschilds there were other Jewish banks in existence as well. One originated with a Jew from Hamburg, Calmer Levy, who married his cousin in Copenhagen in 1778. Like all Jews, Calmer's Hebrew name was 'Calmer son of so-and-so'. 'Levy' recognizes the fact that his ancestors were priests. A Jew's Hebrew name doesn't have a surname as such, so when one was needed, for instance when they were engaged in trade in non-Jewish circles, they often decided to take the name of the town where they were born; in Calmer's case, Hamburg. When, however, he applied for a licence to trade, the registrar spelt his name as Hambro, so he settled for that.[1]

His son, Joachim, became a silk merchant while his other son, Joseph (1780–1848), went into banking and grew the business, to become banker to the kings of Denmark, Norway and Sweden.[2] Joseph had a happy marriage, but when his son Carl Joachim (1807–77) was quite young, his wife started to suffer from melancholia, and it was decided to send the boy to foster parents. They looked after him very well, but persuaded his father to allow them to have him baptized at the age of 15. Later Joseph took Carl Joachim into the business and, after a visit to England, the young man decided to settle down in London as a merchant banker. He is recognized as the founder of the banking house in London in 1838.[3]

Hambros isn't thought of today as of Jewish origin but Carl Joachim was born Jewish and retained a large number of Jewish traits. He was always keen to learn and took himself off to America as a youngster, where he found a new method of milling flour and sold it back in Europe. As a banker, from the beginning, Carl Joachim set out to compete with Rothschilds. There were plenty of non-Jewish banks, but Carl Joachim set his sights on Rothschilds. If they didn't want to handle a loan or an issue, he was keen to prove them wrong. He did it with a major loan for Denmark. In later years he also raised the money for the issue needed by Camillo Cavour, the leader of the movement for Italian independence, to finance his efforts to unify the country.

Which brought into play another Jewish trait. Both the Danish and the Italian issues were highly speculative, but Carl Joachim was always prepared to take a gamble. Cavour was based in Piedmont, and Piedmont was Rothschild territory. The Rothschilds refused to get involved with Cavour, however, and so Carl Joachim launched a £4-million-pound bond issue and took up £400,000 of it himself. Which was more than he was worth. The £100 bonds did, in fact, fall to under £80, but they eventually recovered and Carl Joachim made a fortune.

Although officially a Christian, Carl Joachim was subject to the same difficulties that all prominent Jews had in getting away from their origins. Disraeli was always known and criticized as being Jewish, the Portuguese

Marranos had been treated as Jews, and Carl Joachim was not accepted in society because he was considered a nouveau-riche Jewish banker. The bank itself flourished, however, and 150 years later, in 1998 was bought by the French bank, Société Générale, for £300 million. Much of its core business was still in Scandinavia, which had strengthened the economic ties with Britain very satisfactorily.

If one of the most lucrative avenues for nineteenth-century merchant-bank profits was sovereign debt, one of the problems was that the principals who wanted to raise the loans were not always entirely honest. As James de Rothschild said when dealing with a loan to the Portuguese government, 'We are dealing here with thoroughly disreputable people'.[4] The bankers often knew that the public's funds were at risk if they bought the bonds, but as most of them were kosher, sufficiently glowing prospectuses brought in the punters. The Rothschilds raised £4 million for the Portuguese in 1835.

Another prominent Jewish merchant bank was Bisschoffsheim and Goldschmidt, which originated in Belgium but opened an office in London in 1857 with a family member in charge, Henri Louis Bischoffsheim (1829–1908). Associated with the bank in later years were such Jewish banking luminaries as Sir Ernest Cassel, Maurice de Hirsch and Jacob Schiff.

Bischoffsheim sailed close to the wind on a number of occasions. From 1867 to 1870 he raised £4.8 million for Honduras, which was at the time in default on servicing a loan, on which, in fact, they hadn't paid the interest for forty years. The public were encouraged to invest in the new issue by the arrival of two ships with cargoes of mahogany which were announced to be the method by which Honduras would now pay the interest. The cargoes had not, however, come from Honduras. The flotation was successful, as the prospectus said the money would be used to build a railway in Honduras, which was a fashionable reason for investment. Only fifty-six miles were ever completed, at a cost of £500,000. The other £4 million disappeared and Honduras defaulted again. Bischoffsheim and Goldschmidt, however, made 10-per-cent commission.

The firm also took in $825,000 commission on selling $30 million worth of Erie Railway bonds in 1870, which came under a distinct cloud. Their American associates, like other similar entrepreneurs, have come down in history as 'The Robber Barons', and not without good reason.

The other side of the coin with Bischoffsheim, however, was his creation in 1889 of the Hospital Association Street Ambulances Service in London. He donated no less than sixty-two ambulances and, by his death, there were 400 of them. In pre-NHS days only a charitable donation of that size could have created a facility by which so many lives have been saved. In addition, to mark his golden wedding in 1906, Bischoffsheim gave £120,000 (£3 million today) to the Imperial Cancer Research Association. For her part, his wife, as president of the Daneswood Jewish Sanatorium, went on to create Norwood, the most important Jewish charity today for people with special needs.

While banks and merchant banks were respectable, moneylenders were definitely not. Perhaps the one exception was Samuel Lewis (1837–1901) who had an extraordinary numbers of members of Debrett's among his clients. The Earl of Shrewsbury, for example, borrowed £370,000 from him (about £13 million today). Without Lewis, the lifestyle of a large number of the good-and-great Victorian families would have been unsustainable.

Lewis went to work at the age of 13, when his father died and left his mother impoverished. He sold steel pens and developed into a jeweller. His reputation was endorsed later in his life in a court case, when the Lord Chief Justice, Lord Russell, said:

> His business of bill discounting and money lending was not a very popular one, but let them at least be just to those who carried it on. The plaintiff has been for 30 years at the same address in Cork Street, and there had been no attempt to show that he deserved other than the name of a man who was honourably engaged.[5]

Lewis earned the nickname 'Prince of Money Lenders' because of his generosity to his clients. He was immensely philanthropic and, when he died, he left £1 million to his wife, and control over a further £3 million till she died. In his will he left £670,000 for housing for the poor, besides £100,000 to the Board of Guardians for the Jewish poor. Nine London hospitals were left £10,000 each and the Prince of Wales Hospital Fund benefited from a legacy of £250,000. He had no children, and the Samuel Lewis Housing Trust, which was set up to handle the gift to the poor, did a great deal of good. In 2001 it changed its name to the Southern Housing

Group. The poor seem to have improved their lot, however, over the years, because one flat available for rent in its latest marketing material is on offer for £730 a calendar month.

By contrast with merchant banking, Jews have had little to do with the development of the high-street banks. This was partially because such banks were more hidebound than the merchant banks, which could act much more quickly and without as much red tape. A commitment to leadership rather than teamwork is the mark of a lot of Jewish businessmen. A major exception with the high-street banks, however, was the London and Westminster Bank, whose chairman from 1859 to 1867 was Sir David Salomons (1797–1873).

Sir David was one of its architects and the London and Westminster was the first joint stock bank, created after the rules for the structure of banks was changed by the Bank Charter Act in 1833. Salomons, though, was never worried about needing to be the first to do anything. In battling for the emancipation of the Jews, he was the first Jewish county magistrate, sheriff, alderman and Lord Mayor – of London. He was elected MP for Greenwich before the law was altered on the oath you had to swear on taking your seat. He refused to say the words 'as a true Christian' and was removed from the chamber – and fined £500 for sitting down in it. But then, as he said, 'I don't mind inserting a wedge when I have to break through a solid mass of prejudice and ignorance'.[6]

Salomons fought the good fight, both for his co-religionists and his banking colleagues. Although allowed by the act of Parliament, there was a great deal of opposition to the creation of the high-street bank. When he died in July 1873, *The Times* acknowledged 'to his unremitting care and attention to its interests and progress are greatly due the wonderful success of the London and Westminster Bank and even more the development and importance of the body of Joint Stock banks in London'.[7] Salomons laid the foundations on which the joint stock banks have subsequently flourished. Even so, today, very few Jews are directors of such banks. Disastrous decisions in so many banking boardrooms in recent years might change this situation.

A few minor Jewish banks, like the Haverfordwest Bank and the Milford Bank in Wales, were created by Samuel Levi Phillips (1730–1812).

Another important Jewish bank was S.L. Behrens and Co., which was founded by the uncle of Sir Jacob Behrens (1806–89), Solomon Levi Behrens (1787–1873). The older Behrens had roots in finance, as the family owned a major bank in Hamburg, Germany. He came to England in 1814 to set up as a cloth merchant in Manchester, but diversified into banking after a number of years in Bradford, Leeds and Glasgow. He was associated with Rothschilds.

A small merchant bank in the provinces may not seem very important in today's world. Before mass communications, the telephone, Internet and emails, however, it was a vital component in the growth of an area. A local company, needing capital or financial support, would find the distance to the City of London interminable, by comparison with the friendly bank on their doorstep, which would understand their problems because its management lived among them. When local banks were bought by the giant high-street banks in the latter half of the twentieth century, the local economies found it much harder to make progress.

In Germany, Behrens was 'Aryanized' in 1938, and Behrens' descendants had to surrender all their belongings in exchange for visas to get out of the country. After the war, there was something of a return, but the firm went into liquidation in 1970. The value of what was stolen from the Behrens can be seen from just one result of their tremendous struggle over many years to recover their possessions. In 2011, the family were able to regain a painting that had been sold by the Nazis to a museum in Holland. Sixty-six years later, the Dutch government decided that the picture had, effectively, been stolen from its owner, and it was returned to the Behrens family. Corot's 'Jeune Femme à la Fontaine' was sold at Sotheby's in 2010 to a Swiss museum for £1.6 million.

Another of the major City merchant banks to be started in Victorian times was Stern Brothers, founded by two German-Jewish brothers, David (c.1810–77) and Hermann (1815–87) Stern. They came from a prominent banking family in Frankfurt but migrated to England in 1844. Stern Brothers became well known for launching foreign loans, in particular for Portugal which, in 1869, created Hermann a baron and David a viscount. Among the other varied loans in which they were involved were the Danubian 7-per-cent loan, the Spanish mortgage loan and the Italian tobacco-monopoly loan. Hermann left £3.5 million when he died. The family were members of the Western Synagogue and David's son, Sidney (1845–1912), was created Baron Wandsworth. He left £1 million to charity from his £1.5 million estate, when he died just before the Great War.

At the end of the nineteenth century, the world of banking was in need of reconstruction. There were too many small country banks, which had the greatest difficulty in surviving the storms of slump and boom. There were also notorious cases of fraud by bank directors, which undermined confidence in the system. One of the worst examples was the City of Glasgow Bank, which collapsed in 1878. It was not a limited liability company and the shareholders were fully responsible for the debts. The result was that 1,000 out of 1,200 of them were ruined. The directors were prosecuted and received prison terms.

A bank company doctor emerged: Felix Schuster (1854–1936), born in Frankfurt. His father came to Britain when Frankfurt was absorbed into the German Empire. Young Schuster started in the family business of banking at the age of 18 and the company was partially taken over by the Union Bank of London in 1887. Schuster became a director of Union, and in 1895 its governor. Building on this experience, he addressed the problems of small banks and decided to try to persuade them to amalgamate. Banks like Smith, Rayner and Smith and the London and Yorkshire Bank were among the first to join and, in 1919, with other banks, he formed the National Provincial. 'He was, by nature, shy and this, with the intense earnestness with which he addressed himself to every problem, made him abrupt and formidable in ordinary conversation. He made excessive demands on himself and was prone to make excessive demands on others.'[8]

Knighted in 1906, Schuster did a lot of work for the government as well. He was on the Royal Commission on London Traffic, the Board of Trade commission for the amendment of company law, the India Office committee on Indian railway finance, and served as chairman of the Council of the Institute of Bankers and the Central Association of Bankers. 'His face, of a peculiar pallor, his square black beard and his very deep brown eyes made him a striking figure.'[9] When he died in 1936 at the age of 82, he left over £600,000.

As we've seen, the First World War had thrown doubt upon the loyalty of those Jewish families who had originally come from Germany. These were still the days when there was a quota for Jewish children at good schools, when they were depicted as the villains in popular novels and mocked in music hall acts. It was, therefore, ironic that on 12 September 1919, a group of five men gathered in London to fix the price of gold for the whole world – and three of them were Jewish; a Rothschild was in the chair and also represented were Samuel Montagu and Co. and Mocatta and Goldsmid. The non-Jewish Pixley and Abell, and Sharps Wilkins made up the cabal.

The objective was to kick-start the London gold market after the war and the five companies were the principal gold-bullion traders and refiners. Rothschilds chaired the meeting, as they were to do for the next eighty-five years, and each representative sat behind a small union jack. Negotiations for buying and selling were conducted and, when agreement had been reached, the individual company would lower its flag. When all was agreed, the chairman would announce, 'There are no flags and we're fixed.' It works the same way as it ever did, but the Rothschilds gave up commodity trading in 2004. The five companies now carrying out the gold fix twice a day are Deutsches Bank, Barclays Capital, HSBC, Société Générale and Scotia Mocatta. Recent banking scandals haven't helped.

Another Jewish City merchant to make a major contribution to the life of the nation was Sir Robert Mayer (1879–1985). Mayer was born in Germany but was sent by his father to Britain in 1896 because his father disliked Prussian militarism. Mayer was a musical prodigy, but his father insisted that he went into the City rather than make music his career. As a broker, Mayer made a fortune in non-ferrous metal trading in the City and the United States. This enabled him to retire after service in the First World War and, in 1923, he started the organization with which his name would always thereafter be linked: the Robert Mayer Concerts for Children.

In 1932, he also became one of the founders of the London Philharmonic Orchestra and in 1951 he founded the London Schools Symphony Orchestra. It was, however, through his children's concerts that generations of young people were introduced to classical music. Mayer was the oldest man ever to be knighted, at the age of 100, and the Queen attended a concert in his honour in that year.

There was to be one seriously major Jewish merchant bank founded after the Second World War – S.G. Warburg. There are few better examples of the stupidity of Hitler's laws against Jewish businesses in Germany, or the benefits to Britain of its humanitarian attitude towards the sufferers before the war, than the development of S.G. Warburg in London. The Warburg family had started moneylending in the 1640s and were linked by marriage to the bankers, Kuhn Loeb, in America. That nineteenth-century creation had been led by Jacob Schiff, the banker who would effectively start the process of bringing down the czar. When the German Warburg bank was 'Aryanized' by Hitler, Siegmund Warburg (1902–82), got out in 1935 with only £5,000 of the German firm's capital.

It wasn't until 1946 that he set up Warburgs in London. Britain still looked to the British Empire for its major trading and its financial investments, even though these assets had been massively reduced by the need to pay for the war. Siegmund Warburg was different. As a European, he knew the potential of European investments and it was Warburg who created the Eurobond market.

The benefit to the City of London of being in on the ground floor of this new development did much to cement the City's position as the preeminent European financial centre: 'Today Eurobonds comprise around 90 per cent of international bond issues.' About 70% of them are issued in London.[10] Warburg was one of the key figures in London's revival as a primary financial centre after the war. Initially, he was looked down upon by the established City firms as a parvenu, but it was his innovations which underpinned much of the City's post-war success. Warburg also came up with the idea that merchant banks could have a major role to play in advising companies on how and whether to buy other organizations. As a consequence, he was responsible for much of the development of what is now known in the City as Mergers and Acquisitions. It was Warburg who introduced the concept of the hostile takeover bid, when he helped American Metal buy British Aluminium in 1956. It was a bitter battle. Warburg recalled, 'A major factor in the bitterness was the aspect of the damned foreigner, the newcomer, the fact that I was not a member of the Establishment and held non-Establishment views.'[11]

The idea of purchasing shares in order to gain control of a company and oust the existing management was totally foreign to the City's attitude at the time. A gentleman's agreement was acceptable, but a hostile takeover was the behaviour of what the City would, at best, label a bounder. No matter how inadequate the performance of the existing board of directors, or the resulting depletion of the shareholders' funds, takeovers were expected to be welcomed by both sides. When American Metal was successful, against the wishes of British Aluminium, it established Warburgs as the bank that a board would choose, or at least seriously consider retaining, if there was likely to be substantial opposition to their plans.

In small ways too, Warburg set new standards for the City. Warburg's directors would be at their desks by 8 o'clock in the morning and it was Warburg's policy for everybody senior to know exactly what was going on in all the company's negotiations. Warburg was noted as a man of rigid principles. He said in 1959, 'what matters even more is ... adherence to high moral and aesthetic standards'.[12] He also said that it was a good idea to cry over spilt milk.

Warburg was an obsessive perfectionist with, unusually for a Jewish banker, an aversion to excessive risk. He specialized in giving excellent advice and saw to it that he was in on the ground floor with developing companies, like Max Joseph's Grand Metropolitan. It was said of Warburg that he was 'as much a psychologist, politician and actor-manager as he was a banker'.[13] Some years after Warburg's death, the bank was sold to UBS at rather more than the £5,000 he had arrived with in Britain: £860 million!

If takeover bids are contested nowadays, the shareholders must choose whether to accept the offer being made, or remain loyal to the existing directors. This gives major shareholders the power to swing the day for one or the other party. This situation emerged more and more as the twentieth century drew to a close, and it coincided with Margaret Thatcher's wish to increase the number of people who held shares.

The combination made an ideal opening for City experts who could offer investors sound advice on what to do with their money. Siegmund Warburg would have been delighted that one of the most prominent companies created for this purpose was Warburg's Asset Management, which soon became Mercury Asset Management. Twenty-five per cent of the company was sold in a Stock Exchange listing in 1987.

One of the two moving spirits of Mercury thereafter was Carol Galley (1949–), whose Jewish mother was a refugee from Austria. Educated in Newcastle, Galley gained a degree in Modern Languages from Leicester University and joined Warburgs on graduation – as a librarian! She climbed the greasy pole for the next fifteen years, until she became vice chairman of the new company. She was described in the 1990s as 'The Ice Maiden' and the most powerful woman in the City. In the press, her immaculate dress sense was often remarked upon, which is hardly a judgement of an executive's ability, but is a cross that executive women still have to bear.

On her watch, two of the hottest contested takeovers were Granada's bid for the major television company, London Weekend Television, in 1994, and for the major hotel group, Trust House Forte, in 1996. In both cases, it was Galley's choice of Granada, for the shares Mercury held, that enabled Granada to win the day. More and more companies, as well as individuals, sought expert advice for their asset management and, at its peak, Mercury was advising more than half the companies in the FTSE 100. In 1997, Merrell Lynch paid £3.1 billion for the firm.

The rewards for the most senior executives were substantial. Galley earned £16 million in 1997 and that rose substantially thereafter. Salaries of this kind are, however, usually based on performance, and the shareholders and investors had much to thank her for. Galley stayed with the new owners, who were known in their early days, when they were Merrell, Lynch, Pierce, Fenner and Smith, as 'The Thundering Herd'. She was made joint chief operating officer until she eventually retired. She is still comfortably ensconced in the *Sunday Times* Rich List.

Another Jewish bank was Guinness Peat, which was the creation of Harry Kissin (1912–97). Kissin was a very colourful character who studied for a Law degree at Basle University and came to Britain in 1933 from Gdansk, Poland, where he was born. He spoke Russian, French and German and was drafted into military intelligence during the war, which he ended as a colonel. After the war, he was sent to study technological advances in Germany and, when he was demobilized, he started commodity trading with the Eastern Bloc, notably Poland.[14]

It was through those activities that he met Harold Wilson, who was president of the Board of Trade at the time, and a firm friendship was built between the two men. Kissin was a socialist and supported Harold Wilson's private office before he became prime minister. In 1954, Kissin bought Lewis and Peat, which he built up to be one of the world's largest commodity houses.

While, on the one hand, Kissin was eminently respectable and very charitable, he came under suspicion by MI5 because he did business with the Iron Curtain countries. A lot of prostitutes were allowed to be involved on both sides in securing business, and MI5 were concerned that Kissin would be blackmailed by the Russians. As Harold Wilson was paranoid about plots against him when he was prime minister, his continuing friendship with Kissin was fraught with claim and counterclaim.

In 1973, Kissin bought the bankers, Guinness Mahon, changed its name to Guinness Peat and became life president in 1979. He was made a peer by Harold Wilson in 1974 and also received honours from the governments of France, Brazil and Bulgaria. He had many international interests, including Singapore Land, the most influential property company on the island, and he gave a great deal of financial support to the Jewish charity, Boys' Town, in Jerusalem. Unfortunately, Kissin was a better commodity trader than he was a banker, and Guinness Peat had to be rescued in 1982. Kissin died at the age of 85 in 1997.

Guinness Peat wasn't the only story of a Jewish company without a happy ending. The crisis of 1973 brought down Nation Life, which was part of the Stern Group of Companies. William Stern (1934–) survived Belsen, came to Britain and married into a wealthy, Orthodox family.[15] In the 1960s, a new branch of banking emerged, called unit trusts. These trusts enabled the investor to join with others in buying stocks of all kinds, with the money being handled by professionals who were supposed to know more about the subject than the amateur. Well, a great many did, but when property values crashed, Nation Life was deeply invested in diminishing assets. As a result, Stern won the unwelcome title of the biggest bankrupt in the country, at £118 million, and the investors lost their money.

One good thing that emerged from the fiasco was the passing of the Policyholders Protection Act in 1975, which ensured that the same thing couldn't happen again. Admittedly, doors and bolting horses spring to mind. Stern could point to the vagaries of business as an explanation for the disaster, but his continuing extravagant way of life made for very bad publicity. He was discharged from bankruptcy in 1987, started up again, and crashed again in the 1990s, for £11 million. Stern was alleged to still have a large house in North London, a home in Jerusalem and a villa in the south of France. The Jewish community winced; this was not the kind of behaviour that was laid down in the Babylonian Talmud.

In the high-pressure world of the City in the 1970s, Patsy Bloom (1940–) had a very untypical CV. A Jewish charity secretary in her 30s, a woman who invested only £250 of her own money and yet built, from scratch, a massive insurance business which was worth £32 million, twenty years later. It would seem a pretty far-fetched story in a highly competitive industry, where there are any number of big guns fighting for their share of the market. Yet this was precisely what she achieved.

Bloom was born in London's Maida Vale where her parents ran a sweet shop. She left school at 14 and became a secretary. When she was 30, she got a job as the London organizer of a Jewish charity, the Central British Fund, and enjoyed that for a number of years. One day, however, she received a bill from a vet who had treated her Shih Tzu dog, and she complained to a friend that it was going to be difficult to pay. The friend asked, quite innocently, whether there was some kind of animal BUPA, a way of getting insurance in case your pet went sick.

Giving that some thought, Bloom decided it was a good idea and, with her experience in raising money for charity, she decided that she had the skill needed to knock on doors and sell animal insurance. By 1989, the first health-insurance company for animals, Pet Plan, had a turnover of £7 million and by 1993 it was £30 million. Pet Plan filled a substantial hole in the market and Bloom was nothing if not innovative. 'We introduced an "accidental damage" cover after a dog chewed up an entire three-piece suite. We pay on dog psychiatry and homeopathy. We have a burglar award. If your dog catches a burglar we give £100 in pet food as a thank you.'[16]

Before selling the business in 1996 to one of the City insurance companies, which should have thought up the idea for itself, Pet Plan insured well over 300,000 pets – over half the market – and handled up to

2,000 claims a week. It was not surprising that she was voted Veuve Cliquot Businesswoman of the Year in 1993. The Patsy Bloom Charitable Trust, which she created, has now given donations of over £5 million to animal charities, as well as sponsoring veterinarian education and creating an all-weather outdoor riding area for Norwood, the Jewish charity. She was also made an honorary associate of the Royal College of Veterinary Surgeons.

Provincial economies still need financing in a Britain dominated by London. Local companies retain the advantage in that they often know the territory better than the national banks, and attract the business of local entrepreneurs, who realize they may well receive a more sympathetic ear. Where such organizations don't exist, the local economy can struggle. A typical example of help-at-hand is Jerrold Holdings, a Manchester company created by Henry Moser (1950–).

Moser is from Bury and left school at 16 to go to work as a market trader. He is in the tradition of Jack Cohen and Alan Sugar. The company began as the Blemain Group in 1973 and it specialized in providing funding for residential and commercial concerns. It is the old Jewish moneylender writ large, and it has been so successful that Barclays paid £113 million in 2006 for 30 per cent of the equity. Moser has always kept a low profile, but, as a finance specialist, his value to the renewal of Manchester after the collapse of the cotton industry has been very considerable.

Banks have, traditionally, been the financiers of new companies, but the latter half of the twentieth century saw the beginnings of companies which specialized in that field. Known as venture capitalists, their expertise is strongly focused on identifying which new ideas are worth supporting with hard cash. If they are right, their share in the new company is going to grow in value. If they are wrong, they are going to lose their money. It is just the kind of new field, with an element of gambling, which would attract Jewish involvement.

The most successful venture capitalist in Britain has been a company called Apax Partners, which was the brainchild of Sir Ronald Cohen (1945–). Cohen's family were originally from Aleppo in Syria, but they were living in Egypt when Colonel Nasser took over. After Suez, the Jewish community was persecuted and the Cohens fled to England in 1957.

Ronald Cohen was 12 years old and went to the local school in North London. Some years later he was at Exeter College, Oxford and president of the Union. He read PPE and went on to Harvard.

Cohen gained his business experience with McKinseys but, in 1972, set out on his own and founded Apax when he was still under 30. By the 1990s, it was 'One of three truly global capital firms'.[17] In the intervening years Apax had financed the start-up of 500 companies, including ones as varied as AOL, Virgin Radio and Waterstones, and Cohen had earned the title of 'father of British venture capital'.[18] In 2004, Apax were the fourth-largest financial supporter of the Labour Party.

The largest investment at the time for Apax was the brainchild of another Jewish entrepreneur, Lloyd Dorfman (1953–). Dorfman had a much quieter upbringing than Cohen, being comfortably educated at St Paul's. He didn't want to go on to university and decided that he didn't like investment banking either, which was his first attempt to find a job in life. So in 1976, when he was 23, he opened a shop in Central London to exchange currency for tourists and holidaymakers.

The normal practice at the time was to obtain the money you needed from your bank or from a provider like American Express. To be able to get it from a shop in the high street was an innovation and Dorfman set out to build the company, which he called Travelex. He was asked a few years ago what was the secret of his success and he itemized four things he felt essential: persistence, self-belief, a capacity for innovation and a determination not to take 'no' for an answer.

The persistence was much needed, because what Dorfman wanted was to open a currency-exchange bureau in airports. It took him until 1986 to get his foot in the door, but at Heathrow Terminal 4 he finally got permission. It was the first independent currency operation at a British airport. Today Travelex is in 105 airports.[19] The firm began to grow impressively and, in 2001, spent £440 million on buying the financial division of Thomas Cook. Turnover that year was £21 billion, making it the world's largest, non-bank, foreign-exchange business.

In 2001, Travelex was still a private company, supported by the venture capitalists, 3I. In 2005, Dorfman sold 63 per cent of the company to Apax for £1.06 billion. It had 4,000 staff in thirty-five countries and would retain Dorfman as its chairman; he kept a 30-per-cent stake in the company and is now in the top 800 of the *Forbes* magazine richest men in the world. Dorfman, however, doesn't fit the stereotype. 'With his pinstripe suit trousers hitched high on his blue monogrammed shirt and his brown eyes blinking behind glasses on his bald boiled-egg head, he seems ... more like an amiable uncle than an avaricious empire builder.'[20]

Away from the office, Dorfman has helped a wide variety of good causes. When asked to reminisce on the day he bought Cooks, he recalled that he had chaired a review that same day of the cleaning committee of the Jewish Care charity! He has sponsored the Australian cricket team, taken the rugby icon, Jonny Wilkinson, on board as a brand ambassador, and given the National Theatre £10 million. The Cottesloe Theatre will in future be called the Dorfman in recognition of his munificence.

In 1986, the chancellor, Nigel Lawson, wanted to widen share owner-ship in the population. So he created personal equity plans, which gave small investors considerable tax advantages. One of the companies which took over the baton and offered the public their professional advice on which shares to buy, was the Perpetual Fund Management Company, led by its Jewish founder, Sir Martyn Arbib (1939–). When he sold the company in 2001, it was for over a billion pounds and the Arbib family had about 45 per cent of the stock.

Arbib was a Thames Valley man, educated at Felsted, and operating his business from Henley-on-Thames rather than the City. He had started the company in 1974 with the favoured Jewish overhead of two phones and a secretary. Over the years, he launched a very large number of investment plans which enabled shareholders to invest in companies all over the world. The funds performed well and the company grew from the results.

Arbib used his money to buy racehorses – his horse, Snurge, won the St Leger in 1990 – and for many charitable purposes. He was knighted by Tony Blair for financing the Slough Academy to improve education, and he has also helped create the River and Rowing Museum at Henley, which now attracts more than 100,000 visitors a year. Bringing that many people into a town has, of course, a marked effect on the local economy.

The new generation of bankers includes some very substantial hedge-fund managers who invest other people's money more intelligently than they can themselves; well, that's the principle, and if often works. The 'godfather' of London's hedge-fund community is said to be Stanley Fink (1952–), whose father ran a grocery shop. Fink went to Manchester Grammar, read Law at Cambridge but started off with Arthur Anderson, the accountants. He went on to Mars and Citibank, and was appointed to the board of the Man Group when he was 29. The Man Group were commodity brokers, but went into hedge-fund operation and appointed Fink their financial director in 1986. From 2000 to 2007 he was their CEO, and the Man Group became the world's largest listed hedge fund. Just about the only blot on the copybook was a decision to invest $360 million with Bernie Madoff, the Jewish American with the notorious Ponzi investment scheme. That blew up spectacularly in December 2008.

Fink joined the Rich List with ease and was then struck down with a benign brain tumour. It gave him cause for serious thought and he decided that there were better things to devote your life to than making money. In 2008, Philip Beresford, compiler of the *Sunday Times* Rich List, said of Fink, 'He is one of the finest brains in the City, who is now striking out on a new career, trying to mobilise the City to think of disadvantaged communities here and around the world.'

The beneficiaries of Fink's largesse have been very varied. Man had already given £13.75 million to found the Oxford-Man Institution of Quantitative Finance. The Booker Prize for literature became the Man Booker prize. Fink also raised millions for the Evelina Children's Hospital Appeal Committee, which is attached to Guy's and St Thomas' Hospital. By coincidence, the original hospital had been donated by Ferdinand James de Rothschild in memory of his wife, Evelina, who had died in childbirth when only 29 years old in 1866.

In the 2008 *Sunday Times* Rich Giving List, Fink ranked eighteenth in the country. He moved on to be joint treasurer of the Conservative Party; he has also returned to hedge funds in partnership with Lord Michael Levy, with International Standard Asset Management. It must be unusual for the two senior officers in a company to be ex-treasurers of the Conservative and Labour Parties. Fink was made a peer in 2010.

Other hedge funds created by Jews include one of the greatest, Soros Fund Management. Although George Soros (1930–) is known as an American financier, he was born Soros György. He managed to survive the war in Hungary, when so many Hungarian Jews were victims of the Holocaust, and migrated to London in 1947.

His Orthodox uncle took him in, and he went to the London School of Economics where, in 1952, he gained his degree as a Bachelor of Science in Philosophy. After college, where he supported himself by working at times as a railway porter and a waiter, he took a job with the merchant bank, Singer and Friedlander, created by two Orthodox German Jews, Julius Singer and Ernest Friedlander, in 1920. Singer had started a brokerage business in London in 1907 and was joined by Friedlander who had been the chairman of the Johannesburg Stock Exchange in a distinguished career. The brokerage did well, but had to withdraw from the London Exchange during the First World War because of its German origins. Singer and Friedlander remained for many years thereafter one of the few independent merchant banks.

It was only in 1956 that Soros migrated to America and began a career which led to the creation of his hedge fund. It has to be said that he was one refugee who did not exactly help the British economy. In 1992 he sold the pound short in the expectation that sterling would have to be devalued, which it was. Known thereafter as 'The Man who Broke the Bank of England', he was said to have made a profit of £1 billion from the exercise.

In the hedge-fund world today, among many other Jewish companies, Alan Howard begat Brevan Howard, Stuart Roden begat Lansdowne Partners, Hilton Nathanson begat Marble Bar and Nat Rothschild begat the Atticus Fund.

Where banks deal in money and stocks and shares, there are other forms of investment. One of the most popular is Old Master paintings. London is recognized as a major centre for their sale, but much of the credit for the foundation of this modern international status is down to the Duveens. Sir Joseph Joel Duveen (1843–1908) was a Dutch antiques dealer who came to Hull to start an import business, specializing in Delftware. He opened an office in London in 1879 and moved into selling pictures. His eldest son, Joe (1869–1939) went to University College School in Hampstead and then into the family business.

Sir Joseph's brother, Henry, had also migrated, but to New York, where he opened the American branch of the firm. Joe joined him and learned the antiques business. What became obvious to the family was the amount of money the Robber Barons were making as American industrialization flourished, and the number of Old Master paintings in Europe which would give a veneer of culture to the homes of the nouveau riche. Putting demand and supply together, Duveen Brothers dominated the American art market for the next fifty years, and Joe's offices in London and New York became magnets for the new American millionaires.

Duveen was a great salesman; he was an expert at everything from flattering the ladies to keeping the men's favourite cigars in his office. The paintings he sold improved the collections of the Frick, Huntington and many other American museums. There was, however, a snag. One of the problems with Old Masters is their provenance: are they the genuine article or not? Obviously, it helps if their authenticity is confirmed by a great expert. In such cases, Duveen turned to the advice of Bernard Berenson (1865–1959).

Berenson was born Bernhard Valvrojenski in Lithuania and migrated to Boston, where he became famous as an expert on Renaissance art. For many years, if Berenson said a painting was genuine, that settled matters. However, in the course of a court case between Duveen and a customer between 1920 and 1928, it emerged that Berenson was being paid by Duveen for his opinion. The agreement had, in fact, been reached in 1907 that Berenson would receive 25 per cent of whatever profit was realized on the paintings he authenticated.[21]

Duveen was made a peer in 1933, partially at least because of the munificent donations he made. His father had endowed the Turner Wing at the Tate and the Duveen Gallery at the British Museum houses the Elgin Marbles. Duveen also donated many fine paintings to British museums and art galleries. The firm carried on after his death, but was sold in 1964. Duveen was prominent to the end. He has a magnificent plot at Willesden Jewish cemetery, but a considerable number of the paintings he sold have been re-evaluated and found not to be the genuine article. Duveen could well have said that this was Berenson's fault, rather than his own. Whatever the truth, London's position as a major centre for art sales was not affected.

The City of London is also the centre for a number of other international markets and the commissions on the deals done every day make a handsome contribution to the balance of trade. The professionalism, integrity and efficiency of the people involved are essential ingredients in ensuring that London remains the centre of choice. One of these markets is the London Metal Exchange, where the turnover every day averages $46 billion, and 95 per cent of the business comes from overseas. The work is carried out by the Ring dealers, and one of those privileged to deal in the Ring after the Second World War was Sigmund Sternberg (1921–).

Sternberg was born in Hungary and migrated to Britain in 1939. As an alien he was only allowed to serve in Civil Defence but, in addition, he was able to go into the metal-recycling business. In just a few years, he became one of the companies making up the Ring in the Exchange, and that was where he made his fortune.

The Holocaust affected people in different ways. Sternberg's reaction to the intolerance of religious fanatics was to set out to try to build bridges between faiths. In this he has been remarkably successful; he helped to arrange the first papal visit to Israel in 1986 and negotiated the recognition by the Vatican of the State. He was the co-founder of the Three Faiths Forum – Judaism, Christianity and Islam (in foundation order!) – and was made a Papal Knight of the Order of St Gregory the Great by Pope John Paul II. He was knighted in 1976 and has been a generous supporter of the Labour Party.

To complement the Nobel Prizes, the Templeton Prize was created in 1973. It honours a living person who has made an exceptional contribution to affirming life's spiritual dimension, whether through insight, discovery or practical works. The prize was worth $1,230,000 when it was awarded to Sternberg in 1998. He gave the money to the Sternberg Foundation he had established in 1968 to further its work. As he told the *Church Times* in 2007, 'I think it much better to give most of one's money away.'[22] There are endless charity and interfaith committees on which Sternberg has sat, chaired or supported. He has really done a remarkable amount of good for both Jewish and non-Jewish charities.

Sternberg traded metals. The Reuben brothers financed aluminium-manufacturing companies. David Reuben (1938–) and Simon Reuben

(1941–) were born in Bombay to a Jewish family from Iran. It was the same combination that had produced the Sassoons in the nineteenth century. They were raised by their mother and grandmother in England after their parents divorced. When they grew up, David went into the metal trade and Simon started off on his own in property. They decided to join together in 1977 by creating a property company called Transworld, and it did very well.

They changed course, however, when glasnost arrived in Russia. All of a sudden the Communist Russians had to deal with privatization and capitalism, and the result was a degree of chaos. One element of this was that the aluminium factories in the country didn't have the money they needed to buy the raw materials. As the *Observer* reported: 'The brothers jumped feet first into the chaotic capitalist system that was taking hold in post-Soviet Russia in 1991, when more cautious investors were too nervous to dip their toes in the water.'[23] At its peak, the brothers' Transworld Metals controlled 5 per cent of the world's aluminium production, by paying for the raw materials up-front for the factories, and being repaid in finished aluminium. The profits were very large indeed and for a time Transworld became Russia's biggest foreign investor. In 1995 the company made a profit of £1 billion on a turnover of £5 billion.

When life started to get more difficult for foreign investors in Russia, the Reubens sold out in 2000 for £300 million. Part of it they spent on financing the N. Reuben Primary School in North London in 2004, the Breast Cancer Unit in Meir Hospital, Israel in 2005, the largest children's cancer clinic in Europe at Great Ormond Street in 2008, as well as many other large donations from their Reuben Foundation. In their origins and careers, the Reubens mirror more elements of Jewish entrepreneurial life than most.

NOTES

1. Obituary, *Independent*, 12 December 2002.
2. Joseph Wechsberg, *The Merchant Bankers* (London: Weidenfeld and Nicolson, 1967), p.21.
3. Ibid.
4. Derek Taylor, *Don Pacifico: The Acceptable Face of Gunboat Diplomacy* (London and Portland, OR: Vallentine Mitchell, 2008).
5. *Jewish Chronicle*, 18 January 1901.

6. Canterbury Christ Church University, Salomons Museum, Archive.
7. *The Times*, 13 July 1873.
8. *The Times*, 15 May 1936.
9. Ibid.
10. Niall Ferguson, *High Financier: The Lives and Time of Siegmund Warburg* (Harmondsworth: Allen Lane, 2010).
11. Ibid.
12. Ibid.
13. Ibid.
14. *Jewish Chronicle*, 26 December 1997.
15. Dan Atkinson, *Guardian*, 19 April 2000.
16. *Jewish Chronicle*, 2 October 1992.
17. *Sunday Times*, 23 January 2005.
18. http://en.wikipedia.org/wiki/Ronald_Cohen.
19. *Management Today*, 1 December 2009.
20. Andrew Davidson, *Sunday Times*, 28 September 2003.
21. dictionaryofarthistorians.org/berensonb.htm.
22. *Church Times*, 16 March 2007.
23. James Robinson, *Observer*, 27 June 2004.

Chapter four

Looking after the Ladies

One of the most serious problems for the Jews over the centuries was that they didn't always get enough warning. Agreed, they might be able to anticipate a new ruler throwing them out of the city or country in which they had lived for years. It was much more difficult to know when there might be a spontaneous pogrom, the destruction of their homes and an urgent need to flee the country at practically no notice.

If that happened they needed to be able to travel light. Escaping with their lives might well be regarded as a major victory over their oppressors. They knew it was almost inevitable that their homes and possessions would have to be abandoned to the arsonists, looters and pillagers. What could be rescued? And that was how the Jews grew to love the jewellery business. Jewels were easy to carry about and they were hard to detect. Today, you might see any number of men dressed in Orthodox Jewish clothes, wandering about Hatton Garden or the New York jewellery district. Blue trilbies, dark suits, black shoes and *tsitsis*, fringed garments hanging down their sides. They almost all have brief cases, but which have diamonds in them is anybody's guess.

Happily, wherever the fleeing Jews finished up, there was likely to be a demand for jewellery. Moreover, if they could acquire the skills to value them, polish and cut them, or mount them attractively, the finished products would be worth far more than they paid for the raw materials.

As has already been described, the involvement of the Jews in the British diamond world started even before Cromwell told his people not to harass them. The main polishing centre in Europe at that time was Amsterdam and the majority of the gemstone merchants were Portuguese Jews.[1] To protect themselves from Dutch sea power, the

Portuguese arranged a marriage between Charles II and Catherine of Braganza. She arrived in London in 1662, together with Duarte da Silva and two other Jewish merchants, who had been responsible for arranging her dowry. Which included, among other baubles, Bombay and Tangiers. When the East India Company allowed the Jews to trade diamonds in India, the opportunity became official, and merchants like da Silva took advantage of it.

It is significant that Sir Samuel Barnardiston, on behalf of the East India Company, specifically said, 'the company giving leave to the Jews to trade in diamonds',[2] as if the members of the religion were a nation. Indeed, in Cromwell's time, England was at war with Spain and Portugal and the question arose of whether the possessions of enemy aliens, like the Portuguese Jews, should be confiscated. Legally they could, but Cromwell got round the problem by declaring that the Jews were, in fact, a separate nation unto themselves, never mind that they lived or were born in Spain or Portugal. In that way their goods were safeguarded.

For the Jews, there was another advantage to the jewellery trade in Britain. The diamonds were only to be found overseas in countries like India or, from the late nineteenth century onwards, in South Africa. Discrimination was less likely in those countries where the Jews were out of sight of European capitals, and hoped they were out of mind. Even when they also had to buy from the East India Company overseas, there were far fewer restrictions on Jewish participation in the finished products than might have been the case nearer Head Office. Jewellery also came into the equation when people wanted to raise ready cash by pawning something. A pawnbroker's stock would automatically include some jewellery; it's back to the Jewish moneylenders – or banks and merchant banks, as they are called today.

On a smaller scale, when the occupations of early Jewish citizens in small British towns in the early days of the communities are analysed, there are very often jewellers, pawnbrokers and watchmakers among them. For instance, one such immigrant to London in the late eighteenth century was Menachem Samuel, whose son, Louis Samuel, married his maternal cousin, Harriet Israel (1793–1860). The business moved to Liverpool and when Menachem and Louis passed away, it was Harriet who took over the running of the company until she died.[3]

Louis Samuel's son, Montagu, changed his name to Samuel Montagu and became that Lord Swaythling who appeared in Chapter 3, 'Grown-up Moneylending'. Harriet moved the business to the Market Street area of Manchester and took a particular interest in the mail-order side. Which, of course, links in with the tallymen pedlars; only tallymen in the eighteenth century usually hadn't carried expensive jewellery; it would have been far too dangerous with highwaymen around. As the railways and the penny post made the transportation of goods easier, mail order started to replace the tallymen. Harriet's sons ran the shop and opened a new store in Preston in 1890 and then more throughout Lancashire. They moved on to Birmingham in 1912, and H. Samuel is now probably the best-known name in jewellery shops in the country. The company went public in 1948 and today has 375 branches.

Leslie Ratner started much later than the Samuels. He opened a shop in Richmond, London in 1949. His son, Gerald Ratner (1949–), replaced him in 1984, when the company had 130 branches and was losing £350,000 a year. Gerald Ratner then went on a buying spree. In quick succession he bought H. Samuel and, in 1987, another multiple, Ernest Jones, which was more into the carriage trade. He employed 27,000 people and, in 1987, he expanded into America. Today the company has 1,600 stores in the USA and UK. Only Gerald Ratner isn't running them any more.

In 1991, as chairman of his company, he was invited to speak at the annual conference of the Institute of Directors. For a man who had decided to learn his trade in the Pettycoat Lane market in the East End of London, it was a well-merited recognition of glittering progress. Ratner's problem, however, was that he was either very ill-advised or inadvertently dug his own grave, because the speech he delivered totally denigrated his own products. He told the audience that a prawn sandwich would outlast the earrings he was selling in his shops, that an invitation book was 'in the worst possible taste' and that another popular line was 'total crap'.

The company received enormous publicity as a result, and all of it was bad. The value of the shares dropped by £500 million and Ratner, the chairman, was first demoted to chief executive officer and then had to resign. As he was a very able businessman, if somewhat inadequate at preparing or approving speeches for public consumption, he now has a successful internet company selling jewellery, and the diamonds once again come from India. Meanwhile, the original Ratners changed its name to Signet and is doing very well.

Gerald Ratner was another example of the Jewish businessman who is at his best when creating and leading a company, rather than being a company man. The restraints of the boardroom, where consensus is important and progress is often cautious, demand disciplines which often don't suit an entrepreneur.

Antwerp is, of course, a major diamond centre and had many Jewish companies. When the Second World War loomed, many Jews in the diamond industry escaped to Britain, including Leon Fiszman (1906–2004). In 1948, after the war, he started a company called Star Diamonds, which is now one of the biggest distributors of rough diamonds in the world.

Fiszman *père* remained as chairman until he reached old age, but handed over to his son, Danny (1945–2011), thereafter. The family opened an office back in Antwerp in the 1950s, and further offices in Bombay and Tel Aviv in 1962. Fiszman *père* was a very strong personality and he had the Jewish gambling streak firmly instilled in his personality. When the diamond market collapsed in the 1980s, the employment prospects of diamond polishers in Israel looked gloomy indeed. Leon Fiszman tackled the problem head-on and employed no less than 2,500 of them. Danny Fiszman sold the company in 2004 and, in 2006, the *Sunday Times* Rich List estimated his fortune at £150 million. His main outside interest was the Arsenal football club where he was a non-executive director, but he died quite young in 2011.

One of the most charming aspects of jewellery is the enamel box, and Susan Benjamin (1921–2010) resuscitated the art of making them when she came across an antique example in 1950. She began to design new ones and started a shop called Halcyon Days, which became well known for them. So good were her products that she received no less than four royal warrants from the Queen, the Queen Mother, the Duke of Edinburgh and the Prince of Wales.

Another favourite with Queen Mary, the Queen Mother and Princess Margaret was Moshe Oved (1885–1958), who ran a jeweller's shop near the British Museum called Cameo Corner. He had come to Britain from Poland as a trained watchmaker in 1903, and started in Black Lion Yard in the East End where the Jewish jewellery artisans originally congregated. Resplendent in a purple velvet caftan, Oved was a great character and a founder of the Ben Uri art gallery.

When the subject of diamonds comes up, one's thoughts are directed to great names like Van Cleef and Arpels, Cartier and the vastly wealthy South African Randlords. To attempt to make a mark in the rarefied domain of high-class jewellers, it would not seem ideal to start with a Russian-Jewish refugee father who made suits in the East End, and a Romanian newsagent mother. Leaving school at 15 to obtain work in Hatton Garden and being fired after three months wouldn't improve matters either, and if the next jeweller employer went bankrupt, the odds would seem to be stacked even higher against the candidate.

This, though, was the background of Laurence Graff (1938–), who is now estimated to be worth £1.5 billion. From such an early CV, he began to design jewellery before he was out of his teens, and sold the concepts to jewellers all over England. By the time he was 22, he had formed his own company, Graff Diamonds and, by 24, he had been able to open two small jewellery shops for himself. By the age of 30, he was one of the largest jewellery manufacturers in Britain, and in 1973 he was the first jeweller to win the Queen's Award for Industry.

Graff moved on to a prestigious shop in Knightsbridge and then to an even better address in New Bond Street. Like his forebears, however, his view was international and shops were opened in Monte Carlo, New York and Chicago. He now has thirty stores, including outlets in Geneva, Tokyo and Hong Kong.

Much came to depend on the supply of good diamonds, and Graff didn't want to rely on others if he could avoid it. So he started the South African Diamond Corporation with branches in Johannesburg, Antwerp, New York and Botswana. There he created the SAFDICO

Business Park, which now cuts and polishes the raw diamonds and employs over 500 staff. For a small African country it is a vital economic asset.

The fame of a jeweller-designer depends to some extent on the great diamonds he has handled. Graf has had in his hands the Porter Rhodes, the Star of America, Delaire Sunrise and the Begum Blue stones, among many other great names. In 2008, he paid the largest sum ever for a diamond, £16.4 million for the Wittelsbach Diamond.

Graff has been a generous benefactor as well, with his Graff Foundation. His FACET (For Africa Children Every Time) organization has developed Leadership Centres and helped poor black communities in many ways. A charity auction he organized in London in 2009 raised over £1 million for the projects. Graff is one of the much-needed industrialists dedicated to helping the poorest continents.

If a woman can't afford Graff's jewellery, she can at least have her hair done, but in the 1960s it was acknowledged that the best hairdressers were to be found in France. That all changed through the efforts of a number of British celebrity hairdressers, of whom the most influential was Vidal Sassoon (1928–2012).

Sassoon was born in Hammersmith, London to a Greek–Sephardi father and a Spanish–Sephardi mother. He had a miserable childhood; his father deserted his mother, when he was 3, and left her destitute. The family finished up sleeping on mattresses in their aunt's cold-water tenement in London's Petticoat Lane in the East End. Even that effort to keep the family together failed and Sassoon was sent to the Sephardi Orphanage, where he spent the next seven years. He left school at 14, and was persuaded by his mother to take an apprentice hairdresser's job at Alf Cohen's salon, next to a gasworks in Whitechapel.

At an early age Sassoon was very conscious of anti-Semitism, and took part in efforts to stop the fascists parading in the East End after the war. He had also served in the army and, in 1948, went off to Israel to fight in the War of Independence. His small force held a hill for seventeen days and suffered 40 per cent casualties, killed and wounded. Oddly, he was bombed by Egyptian Spitfires and protected by Israeli Messerschmitts. Arms' supplies were very much catch-as-catch-can in that conflict.

He came back to England to restart his career as a hairdresser and got on the ladder to better things when he persuaded a celebrity hairdresser, known as Mr Teasy Weasy, to give him a job. By 1954 he felt confident enough to start his own salon at what he described as 'the wrong end of Bond Street'. He decided that what he needed was to be different; his objective was to create a new hairstyle for women which would become all the rage; the pot of gold at the end of the rainbow. As he remembered in later years, 'It's true that, in the Sixties, we worked very hard to make British hairdressing the best in the world because, until then, it was always about France. You had to have enormous stamina. We were doing 14 hour days – you couldn't be druggy.'[4]

Sassoon had developed into a brilliant hairdresser. He invented a particular style, which was known as the geometric cut. It was modern, low maintenance and cut very short in geometric patterns. He went on to invent the Bob Cut, which also became extremely fashionable. He even set about polishing his image, talking later of improving his cockney accent by getting tuition from Laurence Olivier's voice coach. As a top West End hairdresser, he became very famous.

Sassoon was, however, also an astute businessman. In the 1970s, he developed his own products in conjunction with the Daz company, Proctor and Gamble. The strapline for the advertising was, 'If you don't look good, we don't look good.' Salons were also franchised and Sassoon remained one of the best-known members of his industry. His worries about anti-Semitism never left him. In 1982, he founded, in Israel, the Vidal Sassoon International Center for the Study of anti-Semitism, and financed the body from then on. In 2009 he was awarded the CBE. He died at 84.

Young mothers were perhaps less concerned about hair products than baby products. Their lives were made much easier by the son of a Latvian-Jewish immigrant called David Atkin (1915–72). In the 1930s, Atkin started a company producing hot-water bottles in a factory originally designed to produce billiard cues; he called the company Cannon after the cues. In 1965, his son, Edward (1945–), joined the company when the firm had widened its product range to include more rubber products, such as bottle teats, bathing caps, car mats and shoe soles.

When Atkin died in 1972, Edward and his brother, Robert, took over the firm. Edward handled the product development and Robert the sales. Eventually there was a massive falling-out, and the two brothers parted company. Edward bought Robert's shares and by this time the company was called Cannon Avent and it specialized in baby-feeding products.

For working mothers who want their babies to have breast milk, a safe sterilized container from which the baby can feed is an essential. It is also an essential all over the world and, as a result, a small family business became a global consumer brand. In 2005, 80 per cent of Cannon Avent's turnover of more than £100 million would go overseas, half of it to America. With so much manufacturing taking place in the Far East because of their lower wages, it might have been thought that Cannon Avent would soon be under threat, but Atkin had the solution.

The labour costs of the company are only 5 per cent because the products are made by automation. It takes fifteen minutes to make a bottle and no human hand is involved in the process.[5] The manufacturing centre is state-of-the-art, in Glemsford, Suffolk. Atkin was always passionate about the products. As he told a London Business School audience, 'If you do not really believe what you are offering is the best in the world, then it is most unlikely that anyone else will.'[6] A lot of credit for the successful running of the company has to go to his wife, Celia, as well.

The Atkins sold out in 2005, and made a personal fortune of £225 million. They created the Atkin Foundation and give substantial support to the Jewish Community Security Trust, Jewish Care and Norwood. There are also, however, Atkin Fellowships at King's College, London, to enable both Arab and Jewish postgraduates to study together. The Camden Roundhouse, the Old Vic and the Tate Gallery have also received generous donations. In 2009 the Foundation gave away almost £1 million.

When it comes to beauty and health, Boots, established in 1849, dominated the pharmaceutical and healthcare high street after the Second World War. Nevertheless, Ronald (1937–) and Peter (1940–) Goldstein decided to take them on. Their father had sold his supermarkets to Tesco, so the funds were available and, in 1966, their first Superdrug store was opened in Putney, London. 'They found the premises, fitted it out, stocked the shelves and manned the tills.'[7] It was very much a hands-on operation.

As standards of living improved, the amount of disposable income that could be spent on luxury products went up as well. Beauty products, in particular, had a great appeal for women, but they were expensive; perfumes and cosmetics came beautifully packaged but with large price tags. So Superdrug offered self-service and reduced prices. The company did well and, twenty years after Putney, it had 289 stores. Superdrug was the drugstore Woolworths. Furthermore, a quarter of its sales came from own-label products, which could be much cheaper than the branded equivalents. The reputation Superdrug acquired for quality and good value proved – as it always will – a winning combination.

When it launched on the Stock Exchange in 1983, the issue was over-subscribed ninety-six times and the price obtained was an astonishing forty-two times earnings; Boots shares at the time were on about fifteen times earnings. In 1987 the brothers did, in fact, sell out to Woolworths and in 1990 they retired. Superdrug is still the second-largest beauty retailer in the UK.

While Superdrug is very well known, the founder of the 'world's leading manufacturers of mouthwash tablets' keeps a much lower profile. Ernst Tell (1889–1954) had a pharmacy in Germany but left in 1936 to escape the Nazis. His son, Wernher (1921–), started manufacturing the mouthwash tablets after the war, and is still at the helm at the age of 90, selling the tablets around the world. For every time a dentist has a new patient, there is a need for a Tellodont.

One of the benefits of living in the twenty-first century is that much of the drudgery has been taken out of the work in the kitchen and homes are pleasanter places to live in. For many of these timesaving improvements and our increase in comfort, the credit should go to Arthur (Turi) Goldstein (1902–84).

Goldstein was born in the old Austro-Hungarian Empire and was fortunate enough to reach Britain in 1938. Tragically, his wife remained behind and died in the Holocaust. Goldstein went to live in Cambridge and created a company called Warmex. He was an engineer by training and a prolific inventor. By the time he had finished, he had taken out thirty-six patents. These included under-seat heating in cars, a better hair dryer, a pop-up toaster and a new form of coffee maker. Goldstein was a pillar of the Cambridge Jewish community and chairman of the *Chevra Kadisha* (the burial society) for many years. He was considered a model employer and a very charitable man. The firm is still in business.

Where there are families, there are children, and children want toys. Here was a major international market, and there were Jewish companies deeply involved in satisfying the demand. For many Jews, simply to survive between the world wars demanded enormous resilience. Time and again, if you were in the wrong country at the wrong time, it was necessary to flee and start again. Typical of this kind of peripatetic refugee was Miklos Klein (1891–1958), a Hungarian Jew who, at 29, served briefly as a junior minister in the communist government of Bela Kun after the First World War. When the government collapsed and Admiral Horthy started a reign of terror, Klein took his family to Algeria and then on to Spain where he started a plastics factory. The Spanish Civil War drove him out of there and he came, via Italy, to England where he finally settled, and reinvented himself as Nicholas Kove.[8]

In 1939, Kove started a company to produce rubber inflatable toys and called it Airfix, partly because of the air in the toys and partly because he felt that there was an advantage to being listed at the beginning of a business directory; 'AI ...' was early enough. Another of the firm's products, which proved particularly successful, was the Lilo, a kind of outdoor sunbed.

During the war he turned to making army buckles and, after the war ended, he imported the first injection-moulding machine into Britain, to enable him to become the largest producer of plastic combs in the country. If something was new and potentially profitable, Kove would give it consideration. At which point it so happened that Ferguson, the tractor company, came up with the idea of giving their sales staff plastic models of their vehicles to leave with the customers. Kove got the contract to produce them and, spotting a good potential product, agreed with Ferguson that he could manufacture a kit for the public, to construct the tractors for themselves.

That was the beginning of Airfix as a famous company. In 1950, however, Kove contracted cancer and had to live a quieter life. He took on as managing director an ex-member of Bomber Command, Ralph Ehrman (1925–), a German Jew who was born in Leipzig and came to Britain at the age of 6. It was Ehrman who brought to the market the model kit of a Spitfire. For kit builders, this was one of the icons of all time. Kove died in 1958 and his wife a few months later. Ehrman led the company as chairman through twenty years of expansion. It was only in the 1980s that the market shrank, as new hobbies, like computer games, emerged. Airfix went into administration but is now, after various vicissitudes, part of Hornby.

Just before Kove reached Britain, the Slump of the 1930s was causing enormous suffering. Every country wanted more manufacturers who could produce saleable products in the depressed world market. If they were successful, that happy result would produce jobs. In Germany, one of the most successful light industries for many years had been the making of toys, of which Steiff teddy bears were probably the most famous. Manufacturing was centred in Nuremberg, and in 1912 a new company was created there, called Tipp & Co. By 1919 Philipp Ullmann (1883–1971), who came from a toy-making family, was the sole proprietor and the firm became well known for producing metal toys.

In 1933, when Hitler came to power, Ullmann and his son, Henry, decided to get out. With them went Ullmann's nephew, Arthur Katz (1908–99). They left behind a thriving business which the Nazis sequestered and which continued to make excellent model cars for many years. In England, with the help of Simon Marks, of Marks & Spencer, Ullmann set up a new company in Northampton which he called Mettoy, because that was what it did: clockwork metal toys. Marks & Spencer was one of their major customers, and Ullmann gave the profits to rescue more German-Jewish refugees. Six hundred new jobs were very welcome in Northampton, but toy production had to stop at the outbreak of war, as the company moved to producing shell fuses, sten-gun magazines, landmines and other military hardware.

The Ministry of Supply was impressed by Ullmann's efficiency and built him a 28,000 square-foot factory in Swansea to increase production. Swansea had been hard hit by the decline in demand for Welsh coal and there was serious unemployment. After the war Colonel Katz was sent by the government to investigate the German toy industry, and Ullmann got his company back. By 1952, the factory in Wales at Fforestfach had grown to 200,000 square feet and was set to employ 1,000 staff.

It was in 1956 that Arthur Katz, now managing director, launched the product that was to make the company famous: Corgi cars. They were so named in an attempt to benefit from the royal family's fondness for the breed, and Corgi went into competition with the market leader for many years, Dinky Toys. Corgi cars were made by pressure die casting in zinc and plastic injection moulding, much superior to the old 'tin' toys. They were designed to be more sophisticated than Dinky. The strapline was, 'The one with the windows'. There was more than that though. 'Plastic windshields, diamond crystal headlights, spring mounted wheels, door, trunks and hoods that opened.'[9]

The company made models of famous cars, like the Batmobile, Chitty Chitty Bang Bang, and the James Bond Aston Martin DB5, which was to be the largest selling toy car ever. The DB5 had rotating licence plates, hubcaps with Ben Hur-style tyre slashers, machine-gun turrets behind the headlights, and an ejection seat that sent the passenger flying through the car's roof. Today it is worth about £300. By the end of the 1950s, Corgi was exporting to over 100 countries. The company was floated on the stock market in 1963 for £40 million. By 1968 it had 385,000 square feet and employed 3,500. 'It was like General Motors', said the American distributor of Corgi, 'There were people creating thousands and thousands of cars.'[10]

Philipp Ullmann remained chairman of the company until he was 86 in 1969; he died in 1971. Arthur Katz remained managing director from 1944 to 1976, received the CBE in 1973, and died in 1999 at 91. Unfortunately for the company, children's tastes in toys now became more sophisticated, and a combination of high inflation and the value of sterling made the toys far more expensive than the Asian competition. 'There was no way you could cut your costs fast enough', said Peter Katz, Arthur's son and Mettoy's managing director at the time. Mettoy called in the liquidators in 1983 and Swansea was closed in 1991. It was another Jewish business that didn't survive the death of the founders.

Another major toy company after the war was Dunbee-Combex, the creation in 1946 of Basil Feldman (1926–). Feldman had been educated at the Grocers' School, which was the preferred choice of Jewish parents with clever children, in London's Stamford Hill. He was only 20 when, with his partner, Richard Beecham, he started making bathing caps and manufacturing plastic products.

In the late 1950s, they decided to go into the toy business and this was mostly achieved by a series of purchases, such as Combex in 1960. In 1962 they went public and, by 1971, had bought the manufacturers of the iconic Hornby trains, Scalextric, the car-racing game, Sindy dolls and Pedigree toys. Their profits peaked at £6.5 million in 1977 when they were the largest independent toy company in Britain. Then came disaster. One of the most famous toy companies in the United States was Louis Marx Inc., and in 1967 Dunbee-Combex bought the British division of the company. Marx got into trouble and was sold to Quaker Oats for $56 million in 1972. They couldn't recover the situation and when it was offered to Feldman for $15 million in 1976 it must have seemed a snip.

Unfortunately Dunbee-Combex-Marx couldn't reverse the losses either and, together with losses in Europe, the profitable British end of the business couldn't prevent the overdrafts rising to alarming levels. In 1979, the company lost £5 million and in 1980 it went into liquidation. Feldman had a distinguished career in the Conservative Party, alongside his business activities, and was both knighted and made a peer. Many of the Dunbee-Combex-Marx products are still being made under new ownership.

When it comes to homemaking, Jewish women are as involved as any other wife and mother. One of the necessities is furniture and this was a Jewish trade for centuries. For Ashkenazi Jews living in small villages and towns on the Continent during the eighteenth century, life was very hard. Living in ghettos, prohibited from membership of the guilds and unable to own land to farm, most lived in poverty. During the summer, the men would tramp the countryside as pedlars, but when the winter came, the cold, the dangers of the dark on empty roads, and the byways churned into mud, made peddling hazardous.

It was from that background that Jews started to make furniture in their homes during the winter. It was not difficult to gather free timber in the forest during the summer, and there was a need in most homes for more chairs, tables and beds. When the spring came, the furniture would be put on sale. Jews worked to acquire the necessary skills to make serviceable products. It wasn't Chippendale and it wasn't the standard of woodwork of Grinling Gibbons, but it served its purpose and it was affordable for the villagers.

In Lithuania, there was a thriving Jewish timber-export trade to Britain and, when 12,000 Jews from Russia and Poland arrived in London between 1861 and 1868, a considerable number set up as small timber merchants. One such firm was started about 1880 by Jacob Gliksten, whose sons, Stanley (1892–1962) and Albert (1898–1951), built it up into one of the largest in the country. So well regarded was Albert Gliksten that, during the Second World War, he was appointed assistant director of timber control.

The Glikstens are best remembered for their investment in Charlton Athletic FC. They took over the club in 1931 and, in just three seasons, saw it promoted from the third to the first division. They also reached the FA Cup Final on two occasions, losing in 1946 but winning in 1947. The Glikstens' company went public in 1946, and the business continued to thrive for many years under Michael Gliksten (1939–2009).

In the First World War, the timber buyer for every government department was Louis Bamberger (c.1849–c.1932). He had taken over his father's timber business, which had been started in 1851. He retired in 1919, but the business continued to flourish. It was the largest supplier of timber to the RAF and worked with car companies such as Vauxhall Bedford. The quality of the wood finishes in cars at the time was an important selling point; as Bambergers advertised in 1933,

'Situated alongside a public park and unenclosed on three sides, these wharves make ideal drying grounds. Visitors will be able to see the care with which the timber is stored and two distinct processes of selection which every piece undergoes before being delivered.'

The family continued to run the company after Bamberger's death, though they had lost two sons in the Great War. They went public in 1948, and had one record that they could have done without; in 1966, their main timber yard caught fire and 50,000 tons was lost. It took 500 firemen to contain the blaze, which was the largest since the Second World War.

When the Jews migrated to Britain, many also brought their furniture-making skills with them; a very large number started small businesses in the East End of London. One of the main ports for importing timber was – and remains – Hull. One of the earliest Jewish furniture makers was Louis Lebus (c.1810–79), who arrived in 1840 from Breslau in Germany. He started making furniture in his home in Hull and moved to London, where the firm eventually finished up in Tottenham, in the north of the city. The advantage of Tottenham was its closeness to the River Lea. It was possible to unload timber at the London Docks, and transport it by barge to the factory, which his son, Harris Lebus (1852–1907), built after his father died.

By the 1890s, the company was employing 1,000 workers and had become one of the largest furniture manufacturers in the world. When Harris Lebus died, his son, Herman took over until 1957, latterly as Sir Herman. The company sold its products to high quality furniture stores like Maples, and played a major role in bringing the designs of the Arts and Crafts movement to the general public.

As standards of living rose throughout the country, there was an enormous demand for cheap, well-made furniture. Because of the bulkiness of the finished products, home manufacturers had an advantage over those overseas. Buying raw materials and selling finished goods is what a sound manufacturing economy is all about, and the country's balance of payments benefited.

The Lebus Tottenham site was a massive nineteen acres and the factories proved invaluable to the war efforts in both 1914–18 and

1939–45. In the First World War they were turned over to producing the Handley Page 0100 and V1500 biplanes, as well as the Vickers Vimy monoplane. The fledgling Royal Flying Corps got the machines they needed to support the troops in the trenches in France.

During the Second World War, the Lebus factory went over to producing the Airspeed Horsa glider and the Mosquito fighter aircraft, though in the early days their furniture production expertise was used to create imitation wooden tanks! So many had been lost in France by the time of the evacuation from Dunkirk that, without the imitations, German reconnaissance aircraft would soon have noticed the resulting complete absence of tanks in Britain. So the mock wooden ones were ordered by the government to fool the enemy.

In the aftermath of the war, Lebus produced a mass of cheap furniture, which went under the general name of Utility, government regulations laying down what standards could be set. In 1947, the company went public and Sir Herman died in 1957. In 1966, their market share collapsed from 7 per cent to 3 per cent and, in 1970, after sustaining heavy losses, it was decided to close the factory. Over 1,000 staff lost their jobs. In 1972, the leadership of the firm went to Oliver Lebus (1925–2009), and he served as president of the Worshipful Company of Furniture Makers in 1979, dying at nearly 90.

Furniture sales really took off in the period between the wars. The main reasons for this were threefold: the development of the mass production of wooden objects during the First World War; the development of hire-purchase terms sufficiently attractive to bring the poorer sections of the public into the market, and massive advertising by retail chains to attract the customers.

Many of the major chains of furniture shops were started by Jews: Benjamin Drage of Drages, Sampson J. Goldberg of Smart Brothers, John Jacobs of the Times Furnishing Company and Sir Julian Cahn (1882–1944) and Joseph Freedman (1860–1949) of Jays and Campbells. The chains managed to raise the number of hire-purchase agreements from about a million in 1891 to six million in 1924 and 24 million by 1936.[11]

The overheads were high; up to 10 per cent of turnover was spent on advertising and there were substantial administrative costs involved in hire purchase. Even so, the profit margins could reach 150 per cent; indeed, Joseph Freedman was on record during the Slump as saying, 'The day profits fall below 200 per cent we'll all be ruined!'[12]

The poorer sections of the public had to be coaxed into spending what were large sums, by their standards, to furnish their houses. The methods used were not always very scrupulous and dicey legal agreements, misleading advertising and poor-quality furniture were all to be found on occasions. There were the usual internal problems as well: one day during the Slump, Joseph Freedman's son told his father that it was necessary to fire one of their managers in Cardiff; he said he was fiddling the books. His father said that was ridiculous. 'No', said his son, 'I can prove he's fiddling the books.' His father sighed, 'You don't understand. I know he's fiddling the books. He's been fiddling the books for years. But we're making a profit in his shop!'[13]

Julian Cahn had, in fact, inherited a fortune from his father, Albert, a German refugee who had decided to set up the Nottingham Furnishing Company, because Nottingham seemed to him to be in the middle of England. The son grew the business, but devoted much of his spare time to cricket. He formed his own team to tour the dominions and paid for the stands at Trent Bridge, the home of Nottinghamshire cricket. At its peak, Jays and Campbell had about 400 stores and Cahn was made a baronet in 1934.

The war sounded the death knell for many of the chains. Factories that had been manufacturing furniture were changed over to war work, and demand slackened as people became concerned that their homes would be bombed, and the furniture destroyed with everything else. Sir Isaac Wolfson (1897–1991), the head of Great Universal Stores, took the opportunity to move in and buy most of the major retail chains. His reasoning was that their hire-purchase debts would produce large sums of cash-flow capital, and their properties could be sold to other retailers in due course at a good price. It was another example of Jews recognizing that they were dead if the Nazis won and, therefore, might just as well gamble that the Nazis would lose, at which point the value of the properties would rebound.

One major organization in the north of England was the Cussins Group. Menassah (Manny) Cussins (1906–87) came from a Lithuanian family called Rakusen, but Israel Rakusen shortened it to Cussins. Manny Cussins was born in Hull and started in the furniture business at the age of 13, pushing a handcart around the streets. He went on to build up a group of furniture shops, before selling out for £1 million in 1954. His second business career was the creation of the John Peters Company which, by 1975, had 100 shops, sixteen cloth factories and a building business. He went on to become chairman of Waring and Gillow, one of the most famous names in the furniture world and merged it with Maples, which was probably the second best known.

In Leeds, though, where he had set up home, Manny Cussins was known as the chairman of Leeds United FC from 1972 to 1983. He had been a director since 1961 and, under the management of Don Revie, the club had won the top division title twice, the FA Cup, the Inter City Fairs Cup twice and the League Cup. Unfortunately for Leeds, Revie left to manage England in 1974 and Cussins was never able to replace him; indeed he fired four managers in his ten years of trying to do so, including the iconic Brian Clough.

Cussins was a well-regarded fixture in Leeds and gave £100,000 for a centre to treat diabetes and vascular diseases. He also provided a house for Jewish children who had been put in care by the local council, and he was president of the Leeds Home for Aged Jews. Cussins managed to struggle through the difficult years of the 1970s and early 1980s but, after his death, the resuscitated John Peters staggered from crisis to crisis and went into temporary administration in 2007. It was just the latest example of a trend but, for the older generation, trends were there to be bucked. Cussins had built his original empire through the Slump.

Schreiber Furniture was founded by Chaim Schreiber (1918–84) in 1957. Schreiber was a refugee from the Nazis and in the 1960s produced furniture for the cheaper end of the market, which did very well. He was, like Simon Marks at Marks & Spencer, very solicitous of his staff. In 1970 he abolished clocking-in, a system of proving at what time the employees arrived for work. It normally only applied to lower-paid staff, rather than management, and was, therefore, he considered, divisive.

Schreiber also abolished wage packets for the lower paid staff and paid them in the same way as management.

Schreibers was only one of the furniture firms founded by Jews. A German refugee, Abraham Myers (1796–1872), came to Britain and set up as a pawnbroker. When he was 54 his son, Horatio Myers (1850–1916), was born and when the youngster was 26 he decided to go into the bedspread business. With help from his relations he bought a company, and this is still in existence today. His great grandson is the operations manager.

Surviving for nearly 150 years is no mean achievement, but the company was firmly established by the time Myers died. He was a religious man, a warden of the Bayswater synagogue and a great supporter in its infancy of the Jewish Historical Society of England. He also served as MP for Lambeth North in 1906. When he died it was said that he was 'Honoured by all who knew him, upright in his dealings, never saying an unkind word, but trying to do all the good he could.'[14] Even if the *Jewish Chronicle* doesn't speak ill of the dead, it was a considerable encomium. In 1982, Myers moved to Huntingdon where it still manufactures beds on a thirteen-acre site with 600 staff – the largest manufacturing business in the town. As the company bought Staples, it has the Royal Warrant.

In 1916 a Russian refugee, Barnett Nathan (1896–1968), set up B. and I. Nathan in Hackney. During the war they made munitions boxes, as they would in the Second World War. After 1918, they flourished and moved to a bigger factory in Edmonton in the 1930s. Nathans specialized in dining-room furniture and was chosen in 1954 to represent the best-of-British furniture design at an exhibition to promote British goods in New York. The furniture was made in Tola (African mahogany) with black diamond legs and brass handles. In the 1960s, the company went over to Scandinavian design, using teak instead. It is still in business today, though under different ownership. A great deal of modern furniture, however, is now made abroad and imports have adversely affected the balance of trade.

After the Second World War, there came a time when the government could relax the restrictions that had created the basic Utility furniture. Designers could now be less inhibited, but the problem for all of them was to find a manufacturer who was prepared to risk the cost of investing in a new production line, which might not gain the public's approval.

The company which became the centre of new design in Britain was Hille. As the Editor of *Building Design* put it in 1981, 'Invitations to the Hille annual party came to be seen as the gauge of a designer's current standing among his peers.' Hille was a family business, founded by Salamon Hille when he fled Russia in 1900. His daughter, Ray, took over the company in 1932 when it was making reproduction Chippendale, Hepplewhite and other classic styles. Not content with these, Ray Hille also offered German Bauhaus, Chinese Lacquer and her own Art Deco designs.[15]

The next generation was Ray's daughter, Rosamund, who joined the family firm when the Second World War ended and she discovered modern art and architecture on a sales trip to America soon after. She also found Robin Day, a particularly good innovator; with her husband, Leslie Julius, they started producing furniture according to his designs. In the years to come, if you visited a modern building such as the Festival Hall or Gatwick Airport, you would be likely to sit on a Hille chair. The difficulty they encountered was to get retailers to stock the furniture, so they opened their own emporium in the West End of London, much to the annoyance of other furniture shops. Manufacturers at the time were not supposed to be retailers as well. Another daughter, Cherrell Scheer, is known today as the 'grand dame' of the British contract-furniture industry.[16]

Fortunately for the Juliuses, other organizations wanted to make a fashion statement as well. Contracts for the Istanbul Hilton Hotel, Chelsea FC and the Nottingham Playhouse made the furniture better known and even more fashionable. Among the most successful designs was a polypropylene plastic chair that sold phenomenally well. In 1963, the *Architect's Journal* called it, 'The most significant development in British mass-produced design since the war.' Not that Hille was the only Jewish furniture company to try to modernize the appearance of British products. Frank Austin (Austin Furniture) for example, was the first to manufacture in teak.

As companies like Lebus and Schreiber declined, because other countries could produce the furniture more cheaply, Hille pointed the way to successfully surviving in a competitive world. More than fifty countries took up licences to produce the polypropylene chair. In reverse, famous designers invited Hille to make the furniture for the US Embassy in London and the UNESCO building in Paris. The company was sold in 1986, Leslie Julius died in 1989 and Rosamund in 2010. She would have been delighted that one of her chairs was chosen for a set of British stamps celebrating British design classics.

Few furniture creations finish up in the Victoria and Albert Museum, and equally few become almost instant classics. One exception is the furniture designed by Robert Heritage for Archie Shine (1910–93) in the 1960s. Shine was a throwback to the Jewish winter furniture-makers in Eastern Europe. He started a small factory in a converted horse-tram stable in the East End of London and was introduced to Heritage by the newly formed Design Council.

Heritage created simple, elegant furniture with long, low lines, much influenced by the Danes. He used teak, afrormosia and rosewood, and the results were very much what the old established Heal's store was looking for, to get away from the traditional products. It was, however, a major act of faith to back a new, young designer, because the hard cash had to come from Shine to make the furniture. The *Guardian* commented at the time: 'Archie Shine has faith in everything Robert Heritage does; an idyllic and very unusual client\designer relationship.'[17] In 1976 Heal's bought Shine out, but the name lives on in antique furniture auctions all over the country.

NOTES

1. Samuel Edgar, *At the End of the Earth: Essays on the History of the Jews of England and Portugal* (London: Jewish Historical Society of England, 2004).
2. Ibid., p.245.
3. www.hsamuel.co.uk/webstore/static/about/today.do
4. Lisa Armstrong, *The Times*, 21 October 2009.
5. *Real Business*, 30 August 2007.
6. Ibid.

7. dave-beentheredonethat.blogspot.com.2010/03/superdrug.html.
8. Helen Peck, *Relationship Marketing*, Chartered Institute of Marketing.
9. Lawrence Zuckerman, *New York Times*, 21 July 1999.
10. Ibid.
11. Peter Scott, *Mr Drage, Mr Everyman, and the Creation of a Mass Market for Domestic Furniture in Interwar Britain* (Reading: University of Reading Business School, 2007).
12. Freedman family folklore.
13. Ibid.
14. *Jewish Chronicle*, 14 January 1916.
15. *The Times*, 22 May 2010.
16. World International Design Network, 8 November 2010.
17. *Guardian*, 9 February 1965.

Chapter five

Whatever Happened to the Old Clo' Man?

The Jew as the 'Old Clo' man was a familiar stereotype in the eighteenth century and it was natural that the community would become part of the clothing industry as it expanded. The Old Clothes Man would go from door to door, buying worn-out or discarded garments, and then repair them and patch them before selling them on. So the typical Old Clothes family would be both manufacturer and retailer. For many people in the eighteenth century, the most expensive item of expenditure in a lifetime might be a new coat, but mass production meant that more and better clothing was increasingly available to poorer people, as the nineteenth century progressed.

Hart & Levy, a Leicester firm, built on this market to become one of the largest clothing manufacturers in the country. Sir Israel Hart (1835–1911), the founder, also recognized the potential of the new invention of the sewing machine. His company expanded until it was a major player, with the motto, 'Every man his own coat'.

Hart was the first Jewish mayor of Leicester and was elected no less than four times. When he finally retired, the Council passed a resolution:

> The council recognizes the unique and interesting fact that never before in the history of Great Britain has a member of the ancient and noble race of Judah held for four years, by the free election of his fellow-citizens, the Mayoralty of a Christian municipality, and rejoices that he has been among the first to put into practice the spirit of universal brotherhood.

The factory had a substantial influence on the employment statistics in

Leicester. After the repeal of the Corn Laws, successive British governments concentrated on promoting the manufacturing industry, as against agriculture. As a consequence, the need for factories to provide work for displaced farm labour was vital to the survival of those forced out of the countryside. There were no unions, however, to protect any form of worker and so their conditions were very much dependent on the whim of the employers.

From Hart's point of view, he was most proud of the company's good labour relations. The reason was that, in a world of so many Victorian sweatshops, the benevolent provision on offer at Hart & Levy was a welcome contrast. The firm had a good canteen, sports teams, a ladies' choir and many other social clubs; Hart believed in looking after his employees. But then, as an old friend said after Hart's death, 'He was a Jew of the old type, whose religion was the motivating force and incentive to every good and noble action.'[1] Hart & Levy continued to be run by the family till 1936, and vanished in the 1960s because of foreign competition. You can, however, still see the fine fountain that Hart gave to the town.

If Hart was the manufacturer, Elias Moses (1783–1868) epitomized the move from tallyman[2] to retailer. He was the son of an Alsatian leather merchant, but he started as a tallyman, selling old clothes, and came to London as a comparatively elderly man in the 1830s. With his son, Isaac, he was able to start the firm of E. Moses & Son in the East End. Business was good and he moved to the City, with a shop called the Ready Made Clothing Emporium. This also flourished, to such an extent that he multiplied the shop floor space seven times. It became the largest shop in London, with its success based on low profit margins, but a very high turnover.

Moses got the clothes made by outworkers in conditions which, by contrast with Hart, were rightly characterized as sweated labour. In 1851, a quarter of all the female seamstresses in the country were located in the East End and conditions were often brutal. The Moses family were also related to Hart by marriage, which cemented their business association. One of the reasons for Moses' success was his new approach to marketing. The shop was very impressive, with a high classical portico and tall ground-floor windows. The service was acknowledged to be impeccable and Moses produced booklets advertising his wares, using his house poet to produce doggerel verses to make the material more readable. One read:

> How that old picture brings before the eye
> The Dress peculiar to days gone by!
> Look at the figures! such outlandish styles
> Seem's old fashioned only to provoke smiles.
>
> How very diff'rent were the dresses worn
> When the old fashion'd picture first was drawn.
> See! There's a curious coat – and there's a hat!
> And there's a bonnie waistcoat! Look at that!

The somewhat amateur message being that, for a modern appearance, you needed to go to E. Moses. He also made sure that the prices of the garments were clearly displayed, thus eliminating the haggling that was a feature of the old-clothes business.

While London was the hub of commerce, the provincial cities also needed the kind of large shops that were eventually transformed into department stores. Among the pioneers of these was David Lewis (1823–85), who was born in London but went to live in Liverpool when he was 17. He started on his own as a boys' clothier in 1856 and gradually expanded, until the Lewis department store was the pride of Liverpool shopping. He also opened equally imposing emporia in Manchester, Sheffield and Birmingham, though not always with the same degree of success. His innovative thinking was well illustrated by the building of a full-scale ballroom on the fifth floor of the Manchester store. The fame of the huge shops was such that Joseph Chamberlain, head of the ruling political family in Birmingham, personally asked him to open one in the city.

One of the most beautiful synagogues in Britain is Princes Road in Liverpool and Lewis paid for the marble almemar (an ornate platform), as well as giving £1,000 to the building fund. He was the warden of the Old Hebrew Congregation for many years, and his involvement in Jewry extended to giving £1,000 for the relief of persecuted Jews in Russia. When he died he left £500,000 in his will to be used for the erection of hospitals and similar institutions. The David Lewis Centre in Cheshire would provide residential accommodation for those suffering from epilepsy; by 1916 it had taken in 1,000 residents.

The company continued successfully after Lewis' death and went public in 1924. New stores were opened in Glasgow (1929), Leeds (1932) and Hanley (1934). In 1951 the company bought Selfridges, but it was taken over, in its turn, by Charles Clore and slowly faded away. The last store to close was the Liverpool branch in 2010.

Fashion is fickle, but few crazes were as popular in the years between 1880 and 1914 as the use of ostrich feathers in hats. The ancient Egyptians had used ostrich feathers for decoration, and the feather was chosen by the fourteenth-century king of Bohemia as a part of his crest; when he died at the battle of Crecy in 1346, it was adopted by the Prince of Wales, together with the king's motto, 'Ich Dien' (I serve). In South Africa, the ostrich was first domesticated in 1863 and by 1900, '90% of the feather merchants (in South Africa) were Yiddish speaking emigrants from Lithuania'.[3] In the list of South Africa's most valuable exports at the time, ostrich feathers came fourth, after gold, diamonds and wool.

The feathers were cut from the ostrich tails – for an ostrich it was like having a haircut – and the value per pound was approximately that of diamonds. It was a large industry, with 20,000 women and 2,000 men employed in the trade in 1912 in London alone. £2.2 million worth of feathers were imported in that year (about £175 million today), and over £20,000 worth of feathers were lost (about £1.5 million) when the *Titanic* sank. As a product, it is soft, durable and flexible and it cannot be produced synthetically. An ostrich feather hat at the time would cost about £5 (£400 today).

Among the ostrich merchants in London were Myer and Nathan Salomon, who died in 1896 and 1905 respectively, their family having migrated to Britain in the early eighteenth century.[4] Myer left £289,000 and Nathan £374,000.[5] In Myer's memory, with something less than overwhelming generosity, his wife gave £40 to the Jewish Soup Kitchen. Myer died at the right time, however, because the bottom fell out of the market in 1913, the war ended the fashion and a serious drought in South Africa in 1916 decimated the flock. Already, by 1914, 80 per cent of the ostrich-feather farmers were bankrupt.

Suits were another matter, and Montagu Burton (Moshe Osinsky 1885–1952), was the creation of an entrepreneur who was the backbone of the Harrogate Jewish community for many years. He was born in Lithuania of a well-to-do family and was sent to the famous Slobodka yeshiva as a young man. In 1900, he came to the north of England and started work as a pedlar. With a borrowed £100, he opened his first shop in Chesterfield selling men's clothing, and decided to concentrate on producing good quality, made-to-measure suits for the working man. It was another example of spotting the hole in the market.

The idea was revolutionary, and his motto, 'A 5 guinea (£5.25) suit for 55 shillings (£2.75)', defined his policy. An alternative way of buying his products was that a three-piece suit (with waistcoat) could be had for the price of a two-piece. The expression, 'The Full Monty', could have come from this. Although he was now known as Montague Burton, he hadn't changed his name officially, and this created the usual problems for him during the First World War. In 1910, he had decided to make the suits himself and, by 1919, he had expanded his retail outlets to forty shops. In that same year he combined his small manufacturing units into one large factory in Leeds.

It was a production centre with industrial-relations policies far ahead of its time. It paid good wages and had the largest factory canteen in the world. When jobs for women were generally difficult to find, they outnumbered male employees in the factory by 10:1. There was a health-and-pension scheme for the workers, and free dentists, chiropodists and even sun-ray treatment. It became the biggest clothing factory in the world, with 10,000 staff producing 30,000 suits a week. The idea was that you were measured for your suit in a Burton's shop and the garments were made to your specifications in Leeds.

The firm was floated on the Stock Exchange in 1929 when Burton had 200 shops, and he was knighted in 1931 for services to industrial relations. These included the endowment of many university chairs: Leeds, Cardiff and Jerusalem in 1929, Oxford and Cambridge in 1930, the London School of Economics in 1936 and Edinburgh in 1948. The sheer volume of Burton's output was astonishing. It made a quarter of the uniforms for the armed forces during the war. When the war ended, everybody got a 'demob' (demobilization) suit and Burtons made a third of those. Still not satisfied, in 1947 the company diversified into women's clothing by buying Peter Robinson, but this was not a great success.

Sir Montagu gave a great deal to Jewish charities and he was happy that he could afford to be generous; by the time he died at the age of 67, every fifth man in Britain was wearing a Burton's suit. The question of the succession was solved by buying Jacksons the Tailors, which came with its founder, Lionel Jacobson (1904–78), another Jewish entrepreneur who had built up a thriving business. Burtons eventually changed its name to Arcadia and is now part of Sir Philip Green's empire.

British suit manufacturers ran into serious difficulties in the 1980s when the lower labour costs of foreign competitors made manufacturing in the UK far too costly. One company which had to deal with this problem was Berwin & Berwin, which had been founded by a Russian refugee, Barnett Berwin, in 1885. The firm opened its factory in Leeds in 1920 and was chosen to make United States army officers' uniforms in the Second World War. The latest scion of the family to take charge is Simon Berwin (1954–). Many Jewish companies facing similar challenges to Berwins in recent years saw the founders retire, or their successors go into administration. Simon Berwin grasped the nettle and moved the company's production to Hungary.

When labour costs in the Far East made even Hungarian labour too expensive, he went into partnership with a Chinese company and today they make 18,000 suits a week, while retaining the family company name. Firms like Debenhams, Ted Baker and Topshop are among their many High Street customers and the firm survives and flourishes.

The loss of jobs in British manufacturing mirrors the loss of jobs in Indian companies in the nineteenth century, when superior British manufacturing technology in the making of cloth drove many Indian companies into bankruptcy. The benefit to the British economy of Berwin & Berwin's solution is that only a small percentage of the cost of the suits goes into the Chinese economy. The majority of the cost goes to support the profits and staff levels of Berwin & Berwin and its shareholders in Britain.

The industrial revolution had identified Bradford as an ideal location for the growth of the wool industry. The land was good for sheep and there was enough water to clean the wool. Where the town only had 6,000 inhabitants in 1801, by 1851 that number had swelled to 103,000. Bradford for a while would be the 'wool capital of the world'. As such it attracted many Jewish wool merchants, none more important than Jacob Behrens (1806–89), who arrived in Britain from Hamburg when the family company fell on hard times. He went first to Manchester, but moved to Bradford in 1838 and built a mill. He was by no means unique. So many other Germans set up woollen businesses in Bradford in those days that part of the town is still known as Little Germany. It is a preservation area with a number of Grade II listed buildings.

For the rest of his life Behrens was a key figure in the growth of the town. He was fluent in many languages and established the Bradford Chamber of Commerce. He was chairman of its tariff committee for forty years and, in 1872, was instrumental in persuading the government to create a commercial department in the Foreign Office; he was often consulted by the ministers on tariffs and commercial treaties. Behrens was a natural choice, for his breadth of vision saw him trading as happily in China and Japan as in exporting to his native Germany.

As was to be expected, initially he had some difficulty in getting accepted in Yorkshire circles; his eventual popularity was due to the fact that, as the Bradford Chamber of Commerce eulogised on his death, 'He seemed to exist only to be of service to his fellow man.' Behrens founded the Bradford Eye and Ear Hospital and was knighted in 1882 for the work he had done on agreeing a trade treaty with France in 1860. He was a prominent member of the Anglo-Jewish Association and his son helped establish the Hallé orchestra in Manchester; the firm continues as Sir Jacob Behrens & Co.

Where Gustav Wolff was responsible for a sizeable percentage of the employment in Belfast with Harland & Wolff (Chapter 11, 'The Motor Age'), there was also a need for financial expertise to maintain the Irish linen industry. Here much of the credit must go to David Joseph Jaffe (1809–74), who came from Hamburg to buy linen in 1845 and, in 1850, decided to move to Belfast permanently. He built up a very large linen exporting company and left £140,000 when he died in 1874. In his memory a fountain was erected in Victoria Square, which has recently been restored. His grave, however, has been vandalised, as have those of the other members of the family. Daniel's son, Otto (1846–1929), did even better, building the family business into the largest linen exporting company and one of the chief industrial concerns in Ireland. He built the Jaffe Spinning Mill, which employed 650 workers in 1914.

The first Jewish religious services in Belfast were held in 1871 in the home of Jaffe's son, Martin. Sir Otto, as his father became, built the first synagogue in Belfast, and joined the Russian and German immigrants together into one community when he built a second in 1904. Otto was a very charitable benefactor. He gave £4,000 to Queen's University (about £2 million today). According to a contemporary, he was 'shrewd, sharp-witted, far-seeing, and (whilst) almost parsimonious in business, he is lavish in unostentatious charities'.[6] In 1899, he became the first lord mayor of Belfast (as against simple 'mayor') and, in 1904, was elected again. He had been born in Germany and it seemed perfectly reasonable to accept an invitation to act as German consul in Ireland. Unhappily, years later with the anti-German feeling of the First World War naturally virulent, Sir Otto was suspected of being a German spy. He was very hurt by this attack on his patriotism: 'How anyone who has any knowledge of me and my life could think that I could approve of the horrible and detestable actions of which she (Germany) has been guilty, is beyond my comprehension.'[7] With regret, he moved to London where he died in 1929.

The main concern of housewives today, as far as fabrics are concerned, is whether they will wash well in a machine. There's rather more to it if you're a manufacturer. One Swiss-Jewish chemist was Henry Dreyfus (1882–1944) who had a degree from the University of Basle. In 1912, he started a company to manufacture cellulose acetate, which is the basis for cinematography film and was used for treating the skins of early aircraft. It could, however, also be spun into artificial silk. In 1915, the War Office accepted a tender for that material from Dreyfus and he came to Britain to set up a factory in Derby. It began production in 1917 as the British Cellulose Chemical Manufacturing Company.

After the war, Dreyfus floated the company as a maker of artificial silk and by 1927 he was chairman and managing director. What Dreyfus aimed for was a vertically integrated company, able to do everything from spinning the material to making the garments; Joe Hyman would have the same idea fifty years later with Viyella. British Cellulose became a major supplier of women's underwear in the 1930s and should have made handsome profits. Unfortunately, Dreyfus was autocratic and very difficult to work with. He paid insufficient regard to costs and, as a result, there was financial chaos and the company suffered from a disastrous profit record. In fact the company didn't pay a dividend until 1944.

Like many other entrepreneurs of his kind, Dreyfus was pugnacious, determined and constantly at war to protect his market. This involved, primarily, retaining his patents, but he was unsuccessful in suing his major competitor, Courtaulds, for infringing them. Eventually, some years after he died, the company was taken over by Courtaulds in 1957, but the benefits to the balance of trade had come from the initial skill and imagination of Dreyfus.

Nottingham was another city that benefited greatly from its Jewish citizens. It had a great tradition for making lace, but this was a very competitive industry and its commercial success ebbed and flowed. One of the most successful companies was Hyman & Alexander, founded by Lewis Heymann (1802–69), for it was Heymann who pioneered lace curtains.

Another was Jacob Weinberg (1830–1900) who came over from Hamburg in 1849 as an agent. As the *Nottingham Trader* said of him later, 'by his strict integrity, industry and zeal, and his business capacity, he built up an organization which has for many years held a world-wide reputation'. In strong competition with German lace manufacturers, Weinberg's Simon May & Co. more than held its own.

Where many German-Jewish immigrants were not Orthodox, Weinberg was an exception: 'Whenever in England a movement was set afoot which had for its object the strengthening of Orthodoxy, there Weinberg's aid was readily and unstintingly given.'[8] Perhaps the most typical example of this was when, in 1897, the Nottingham council decided to put up public baths. Weinberg wanted part of them set aside for a Mikveh – a Jewish ritual bath. He gave the marble for the baths and got the council to provide the Mikveh, but he went one step further. For a payment of 100 guineas (£105) the council agreed to provide water to the Mikveh in perpetuity, without charging water rates. Simon May is still in business.

In Leeds the greatest Jewish firm to be founded by an immigrant was Marks & Spencer, which started life as a stall in Leeds' Kirkgate market.

The stallholder was Michael Marks (1861–1907) who had fled the pogroms in Russia after 1881. He had taken the stall because it offered shelter from the elements, which was not available to him as a pedlar. In a 50:50 partnership with a non-Jewish friend, Tom Spencer, he built the business up, opening a considerable number of Penny Bazaars, and when he died he left £30,000 (over £2 million today). The Penny Bazaars sold everything for a penny (0.5p). The merchandise was varied and its cheapness proved very attractive to poor people, particularly as Marks laid great emphasis on offering the highest quality possible.

After the death of Marks, it took his son, Simon (1888–1964), until 1917 to gain full control of the company from the Spencer interests. After the war, the company faced the competition of Woolworths for the same markets on which Marks & Spencer depended. Woolworths was bigger and could buy its stock more cheaply. This led to Marks making a number of major decisions, the most important of which was to buy directly from manufacturers and cut out the wholesalers. In memory of his father, Simon introduced the St Michael brand in 1928 and thus, effectively, created 'own-brand' merchandise; this gave the public branded products at a lower price, as he didn't have to build in the manufacturers' marketing costs.

Marks was always determined to give his customers good service, but he recognized that this depended on good staff. Talking to an assistant one day, he discovered that she couldn't afford lunch. So he set up staff restaurants with heavily subsidized meals, and went on to extend the staff facilities until they were widely recognized as being among the best in the country. Setting a high standard was an example for the rest of British industry.

Marks & Spencer developed more and bigger stores as they steadily expanded. Though they remained wedded to low prices – the Penny Bazaars translated into 5 shilling (25p) maximum prices in the 1930s – Marks was always, like his father, intent on providing the best possible value for money.

Throughout his life, Marks was noted for being fiercely outspoken when he found his management falling below the standards he wanted set. Management were terrified of his wrath, which could arise from the smallest faults. The same attitude can be seen in the history of many Jewish company chairmen, but it is necessary to look behind the scenes. As chairman of a major chain of stores, Marks could only be seen a few times a year in almost all of them. Now, it is axiomatic among junior management that, if you can fob off Head Office when they do appear, you can then go back to running the branch or department as you think fit. Only if the consequences of so doing can be recognized as potentially dire will poor local management stick to the company line. One manager remarked that the education he got at Marks & Spencer was 'better than a university although more frightening'.[9] Marks needed to be an autocrat.

Marks had also introduced quality control before the Second World War, which meant that his inspectors would lay down exactly what standards he wanted from suppliers, if they wanted to retain his business. This was revolutionary at the time, but it also meant that the suppliers got the benefit of the advice of experts in Marks & Spencer's own research department.

Outside the business, Marks' main interest was in Zionism, and he served Chaim Weizmann, who would become the first president of Israel, with real devotion. They had met as young men and the survival of Zionism as a movement owed much to the time and money Marks put into its progress. In Britain, Marks was also responsible for largely financing the creation of the Air Cadet organization in the 1930s, which started tens of thousands of young men on their way to keeping the RAF supplied with sufficient expert personnel when war came.

The growth of Marks & Spencer owed much to the chairman's recognition that new fabrics would make it easier for poorer women to improve on the very basic standards of clothing, which were all that was available before the 1920s. Marks & Spencer became, primarily, clothing shops, leaving behind the other items sold in the Penny Bazaars. Perhaps the last great lesson Lord Marks, as he became in 1961, gave to British industry was the need to avoid wasteful paperwork. In 1957 he launched a Simplification Exhibition and could prove to have saved his company overheads of £4 million in just two years.

The roll-call of Jewish entrepreneurs is male-dominated, but the courage and determination of the Jewish female members of the family, or the women they married, was usually a vital part of their success. Such a woman was Fanny Ziff (1890–1973), who came to Britain on her own in

1904 when she was 14. She then worked in the family clothing business until she had enough money saved up to go back to Lithuania and bring all her family to England. What a wonderful day that must have been for her.

When the war started, Fanny's brothers went off to the front and she decided to start a shoe shop so that they would have something to come back to when the war ended. This was, by no means, the first time that Jews had been involved in shoe manufacturing. In the nineteenth century, 'the first recognizable factories were built in Northampton, one by Isaacs, Campbell & Co. of London'.[10] This was the same Samuel Isaac who later built the Mersey Tunnel (Chapter 11, 'The Motor Age'). Fanny named the shop after her fountain pen – Stylo.

The siblings came home to find a business waiting for them and expanded it slowly until, in 1936, they had fifty-nine shops, and formed the Stylo Boot Company. Fanny's brother, Max, had a son, Arnold (1927–2004), who came into the business after service in the Second World War. He had tried reading Economics at Leeds University but dropped out after a year. He found with the family business that, with his father and several uncles running the company, his job was to discover new sites for additional shops. But when his father died in 1955, Arnold took over as managing director and served in that capacity till 2000. He also used his property expertise to found Town Centre Securities in 1957. This was started with £1,000 of capital and launched on the Stock Exchange eighteen months later with a value of £250,000.

Stylo eventually grew to hundreds of shops and Arnold was a hands-on MD. When you have an empire of shops, the company style is often created by folklore. So there was a widely publicized story of Arnold visiting the Walsall store and finding the front steps dirty. He looked for the manager and found he was drinking coffee nearby. When the manager was told the MD was on site, he rushed back and found his boss with a pail and a brush, on his knees, scrubbing the steps. When he protested that he shouldn't be doing such a demeaning task, Arnold said, 'Well, I can't wait for you to finish your coffee!'

Ziff was well known for his 'no-nonsense, gritty, Yorkshire style'. Ziff was devoted to Leeds and wanted to do all he could for the town to which his family owed so much. He developed the Merrion shopping centre, raised £1 million for a body scanner for the hospital, and made very substantial donations to the Yorkshire Cricket School, the Tropical World Gardens, the Salvation Army and the Leeds Parish Church; he was made high sheriff of West Yorkshire in 1991. The *Guardian* called him the 'leading benefactor of his generation to Leeds'.[11]

When Arnold Ziff died in 2004 his son, Michael, took over but the pension fund was inadequate for its obligations. There was £7 million earmarked for the company's own balance sheet, but it was decided to bolster the fund with this sum instead. This, together with the refusal of the landlords of the shops to help with lower rents, resulted in the company running into serious cash-flow problems, and Ziff had no alternative but to put it into administration. He then negotiated a management buy-out from the liquidator and 160 of the 400 shops were saved from closure. Stylo still trades enthusiastically and staff loyalty was rewarded. This is in marked contrast to a large number of other UK companies, who have avoided the pension obligations their loyal old employees expected to see honoured.

There was another part of the clothing industry where Britain benefited greatly from the Nazi persecution of the Jews. In the 1920s, one third of the world trade in furs was located in Leipzig. In the Bruhlstrasse there were, literally, hundreds of fur companies, but the Jewish ones were 'Aryanized' by the Nazis, and their owners had their companies stolen and their own lives put in danger. After the enormities of Kristellnacht in 1938, a large number of these Jewish fur companies migrated to London. Perhaps as many as eighty of them relocated, and the capital became the European centre for the fur trade. Leipzig never recovered its position, but where there were 11,500 Jews in the town in 1933, only 1,100 lived there in 2005, and most of those came from Russia after glasnost.

The industry in recent years in Britain has been adversely affected by the successful campaign of animal rights activists to turn the public away from the killing of animals for their fur. The arguments were different before the welfare state, central heating and in the days when the production of fur garments was one of the few ways of making a living in a harsh environment. The country peasant could earn some money by selling the pelts and the furrier could make some by turning them into clothing.

The German corsetieres were under pressure as well. One of the largest German firms was founded in 1887 by Max Lobbenberg (1856–1939) and Emil Blumenau (1857–1931). It too was undermined by the anti-Jewish programme of the Nazis when they came to power; salesmen were restricted in their travels, it was made difficult to buy the materials needed and there was a state-sponsored campaign to boycott the products of Jewish companies. Lobbenberg countered the pressure by setting up branches abroad. Otto Lobbenberg went to Paris and came up with a radioactive corset, approved by the Curie Institute. It was supposed to keep you warm and help your rheumatism.

When the Nazis made Max Lobbenberg sell the firm for a fraction of its worth, he came to Britain, where his son, Hans (1896–1955), and Hans Blumenau (1896–1976) had set up a firm called Corset Silhouette as joint managing directors. Max died within a few weeks, but the sons continued to manufacture in Islington, London. During the war they had to move, as they were now producing garments for the women's armed forces, and London was a prime target for bombing. They were offered factories in Coventry or Shrewsbury and chose Shrewsbury. It was the right decision for both the company and the town.

After the war, Corset Silhouette continued to have a healthy turnover, partly because clothes were still rationed and in short supply. What inflated the profits by 50 per cent was the invention of their designer, Anne Marie Lobbenberg (1908–71). She created the Little X corset, which proved immensely popular. The company went public in 1959, the issue being oversubscribed twenty-eight times. At its peak, Corset Silhouette ran five factories employing 3,500 staff; in Shrewsbury it was the largest employer. It exported to over sixty countries, was the largest manufacturer of swimwear in Britain and was a major supplier to Marks & Spencer.

By the late 1970s, Anne Marie Lobbenberg and Hans Blumenau had died and the next generation decided to sell the company. It went for £15 million, but within two years the new owners had to go into administration and the company was sold on by the liquidator for £400,000. Various organizations ran the company with little long-term success for the next thirty years. It is still operating, however, though the economy in Shrewsbury has lost one of its main supports.

Another German refugee was Max Bruh (1907–94), who escaped to Switzerland in 1938 and managed to reach Britain in 1939. Bruh had been the export director of a German fashion house between the wars and had built up a wide range of foreign contacts. In 1944 he bought a company off the shelf called Frank Usher, and started to create high-fashion clothes at much more reasonable prices than were normal. Much of his production was exported after the war, helped by his pre-war contacts. In 1961 he sold out to Selincourt, though he remained at the helm; Lou Mintz knew a good professional when he saw one (Chapter 14, 'The New Clo' Man'). In 1986 Bruh bought the company back, and it continues to trade to this day.

A number of German-Jewish hat manufacturers also escaped before the war and opened factories in Luton where the British hat industry was primarily located. Lutz Heymann came from Dresden and his Marida company still exists, but the industry has suffered from the fact that hats have largely gone out of fashion. There were 250 hat manufacturers in Luton in the early 1950s, but only thirty were left in the early 1980s.

Another aid to feminine beauty was the invention of nylon and its use in making stockings. At its birth in Britain, one of the largest companies was Kayser Bondor, transformed from the tiny Fully Fashioned Hosiery Company by its financial director (1929), later managing director (1931), John Goodenday (1894–1961). Goodenday's father was a master tailor in Bolton, (Charlie) Kadious Goodenday (1868–1939). The boy left school at 13, and by 15 was the secretary of the local synagogue.

Over the next twenty years, Goodenday climbed the greasy pole. Reports of how he did it are very vague; 'after many ventures – some successful, some unsuccessful – into the business world',[12] he is next found as one of the first directors of the Lex Group of garages in 1928. At the age of 23 he had changed his name from Jacob Nathan to John Goodenday and his post of financial director would suggest he had acquired a deal of accountancy knowledge. He left Lex to become financial director of Fully Fashioned a year later.

The company flourished sufficiently to build a new factory in Biggleswade in 1938, and eventually provided Marks & Spencer with 95 per cent of the underwear it sold. Those were the days when companies tried to encourage their staff to play together as well as work together. There would be company sports grounds and, at Kayser Bondor, you could join the company sports team to play darts, cricket, tennis, golf, swimming, bowls, badminton and football, or enjoy the motoring, angling or amateur dramatic clubs.

During the war, the factory was used to build Spitfires and Lancaster bombers, so the hosiery products were manufactured in a nearby converted cowshed. Eventually they produced 1,200,000 items a week. The Queen and Princess Elizabeth came to visit the restored factory in 1946 and were presented with the new nylon stockings. By 1949, Kayser Bondor had 12 per cent of British hosiery production and 14 per cent of its exports. They could boast the largest hosiery mills in Europe. In 1961, a few months before he died, Goodenday was able to announce profits of over half a million pounds, but the company was taken over by Courtaulds in 1966. By 1991, it had gone the way of so many British clothing companies and the factory was closed. Goodenday's son, David, eventually became Master of the Worshipful Company of Framework Knitters in 1998.

John Goodenday never forgot his humble origins. He set up a fund with his own money within the company for those of his staff who fell on hard times. He also created a home for sixty elderly Jews in Earls Court and served as treasurer of the English Friends of the Hebrew University of Jerusalem.

It wasn't just the German refugees who founded companies that benefited the economy. Lionel Green (1914–91) found them vital to the success of his Windsmoor company when he started the business in 1933. Green was the son of a Polish–Jewish tailor and started by selling clothing to retailers. He had, however, spent a year in Berlin in 1930 studying the techniques of their clothing industry, for which he developed a great admiration.

When he founded his own company, the need was to produce fashionable clothes when he couldn't afford designers. The solution for Windsmoor, as for many companies, was to copy the French fashions. For Green, the German refugees 'were some of the finest copiers of the Paris collections – perfectionists – thorough in everything from the choice of the cloth to the sewing of the buttons'.[13]

Windsmoor made traditional tailored clothes and there were many innovations in their marketing. They sponsored a weekly radio show and had imaginative advertising. Their slogan, 'Look Your Best in Windsmoor', became well known to women. They also started taking up concessions in stores, beginning with London's Swan & Edgar in 1955; eventually there were nearly 250 outlets of this kind. Business was so good in that year that Green bought himself an Aston Martin DB2, which shows considerable taste in cars.

In 1980 the company went public when its turnover was £54 million, but Green was getting older, and the business today is part of Jacques Vert. His son didn't join the firm, but did become the Director of Public Prosecutions. When Green died, the *Daily Telegraph* said, 'he is remembered as a man who had time to listen and who lived his life by the standards of his religion'.[14] Which seemed to stand him in good stead.

One of the largest sports goods' manufacturers in the country emerged from a company founded, in 1932, by the 19-year-old Berko Rubin (1913–69) in Liverpool. The Liverpool Shoe Company was set up to sell shoes to retail stores and had grown sufficiently to go public in 1964. Rubin died soon after and his son, Stephen Rubin (1938–), took over the reins. Rubin qualified as a barrister at the age of 21 and adopted a wider view of business opportunities. He used the company to diversify into ship broking and venture capitalism. The firm's name was changed to Pentland and, on the shoe front, Rubin was responsible for the first woman's tennis shoes, made on a last specifically shaped for the female foot. Venture capitalism is all about spotting the up-and-coming firms, and in an early venture, £51 bought a 51 per cent interest in a home-brewing and wine company, which was sold four years later for £1 million.

Recognizing the dangers of competition from cheap Asian labour far earlier than others, Rubin set up a Hong Kong manufacturing base almost as soon as he took over. The company really took off in 1981, however, when he bought 55.5 per cent of a struggling American sports shoe company called Reebok for £50,000. A Reebok is an African gazelle and the company had been making expensive running shoes for world-class athletes. Rubin's contribution was better marketing and the Asian sourcing. In 1982 the company launched the first shoe specifically designed for aerobics, and used glove leather to eliminate the irritation of a breaking-in period. Sales rose from $300,000 in 1980 to $66 million in 1984. By 1986 that was $919 million and 34 per cent of the total American athletic footwear market.

British firms often flounder in America but, by 1990, Pentland's share of Reebok was worth $500 million. Rubin expanded into many other fields as well, including the production of the first-ever oscillating fan heater. In 1999, he took the company private again. The Speedo brand followed, plus the global shoe and sportswear subsidiary of Adidas, the global Lacoste licence and many other major international names – Ellesse, Reusch (Germany) and Olympico (Italy). Pentland is today a major player in the sportswear industry and the Rubin family own it, the forty-second largest private company in the UK.

Rubin has used his fortune to support many good causes, such as the industry's efforts to eliminate the exploitation of child labour, action for climate change, outfitting British and Israeli sporting teams and supporting such Israeli charities as the Wingate Institute of Physical Education and Sport. He was elected world chairman of the Textile Institute from 1994 to 1996 and president of the World Federation of the Sporting Goods Industry from 1995 to 2001. Thanks to his company, Britain has a major piece of the industry.

Undoubtedly the most famous clothes hire company in the country is Moss Bros, founded by Moses Moses (c.1825–94), a Dutch Jew who came from the world of second-hand clothes selling. In 1851, he gave up his cart and opened a shop in Covent Garden. He had decided that there was a market between those who could afford Savile Row and those who bought from the Old Clo' Man. Moses had a mission statement for his shop before mission statements were ever considered: 'Sell only the best stuff; give only the best service.'

Moses had three sons, George (1855–1906), Alfred (1862–1937) and Lewis (1864–1914). George was the cutter, Alfred the clothes buyer from tailors and Lewis the salesman. The shop would buy rejects from the Savile Row tailors and then bring them up to a good enough standard to sell as ready-to-wear. For many years this was the formula, and Moss Bros suits were always hand-finished.

When Moses died in 1894, George and Alfred took over and changed their name to Moss in 1898; it was very common for Jews to anglicize their names. In 1897, there came the moment which would mark Moss Bros out for the future. A friend of George was down on his luck and singing at social functions to keep himself going. In order to look the part, he borrowed clothes from the shop, and eventually George decided that he ought to pay for the hire; 37½ pence was the agreed price and, from hiring to that one friend would come millions of customers in future years.

The next two generations gave no thought to doing anything except joining the family firm. Harry Moss (1896–1982) started working in the shop when he was 13 and Monty Moss (1924–) took over from him. He went to Harrow but always worked in the shop during the holidays. The firm expanded mightily, and now has 116 mainstream stores and thirty-five fashion stores all over the country; it is still nearly 20 per cent owned by the family.

Hiring clothes for special occasions raises no eyebrows today, but it was totally novel when Moss Bros offered the service. When Ramsay Macdonald's government took office in 1924, the king insisted that the Labour ministers be properly dressed for court. Few of the government could afford the expense of buying court dress, but the solution was to go to Moss Bros where the complete outfit could be hired for £30 (though that's about £1,300 in today's money!). While Moss Bros has a much larger business selling high-quality clothes today, it is still the hire side for which it is best known. All the companies in the same field stem from Moses Moss.

Where Moss Bros specialized in the hiring of morning dress and tails, the lowly sock was not high on anybody's sartorial wish list. Which, of course, creates a hole in the market if you decide there is a market for socks as a luxury product. In 1937 Louis Goldschmidt (1890–1961) got out of Austria ahead of the Anschluss and made his way to Leicester. He had been in the hosiery business for some years and, in England, he started the Midland Hosiery Mills and produced stockings. So did a lot of other companies, however, and it occurred to Goldschmidt that there might be less competition and greater prospects if he switched to socks. At the time these were only available if you liked the thick and heavy variety. Goldschmidt decided to buck the trend and have a machine produced which could make thin, elegant socks out of the best material, Sea Island Cotton.

It is a truism that there is always a market for quality, and Pantherella socks are further conclusive evidence that this remains true. The factory in Leicester has now been producing them for seventy-five years and they are that rare company in British clothing manufacturing today, one which still makes its products in the UK. In 2011, there was a choice of 1,350 styles, seventy more being created every season. From a staff of only 100 come 1.3 million pairs a year and 60 per cent of the production is sold overseas, mostly in America. It proves it can still be done. The firm was sold in 2001, but the elegance of Pantherella socks continues to attract those who can afford the best on the market.

NOTES

1. In conversation with the author.
2. A tallyman is a door-to-door salesman who keeps a 'tally' of credit.
3. Sarah Abreyava Stein, *Plumes: Ostrich Feathers, Jews and a Lost World of Global Commerce* (New Haven, CT: Yale University Press, 2008).
4. William Rubinstein, 'Jewish Top Wealth-holders in Britain, 1809–1909', www.jhse.org/book/export/article/21930.
5. Ibid.
6. Louis Hyman, *The Jews of Ireland: From Earliest Times to the Year 1910* (London and Jerusalem: Jewish Historical Society of England and Israel Universities Press, 1972).
7. *Northern Whig*, May 1915.
8. *Jewish Chronicle*, 23 March 1900.
9. Paul Bookbinder, *Simon Marks, Retail Revolutionary* (London: Weidenfeld and Nicholson, 1993).
10. June Swann, *Shoemaking* (Oxford: Shire Publications Ltd, 1986).
11. Martin Wainwright, *Guardian*, 30 July 2004.
12. *Jewish Chronicle*, 16 June 1961.
13. *Jewish Chronicle*, 25 November 1977.
14. *Daily Telegraph*, May 1991.

Chapter six

Where There's Muck There's Brass

The Industrial Revolution was made possible by the brilliant inventions of a number of great men. The difficulty that often arose was how to translate those innovations into commercial successes; an inventor is not, automatically, a practical man of business. It is not surprising that there were occasions when success was only achieved because the inventor found a Jewish entrepreneur who could handle the business side for him.

One example was the creation of the Usworth Colliery in Durham by the firm of Elliott and Jonassohn, which was formed in 1840. George Elliott (1814–93) was a non-Jewish, practical coal-industry worker, who had done his apprenticeship thoroughly and recognized that the open-cast mine at Usworth had deep reserves. David Jonassohn (1794–1859) was a Sunderland Jew who had built his business up from that of a tallyman to become a merchant, servicing tallymen. He had sufficient financial experience to be the ideal partner for Elliott. The Usworth colliery provided employment for over 100 years, and the company improved the standard of living of its workers significantly.

An even more obscure entry into coal mining came when Colonel Joseph Joel Ellis (1816–85) decided to give up his business as a successful jeweller in the Strand, London and move from his home, in what is now the Chinese Embassy, to Leicestershire where, in 1869, he bought the Nailstone Colliery and started mining. Joel Ellis' rank came from his position as honorary colonel of the 1st Tower Hamlet Artillery Volunteer Corps in the East End of London. His parents were from Krotoschin in Bohemia and they had migrated to Bristol, where Ellis was born. The very upper-crust name came, in 1863, from the deed poll, as the Colonel was born Joseph Joel. He rose to be consul general for Persia. His life seemed to involve a somewhat laborious journey trying to climb the greasy pole.

In 1876 Joel Ellis sold Nailstone and sunk a pit in nearby Ellistone. He had been able to go public with Nailstone in 1871 and the Ellistone pit was sunk in 1873, producing coal from 1875. It employed 200 staff, slightly fewer than Nailstone. Joel Ellis lived the life of an English gentleman in rural Leicestershire until he died in 1885, and the Ellistone colliery finally ceased production in 1952.

Manufacturing iron was also tremendously important in the nineteenth century and the foremost position Britain held in the field was due, to a considerable extent, to Sir Bernhard Samuelson (1820–1905). He came from a family of German merchants who had emigrated to Hull. After school he went to the continent to work for an engineering machinery company and 'he amassed a considerable fortune in private speculations'.[1]

Returning to England, he began making agricultural implements in Banbury in Oxfordshire, and transformed the little market town into a major industrial centre. By 1872, he was manufacturing 8,000 reaping machines a year. He was elected to Parliament for the constituency but, in 1865, his victory was questioned because it was said he was an 'alien'. A parliamentary commission threw the accusation out, however, and he served as an MP until 1895.

In 1853 he had branched out into iron production in Middlesborough and built both the Britannia Works on a twenty-acre site and the Newport Works on a forty-acre site. 'He transformed Cleveland into the greatest iron-producing centre in the world.'[2] Even as early as 1870, it was producing 3,000 tons of pig iron a week. When he died, *The Times* wrote, 'In Sir Bernhard Samuelson, probably, the nation is indebted more than to any other man for its knowledge of the relative position which England occupies among the competing industrial peoples of the European continent and the Transatlantic nations.'[3]

Samuelson, however, did more than build a great company, whose output of iron, tar and by-products was colossal. He also spent £25,000 (£2 million pounds today) on developing steel production, and was a great advocate of technical and scientific education in the country. He sat on parliamentary committees on the subject and chaired them as well. In

1884, he was made a baronet. After his death, the company became part of Dorman Long which had supplied the company with its materials for a number of years.

Samuelson's brother was Martin Samuelson (1825–1903). He started his business life in Hull as a railway engineer and, in 1849, established his own works. By 1853, he had turned to iron shipbuilding on reclaimed land at Sammy's Point, which was named after him. Ten years later, he was building more ships than any other firm in Britain, sometimes four at a time. He had been elected mayor of Hull in 1858 when he was only 33, and was highly regarded in the town.

In 1864, the company launched ninety-five ships, but then ran into such serious cash-flow problems that Samuelson sold out to another local shipbuilding company, which collapsed only one year after Samuelson's bankruptcy in 1865. When the dust settled, Samuelson's reputation hardly suffered and, in 1870, he was asked to design the North Bridge over the River Hull. He went on to be the engineer of the Humber Conservancy Commission and died at the age of 78.

One city whose economy needed reinventing in the nineteenth century was Norwich. The wool- and silk-weaving industries, which had been a mainstay for the local workforce, seriously declined in the 1830s as mass production became easier. One company, which had been established by a French Jew, David Soman, produced fur caps, but Soman recognized the potential of making boots and shoes. This had been an outworkers' occupation in Norwich for centuries, but now there was the possibility of factory production. In 1853, the business passed into the hands of his son-in-law, Philip Haldinstein (1823–1901), and it expanded rapidly over the next fifty years. Eventually it employed 2,000 staff, though often in conditions which would not pass muster today. In 1897, the bootmakers went on strike for a fifty-four-hour week, a minimum wage and a constraint on the employment of boy labour. The strike lasted thirty-four weeks but, unhappily, achieved very little.

Haldinstein became the first Jewish sheriff of Norwich and a pillar of the community. When he died in 1901, the *Jewish Chronicle* recorded, 'Mr Haldinstein was a man of strong, if narrow, intelligence; and of the strictest integrity in the fulfilment of the bargains which he keenly contested'.[4]

Haldenstein left £134,000 and his eldest daughter married the future Lord Mancroft, a government minister in Macmillan's time who became mayor of Norwich. P. Haldinstein & Co. was purchased by Bally in 1933. The Norwich shoe industry had thirty factories in 1960 but only three in 1990; the factories are now, primarily, located in India.

If Jewish companies were important in the shoe industry, George Cohen tried his luck in quite another direction. In 1834, he founded George Cohen, Sons & Co., a firm 'for the purchase and sale of scrap cast and wrought iron'. Over the years, he brought in his sons and his relatives in the Levy family. All had to serve seven-year apprenticeships and the company became the George Cohen 600 Group, after it moved its head office in 1869 to 600, Commercial Road in the East End of London.

George Cohen 600 Group grew to handle enormous metal-recovery projects. Among their contracts in the future would be the removal of the giant Ferris wheel at Earl's Court in London, a predecessor of the London Eye. They also dismantled the water towers at the Crystal Palace after they had been moved to South London from their 1851 Great Exhibition site in Hyde Park. After the Great War, the company dealt with the disposal of 500,000 tons of surplus ammunition and, in 1931, they disposed of 1,500 tons of a metre-gauge railway in Aden, including the rails, goods wagons, passenger coaches and the trains themselves. In 1959, the company broke up the London trolley buses when they went out of service, as well as the Festival of Britain Dome of Discovery. Nothing was too large for them to handle.

After George Cohen came his sons, Moss and Michael, who were made partners in 1883 and, in 1908, George Levy became a partner and later vice chairman. Cohen was Orthodox, and the Cohen and Levy families held all the shares in the company until it went public in 1947. By that time there were 6,000 staff and the issue was heavily oversubscribed. The board consisted of three Cohens and five Levys, headed by Cyril Cohen (1901–69), George Cohen's grandson, as chairman and managing director. In addition, however, they had a woman director who was not related to the family, and a director who had started in the 1920s at 2½p an hour.

The firm was now a big player in the machine-tool industry and, although the family control ended with Cyril's death, the company still operates out of Britain, Europe, North America, Australia and South Africa. It has also moved with the times and plays a major international role in lasers. It is the largest machine-tool maker in the country. One commentator said in 2009, 'The group today is a real rarity in the UK; a company that makes real things out of metal and sells in more than 180 countries'.[5]

Another example of the effect of new technology was the exploitation of the invention of the sewing machine in Britain. The successful inventor was an American, Elias Howe, but he had the greatest difficulty in marketing and financing his invention. Eventually he met Nahum Salamon (1829–1900) in London and, in 1859, Salamon became the patent agent for the Howe Sewing Machine in Britain. In 1862, at the International Exhibition in Kensington, the machine won a gold medal and after that it began to be accepted.

The transformation of the lives of working women and the manufacture of clothing, by the invention of the sewing machine, was enormous. Salamon, however, recognized that the British preferred a hand-operated system rather than the Howe treadle machine, and wanted to avoid the cost of bringing them from America. So he joined up with James Starley, who had moved from working in industry to having his own small factory in Coventry. Salamon acted as company secretary and then chairman. Between the two men, the Coventry Machinist Company flourished, but it is significant that, initially, every purchaser of a machine had to make the cheque payable to Nahum Salamon. Starley was a technician rather than a financier. One side effect of the company was to bring much-needed work to Coventry, which had been badly hit by foreign competition to its traditional silk and watch industries.

Salamon, however, diversified. He recognized the potential of another new invention – the bicycle. In 1873, it was Salamon who built the first bicycle factory in Britain, also in Coventry. He retired in 1881 and died in 1900. His son, Alfred Salamon (c.1850–1919), had shown an early talent for science and so his father sent him to the Royal School of Mines. There he became a chemist and, with his father, bought the British patents for a new American invention, saccharin. He was a director of the Saccharin Corporation and, from 1887 till his death in 1919, a member of the Royal Society of Chemistry.

Over the years improvements were also made to the quality of paints, and a German–Jewish chemist, Louis Amelius Christianus Adolphus Steigenberger (1741–1814), came to London and began producing pigments in 1770. He specialized in Prussian blue and shortened his name to Lewis Berger, creating Berger Paints, which still exists.

Another great Jewish chemist was Ludwig Mond (1839–1909) who was born in Germany and educated at the universities of Marburg and Heidelberg. Though he never received his degree, he was highly regarded and arrived in Britain in 1862 to take up a job in Widnes in Lancashire. In 1867, he started on his own with a company to manufacture soda. Now soda may be taken for granted, but it has a wide variety of uses. These include the production of glass, as a water softener, for washing and baking, and as a descaling agent. By 1900, Brunner Mond was the largest producer of soda in the world. By 2005, 42 billion kilos of the product were made internationally. Mond took advantage of the invention of the Solvay process, where the basic ingredients required are simply salt-water brine and limestone. He also discovered nickel carbonyl, from which nickel can be made. He was the somewhat unusual mixture of a businessman and an academic.

As a member of the chemical industry, Mond developed the local Lancashire Chemical Association into the Society of the Chemical Industry, and was elected president in 1888. He was a generous benefactor to the Royal Society and the Royal Institute of Great Britain and, even if he hadn't gained an ordinary degree, he still ended up with the Honorary variety from Padua, Heidelberg, Oxford and Manchester.

Another major innovation at the end of the nineteenth century was the invention of the electric lamp. Britain's bulb industry was effectively created by two German–Jewish immigrants, Gustav Binswanger (Gustav Byng 1855–1910) and Hugo Hirsch (Lord Hirst, 1862–1943). Hirst came to London when he was 16 because he hated what he felt was the 'Prussianization' of Germany; it was said that many, if not most, migrants came to England because they hoped to find freedom. He worked for Byng in the Electric Apparatus Company, which was producing equipment for steam generation. In 1889, the two men took over a defunct factory and started making bulbs. The firm was called the General Electric Company.

The major international competition in Europe came from Germany but in 1909, Hirst obtained the British rights to manufacturer tungsten-filament lamps. The controlling interest in the company at the time was owned by German investors, but for years the German lamp manufacturers still tried to ruin the company by undercutting its prices. The motto of the company was 'Everything Electrical' and the trademark for the lamps was Osram. In those days, GEC employed 1,500 workers in their Hammersmith factory in London and Hirst sent hundreds of his staff to Germany for training. In spite of the competition, the works produced seven to eight million lamps a year, and other companies were created to form a British industry.

During the First World War, Hirst was accused of being loyal to his native country, but he defended himself stoutly and rode out the attacks. In the 1920s, the company was deeply involved in creating the national grid, and was a major player in the industry right up to Hirst's death in 1943. He had been chairman since 1910. It was not until 1961 that General Electric merged with Michael Sobell's company, Radio and Allied, to create the company which Lord Weinstock led for so many years (Chapter 7, 'The Sum of the Whole ...').

It might seem unlikely that a major Anglo-Jewish technology company would emerge from a family of Bavarian bankers. This family was the Seligmans, who emigrated to Britain in Victorian times and settled down to trade in the City. One of their sons was Richard Seligman (1878–1972) and, as befitted the son of a banker, he was sent to Harrow. There he developed a passion for science. When the time came to go on to higher education, he chose the recently founded City and Guilds Technical Institute rather than a prestigious university (it wasn't until 1907 that Imperial College was founded).

After City and Guilds, Seligman went on to Heidelberg and Zurich Universities, where he gained his doctorate, and by 1904 he had a job as a chief chemist at British Aluminium. In 1910, he struck out on his own by starting the Aluminium Plant and Vessel Company with a staff of seven. This provided welded containers for various industries, but the company's phenomenal growth came when Seligman invented a plate heat-exchanger in 1923.

This revolutionized the heating and cooling of fluids; it set the standard for the computer-designed, thin metal-plate heat exchangers, which are known around the world today. Basically, it made possible the heating and cooling of fluids in bulk and much more quickly than before, and the APV Paraflow is still the leading make. APV provides machinery for the pasteurization of milk, and for the beverage, pharmaceutical and health-care industries. The company went on to employ 2,750 people and, in 1958, Seligman retired to the role of president. In his time he was the first gold medalist of the Society of Dairy Technology and president of the Institute of Metal. He died at his desk in 1972 when the company was worth £30 million. APV was sold to Siebe in 1997 for £331 million.

The key to safety for Jews under threat in Europe before the war was a visa to emigrate. To obtain one for the UK was time-consuming and, in 1938, as the likelihood of a coming war loomed ever larger, the urgency became ever greater. At which point an official in the Home Office came up with a cunning wheeze. It involved Jewish manufacturers from Germany and Austria who wanted to get into Britain. It was made clear to them that, if a visa was granted, the manufacturers could set up in any part of the country they wanted: Greater London was the favourite by a distance. From the government's point of view, however, the problem of unemployment wasn't in the south of the country. It was in the North East, Scotland and Wales, so those three areas were identified as the ones which needed special help.

The government had tried to get their own British manufacturers interested in setting up in these new development areas, but with very little success. Over 5,000 were contacted, 200 replied but only twelve agreed even to consider the possibility. As a result, it quickly became clear on the grapevine that if a German–Jewish manufacturer said he would set up a business in one of the development areas, he was very likely to get a visa. Moreover, he would be given it much more quickly than if he preferred a London location: the pressure thus put on German–Jewish and Austrian potential manufacturers was very effective.

A detailed study of the impact of the consequent formation of the Jewish companies in the North East shows that about 17,000 jobs were created directly by refugees. If you add the numbers of jobs produced for subcontractors, the result was certainly helpful for the local unemployed. The side effects were worth having too. It was current economic wisdom that the unemployed from declining heavy industry would be ill-suited for jobs in light industry. The Jewish refugee companies proved this philosophy false. The belief was also that the development areas were too far off the beaten track for transporting goods to where they were needed. This also proved fallacious. It was further suggested that the jobs would be taken up by women, which wouldn't help reduce the hard-core male unemployment. In fact, the number of men employed outnumbered the women.[6]

In 1945, the Association of Jewish Refugees produced a tenth-anniversary pamphlet that told the story of what happened next. No less than 160 companies were created by Jews. Of course, not all of them flourished and some of their founders were interned as enemy aliens when the war started, which finished the business. Others joined up and served in the forces. Still, the pamphlet has no less than 150 advertisements for refugee companies throughout the country which were still in business at the end of the war. In 1974, three of the companies started by the refugees in the North East were employing more than 1,000 staff each.

For the safety of the UK, perhaps the most important refugee firm was Sigmund Pumps. The business was started in 1868 in Moravia, now the Czech republic. It specialized in water pumps, and when the Second World War could be seen looming, Miroslav Sigmund (1908–2004) was sent to find a new haven. In 1938, he chose Britain and was welcomed by the government, who foresaw that they would need a large number of fire-fighting pumps if the worst happened. Sigmund was given the contract and built a factory in Gateshead to produce them. By the time war broke out, the firm had 420 employees and had delivered 3,000 fire pumps to fire brigades all over the country. Sigmund's brother also bravely smuggled forty essential manufacturing machines to Britain but, in 1942, he was executed by the Nazis.

During the war Sigmund Pumps manufactured Bren-gun parts, with a team of refugees from the Bren factory in Czechoslovakia. By the end of the war the company, now with 2,000 staff, had produced 8,000 fire pumps, 4,000 more for ships, 800,000 stirrup pumps for the general public,

200,000 six-pounder guns, and 3,000 engine parts for tank landing craft.[7]

After the war, they also produced for the government the 5,000 'Green Goddess' fire engines built between 1952 and 1964. Sigmund was a prolific inventor with a lifetime achievement of more than fifty patents, and he was also responsible for the development of the market for plastic spectacle lenses. He retired finally in 1974 when he was 66, but lived another thirty years.

Another refugee who made a real difference was John Somerfeld (1914–85), who was born Kurt Joachim in Berlin. In 1938, he escaped to London after the family firm had been confiscated, and became a student at Imperial College. It was Somerfeld who invented the Somerfeld track, a heavy-duty portable road which could be in service within twenty-four hours. Initially, it was used to repair aerodrome runways destroyed in attacks by the Luftwaffe. Without such a concept it would have been impossible to get the fighters into the air again. Later it was used to build bomber runways, helping the Allies achieve their objectives overseas.

One of the Jewish firms that came to prominence some time after the war was Sterilin, which was the creation of Richard (1925–) and Thomas (1921–) Tait. They came from a Berlin family and got out just before the war began. Their mother was on the last plane from Berlin at the end of August 1939. In the 1960s, Richard Tait's Swedish cousin told him about an idea she'd had for the use of plastics. Tait spotted the possibility of using plastic containers for laboratory purposes, rather than glass. At the time he was the sales manager of a plastics importer called Hamlin, and Thomas was an engineer. Richard persuaded Hamlin to diversify into the field. Eventually they formed a separate company, Sterilin – Sterile-Hamlin – and, in 1966, built a factory in South Wales at Aberbargoed, which flourishes in a new location a few miles down the road to this day.

Although it only employs 250 staff, its turnover is in excess of £38 million and it goes some way to replace defunct coalmines in the Welsh economy. There were a number of other pharmaceutical firms created by refugee Jews, like Paul Somlo with Somportex, Victor Fox with Medopharma and R.J. Hulse with Medo Chemicals.

Jewish immigrants are not always motivated by oppression. There was a considerable influx of Jews from South Africa before the end of apartheid, simply because they hated the regime they were living under. The Jews were treated perfectly well in South Africa by the government, but the treatment of the Blacks and Cape Coloureds was too much for a lot of Jews to stomach. Among those who left in 1969 was David Tabaznik (1948–) whose grandfather, Mendel, was a renowned Yiddish writer, and whose father, David, had an important role in looking after mentally ill Blacks on behalf of the government.

The hole in the market that David Tabaznik spotted was the manufacture of medicines after the patents of the pharmaceutical companies which first invented them had run out. Exact copies of the medication could then be made and would sell at about a fifth of the original price. Within a year, these generic products would have about half the market. The firm which he created was called Arrow Generics, and the secret of its success was the speed with which it came into the market after the patents had expired. It's easy enough to find out the day on which this will happen, but Arrow was geared to producing the generic copy the day after! And they did it for 275 medicines!

Today they operate in twenty countries as the subsidiary of an American corporation. Their development was materially assisted by Jacob Rothschild who bought 20 per cent of the holding company in 1989 for $14 million. In 2009, the American Watson Pharmaceuticals paid $1.75 billion for what had become the Arrow Group. Apart from donating to the Labour Party, the Tabazniks have taken a particular interest in the Oxford Institute of Yiddish Studies, as a tribute to the work of Grandpa.

For another town in trouble during the Second World War, a Jewish entrepreneur arrived like a white knight. This time it was a refugee who escaped to London in 1938 at the age of 26 and was bombed out in 1940. He moved to a small town in Cumbria which was suffering badly from the unemployment of the Slump, and was in such a desperate state that the government had also designated it a development area.

Frank Schon (1912–95) was the son of a German lawyer and had studied Law at university. When he graduated, he went into a family chemical company and learned there of a German firm which was pioneering synthetic detergents. When he got to England he first started making firelighters with a friend, Fred Marzwillier, and they started a company called

Marchon, culled from their surnames. After being blitzed, they were attracted to Whitehaven in Cumbria, because they could obtain a government grant if they set up in business there.[8]

A friendly farmer sold them a dilapidated house on some of his land so that they would have somewhere to manufacture the chemicals. Which might well have been the end of the story if a local ex-miner hadn't pointed out to them that the land was sitting on deposits of anhydrite, which is the key ingredient in making sulphuric acid. The two young men saw the possibilities opening up. In 1943, they created Solway Chemicals and Schon remained its chairman until 1968. After the war, Schon went over to Vienna to find the scientist who had invented the anhydrite process and, in 1951, during the Korean War, when there was a major shortage of the acid, the firm really took off. The Marchon works in Whitehaven became the largest employer in the town, with over 2,000 staff, apart from contractors. It now made synthetic detergents and it was the largest single-site producer of sodium tripolyphosphate in the world. This, in a town with only 25,000 inhabitants. It also developed ten factories abroad and broadened its chemical base to include many other products.

Albright and Wilson, the second-largest chemical company in the country, recognized Schon's competitive edge and bought Marchon in 1955. Marzwillier retired in 1957 and Schon moved onto the Board of A&W. He continued to run Marchon, which became responsible for more than a third of the holding company's profits. Schon was acknowledged to be a brilliant negotiator and the Whitehaven plant remained very much his baby.

For the next twelve years, Schon defended the status quo fiercely, but Albright and Wilson eventually brought in consultants to see how the parent company could be run more efficiently. The result was a decision to appoint regional managers under a chief executive officer. This would have reduced Schon's influence, and he was only 57 years old. In addition, the company had received a good offer from the Canadian government to build a new plant in Newfoundland, where the cost of electricity, a key factor in Marchon's production, would be far lower.

The Albright & Wilson board decided to adopt both recommendations and Schon resigned in protest. Out of loyalty to him, the rest of the Marchon board, bar one director, resigned as well. Schon's concerns were soon proved well founded as the Newfoundland plant effluent started to poison the local fish. Within two years it was closed, and the company had to settle down to a prolonged period of retrenchment.

The employment prospects for the families in Whitehaven depended very much on the Marchon plant and the nearby Sellafield nuclear reactor. The plant continued in operation for many years but, in 1999, it was sold to a French company, then on to an American firm and eventually, in 2005, it was closed. The memorial to Frank Schon is a plaque at the Civic Centre marking his contribution to the town. The fairy story of the Jewish refugee is also to be found in the local museum, as the town turns to tourism and fishing to rebuild its infrastructure. Unhappily, Whitehaven now has some of the worst deprivation in the country with poor educational attainment, unemployment and crime figures.

Schon himself went on to advise Israel on marketing its chemicals, and did a lot of good work as chairman of the National Research Development Council and chairman of the Cumberland Development Corporation. In 1976, he was made a peer and, when he was introduced to the Lords, he said, 'The debt that I owe to the kindness and humanity of the British people cannot be discharged'.[9] He died in 1995 at the age of 83, and the gap he left in supporting the standard of living of the citizens of Whitehaven has not been filled since he resigned.

Most Jewish businessmen stayed clear of politics, and even fewer got involved in matters of national security. One exception was Rudy Sternberg (1917–78) who was born in Austria and came to England when he was 21 to study chemical engineering at London University. This was one way of getting a visa to escape from Europe. It was on the basis of his studies that he first saw the possibilities of Bakelite. This was the first synthetic plastic and was used, initially, for everything from saxophone mouthpieces and cameras to rotary dial telephones and children's toys. In 1948, when the war was over, Sternberg bought a disused mill in Stalybridge in Lancashire. There were plenty of them empty and eventually he manufactured in six, employing 1,000 people.

Over the years Sternberg built up his new company, the Sterling Group, into the fourth-largest petrochemical company in Europe. The foundation of his success was his concentration on doing business with the Communist Eastern Bloc countries, particularly East Germany. For example, he obtained a contract to export its potash, and made friends with the head of the government, Walter Ulbrecht, which few in the West were prepared to do at the time. Sternberg was a flamboyant character. On one occasion he took a stand at the Leipzig Trade Fair and could be seen driving round the town in a Rolls Royce, flying the Union Jack.

The firm grew massively and Sternberg made a fortune, but part of the cost was arousing suspicion within MI5 that he could be a Communist agent. He had become friends with the prime minister, Harold Wilson, when Wilson was president of the Board of Trade and, when Wilson was defeated in the 1970 general election, Sternberg was one of the businessmen who financed his private office thereafter. Rumours of all kinds were spread, though nothing was ever proved against Sternberg, except that he was a very astute businessman. Sternberg was knighted in 1970 and made a peer in 1975 as Lord Plurendon. He had another string to his bow as chairman of the British Agricultural Export Council (1968–75), and was later elected president. He died in 1978.

Another atypical Jewish company was founded in 1932 by Eric Weiss (1908–90) who came to Britain in 1931. The family business in Germany had failed, but its chemical products were still needed by the metal industries. In a small room in Birmingham, Weiss started Foseco (FOundry SErvices COmpany). It claims – probably fairly – that it has produced more products and service innovations than any other company in the foundry industry, inventions such as hexachloroethane tablets to remove undesirable gases from aluminium, and exothermic sleeves.[10]

For the uninitiated, the key point about Foseco was that it dealt with the foundry industry rather than the general public. It succeeded because it really could improve a foundry's productivity and profits. Weiss, from the age of 17, had worked in the industry. He was an experienced manager. In 1933, the other half of the equation arrived in Britain; Dr Kossy Strauss (1905–85), a brilliant Jewish chemist and a friend of Weiss, also left Germany for safer shores.

The initial capital they employed was £500 and, to begin with, what was on offer was pretty primitive: a weighing machine, a sieve and two shovels were part of the package. One of Weiss's best ideas was to produce a free magazine for the foundry industries, which would deal with complex issues in simple terms. This proved very popular and the firm started to grow. During the war the government built the company a factory in Staffordshire, which was used for the production of torpedoes and aircraft frames. By 1952, it had a turnover of over £1 million. It went public in 1964, had a turnover of £20 million in 1967 and employed 3,500 people all over the world.

Weiss was not a dictator. The *Foseco Group News*, commenting on his passing, focused on 'this unfailingly courteous man; one of the rare business leaders who was also an excellent listener'.[11] The chairman added, 'he was the creator, for many years the leader and always its inspiration. A kindly caring man, he was loved and respected by all who knew him.' Which isn't a typical picture of entrepreneurial founders.

In 1980 Weiss received a knighthood, and the company became a world leader in the supply of products to the foundry industry. Eventually it was sold to Burmah Castrol and Weiss became life president. Today Foseco is in the FTSE 100. Kossy Strauss, for his part, was the founder of the Singers Hill Synagogue Zionist Council and the family gave a *sefer torah*[12] to the congregation in his memory, which is an expensive gift. Both Weiss and Strauss were well known for their charity work and generosity.

Another major British company which supported the economy after the war was Lansing Bagnall, who became the largest manufacturers of fork-lift trucks in Europe. It was in bankruptcy when Emmanuel Kaye (1914–99) bought it with his partner, John Sharp, in 1943. Kaye had been born in Russia, where his father was a wheat merchant. The family came to Britain when Kaye was very young and he attended the Twickenham Technical College. He left school at 15 and, after starting his business life as an office boy in the City, he joined a small engineering company and met Sharp. The two of them decided to set up a precision tool and instrument company called J. (John) E. (Emmanuel) Shay (Sharp and Kaye), but it was an act of considerable faith to buy Lansing Bagnall.

After the war they were able to obtain planning permission for a factory in Basingstoke, which eventually sprawled over forty acres. Fork-lift trucks were still in their infancy, but Lansing Bagnall took the counterbalanced truck and redesigned it. The result was the first reach truck that could be used in narrow aisles. It lifted pallets and deposited them on shelves – simple and efficient.

At its peak in the 1970s, the company employed 3,000 people and had a new parts-and-services division that was housed in a building which could, alternatively, have taken two Jumbo jets. Sharp died young, but Kaye was knighted in 1974 and chaired the company for forty-six years until, in 1989, he sold it to a German firm. Kaye left over £45 million when he died at 84 in 1999.

Kaye was a well-liked man and served on the council of the CBI for many years. He was extremely keen on homeopathic medicine and healthy eating, once sending a memo to seventy of his executives telling them to eat more fish. He was chairman of the Thrombosis Research Trust from 1985 to 1999, and a major contributor to Emmanuel College, Cambridge. He only once aroused controversy when he was persuaded to support Tony Blair's private office fund with, it was said, a contribution of £50,000.

There are any number of examples of Jews converting to Christianity, but Arthur Hubert, the founder of one of the largest scrap metal merchants in the country, Tom Martin Ltd., came from a rarer background: a Huguenot family which became Jewish in 1670. Hubert (1904–91) was born in Germany and his father had a flourishing business till Kristallnacht in 1938. When the Jews were rounded up afterwards, Hubert was sent to Buchenwald concentration camp. He was released on condition that he signed over his family's company to the Nazis, and so arrived penniless in London on 2 September 1939, which was cutting it very fine indeed. He had intended to go on to America but had left it too late. Instead, he found himself interned on the Isle of Man as an enemy alien.

When he was released, he took a job as a scrap-metal salesman and, in 1948, he set up his own business, Tom Martin, in Blackburn. He ran the company for the next twenty-eight years and retired at 72, though he stayed on the board for a further ten years. The success of the business was ascribed to its being 'a supermarket in a world of Steptoe and Son [a popular TV series about a scrap metal dealer and his son] corner shops'.[13] The Tom Martin juggernauts still collect scrap metal all over the North of England, but Hubert is primarily remembered for the enormous amount of charity work he did for the very Orthodox section of British Jewry. The main rabbinic seminary in Gateshead benefited, as did a very wide range of Jewish institutions.

Germany wasn't the only country which missed out because they drove their Jewish families away. If the Egyptians had looked after their Jewish community, post 1948, they might well have had not only venture capitalism (Sir Ronald Cohen), but also a large stake in the steel-trading industry worldwide. Hans Oppenheimer (1915–85) was born in Stuttgart, but went to work for his uncle in Alexandria, rather than go on to university. He migrated to Britain after 1948 and, in 1951, started a joint steel-trading firm with a German company, Coutinho, Caro & Co. Eventually they were bought out and, after Oppenheimer died in 1985, Ralph Oppenheimer (1941–), his son, agreed with the new owners to buy their shares. The result was a change in company name to Stemcor, roughly from STEel Marketing CORporation.

Today Stemcor is a very large independent trader in steel and raw materials. It has annual sales of over £5 billion and operates out of eighty offices in forty countries. It is the fifth-largest private company in the UK and the shares are either owned by the family or the staff. Margaret Hodge, the former Labour minister for children and culture, is Hans Oppenheimer's daughter.

Inevitably, there are occasions when ground-breaking Jewish firms go bottom-up, whether through ill fortune or ill practice. One of the most high profile was John Bloom (1931–), who in 1958 hit on the ingenious idea of offering home washing-machine demonstrations if the potential customer would like to see what the newfangled invention could do. Like any new product, washing machines were initially very expensive but Bloom had managed to get a Dutch company to sell to him direct. He was, thereby, able to offer the Electromatic twin-tub washer-spin dryer for under £42, which was half the normal price on the high street.

Within a short time, Bloom had 10 per cent of the market and this son of a Polish-born, Orthodox, East End tailor, who had left school at 16, was on his way. In 1963 he joined up with Colston dishwashers and had control of the well-liked Prestcold refrigerator. He bought the Rolls Razor Company to enable him to produce his own washing machines, and his shares doubled within weeks after very favourable prognostications. By the end of 1963 he was operating at a rate of over 200,000 machines a year.

Not surprisingly, the market leaders, such as Hoover and Hotpoint, were not best pleased. What developed was a massive price war. Bloom had to increase his advertising spend and was then hit by a postal strike which prevented coupon orders from reaching him. Isaac Wolfson had been financing the hire-purchase agreements entered into by Bloom customers, but at £10 million plus, decided enough was enough and withdrew his support. By mid July 1964 the company was in administration. Obviously a lot of people lost a lot of money and attempts were made to suggest that Bloom had acted illegally. Official enquiries were instituted and Bloom was fined £30,000 by the courts. That was a comparatively minor penalty and rumours abounded of a stitch-up. The 430-page, 1965 report into Rolls Razor was, allegedly, ordered to be kept secret for eighty years! Till 2046! That didn't look good at all, but Bloom went off to America to start a nightclub and the saga was over. The benefit to the British people was that a very large number of households had been able to own a dishwasher as well as a television set, which had recently become de rigueur in any home of any substance.

As one door closes another one opens. As traditional British industries collapsed, their labour costs undercut or their products becoming out-dated, there was a desperate need for new inventions and new companies. One came in 1973 when Paul Gotley (1925–2009) decided to produce a gas-detection machine. Gotley came to Britain on a Kinder-transport, a train that rescued Jewish children from Germany, though – often tragically – the rest of the family had to be left to their fate. Gotley never saw his parents or his sister again, as they perished in the Holocaust. The boy's formal education effectively finished at that early age, but he took himself to night school and became an engineer. After a number of jobs, he found that there was a problem besetting telephone exchanges; there were too many explosions, and no equipment to give warning that they were likely to happen. Gotley suggested to his company that they try to do something about it, but there was little interest.

So, starting in a converted Nissan hut, Gotley set up Neotronics to manufacture a gas-detection unit. The Nissan hut is now under Stansted

Airport's runway, but Neotronics has its own factory and is the largest gas-detection company in the world. It was launched on the Stock Exchange in 1987, and employed 400 staff before Gotley sold it in 1996. At which point Gotley provided the capital for his daughter, Andrea Gotley, to set up her own gas-sensor manufacturing company, Alphasense, which is helping the UK to maintain its international lead.

Lord Peter Levene (1941–) is a difficult man to pigeonhole because he is part-industrialist, part-City of London man, and part-government adviser. What can be said is that he looks like the American comedian, Phil Silvers, and that he has had a tremendously successful career. Levene's father was an antique silver dealer who lived in Willesden, North London and sent his son to the City of London School, which had been particularly popular with Jewish boys since they first flocked into the East End in Victorian times. The brightest got into the school, and Marcus Samuel of Shell provided it with a great deal of financial support. As Levene recalled, 'In those days the ambition of the Jewish parent was to raise young English gentlemen who were Jews, not Jews who were Englishmen'.[14]

Levene went on to the University of Manchester, but then joined a company that possessed the grand-sounding name of United Scientific Holdings, but little else. There were twenty staff and the company sold army-surplus telescopes and watches. It took twenty years for Levene to become chairman of the board and to build it into a major quoted company. It finally achieved total respectability by buying manufacturers like Alvis Tanks in 1981. As a supplier to the Ministry of Defence, the performance of USH came to the attention of the minister, Michael Heseltine and, in 1985, he asked Levene to become head of defence procurement, a job he did for six years. Levene's contribution to the British economy was to introduce fixed-price contracts, more competition and a harder-nosed approach to purchasing.

Desirable as this methodology is in commercial business, there is a school of thought that it doesn't work in defence procurement, because of the continuing development of research into new weapons systems. What you buy might be improvable – but more costly – while the contract is being fulfilled. In 1998, the Levene reforms were abandoned, but Levene told the Defence Select Committee in 2006 that, 'We did get value for money. We did get projects, almost without exception, delivered on time and on cost.'

The ludicrous position today, when the government is building two aircraft carriers but cannot afford the planes to put on them, is not a situation that would have been likely to occur when Levene was in charge. It was not surprising that, in 2010, the new coalition government set up the Defence Reform Unit under Levene, to sort out the mess. From 1992 to 1997, Levene was appointed adviser on efficiency and effectiveness to the prime minister, John Major, and in 1997, he was made a peer. He was elected the eighth Jewish Lord Mayor of London and, in 2002, was elected chairman of Lloyds of London, the first non-insurance man ever to get the appointment.

Levene is very good at modernization. He has the typical Jewish entrepreneur's suspicion of processes that can only be justified because they are traditional. As Lord Mayor of London, he sold the civic Rolls Royce and abandoned morning dress for meetings. At Lloyds, he cut out waste, 'You had all those people staggering around with all those files. It was absolutely ludicrous.'[15] He also sorted out the teething problems of the Docklands Light Railway and Canary Wharf, when he became their chairman. With such a curriculum vitae, it was not surprising that he went on to be appointed vice chairman of Deutsche Bank and chairman of the Bankers Trust.

It was on his watch that Lloyds finally got an insurance licence from the Chinese government to work in their market. As much of the British economy now depends on the success of the City of London as a financial centre, Levene's contribution has been massive. His feet, however, remain firmly on Jewish ground. He is married to a former pupil of the Orthodox Hasmonean High School for Girls, he asked the senior rabbi of the Sephardi community, Rabbi Abraham Levy, to be his chaplain as Lord Mayor, and he is always ready to help Jewish charities. He is now over 70 but only recently remarked, 'My wife says she married me for better and for worse, but not for lunch. When I get bored I'll tell you.'[16]

Two years after Levene started to head up Lloyds, his namesake but no relation, Peter Levine (1956–) started a company called Imperial Energy. The objective was to prospect for oil in Siberia. It was another opportunity thrown up by the chaos in Russia, as the country grappled with the complexities of the capitalist world after glasnost.

Levine came from a working-class Jewish family with roots in Russia and his father worked as a tailor in Leeds. In 1974, young Levine went up to Oxford to read jurisprudence and, when he graduated, he put together the Peter Levine Law Group over the next ten years. By the time he met the leaders of Kazakhstan, a new 1991 republic formed as the old USSR broke up, he ticked all the boxes for the kind of international lawyer they needed.

Kazakhstan is the ninth-largest country in the world, bigger than Western Europe, but with six inhabitants per square kilometre; it is vast, extremely remote and the climate is dreadful. The new rulers wanted overseas representation. Levine was a British lawyer, charismatic, he spoke fluent Russian, dressed impeccably and was quite prepared to be their honorary consul in the North of England. He was also one of the founders of the British-Kazakhstan Society, formed to further the interests of the country. Levine was also appointed international legal adviser to the Supreme Court of Kazakhstan.[17]

In 2004, on the small AIM market, Levine launched Imperial Energy. The shares were 25p and the total raised was £2.5 million. It was agreed with the Kazakhstan rulers that Imperial Energy could look for oil in the country, and they bought substantial shares in the assets of the Western Siberian Sibinterneft and Allianceneftegaz from their general director.

Imperial struck oil all over Kazakhstan. It was soon estimated that it had 3.5 billion barrels of oil reserves and, as early as 2005, the shares stood at 550p. Sir Tony Brenton, the British ambassador in Moscow, said, 'This is a serious British company, doing serious work in Russia. It's a very good example of Russia and the UK coming together.'[18] In the next few years, however, difficulties arose in working with the authorities in Kazakhstan and, in 2009, Levine sold Imperial Energy to India's Oil and Natural Gas Corporation for £1.5 billion. Levine made about £90 million from the sale. Phenomenal doesn't begin to describe that kind of success. Just as Marcus Samuel beat Standard Oil to the nineteenth-century market in Japan, so Levine was into Siberia before the modern oil giants.

Levine is still involved in oil-exploration companies, but he has now been able to turn his attention to good causes. In 2011, he gave his old college, Trinity, £5 million for fellowships and for bursaries for bereaved undergraduates. Children of members of the armed forces killed abroad are particularly welcome to apply.

NOTES

1. *The Times*, 11 May 1905.
2. Ibid.
3. Ibid.
4. *Jewish Chronicle*, 1 March 1901.
5. David Holding, *The Share Centre*, 28 October 2009.
6. *Daily Telegraph*, 9 April 2004.
7. Herbert Loebel, 'Refugees from the Third Reich and Industry in the Depressed Areas of Britain', in *Second Chance. Two Centuries of German-speaking Jews in the United Kingdom*, ed. Werner Mosse (Tübingen: J.C.B. Mohr, 1991).
8. Tam Dalyell, MP, *Independent,* 12 January 1995.
9. *The Times*, 6 January 1978.
10. *Foseco Group News*, 1990.
11. Ibid.
12. A hand-written copy of the first five books of the Bible. *Jewish Chronicle*, 1991.
13. *Jewish Times Asia*, 27 September 2010.
14. *Daily Telegraph*, 23 June 2009.
15. *Daily Telegraph*, 18 September 2010.
16. Ibid.
17. Kazakhstan Embassy newsletter, 5 May 2003.
18. Ibid.

1. Airfix – the Tiger Moth construction kit was just one best seller.

2. Amstrad's CPC464 – great marketing builds on great inventions. Photograph by Bill Bertram.

3. Archie Shine furniture, designed by Robert Heritage, is in the V&A. Photograph courtesy of Michelle Hanlon: made-good.com.

4. El Horria (Mahroussa) yacht built on the Isle of Dogs by Samuda Brothers. Photograph by Lawrence Dalli.

5. Forman's Smoked Salmon, the best of British haute cuisine.

1934: The largest salmon ever sold in Billingsgate Fish Market weighing in at 74lbs. This beauty came from Norway and was sold for 2/10 a lb when typical prices were 2/3. Louis Forman stands behind the salmon wearing a black Homberg hat.

6. The Gestetner Cyclostyle copying machine, 1910. The ultimate accolade, a generic term: To Gestetner.

7. Glaxo's 'Builds Bonnie Babies' campaign – from impoverished beginnings to international fame.

8. The original Marks & Spencer Penny Bazaar, where it all started.

9. The Multitone VPM Vacuum Tube Hearing Aid, 1937. Multitone provided Winston Churchill with his hearing aids. Photograph courtesy of hearingaidmuseum.com

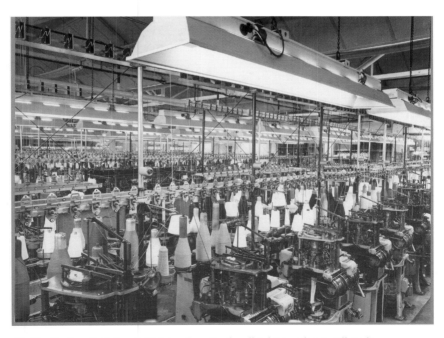

10. The Pantherella factory in Britain where Pantherella's long socks are still made.

THE HOUSE of TUCK

is THE house for

CHRISTMAS CARDS   GIFT BOOKS
CALENDARS   PAINTING BOOKS   TOY BOOKS
AUTO-STATIONERY   JUVENILE BOOKS
POST CARDS   TOY NOVELTIES
VALENTINES   PICTURES
EASTER CARDS   WEDDING BOOKS
CHRISTMAS SEALS, TAGS, Etc.   PAPER DRESSING DOLLS
BIRTHDAY CARDS   BIRTHDAY BOOKS
BABY BOOKS   ZAG-ZAW PICTURE PUZZLES

"There is no influence in the world
so ennobling as that of the Fine Arts"

CULTIVATE a love for the **Beautiful** and the **Best in Art** by insisting
on having the TUCK Publications, always. They are produced by the
best processes of Printing, Engraving, Etching, Photogravure, etc., etc. There
can be no mistaking "TUCK'S"—The quality is there.

Every TUCK Publication bears the impress of the world-famed trade mark—
THE EASEL & PALETTE—recognised as the "Hall-mark of Excellence."

*TUCK'S Art Publications are sold by the leading Dealers, Stationers and Art Stores
throughout the country.*

WRITE FOR CATALOGUE AND LIST OF 75,000 POSTCARDS CONTAINING
TUCK'S POSTCARD EXCHANGE REGISTER or 7,800 COLLECTORS ALL OVER
THE WORLD, WHO WILL EXCHANGE TUCK'S POSTCARDS WITH YOU.

**122-124 FIFTH AVENUE
NEW YORK**   RAPHAEL TUCK & SONS
CO., LTD.   **9-17 ST. ANTOINE ST.
MONTREAL**

London—Paris—Berlin—Bombay—Buenos Ayres—Cape Town

11. Tucks - the populariser of Christmas cards, postcards and jigsaw puzzles. Courtesy of tuckdb.org.

12 Moss Bros store fascia, circa 1920. Moss Bros provided court dress for the first Labour cabinet.
Courtesy of Moss Bros Group PLC.

13. First World War Decca portable gramophone – to while away the terrible hours in the trenches. Courtesy of John Sleep Gramophones.

14. Interior of the Kilburn State Cinema showing stairs to circle, wall, Wurlitzer and screen. The Palaces of the People – and the State Kilburn chandeliers had more bulbs than those at Buckingham Palace. Photograph by Malcolm Barres-Baker. Courtesy of Brent archives.

15. The Triumph 1919 Type H for the motorcycle Formula 1 races of its day. Courtesy of Triumph Motorcycles Ltd.

16. Ford Zodiac MK2 Corgi Car. Corgi produced so many cars that their American Distributor said that their factory looked like General Motors. Courtesy of Sir David Michels.

Chapter seven

The Sum of the Whole is Greater than the Sum of the Individual Parts

Over the centuries, the foundations of a country's economy will change. Texas is running out of oil, the Far East can produce many types of clothing cheaper than Europe, and Korea has become a major car producer. Britain couldn't escape the changes. The Industrial Revolution made it the largest manufacturing nation in the nineteenth century, exporting as much as its next two competitors – Germany and America together – for many years. The twentieth century saw its decline from being the principal Great Power, and many of its manufacturing industries became shadows of their former selves, or even vanished. Much of the lost business was replaced, of course. High-tech industries, mass tourism and the further growth in the international importance of the City of London helped to bridge the gaps, as did the growing proportion of the population employed in the increasing number of new service industries.

As the effects of international competition, slumps and wars took their toll, however, some companies only survived by amalgamating with others. For that process to be a success, a business titan was often needed to draw them together, and some of the most successful in stemming the adverse tide were Jews.

One of the earliest was Ivor Levinstein (1846–1916). Some products we take for granted; among these are salt, but there was a time when the salt companies competed fiercely, with a good deal of price-cutting. So in 1888, the Salt Union was formed and its chairman was Levinstein, who came from a Jewish family of dyestuff manufacturers in Germany and arrived in England in 1864 from Berlin. He set up the Blackley Dye-works outside Manchester and the firm flourished. Levinstein was not only the chairman but the chief salesman as well. He founded and edited the *Chemical Review*, which was one of the first technical journals in the country and, no doubt, plugged his own products.

Levinstein went on to be twice elected president of the Society of the Chemical Industry. He was instrumental in the creation of the Manchester School of Technology, which in 1905 became the Faculty of Technology at Manchester University. His most important contribution to the economy, however, was his determined effort to reform the patent laws. These gave too much power to overseas patent holders, whose terms were so broad that British manufacturers couldn't make the products. Levinstein sued a number of major German chemical manufacturers and eventually won agreement for licences to be awarded. In 1906, he was given an Honorary MSc by Manchester University. As the major shareholder in the £3 million Salt Union, Levinstein guided its progress for a number of years and still found time to open a lager-beer brewery in Wrexham, which was certainly the exception to the rule.

When the government during the First World War realized it had been far too dependent on the supply of dyestuffs from Germany, they initiated the British Dyestuffs Corporation. This was one of the first instances of the government tutoring an industry, and its technical director was Levinstein's son, Herbert (1876–1956). He had previously advised the government on how to deal with the German use of poison gas. Herbert Levinstein followed in his father's footsteps. He fought against the Russian refusal to recognize the patent laws and worked hard in the professional bodies of the industry. As a result, he was twice president of the British Association of Chemists, and 'there were indeed few professional bodies within the chemical industry of which he was not president at one time or another'.[1]

Another of the early Jewish amalgamators was the German, Siegmund Loewe (1856–1903), whose family had a small-arms company which was very successful. The inventors of both the Mauser and the Luger pistols worked for them. In 1897, when Lord Nathan Rothschild brokered a merger to create an armaments company, Vickers Son & Maxim, in

Britain, it was the Loewe family who ended up owning most of the shares. Lord Rothschild's protégé was Siegmund Loewe, who became general manager of the new company and did a good job in establishing the benefits of amalgamation. Unfortunately he also became one of the first car accidents when, in 1903, he swerved to avoid a cyclist and was killed as a result. 'His remarkable ability led to him being invited to give his services to Vickers, by whom his loss will be much felt.'[2]

After the First World War, there was inevitably a dramatic drop in the demand for war materials. At the same time, there was a move in 1925 towards forming major international companies, like the ever-expanding Dupont in America and I.G. Farben in Germany. It was recognized that British exports in the chemical market were likely to come under severe threat and it was Sir Alfred Mond (1868–1930) who set out to achieve rationalization, a term which he claimed to have invented.

Mond's was not a rags-to-riches story. His father was Ludwig Mond of Brunner Mond. The young man was sent to Cheltenham and St John's College, Cambridge, where he failed his Natural Sciences degree. He then changed course and became a barrister, but his ambition was to be an MP. He was elected in 1906 for Chester with a majority of forty-seven, and sat in Parliament for most of the next twenty years, usually representing Welsh constituencies as a Liberal.

Mond was a tough personality. He faced much anti-Semitism on the hustings from Tory opponents, but confronted it with good humour. He was considered blunt, direct, blustering and occasionally distinctly ill-mannered,[3] but, at the same time, he had a powerful intellect and considerable vision. He was listened to with respect in Parliament, in spite of the fact that he never lost a guttural family accent, and had a bad voice as well as a bad delivery. He was one of the first Jews to be a minister, serving as First Commissioner of Works from 1916 to 1921, and the first Minister of Health from 1922 to 1923. He was an early advocate of health insurance. In office, there was a popular piece of doggerel about him: 'The minister bland who rules pro tem, out of Swansea via Jerusalem.'[4]

Mond's philosophy in life was based on that of his father, whom he quoted: 'He said he would not seek success. He would compel it.'[5] So did his son. After the war, Mond conceived the idea of the Imperial War Museum and was its first chairman in 1920. He also put the War Graves Commission on a sound financial footing, and successfully advocated the creation of war memorials, such as the Cenotaph.

He had more difficulty in trying to keep the Welsh mining industry afloat in the face of severe international competition. He took a major part in the creation of the Amalgamated Anthracite Collieries, which was one of the two trusts that eventually owned the South Wales mines. The only way to keep the company afloat was to reduce the wages and extend the hours of the miners, who suffered severe economic hardship as a result. Mond was heavily criticized, not least because he, personally, was awarded a very substantial salary. The Ammanford strike of 1925 led to fifty-eight miners being imprisoned for riotous assembly; the mine owners were blamed for not handling the economic problems more sympathetically.

These were dreadful years for the miners, and some reacted badly. They asked Arthur Horner, the miners' leader, if they could smash Jewish shops. Horner replied, 'If anybody started anti-Jewish activity on this issue I would resign the Presidency of the South Wales miners in protest'.[6]

In addition to his political interests, in 1909 Mond had found himself managing director of Brunner Mond and its sister company, Mond Nickel, after his father died. As such, after the First World War, he foresaw the problems emerging in competing in the international chemical industry. So he set off for America on the *Aquitania* to negotiate cooperation with firms in the American chemical field.

On the boat, however, he found Lord McGowan of Nobel Industries, who had hurried after him, and who was keen on the main British chemical companies sticking together. The voyage gave them time to work out the details and, on four pages of Cunard paper, was typed the eventual agreement which they reached. Brunner Mond, Nobel Industries, United Alkali and British Dyestuffs would merge to become Imperial Chemical Industries, a combine large enough to take on Dupont and I.G. Farben. Mond would be the first chairman.

After that momentous decision, ICI was a major player in the British economy for many years and Mond was its creator. Less well remembered were the Mond-Turner talks after the General Strike. Mond was passionate about the need for management and labour to work in harmony. The TUC, after the General Strike, was anxious to avoid there ever being another. So, in 1928, Ben Turner, the leader of the wool-textile workers, for the TUC, and Mond, with the National Confederation of Employers and the Federation of British Industries, sat down to mend fences. What emerged was known as Mondism, a determination to have a rapprochement between the two sides. It was a pity that the employers remained aloof from the proposed closer cooperation for many years.

Mond was made a Baronet in 1910 and a peer in 1928. He took the title of Lord Melchett and said he didn't want his father's name. He wanted his own name. But it is the name of Mond which is still to be found in a town in Israel he founded. It is called Tel Mond, for he was a keen Zionist at a time when most of the richer Jews in Britain were still reluctant to associate themselves with the concepts in the Balfour Declaration. He was the first president of the Technion in Palestine in 1925 and president of the British Zionist Federation.

A similar recognition that amalgamation might be the best way forward was the view of Lewis Coleman Cohen (1897–1966) who created the Alliance Building Society, by combining his Brighton & Sussex Building Society with a number of others. Cohen was an estate agent who had left school at the age of 13 and gone to work as a clerk for 25p a week. Nineteen years later, he bought the estate agency and was invited to become secretary of the Brighton & Sussex Building Society.

After all the mergers he arranged in the next fifteen years, the Alliance was formed and, in 1945, became the eighth-largest building society in the country, with reserves of £150 million. Unlike Mond, Cohen stood for Parliament unsuccessfully on six occasions, but he did become mayor of Brighton in 1956/57 and, in 1965, was made Lord Cohen. It says much for Cohen's popularity in Brighton that, although he was a socialist, he was still elected mayor by a Tory council.

One of the greatest amalgamators was Sir Isaac Wolfson (1897–1991).

It was Wolfson who grew Great Universal Stores (GUS) into one of the greatest firms in the country, who built up the largest mail-order company, combined 2,200 stores involved in men's, women's and children's clothing, and backed a considerable number of budding entrepreneurs. Folklore can be created in a comparatively short number of years and the accepted story today is that Wolfson took over an ailing direct-mail company and led it to almost immediate success. The facts do not diminish his contribution, but throw light on the customs and mores of the 1930s and 1940s.

Wolfson was the son of Solomon Wolfson, a very Orthodox Polish cabinetmaker, and was brought up in the Gorbals, a very poor part of Glasgow. He showed early talent. His father said, 'I'm not much good at business, but I have a son who is a financial genius'.[7] Young Wolfson was 9 at the time! At 14, he was selling furniture for his father at a salary of 25p a week. When Wolfson was 23, he came to London and started his own company, trading everything from foods to pianos. In 1927, he bought an old car works and turned it into a furniture factory.

It was in 1932 that he joined Great Universal Stores. This was a company formed in 1900 as Universal Stores, by three Jewish brothers, Abraham, George and Jack Rose. The idea was that the public should be able to buy from a warehouse instead of a shop, thus eliminating the cost of having shops in different towns. The brothers Rose took Wolfson on as a merchandise controller. Although it was in the middle of the Slump, Universal Stores was doing well and, in 1931, had launched on the Stock Exchange. Over the previous three years, profits had grown from £110,000 to £410,000, largely on the back of a major advertising campaign in 1928.

Wolfson was appointed joint managing director with George Rose very quickly, but when Abraham Rose stood down as chairman in 1933, his replacement was not Wolfson. The likelihood of the City approving the appointment of a 36-year-old from the Gorbals was remote. The new chairman was Major General Sir Philip Nash, who was probably happier on a battlefield than selling goods from a catalogue. When Nash died in 1936, both Wolfson and his brother, Charles, were members of the board, but another luminary, Sir Archibald Mitchelson took over the chair.

It wasn't until 1946 that Wolfson was considered an appropriate figurehead for the company, even though he had been running it highly successfully for years. Wolfson, himself, would probably have approved the charade to satisfy the City, even though dividends were around 45 to 50 per cent in the years before the war. He remained in office for the next forty-one years.

During his time with the company, he bought and improved such household names as Burberrys, Warings, Jays & Campbell, Hope Brothers and Global Tours. He backed Jimmy Goldsmith (1933–97), John Bloom and Max Joseph, providing finance, at admittedly a high rate of interest, where high-street banks feared to tread. He was the undisputed leader of the Jewish community for many years, and the first really senior leader to come from nineteenth-century refugee antecedents.

Wolfson was immensely charitable. As early as 1936, he had given £13,000 (£2.5 million today, using average earnings as the yardstick) to help German–Jewish refugees. The Wolfson Foundation started in 1955 with a fund of £6 million, and has given away over £100 million to both Jewish and non-Jewish charities. There is a Wolfson College in both Oxford and Cambridge. Wolfson was also a very religious man and was president of the United Synagogue from 1962 to 1973. In that capacity he was responsible for persuading Immanuel Jacobovits to take on the mantle of chief rabbi. Wolfson once said that he would like to be known in history not as a businessman, but as a man who built 50 synagogues in Israel. He died at 93.

Sometimes there are, morally, more important causes than the economy for the government to tackle. In 1944, Ernest Bevin, the Minister of Labour, was agonizing over the employment after the war of severely injured servicemen. As was universally agreed, the country didn't want a repeat of crippled ex-soldiers playing mouth organs for money in the streets, as had happened after the First World War.

Bevin, therefore, decided to set up an organization to provide work for such heroes. A Disabled Persons Act was passed and a company set up, which became known as Remploy. Now Bevin was dyed-in-the-wool Labour, but for chairman of the new organization he approached a former Conservative MP, Sir Jack Brunel-Cohen. The plan was to create 130 factories to employ 13,000 staff and, if Brunel-Cohen only managed ninety by the time he gave up the chairmanship in 1956, it was still a tremendous effort.

Why Brunel-Cohen? When he made his maiden speech in the House of Commons after being elected in 1918, he asked permission to do so sitting down. It was very unusual, but the Speaker agreed immediately. Brunel-Cohen had lost both legs in 1917 at the Battle of Passchendaele.

Brunel-Cohen didn't want to patronize the employees by manufacturing goods with a low skill level in the factories. The ex-servicemen wouldn't just make woven baskets. They would make such products as protection suits, motor components, violins and school furniture. The government might have to subsidise the work – the subsidy grew to over £100 million a year – but very large numbers of disabled ex-servicemen benefited over the years. Sir Ivor Cohen was another Jewish chairman, who followed Brunel-Cohen from 1987 to 1993.

Another of the great Jewish amalgamators was Charlie Clore (1904–79). You could also call him a wheeler-dealer on a heroic scale. For Sir Charles Clore, as he became in 1971, the deal was everything. He was born in the East End of London. His father, Itzhak Israel Clore, had escaped Tsarist pogroms in Riga in Latvia, and set up as a textile merchant when he came to Whitechapel. Initially, Charlie joined him, but soon set out on his own, buying the South African film rights to the Heavyweight Championship fight between Jack Dempsey and Gene Tunney. He was just over 20 years old.

The film made a profit and, in 1928, Clore used the money to buy a derelict ice rink in Cricklewood in London. He liked skating and, once the rink had been refurbished, it became very popular. Clore then branched out into buying the Prince of Wales Theatre, but couldn't sell it, so he ran non-stop revues to keep the investment afloat.

For the next 20 years, Clore dabbled in a wide range of industries. From 1945 to 1947 he owned Jowett Cars, and in 1948 he bought an interest in the New Century Finance Co., which was a West End issuing house. During his lifetime he owned two oil tankers, Furness shipbuilding, William Hill the bookmakers, Bentley Engineering, the knitting-machine company, Mappin & Webb, the jewellers, Lewis

Stores, which included Selfridges, and he had interests in South African gold mines, hotels and farming, besides being a major player in the property world.

Many of the deals were hostile takeovers. These were, not surprisingly, unattractive to the directors under fire, and the City, as Warburg found, did not consider such takeovers were a gentlemanly thing to do. Clore was attacked for his methods but, in 1979 *The Times*, in his obituary, summed up his considerable achievement. They pronounced hostile takeovers as good for the British economy, 'as they increased the pressure for more industrial efficiency and the more intensive exploitation of business assets'.[8]

It was in 1953 that Clore made his most important purchase – J. Sears & Co. Sears had 900 shoe shops and they were mostly freehold. So Clore sold the freeholds to institutions and took long leases instead; sale and leaseback. He then went on the hunt for more shoe companies, creating the British Shoe Corporation, which included Truform, Freeman, Hardy & Willis, Manfield, Dolcis, Saxone, and Lilley & Skinner. The resulting company had 2,000 shops immediately after Clore's death, and sold 25 per cent of the shoes purchased in the country. They did not seem to keep up with the times, however, and some divisions, like Dolcis, have gone into administration in recent years.

It is extremely unlikely, of course, that any captain of industry can reflect at the end of an illustrious career on an unblemished record of success. Manchester United don't win every match and Jewish entrepreneurs, like anybody else, are also to be found licking their wounds.

Clore had found a site in Park Lane for Hilton to open its first London Hotel. He then offered them another site in Grosvenor Square, which they turned down. They pointed out they could only get 150 bedrooms into the area available and this was too small a number for them. So Clore offered the site to another hotelier, Max Joseph, and Joseph pointed out the same thing. The asking price was too high for a site that would only produce a small hotel. Clore saw the sense of this and offered Joseph the site for a far smaller figure, which Joseph accepted. He then built a hotel with 300 smaller bedrooms than Hilton would have found acceptable. Clore would have shrugged at being outsmarted, though he was extremely annoyed when he failed to take over Watneys, the brewers. He only retired in 1977 when he was 73 and he died two years later in 1979.

Almost outstripping his commercial success was Clore's charitable efforts. In 1965, he set up the Clore Israel Foundation, which has so far given away in excess of £60 million. He financed the building of the Clore Gallery at the Tate, which cost £6 million. He twice gave £200,000 to London Zoo, and London University received a donation of £750,000. He also started the British Clore Foundation in 1965 and, during the last ten years alone, in conjunction with his daughter Vivien Duffield's charitable foundation, over £50 million has been given to good causes. Many Jewish charities have benefited. In 2000, Vivien Duffield was made a Dame in recognition of her efforts.

As the entrepreneurs built salt conglomerates, great building societies and major shoe companies, so Joe Hyman (1921–99), a contemporary, attacked the old-fashioned practices of the textile industry with the same vigour. Hyman was the grandson of a Russian émigré textile merchant and his father, Solly Hyman, had followed his father into the family business in Manchester. Joe Hyman went to Manchester Grammar School, but he left at 16 and worked with his father till he was 23. He then started buying and selling cloth on his own account from a small back-street office. He had a capital of £10,000 provided by his father, and the local bank, Martins, came up with an overdraft facility. As Hyman recalled: 'I started with a silver-plated spoon.'[9]

Hyman had a dream. He believed in vertical integration. That you should not just make the raw material, but go on to make the goods and sell them. In the textile industry, at the time, you did one thing or another. Not Hyman, who bought a knitting mill in 1957 and then William Hollins, a company which had a good brand in Viyella, well known for warm pyjamas in an age when central heating was an optional extra. Hyman now had the capacity to spin, weave, produce the cloth and make the clothing.

He was working, of course, in an industry which had at least 200 years of tradition behind it. Hyman did not like the result: 'I object to the idea that top jobs would be the monopoly of the upper middle class.'[10] At the time, the normal rule was for the workers to come from the secondary schools and the management from the public schools.

In 1961, British textile manufacturers were under increasing attack from foreign competition. To achieve strength in size, ICI tried to buy Courtaulds, but the two giants of the textile industry were unable to agree a merger. Courtaulds fought off the ICI bid. Sir Alfred Mond's old company was now concerned that Courtaulds would go after their textile business clients, and they wanted to support a competitor who would be on their side. Hyman saw his opportunity, produced a viable business plan – they were unusual at the time – and persuaded ICI to back him. ICI gave him £13 million for a 20 per cent share of his company and a £10 million loan.

Hyman set out to integrate and rationalize. He bought such companies as Combined English Mills, Bradford Dyers and Clegg & Orr. His company owned brands like Aertex and British Van Heusen. There was also another important factor; Hyman relied heavily on the scientific knowledge of the industry possessed by David Brunnschweilor (1927–), who would become chairman of the Textile Institute Council. Between them they recognized the potential of polyester/cotton as a fabric before the competition woke up to the same conclusion. Viyella went on to sell immense quantities of brushed nylon shirts through Marks & Spencer. Over just a few years, sales went up ten times and profits twelve times. In 1963, the business had been worth £6 million. Two and a half years later it was worth £50 million.

Another key to Hyman's success was that he went for the top end of the market, and left the cheaper side to the Far Eastern manufacturers: 'I got Viyella worn by the jet set.' He associated the products with 'colour, sex, romance, fast cars, that sort of thing'.[11]

It was always a tough market, though, requiring strong direction. Like any other, the Jewish business community also has its fair share of mild – and not so mild – megalomaniacs. At one time, Hyman employed a non-Jewish member of staff, Ernest Sharp, who would become one of Max Joseph's most senior executives at Grand Metropolitan. One day Sharp was in his office in London when he was told that Hyman wanted to see him immediately in Birmingham. Fearing some disaster, Sharp rushed to Birmingham where Hyman kept him waiting for several hours. Eventually ushered into his boss's presence, Hyman proceeded to spell out in some detail how well he had advanced Sharp's career and how well Sharp had been treated by the company.

By now Sharp was petrified at what might be coming and, when Hyman asked him whether he would do him a favour, Sharp was desperately anxious to oblige. Hyman spelt out his major concern 'Ernest', he said, 'Could you please see to it that the secretaries don't leave their umbrellas in the corridors when they come in from the rain!' That was it. Sharp returned to London.[12]

Hyman had imagination, boldness, good marketing skills, a mastery of finance and he was quick to grasp the implications of new technology. He was also autocratic, impatient and a one-man-band, who kept everything in his head. He was a cultured man, very keen on classical music. As *The Times* once said, 'He looks more of a rich Mayfair salesman of antiques than the tough, innovating revolutionary of a traditional industry in need of a purge'.[13]

In an obituary, he was recognized as having been 'influential in establishing many business techniques that have become routine'.[14] Among these was reducing the size of head office, arranging sales and leaseback deals on premises, chasing excess stock levels and, typically, working round the clock. He had, perhaps, the Jewish trait of self-mockery, and once said, 'I saved Viyella by my efforts and the textile industry by my example'.[15] It's more likely, though, that he meant it.

The *New York Times* summed up his approach when it labelled him 'a swashbuckling, impatient autocrat', but within only eight years ICI lost patience with the maverick they couldn't control. In 1969, in an all-night boardroom coup, Hyman was removed by his fellow directors. He tried a comeback with the woollen industry in the 1970s but it didn't work out that well, and he retired in 1980 to the Surrey countryside. To an extent, Hyman was unlucky. He had inherited a life in the textile industry when, in Britain, the business was coming under severe and continuous strain. The same was true for the woollen industry. What Hyman had achieved for Viyella would be picked up by David Alliance and Harry Djanogly long after he had left the scene. He died in 1999.

He hadn't saved the British textile industry by his example, but he had delayed and slowed its decline.

The search for the hole in the market applies as equally in fashion as it does anywhere else. Lou Mintz (1908–87) recognized that at a very early age. He was born on a train in Switzerland while his parents were leaving Poland, and was brought to Britain at the age of 5. At 15 he left school and started work as a buying agent for department stores. He became sufficiently proficient at this to start his own business when he was 18, and he decided to concentrate on clothes for stout women – or 'the fuller figure' as it was more decorously described.

Over the next thirty years the company, Linda Leigh, grew and prospered. Where overweight women had been dismissed as an unimportant market segment in the past, Mintz held fashion shows in upmarket hotels and encouraged fashion editors to take the women more seriously. There are a substantial number of manufacturers looking after their needs today, but Mintz was a pioneer.

When he was in his 50s, he considered accepting a takeover bid from Selincourt, but finished up buying the company instead. When he made his offer, the board of directors minuted that there was concern that the City might not like the idea of the firm being taken over by someone of 'the Jewish persuasion'; Selincourt had been founded in 1852, and that kind of mild anti-Semitism was fairly common in many of the less dynamic companies. When Mintz came to the next board meeting, he told them that he had been going through the directors' expenses, and had found bills for wines, spirits and cigars, that could not possibly have been spent for the good of the business. He compared their behaviour unfavourably with Jewish business ethics.[16]

Mintz now set out to build up Selincourt by taking over other good names in British clothing manufacturing. In the next few years the company bought Harella, Frank Usher, Hardy Amies Ready to Wear, Skirtex, Dorchester Lingerie, Garlain, Margray and a number of others. By 1974, the company had the third-largest turnover in the industry. Mintz retired at 65 in 1972 and died in 1987. Within the Jewish community, Mintz had distinguished religious forebears, like the Vilna Gaon and Rabbi Judah ben Halevi Minz (1408–1508). In his own right, he was president of the Food for the Jewish Poor charity for many years, helped found the Marble Arch Synagogue and created the Barkingside Jewish Youth Centre. A strong supporter of the Labour Party, he bought the last sixteen years of a lease of the Roundhouse in Camden, London, and created an Arts Forum with ties to the TUC.

The need to amalgamate also applied to the carpet industry, and one of the most successful entrepreneurs in that field is Philip Harris (1942–). From a Russian immigrant family, Harris had to leave school at 15 when his father died, and left his only child a London market stall in Rye Lane Market, Peckham and two shops. To make matters worse, his mother died three years later and the adolescent had to pick up the pieces from there. It didn't help either that he was severely dyslexic. Fortunately, there was a consumer boom in the Fifties and Harris flourished. As the CEO of Debenhams, who once worked for him, commented years later, 'He is a workaholic, always running around the stores. He knows every detail about his businesses: all the stores, carpet ranges and sales figures intimately.'[17]

Over the next thirty years, Harris built Harris Carpets into a 1,600-store empire, buying another large company in the trade, Queensway, in 1977. In 1988, however, he lost the company to a hostile takeover, though his personal share of the selling price was £76 million. Harris Queensway collapsed within three years of the takeover and Harris, himself, started again with Carpetright. He remains the chairman and chief executive of the company, which has 600 stores, including branches in Belgium, Poland and the Netherlands.[18]

Harris used his fortune to support educational and medical charities. By 1999, he had given £10 million to these good causes. The Harris Manchester College in Oxford and the Harris City Technology College in Croydon are just two of the institutions which have benefited. He gives 20 per cent of his income to charity every year. Arsenal and the Conservative Party are his two other loves. In 1996, he was made a peer and, in 2007, the company was valued at £850 million.

Working at the top of the government's nationalized industries seldom offered the same financial rewards as working for oneself. Few Jews applied, though there were notable exceptions, like Sir Monty

Finniston (1912–91). Finniston was the fifth son of a haberdashery sales-man in Glasgow. He won a scholarship to grammar school and got a degree in Metallurgy from Glasgow University. He became a metallurgist at the Royal Naval Scientific Service during the war, and went on to be chief metallurgist at the Atomic Energy Authority establishment at Harwell from 1948 to 1958. In 1967, the Labour government, despairing of Britain's performance in the production and sale of steel, created the British Steel Corporation. Finniston was considered one of a rare breed, 'a highly regarded scientist who has more than a dash of commercial tycoonery within him'.[19] He was appointed technical director and a vice chairman of the new organization, coincidentally under the chairman-ship of Lord Melchett, a great-grandson of Sir Alfred Mond, creator of ICI.

It was Finniston who produced the ten-year strategic development plan for the new corporation. The fourteen founding companies, with their more than 200 subsidiaries, were to be reorganized. The plan was to convert the small works with their obsolete equipment into five centres, with more compact and highly competitive plant, in South Wales, Scunthorpe, Teeside, Sheffield and Scotland. In 1973, when Melchett fell ill, Finniston became chairman of the organization, when he was also knighted.

The problem Finniston faced was that the new structure was going to require a serious reduction in the number of steel workers. The unions at the time were very powerful and, when the Labour Party regained office in 1974, the plans became deeply unpopular. Although British Steel was losing money, the steel workers wanted a 30-per-cent pay rise and to retain the unprofitable plants. Finniston fell out with the government ministers responsible in a big way. He had also publicly denounced the unions as 'in a state of anarchy' and 'belonging to the Middle Ages', which equally didn't go down too well.[20] When his term of office expired in 1976, it was not renewed.

Nevertheless, Finniston was only recognizing the inevitable. The rationalization took place under his successors and, in 1987, the indus-try was privatized, when productivity per man-hour had tripled over the days when Finniston took over. By 1989, the Corporation was making over £700 million profit. For some years, British steelmaking had a renaissance in world markets. Undoubtedly, what Finniston will be remembered for is the 1980 Finniston Report on engineering education. This government enquiry was to investigate how engineering could achieve a higher status in the country. The result was that a new degree, BEng, replaced the old BSc and BA, and the Engineering Council was created in 1982. Engineering education is now discussed as Pre- and Post-Finniston.

When he was fired, Finniston had no difficulty in obtaining better-paid directorships, and this 'formidable and forceful intellect but highly approachable'[21] figure remained well-regarded until his death. Finniston was an Orthodox Jew. On Yom Kippur, the Jewish fast, a section from the Prophets (*Haftorah*) is read during the service by a lay member of the congregation. Finniston said that his proudest moment was to be asked to read the *Haftorah* on Yom Kippur in his synagogue. He was always influenced by his religion. He believed 'the ethical standards inculcated by Judaism are the only hope for the world'.[22] He was instrumental in arranging several gatherings at the Chapel Royal, Windsor, with Christian and Moslem representatives, to discuss the ethics of commerce, and Prince Philip attended many of them.

The best-known retailer in Britain today is Sir Philip Green (1952–) who, in the *Sunday Times* Rich List for 2010, was rated ninth in the country, with a fortune of £4.4 billion. Green comes from a middle-class family, went to a Jewish boarding school, lost his father when he was 12 years old, and started work at 15.

There are many kinds of anti-Semite, and one is the snob, who looks down on Jews as not out of the top drawer, extravagant in their behaviour and lacking in social graces. For bigots like this, Green is a gift, a stereotype. He is a heavy man where slim is elegant. He has a prominent Roman nose. He is apt to splash out on family occasions to a degree which usually has few parallels: he was alleged to have spent £4 million on a three-day event for 200 of his friends for his son's Bar Mitzvah.[23] His fiftieth-birthday celebrations were reported to have cost him £5 million.

Green is very tough in his negotiations and accused of being overly aggressive and capable of using colourful language. In 1988, he formed a company called Amber Day and, in 1992, was forced to resign by the directors after poor trading. He never put himself in that position again, relying in future for the money he needed on the banks and wealthy friends. He also failed in a takeover bid for Marks & Spencer. He lives in Monaco and he legitimately avoids paying a lot of tax which would otherwise be due if the family's permanent home was in Britain. This is often commented upon in the press.

A gift to the anti-Semite, and yet a major contributor to the British economy in many ways. It is one thing to create a fine product and a company to make or sell it. There will usually come a time, however, when it grows old and loses some of its efficiency, some of its drive. It is then that a Philip Green is needed. Time and again he has bought failing companies and resuscitated them. He finds their faults seldom differ: 'Bad buying, no discipline, no control, old stock, indecision, time wasting, corporate thinking.'[24]

Correcting these faults has made Green several fortunes. In 1995, he bought a sports retailer, Olympus, for £1 on condition he took on the £30 million they had in debts. In 1998, he sold it for £550 million. In 1999, he bought Sears Retail for £538 million and sold its several parts for £729 million. In 2002, he paid £850 million for Arcadia, who owned a string of famous high-street names, and got the money back in two years. There is nothing wrong with foreign investment, but if a country is able to produce its own entrepreneurs, the jobs of its workforce are probably safer, and the benefits of its growth come to the economy.

There is, of course, another Philip Green. The one who plays tennis with Prince Albert of Monaco, who put £6 million into creating the Fashion Retail Academy, which now has 200 students, the one who was knighted in 2006. For a man who started by buying and selling £20,000 worth of imported Hong Kong jeans in 1979, it is remarkable to have 2,300 shops in Britain and 12 per cent of the UK clothing market only thirty years later.

On the one hand, Green may not be the obvious choice for a Cheltenham soirée. On the other, he was the choice of the prime minister, David Cameron, when he came to office in 2010, to inspect the ways in which Whitehall spent the tax payers' money. The results may not make him any more popular in the public sector, but his recommendations, if they are adopted, could save the country a great deal of revenue just when it is badly needed.

One of the great amalgamators in the advertising industry has been Sir Martin Sorrell (1945–). Sorrell has an MBA from Harvard and was given the Harvard Alumni Achievement Award in 2007, which is their highest accolade. He joined Saatchi & Saatchi in 1975 and was their financial director from 1977 to 1984. He was so close to the Saatchis that he was often known as the third brother. He took responsibility for organizing the purchase of the many companies they took over.

In 1986, he became the CEO of a wire-basket company, but used it to start to buy advertising agencies. He bought eighteen in three years and, in 1989, stunned the industry when he bought J. Walter Thompson for $566 million. As an icon, buying JWT was akin to buying Sainsburys in supermarkets or Macdonalds in restaurants. Sorrell went on to pay $825 million for another major player, Ogilvy & Mather and then, in 2000, bought a third, Young & Rubicam and a fourth, Grey Advertising. By that time, the company had the largest media-buying group in the world, and it is now valued at about £5 billion on the Stock Exchange. It employs 140,000 people in 2,400 offices in 107 countries, which is amalgamation on a heroic scale: 'Many industry observers credit him with the fact that the UK still has an independent vibrant communications industry.'[25] Beyond the advertising industry, in 1997, Sorrell was made a Foreign Office ambassador for British business and knighted in 2000. He is a substantial supporter of Jewish Care and shows no sign of slowing down.

One of the newest and largest Jewish amalgamators is Mick (Mick the Miner) Davis (1958–). Born in South Africa of parents from British and Lithuanian antecedents, Davis went to a Jewish School in Port Elizabeth and became an accountant. He made a career in the mining industry and, in 2002, was poached to become the chief executive of X Strata, a Swiss-registered company, one of the largest mining companies in the world, and part of the FTSE 100.

At the time, the firm was only capitalized at £300 million, but after a frenzied round of takeover bids, costing £30 billion, the company became the largest producer of zinc, the largest exporter of thermal coal, a major part of the copper and nickel industries and the largest producer of ferrochrome. The sheer size of X Strata makes a billion pounds seem like a drop in the ocean. The indebtedness of the company is over £10 billion but, in 2010, it turned in a much-improved profit of £6.6 billion on a turnover of £30.5 billion, up from £1.53 billion in the previous year. It operates in nineteen countries. Paying for the Second World War led to the liquidation of most of Britain's assets overseas. What was needed was to rebuild those investments, and it is companies like X Strata who have repaired some of the damage.

Davis earns about £5 million a year in salary and bonuses, but he devotes a lot of his time to Jewish charities in Britain. He is the chairman of the executive of the Jewish Leadership Council and is devoted to raising money for good causes. A larger-than-life character, he is a worthy successor to the generations of committed fundraisers who have looked after the poorer sections of the community for so many years.

NOTES

1. Obituary, *The Times*, 8 August 1956, p.11.
2. Obituary, *The Times*, 26 November 1903, p.11.
3. Liberal Democratic History Group 53&item=biography.
4. Edward Jamilly, ''Patrons, Clients, Designers and Developers: The Jewish Contribution to Secular Building in England', *Proceedings of the Jewish Historical Society of England*, 38 (September 2003).
5. Ibid.
6. Arthur Horner, *Incorrigible Rebel* (London: McGibbon and Kee, 1960).
7. *Jewish Chronicle*, 28 June 1991, p.15.
8. *The Times*, 19 November 1979.
9. Nicholas Faith, *Independent*, 12 July 1999.
10. Ibid.
11. Ibid.
12. In conversation with the author.
13. Nicholas Faith, *Independent*, 12 July 1999.
14. Robert Heller, *Guardian*, 12 July 1999.
15. Nicholas Faith, *Independent*, 12 July 1999.
16. The author in conversation with Richard Mintz.
17. Rob Templeman, *Daily Telegraph*, 3 November 2007.
18. Richard Fletcher, *Daily Telegraph*, 3 November 2007.
19. *The Times*, 25 July 1967.
20. *The Times*, 20 November 1973.

21. *Jewish Chronicle*, 8 February 1991.
22. Ibid.
23. Sally Vincent, *Guardian*, 23 October 2004.
24. Ibid.
25. *Wikipedia*.

Chapter eight

The Media Story

The theory that the Jewish community owns, or can materially influence, wide sections of the British press, has been given credence by important members of the Establishment over the years. Lord Beaverbrook, for instance, who owned the *Daily Express* and the *Sunday Express* for a large part of the twentieth century, wrote to a newspaper owner in December 1938: 'The Jews have got a big position in the press here. I estimate that one third of the circulation of the *Daily Telegraph* is Jewish. *The Daily Mirror* may be owned by Jews. *The Daily Herald* is owned by Jews. And the *News Chronicle* should really be the *Jews Chronicle*. Not because of ownership, but because of sympathy.'[1]

Writing about news reporting in 2010, John Simpson, a first-rate media expert, commented, 'None of these assertions was true. It was simply that each of the newspapers Beaverbrook named was critical of Hitler. The one proprietor who was actively pro-Hitler was Lord Rothermere who owned the *Daily Mail*.'[2] And for years after the war, many in the Jewish community were reluctant to buy the paper for that reason. If they had, however, constituted one third of the *Telegraph*'s circulation, it would have been necessary for nearly 100 per cent of the community to buy it. It's an example of the public's perception that there are far more Jews in Britain than is actually the case.

In fact, though, John Simpson was wrong on more than one count. It was true that Odhams Press owned the *Daily Herald* and *The People*. Odhams had been built up by Lord Southwood. Now, admittedly, Lord Southwood sounds Eton and Balliol, but he started life as Julius Salter Elias (1873–1946). His family was poverty stricken and, eventually, Elias was reduced to working unpaid for an employee of Odhams, a small printer, in order to have somewhere to sit to keep out of the rain.[3]

At this point, Elias was spotted by the owner who was impressed by his diligence. He gave him a job, and Elias slowly progressed, until he came to be responsible for building up the company. His big break came when he secured the printing contract for *John Bull*, a magazine with a massive circulation, run by a con artist called Horatio Bottomley. When Bottomley was finally exposed in 1922 and went to prison for seven years, Odhams saw their circulation plummet, but Elias had faith in the product and built it up again without the founder.

In 1925, Elias bought the struggling *Sunday People* and with the aid of first-class marketing and gimmicks, like offering free life insurance to the readers, he built up the circulation from under 300,000 to 3 million in a few years. The writing improved as well for although, as a publisher, Elias never pretended to be a journalist, he was expert at spotting great newspapermen.

As the presses were only used once a week, Elias determined to buy a daily paper and, in 1930, he took over the *Daily Herald*. There was a need for a paper that supported the relatively new Labour Party, another niche market for a Jewish entrepreneur to exploit. Guarantees were provided that the paper would support Labour and, with the enthusiastic help of trade unionists all over the country, Elias soon moved the circulation from 250,000 to over two million. His core company was also by now the largest billposters in the country, and Elias was made a peer, Lord Southwood, by Neville Chamberlain.

There remained a poor level of advertising revenue for the *Herald*, because its readership was, primarily, working class, without much disposable income. Elias decided he could not afford to alienate his potential advertisers. So he ensured that the paper supported Appeasement which, in the 1930s, was the populist view of the correct political approach to the dictators, Hitler and Mussolini. Lord Southwood's support for the Labour Party came from conviction, but wider Jewish support for the Labour Party owed something to the fact that Jews were often not made welcome by the selection committees of the country's Conservative Associations.

The most unsavoury instance of this, at the time, was when Daniel Lipson (1886–1963), a former mayor of Cheltenham and a highly respected local head teacher, was not adopted by the constituency Conservative Party. In 1937, they needed a new candidate, but Lipson was rejected because he was Jewish. The ex-mayor, however, had no intention of taking this lying down. He stood as an Independent and won handsomely. The local population did not have the same prejudices as the selectors. Indeed, when all the Jewish Conservative MPs lost their seats in 1945, Lipson was the only Jewish Conservative supporter to retain his.

In 1939 when war broke out, the *Herald* swung from Appeasement to belligerence, like everybody else. When the Labour Party agreed to join a national government with Churchill in 1940, the *Herald* and the *Sunday People* also became less critical of the conduct of the war, which had gone so badly for Chamberlain. Ever the perfect gentle man and gentleman, Southwood asked his editor whether the headline castigating the prime minister could be changed to read 'Mr Chamberlain' instead of 'Chamberlain'.

In 1944, Southwood was appointed Labour chief whip in the Lords and, when he died very suddenly in 1946, he was sincerely mourned. His passing was particularly regretted at Great Ormond Street, the hospital for sick children, where he had been the chairman from 1937 until his death. He had also been responsible for a charity campaign for the Red Cross – 'Penny-a-week'. The peers stood in the House of Lords to pay tribute to him and referred to his 'inexhaustible courage and tremendous industry' and his 'kindliness and good nature'.[4] Some years after his death the *Herald* became *The Sun*.

There was a London evening newspaper called *The Globe* (1803–1921), whose proprietor was at one time Elias Polack (later Goldsmid), whose father was a stalwart of the Jewish Dover community. The first local paper to be started by a Jew, however, was the *Brighton Guardian*, which Levy Emmanuel Cohen ran from 1827 to 1860. The first Jewish national newspaper owner was Joseph Moses Levy (1812–83). He was a printer, and when Colonel Arthur B. Slegh decided to launch a new paper in 1855, Levy agreed to produce it. Unfortunately for the Colonel, hardly anybody bought it or took advertising. As the agreement was that, if he wasn't paid, he could have the paper, Levy became the owner. He set to work to make the *Daily Telegraph* a success. In the same year he also took over the *Sunday Times*, but he only kept it a year before selling it on.

Levy decided that the key to success was to make the *Daily Telegraph* 'the largest, the best and the cheapest newspaper in the world'.[5] It was certainly the cheapest of the British national papers because, where the *Times* sold for 3½p, the *Telegraph* was only ½p. The journalism was voluminous; state occasions would be covered in enormous detail, and the dullest subjects were livened up with imaginative copy. There were also overtones of the salacious material which could confidently be expected to feature in the future *News of the World*.

Levy appointed his son as the editor of the *Telegraph*, and Edward Levy (1833–1916), became a legend in Fleet Street. Lord Northcliffe was once passing the *Telegraph* building and said to a friend, 'Sitting in a room up there is an elderly gentleman who can teach us all our business'. He called him 'the greatest journalist of us all'. As the paper flourished, Edward Levy took over total control after his father died. In 1875, he decided that the name Levy was not quite grand enough to help him establish himself in society. So he changed it to Edward Levy-Lawson, and was knighted in 1892. He finished on top of the greasy pole in 1903, as Lord Burnham. He died in 1916, and the business was sold in 1927.

Initially, the *Telegraph* supported the Liberal Party. This was not surprising, as the Liberals had supported the admission of Jews to Parliament, where the Conservatives had not. This loyalty changed at the time that Gladstone was stumping the country on behalf of the Bulgarian Christians, who were being massacred by the Turks – the famous 1880 Midlothian campaign. The Jews were not in favour of this approach, on the reasonable grounds that, when the Bulgarians were not being massacred by the Turks, they spent much of their time massacring the local Jews.

Lords Southwood and Burnham made a major contribution to the UK newspaper industry. The most significant thing about the ownership of the *Observer* and the *Sunday Times* at the end of the nineteenth century, however, was that they both had the first woman editor of national papers. Rachel Beer, née Sassoon (1858–1927) was a member of that great Jewish family, part of the coterie surrounding Edward VII when he was Prince of Wales. Her father-in-law, Julius Beer (1836–80), was from a Frankfurt clan, and had risen from a poverty-stricken background to great wealth by successful investments on the Stock Exchange.

In 1870 he bought the *Observer*, founded in 1791, but died of apoplexy in 1880. Feeling stigmatized because of his Jewish birth, he had £5,000 spent on producing the 'largest and grandest of all the privately owned buildings in the (Highgate) cemetery'.[6] Based on the tomb of King Mausolus in Turkey (that's where 'mausoleum' comes from), it was broken into many years later and is now a tool shed. Even though he was buried in a proper Christian cemetery, he would have been disappointed that he still didn't get an obituary in *The Times*.

The *Observer* was left to his son, Frederick Beer (1859–1901), who was as weak and vacillating as his wife, Rachel, was strong minded and determined. Rachel moved in as a contributor, was appointed assistant editor and in 1889, when the editor left, she took the vacant position. In 1893, when the *Sunday Times* came on the market, she ensured the family bought it, and became editor of that as well. It all ended in tears, because Frederick died young, Rachel had a breakdown and the two papers were sold on in 1905 for the ridiculously low figures of £4,000 each.[7] Even so, Rachel Beer proved it was possible for women to be newspaper editors, long before it was firmly established in our own times. She could also point to one major scoop on her watch, when Count Esterhazy confessed in an article that he had forged the papers that had condemned Captain Dreyfus.

In a democracy, the press has always been invaluable in exposing corruption and warning the public against financial charlatans. Among its foremost watchdogs in the late nineteenth century was Harry Marks (1835–1916) who started the *Financial News* in 1884. He had also set up the London *Evening News* in 1881, but sold out to the Harmsworths in 1894. That paper, in spite of being printed at first on blue paper and then on yellow and green, had not been a success.

Marks was the fifth son of Rabbi David Woolf Marks, who played a major part in the growth of the Progressive movement in British Jewry. As a youngster, Harry took himself off to America and worked in journalism there. He conceived the idea of a financial newspaper, which would be read because of its exposés. He put his idea into practice, and his paper predated the *Financial Times* by a couple of years. It particularly targeted questionable investment schemes and corruption in local government.

The paper did well and, for example, led to the downfall of a number of senior officials of the Metropolitan Board of Works, who were robbing the public purse. The company was floated in 1898 and, by 1911, was paying a

35 per cent dividend on its shares. It went on to be one of the papers which, in 1912, exposed the Marconi scandal. By that time, however, Marks had given up the editorship through ill health, though he remained influential as the proprietor. He was an extremely dapper man, with a considerable sense of humour and served both as an LCC councillor and an MP. He won his parliamentary seat in 1895 by only four votes, retired in 1900 and was then elected for the Isle of Thanet in 1904 and 1906. He died in 1916 and the paper passed into new ownership in 1928, before itself expiring in 1945.

One of the most notable Victorian journalists was Frederick Greenwood, who edited the *Pall Mall Gazette*. This Tory paper was very influential, and it was Greenwood who wrote to the government to recommend the purchase of the Suez Canal shares, which Disraeli successfully achieved. In 1880, however, Greenwood fell out with the paper's proprietor, and started the *St James's Gazette*. This didn't prove a happy relationship either, and he persuaded Edward Steinkopff (1837–1906) to buy it. Steinkopff was a German Jew who had made a tremendous fortune by buying the export rights of a German mineral water manufacturer, called Apolinnaris, in 1874.

The importance of bottled water in Victorian times was that you could drink it safely. After 50,000 Londoners had died of cholera in the 1860s, the connection between the disease and impure water had finally been recognized. In 1875, Steinkopff imported six million clay jugs by sea and sold the product as 'clear as crystal, soft as velvet and sparkling as champagne'. St Apolinnaris is, in fact, the patron saint of wine.

Steinkopff thought Greenwood extravagant and didn't give him the editorial freedom he wanted. So Greenwood left, but Steinkopff continued to own the paper until he sold it in 1903. The paper was considered to be the intellectual and literary side of Tory journalism, and attracted many great writers to contribute. When Steinkopff died, he left £1,250,000 and gave his daughter instructions in his will that she was to give £1,000,000 to charity. Lady Seaforth – she had married Lord Seaforth in 1899 – did as she was told.

Another son of a rabbi was Paul Reuter (1816–99), who was born in Germany and spotted yet another new opportunity to build a business. The invention of the electric telegraph had increased the speed of communications out of all recognition. It was said you could use the machine to map the progress of the 1848 revolutions, which broke out as fast as the telegraph carried the news of each uprising across the continent; shades of the Middle East in 2011.

Reuter had to flee Germany when the revolutionary movement collapsed, and he decided to come to London. In 1851, he opened an office at the London Stock Exchange for transmitting financial data, and it was no coincidence that the Channel undersea cable began operating that November. Reuter came to an agreement with the Stock Exchange that he would provide them with the prices of continental stocks if they, in their turn, would allow him to transmit data on London stock prices.

That was how Reuters started, and it soon became famous for the speed with which it transmitted the news: it was the first to report the assassination of Abraham Lincoln. In 1883, Reuter sent his offices a memo, setting down what he wanted to be reported, which remained the company's policy thereafter: 'fires, explosions, floods, inundations, railways accidents, destructive storms, earthquakes, shipwrecks attended with loss of life, accidents to war vessels and to mail steamers, street riots of a grave character, disturbances arising from strikes, duels between and suicides of persons of note, social or political, and murders of a sensational and atrocious character'.[8] Reuter died in 1899 but his agency continues in good order.

In the post-war era after 1945, only two Jewish entrepreneurs have been seriously involved in the national press; Robert Maxwell (1923–91) was the first. He ran the *Daily Mirror* Group and died in mysterious circumstances before the courts could decide on his probity. He drowned after apparently falling from his yacht. Subsequently, the pension fund of his company was alleged to be short by several hundred million pounds.

In his lifetime, Robert Maxwell attracted a great deal of criticism. There are, however, few people who are totally good or totally bad. Wallenstein, one of the most ruthless killers in the Thirty Years War (1618–48), was a good son, husband and father. It was the same mixed picture with Ján Ludwik Hoch, which was Maxwell's name when he was born in Czechoslovakia. By 1940, at the age of 17, he was sitting on a roadside in France, among thousands of refugees fleeing south from the German advance.[9] He had escaped his own country and was lucky enough to be picked up by some

Czech soldiers, also trying to reach Marseilles and a possible ship to England. Among them was Fred Kobler, the same hotel genius who would lay the foundations of Max Joseph's Grand Metropolitan (Chapter 9, 'Eat, Drink and be Merry').

Maxwell made it with the Czechs to England and, later in the war, served in the Intelligence Corps. Speaking Czech, he was seconded to that section, made many friends in the Czech resistance and won himself an MC. In 1948, five Arab armies invaded Israel at the end of the British Mandate. The Jews were terribly short of weapons because of an arms embargo enforced by the American, British, French and Russian governments. The additional problem for the Israelis was that the Arabs had the arms they needed already. Prospects were extremely bleak.

Only one major arms-producing country remained – Czechoslovakia. The Czech Communists had just overthrown the country's Liberal government, but the Russians hadn't yet arrived to take over the country. There was a brief window in time when, if they wished, the Czechs could supply the arms the Israelis needed. It was Maxwell who was said to have negotiated the setting up of the Czech airlift of arms to Israel, which played a vital role in the defeat of the Arab armies.[10] This could account for the fact that when Maxwell drowned, the president and prime minister of Israel came to the funeral in Jerusalem, while everybody in England was looking for the lost pension-fund money.

When Maxwell got back to Civvy Street after the war, he went into publishing with a company called Pergamon Press. Pergamon performed an extremely useful role in publishing scientific papers. The progress of science depends on the advances being communicated worldwide so that others working in the same field can benefit from the discoveries made. Before the advent of the Internet, any publishing house willing to print the material inexpensively was a real boon to academics. In addition, it improved their status, because their work had been acknowledged. Maxwell provided a very valuable service.

In facilitating the spread of scientific knowledge through the medium of books, Maxwell was following in one of the oldest Jewish traditions. In Judaism it is books that are revered, rather than soaring spires, splendid vestments, jewelled artefacts and magnificent choral works. There is an ancient Jewish custom that the first time children pick up a book, they should be given a spoonful of honey. In that way, it is hoped, they will always associate learning with sweetness. A new Jewish community will try, before anything else, to obtain a *Sefer Torah*, a scroll which contains the first five books of the Bible.

The other post-war Jewish newspaper proprietor would not have pleased Lord Beaverbrook at all. Richard Desmond (1951–) bought the *Daily Express* and the *Sunday Express* in 2000, when both titles were a shadow of the pre-eminence they enjoyed in Beaverbrook's time. Where Beaverbrook could boast of a circulation of roughly four million, the papers today sell about a third of that.

Desmond was still rated the forty-fourth-equal richest man in the country in the *Sunday Times* Rich List (2009), which is pretty good for a man who left school as soon as he could. By the time he was 21, he owned two record shops, but he got a taste for publishing and, at the age of 23, formed Northern & Shell. This company grew with the successful production of a range of top-shelf magazines, a celebrity magazine called *OK*, and through the increasing relaxation of restrictions on televising pornography: another emerging niche market, if less salubrious than most.

Whatever one's view of the sources of Desmond's wealth and the sensational stories about his business empire, it certainly cannot be denied that he is an extremely charitable man and has spent very large sums of money on philanthropic causes. He is one of the mainstays of the fund-raising efforts of the Jewish community and has two totally different persona, as businessman and benefactor.

One major post-war magazine publisher was Felix Dennis (1947–), the son of a Jewish working-class Kingston-on-Thames family. The 'Swinging Sixties' set new criteria for young people to keep up with the times, and Dennis went from the Harrow School of Art to playing in rhythm-and-blues bands, and then on to getting a nine months' prison sentence in the longest obscenity trial in British history. This was in 1971, and the charge related to material in *Oz* magazine, which he produced with two friends. There were three defendants accused of conspiracy to corrupt public morals, and Dennis got a lesser sentence because the judge said he was 'very much less intelligent' than the others on trial. The appeal court quashed the sentences on the grounds that the judge was biased, and he was certainly a very poor judge of intelligence.

In 1974, Dennis continued in magazine publishing by forming Dennis Publishing and concentrating initially on his *Kung Fu Monthly*. This was at a time when Bruce Lee was making hit kung-fu films and the magazine did very well: Dennis pocketed £40,000 for filling that hole in the market. He went on to serve the new readership of those interested in computers with the magazines *Mac User* and *Personal Computer*, which focused on keeping operating costs down; they did so well that he sold them both. In all, during his career, he launched, acquired, published and sold over 250 magazine titles.

Dennis's major coup, however, was the creation of Microwarehouse, a computer mail-order company delivering purchases the next day. This made him an enormous fortune. It has to be said, though, that even with such success, Dennis was unlikely to be put on a pedestal as a role model due to various incidents in his private life.[11] On a more positive note, Dennis is planting The Forest of Dennis, which he hopes will reach 20,000 acres. He is also a Fellow of the National Library for the Blind, to which he has contributed very generously. Asked to comment on how to be successful, Dennis said, 'Tunnel vision helps. Being a bit of a s... helps. Stamina is crucial, as is a capacity to work so hard that your best friends mock you, your lovers despair and the rest of your acquaintances watch furtively from the sidelines, half in awe and half in contempt.'[12]

When it came to innovation in printing, there was one Jewish company which created enormous new markets. Raphael Tuck (1821–1900) was born in a small town in Prussia and became a carpenter, like so many other Jews at the time. When he was already 44 in 1865, he migrated to London, as a consequence of the war over Schleswig Holstein. He started a small shop in the City, selling prints and frames. To be a good carpenter, you have to be of a creative cast of mind and, within six years, Tuck had spotted the possibilities of a new fashion which many of the well-to-do had adopted – Christmas cards!

The first commercial card had been sent in 1843 by Sir Henry Coles, although the royal family had been sending their own since soon after Victoria and Albert got married. The cards on offer were very expensive;

just one would cost about a workingman's weekly wage. It illustrates the wealth of the base market that in 1846, 1,000 were sold by a shop in London's prestigious Bond Street.

In 1871, Tuck started producing much cheaper cards and, with a drop in the cost of postage at the time, they started to catch on. What really created the mass market, though, was a brilliant piece of marketing; in 1879, Tuck offered a prize of 500 guineas for new Christmas-card designs (about £275,000 today by average earnings). The entries would be judged by no less a distinguished panel than appointed members of the Royal Academy. The resulting publicity was enormous and the Christmas card habit was created.

In 1895, the company used the same gimmick again. This time there would be 4,000 prizes, still judged by Royal Academicians and, as a consequence, there were 10,000 entries. Of course, the cards did not just consist of attractive illustrations. The words were also important and, in 1889, Tuck offered Alfred, Lord Tennyson, the poet laureate, 1,000 guineas (£1,050), for twelve poems of eight lines each. To his regret, Tennyson decided he was too old (80) to do the work. As his salary for being poet laureate was £72 a year, it was a generous offer.

If we owe the mass production of Christmas cards to Tuck, we are also in his debt for picture postcards, the first of which he printed in 1894. It was Tuck's last hurrah, and for four years he lobbied the postmaster general for permission to send postcards instead of letters in envelopes. Eventually he got his way and, in 1900, the year he died, the company was producing 40,000 different varieties.

The sons of Raphael Tuck took on the running of the company. One of their early successes was with the popularization of jigsaw puzzles. These had been in existence since 1760 but, again, were only for the people who could afford such luxuries. The Tucks brought in five innovations; colourful subjects, recognizable shapes for the jigsaw pieces, plywood and thick card instead of wood, more reasonable prices and attractive boxes. Jigsaw puzzles became a very popular pastime and, in 1908, there began a jigsaw-puzzle craze. In 1914, the most famous puzzle was produced: a 1,250-piece giant of the House of Lords.

In 1925, under Sir Adolph Tuck (1854–1926), Raphael's son, a major effort was made to revive the market for Valentine's cards, which also proved very successful. The material Tuck produced is a fascinating history of print-ing in its time but, unfortunately, the archive of the company was destroyed in 1940 in the Blitz, so much of the earliest material is very rare. When Tuck's sons expired, the firm started to fade. It was bought by Purnell in 1962. One grandson of Raphael Tuck was called after the old man, and served as Labour MP for Watford from 1964 to 1979.

The high point of the International Printing Machinery & Allied Trades Exhibition is the presentation of the 'Champions of Print' award. In 2010, the winner was Lord Robert Gavron (1930–), who was the founder of the St Ives Group, and served as its chairman from 1964 to 1993. The encomium recognized him as 'the founder of one of the largest print powerhouses in the world, and avid "Champion of Print", who combined a unique vision for St Ives with his outstanding business acumen'.

Gavron was a barrister by the time he was 25, but he was fascinated by print and took a job as an £8-a-week floor sweeper in that year. Having learned the business and briefly taught at Carmel, the Jewish public school, he started St Ives in 1964 with £5,000. The company are in the marketing, print-and-display services industry. When large posters are needed, they may well be produced by St Ives. The brand advertisements at football grounds are another of their markets. They print magazines and produce window displays for shops. The company flourished to the extent that Gavron, an ardent Labour Party supporter all his life, was able to donate £500,000 for the Party's 1996 election war chest. In 1999, he received a peerage. Gavron retains a £30-million stake in the company and is still chairman of the Fabian Society, the leading centre-left think tank, a post he took on in 1982.

Book publishers were well established in Britain long before the Jews started to arrive in numbers in the nineteenth century. In the world of book publishing, the major Jewish influence came from the refugees who arrived in Britain before the Second World War. There were two major British-born exceptions: Victor Gollancz (1893–1967) and Anthony Blond (1928–2008).

Gollancz was the nephew of the first rabbi to be knighted, Sir Hermann Gollancz. He was educated at St Pauls and New College, Oxford, and was a lifelong socialist. There were many attractions to socialism for Jews in those days, but the most important for many was that the Communists were the sworn enemies of the Fascists; there is an old saying in the world of diplomacy which applies here – the enemy of my enemy is my friend. Gollancz launched his company in 1927 and among the first authors he published was George Orwell. Gollancz was noted for the bright-yellow dust covers he favoured, and he was one of the founders of the Left Wing Book Club.

During the war, his pamphlet, *Let My People Go*, powerfully exposed the horrors of the Holocaust, but after the war he spearheaded a campaign to treat German civilians more humanely. In 1948, he formed a Jewish society to help Arab refugees and, in 1951, he started the charity War on Want. He also became chairman of the national campaign to abolish capital punishment. Although successful as a publisher, Gollancz's main claim to fame was as a campaigner. There are certain personalities who can best be described as 'agin the government', and it seems to have been important to Gollancz that the causes he championed should generally be unpopular ones. That did not make them any the less admirable. He was knighted in 1965, just before his death.

Anthony Blond deserved his nickname as the 'enfant terrible' of the publishing world. Educated at Eton and a conscientious objector, he did not complete his studies at New College, Oxford. He started his publishing house in 1952 and made money from publishing the *History of Orgies*, Harold Robbins' *Carpetbaggers*, being involved in *Private Eye,* and spotting the potential of authors like Spike Milligan. When he sold one company, he started another. CBS, Harlech TV and Hutchinson all bought Blond houses. The obituary in *The Times* referred to him as having 'much flair but little perseverance'.[13] Where he did make a substantial difference was in the publishing of educational books, and here he improved standards very considerably.

The main thrust of the Jewish contribution to British publishing, however, came from the refugees: George Weidenfeld (1919–) of Weidenfeld and Nicholson, André Deutsch (1917–2000), Paul Hamlyn (1926–2001) of Octopus, Paul Elek (1906–76) of Granada Publishing, Bela Horowitz (1898–1955) of Phaidon, Walter Neurath (1904–63) of Thames & Hudson, and Ernest Hecht (1929–), Souvenir Press.

These were men from cultured backgrounds in Europe. They recognized that the book-publishing world in Britain was led by a string of great companies, many of whom had been in existence for many decades or even centuries. They also knew that profits were hard to come by, with booksellers taking a substantial percentage of the cover price of books, not to mention the costs the publishers had to bear of author's royalties, office expenses and salaries. It would be difficult to persuade established authors – the bread-and-butter of successful publishers – to move to their small firms.

If they were to break into the magic circle, they would have to come up with something new. They would have to discover the fine authors of tomorrow who were still unrecognized and in need of a publisher. Many of them worked out that there was one other way through. They might sell books on their subject matter, rather than on the fame of their authors. Was this a hole in the market that they could fill?

The refugee publishers also had in their favour that they were internationalists; they thought outside the United Kingdom. Many of them would achieve great success by producing books that were sold all over the world. Sometimes they reduced their own costs by having them printed in countries which could do the job cheaper.

George Weidenfeld came to London from Vienna and went to work for the BBC monitoring service. As early as 1942, he was a political commentator and he spent the war years building up a very wide range of contacts. These stood him in good stead when he set up Weidenfeld and Nicholson in 1948 with Nigel Nicolson, who was from a prominent establishment family. In 1949, Weidenfeld was chef de cabinet for Chaim Weizmann in the new State of Israel, but was more famous back in London for publishing *Lolita,* a book as controversial as *Lady Chatterley's Lover* had been in its time. It sold 200,000 in hardback. He also showed considerable foresight with the first book he published, *A New Deal for Coal* by Harold Wilson, when the author was president of the Board of Trade; a useful friend for the future.

In the years immediately after the war there was still rationing, and goods were in short supply. Israel Sieff (1889–1972), later Lord Sieff, of Marks & Spencer, was a keen Zionist and knew Weidenfeld well. Sieff needed a new range of products for the stores to increase sales, and Weidenfeld came up with *Illustrated Children's Classics*. He also produced a series entitled *History of Civilization*. As the reputation of his house increased, he was able to persuade Saul Bellow, Mary McCarthy and Edna O'Brien to join his list of authors. He counted two Booker prizewinners among them.

Then there were the politicians: he published Henry Kissinger, Golda Meir, Charles de Gaulle and Konrad Adenauer. He also recognized the great diarists, and had Chips Channon, Alan Clark, Michael Palin and Cecil Beaton sign with him. In 1976, Weidenfeld was made a peer and sold out his British company in 1991. He still negotiates for new authors though and, in 2005, reached agreement to publish Pope John Paul II. The international status of British book publishing owes a lot to Weidenfeld.

André Deutsch was born in Budapest and fled to Britain before the war. He was interned on the Isle of Man where he met Francis Alder, who taught him the basics of book publishing. From 1947, Deutsch tried for five years to make a success of his new firm, Allan & Wingate, and published the very well-received humorous books of George Mikes (*How to be an Alien*, etc.). He fell out with his fellow directors, however and, in 1952, started afresh with André Deutsch. For the next thirty years he published famous authors such as Ogden Nash, Philip Roth, Norman Mailer and John Updike, before selling out to Carlton Publishing.

The hole in the market that Deutsch identified was the publication of the memoirs of former Nazis, like Franz Von Papen. In that particular instance, Deutsch sold the serial rights to a national newspaper for £30,000 (about £500,000 today). Deutsch was particularly well known on the Continent, where he was famous for his mercurial temperament. When he died, an obituarist commented, 'He was quick to sense a slight, suspicious with strangers and unable to conceal a certain arrogance towards those less quick-witted than himself'.[14] But he still produced a lot of overseas earnings for the Exchequer.

Paul Hamlyn was originally Paul Hamburger, and he came from Berlin in 1933 when he was 6 years old. When his father died a few years later, the family was almost destitute. Hamlyn became a Bevin Boy, working down the mines during the latter stages of the war. He was always attracted to books, though, and started his career by selling them off a barrow in Camden Market in London.

In 1947, with £350 he inherited from his grandfather, he started his own business and decided to specialize in books on hobbies. This section of the market was ill served, and Hamlyn also extended the distribution points by persuading department stores to sell books. Cooking and gardening books at reasonable prices did best, and he cut his costs by producing the books in Prague. In 1964, he sold the company, Books for Pleasure, to IPC for £2.25 million. He then did very well with Music For Pleasure records, which he operated with EMI.

In 1972 he started Octopus Books, went public in 1983 and sold that company for £530 million in 1987. The range of reading interests he served was immense: health, antiques, pet care, anything in which large sections of the public took an interest. The secret was to sell mass-market books cheaply. It was significant that two-thirds of his business was international. Hamlyn was very generous indeed. He gave 12,000 books to the British Library, and the Hamlyn Foundation, which he created in 1987, would give £1 million to the Bodleian Library in Oxford and £2 million to the Labour Party. Hamlyn received a peerage in 1998, but died in 2001.

Paul Elek came from Budapest to London as a student in 1929, and then migrated to Britain in 1938. He was the son of a printer and, summarizing his contribution recently, it was said that, 'Paul Elek was one of the many émigrés from Continental Europe who did so much to enrich and stimulate the cultural life of staid provincial Britain in the mid-twentieth century'.[15]

Elek's motivation was his dislike of the modernization of the country. He was an Anglophile who yearned for the Disney image of Britain: ancient pubs, castles and thatched cottages. He wanted to produce the record of an England that was vanishing. Following on from the pre-war success of the *Shell Guides to Britain*, from 1966 onwards he produced a number of illustrated topographical books about the country. In all, he published 1,000 books in a career which spanned thirty years. He had a long scientific and educational list as well.

Bela Horowitz, who created the Phaidon Press, came from Vienna. His gap in the market was telling the story of art to young people; he wanted to produce quality books on the subject at affordable prices. Horowitz achieved this by producing editions in cooperation with other publishers overseas, thereby justifying large print runs. He first came up with large-format art books in 1936 and ensured that the illustrations were of a very high quality. His reputation for good work grew, to the extent that he was commissioned after the war to produce a catalogue of the drawings in the Royal Collection at Windsor.

The company's biggest commercial success was the production of Sir Ernest Gombrich's *Story of Art*. This sold over two million copies in fourteen editions. Lord Clark, a notable intellectual guru in the latter half of the century, labelled Phaidon, 'one of the few civilizing influences of our time'.

Walter Neurath was also Viennese and arrived in Britain in 1938. He too was interned on the Isle of Man when no longer a youngster, and decided to strike out on his own after the war as a publisher. He founded Thames & Hudson in 1949, but didn't go down the famous-author route. Instead he produced a series of *Britain in Pictures*, much like Paul Elek. Neurath was always looking for new ways to sell books: 'His fertile imagination constantly produced ideas for new books and new series of books.'[16] In 1959, he began producing his *World of Art* series. Fifty volumes appeared with a total sale of six million copies. He fitted one stereotype of a Jewish entrepreneur: 'He did not suffer fools gladly and was impatient with incompetence, but extremely generous.'[17]

The longest survivor of this rich flood of continental Jewish publishers was Ernest Hecht from Czechoslovakia, who created the Souvenir Press in 1951 when he was only 22 years old. At the time of writing, he is still running the company, the oldest independent publisher in the country. His original start-up capital was savings of £250, and he started with an office in his parents' bedroom.

Hecht is a pragmatist and an individualist. He has been called 'the Brian Clough of publishing' and is noted for his sayings: 'The first duty of a publisher is to remain solvent'; 'You can't run a publishing company like this by committee'. After fifty years in charge, he announced that he had no plans for the succession: 'I won't be here to worry about it'. Hecht's choice of authors has been, if nothing else, eclectic. He has published five Nobel laureates and Mel Calman, a quirky and much-loved Jewish cartoonist. He also produced the *Playboy* tenth anniversary reader.

The press remains in being because of advertising, and the largest advertising agency in Britain during the 1980s was Saatchi & Saatchi. Charles (1943–) and Maurice (1946 –) were born to a Baghdad Sephardi family, who came to Britain in 1947. Maurice got a First at the LSE and Charles studied at the London School of Communications, which specialized in media studies. Charles started in advertising as a copywriter, but joined with

Maurice to create their own agency, Saatchi & Saatchi, in 1970. They did well, but really made their reputation when, in 1979, they were appointed by the Conservative Party as their advertising agents. Their poster, 'Labour Isn't Working', was a much-discussed and powerful promotion, and when Margaret Thatcher won the election, the Saatchis had arrived in a big way.

Through a process of takeovers, they became the world's largest agency in the 1980s. Their financial director, Martin Sorrell, became a prominent amalgamator in the advertising world. What Saatchi & Saatchi brought to the party of advertising innovation were two main concepts; first, that all media buying should be done by a central department, rather than split among separate account groups. Second, that all a company's marketing needs should be serviced by a single organization, rather than a number of specialist companies. As Maurice Saatchi said, 'Today they call it integration and it is the holy grail of all large marketers'.[18] When he advocated it originally, however, it was pretty revolutionary.

The two brothers were very close and a good team. Their corporate slogan was, 'Nothing is impossible'. Charles was 'all manic energy and visceral intelligence' and Maurice was 'mega-charming and businesslike'.[19] The problem was that their ambitions grew to an extent that alarmed their shareholders: a plan to take over the Midland Bank was just one project. In 1995, there was a shareholder revolt, and Saatchi & Saatchi no longer had a Saatchi on the board.

The result was the creation of M. & C. Saatchi, and a war between the two companies to win control of the company's clients. The Mirror Group and British Airways were among others who went to the new firm. In 2010, Saatchi & Saatchi was the sixteenth-largest advertising company with revenues of £118.5 million, while M. & C. Saatchi was seventh with £193.7 million. By then, though, Charles had decided to devote himself to his love of art. Maurice was made a peer in 1996, and joint chairman of the Conservative Party in 2003; he stood down in 2005, after Michael Howard, who is also Jewish, lost the election.

The Saatchis will certainly be remembered for 'Labour Isn't Working', but not for an advertisement they wrote for the Citrus Marketing Board of Israel. The headline was to be, 'Jaffa – the Chosen Fruit', but it was banned by the television-advertising watchdogs on the grounds that it was anti-Semitic! Now if that was a joke by one of the great Jewish comedians, like Jackie Mason, in front of a Jewish audience, there would be howls of laughter. It's wonderful to see the attention the authorities are giving to trying to stamp out racist remarks, but Jews are famous for their sense of humour, and the Saatchis were not anti-Semites by any stretch of the imagination.

In terms of their work for the Jewish community, the Saatchis gave £250,000 in 1998 to finance the creation of the Saatchi Synagogue in London, under the authority of the senior rabbi of the Sephardi community. Its purpose was to attract younger business people back to synagogue.

Whatever the form of media, it is imperative that it reaches the target audience. That used to be almost solely the responsibility of the Post Office, but in recent years a number of companies have emerged, offering a fast, guaranteed delivery service within a short specified time. The first to recognize the need for this product was Clive Bourne (1942–2007). Bourne was born to a Jewish Ilford family in a Salvation Army hostel. The charge was only 12½p, which his mother considered a great bargain. He left school at 15 to work in a shoe shop and in 1962 he spotted the market he could exploit and started an overnight parcel service. He set up in an old building in a Shoreditch churchyard, and the main attraction of the concept to him was that it didn't require either equipment or money. Just energy and know-how; he even used the local telephone kiosk as his phone.

He called the company Seabourne Express Couriers. By the mid 1970s he had progressed sufficiently to start a daily express-parcel service agency, years before Fedex or UPS. In both 1981 and 1988 the company won the Queen's Awards to Industry. He survived many pressures; for example, the Arab Boycott Office tried to get him to stop delivering to Israel, but he refused. In 1989, he was also instrumental in developing the old RAF station at Manston into Kent Airport; it made for an excellent link in the express-service chain. He named the VIP lounge after the most prominent Jew in Victorian times, Sir Moses Montefiore.

Eventually, in 1990, Bourne sold the company to UPS and, shortly after, he was diagnosed with prostate cancer. With the profit he made from selling the company, Bourne became involved in a string of charitable activities until he died of the disease in 2007. He founded the Prostate Cancer Research

Foundation and, in 1996, he backed the Museum of Dockland. He was a founder-patron of Jewish Care and he was particularly interested in Tony Blair's plans to produce city academies, in place of poorly performing schools.

One of the schools which had educated hundreds of Jewish boys over the years was the Hackney Downs School, but it had fallen on hard times as the population of the East End altered. Bourne sponsored its change to an academy, with a fine new award-winning building. He called it after his father, Mossbourne Community Academy, and it has been one of the ten best performing state schools in the country for three years.

In 2011, the pupils of Mossbourne County achieved twelve places at Cambridge, as well as receiving numerous other university offers; it is now a shining example of what can be achieved in unpromising circumstances. For the British economy to flourish in the future, one element it will require is an increasingly large workforce of educated young people. It is vital to offer this opportunity to children from poorer homes, and the academy projects are one way to achieve the goal. Bourne was knighted in 2005.

NOTES

1. John Simpson, *Unreliable Sources: How the Twentieth Century Was Reported* (Basingstoke: Macmillan, 2010).
2. Ibid.
3. Bernard Falk, *Bouquets for Fleet Street* (London: Hutchinson, 1951), p.250.
4. Hansard, 10 April 1946.
5. Falk, *Bouquets for Fleet Street*, p.211.
6. Loren Rhoads, *Morbid Curiosity Cures the Blues* (New York: Scribner, 2009).
7. Falk, *Bouquets for Fleet Street*, p.330.
8. James Harding, *The Times*, 16 May 2007.
9. Author in conversation with Fred Kobler.
10. Ibid.
11. *Mailonline*, 2 April 2008.
12. *Sunday Times*, 30 July 2006.
13. *The Times*, 1 March 2008.
14. John Calder, *Guardian*, 12 April 2000.
15. *Apollo Magazine*, April 2008.
16. *The Times*, 29 September 1967.
17. Ibid.
18. *Guardian*, 6 September 2010.
19. Jenni Frazer, *Jewish Chronicle*, 17 November 1995.

Chapter nine

Eat, Drink and be Merry

One of the great success stories in post-war Britain's economy has been the growth of tourism. Although often described as a damp offshore island, for many years Britain has been sixth in the world for welcoming tourists. There were fewer than a million incoming visitors in 1946, but well over 25 million today. Much of the credit for this happy state of affairs must go to the airlines, which have made it so easy to come to the country. It's also due to the quality of the entertainment, sightseeing and cultural activities available throughout the land. Even so, a considerable percentage of tourists have no family to accommodate them in a foreign country. Only the growth of the British hotel industry, and its modern reputation for high standards, has made it possible to welcome the vast numbers involved.

The first Jewish hotel company was probably that of Charles Grunhold, who owned the Talbot Hotel in Westminster. He left £142,000 when he died in 1905, so it looks like it was a successful enterprise. The first Jewish hotel company of any national significance, however, was J. Lyons, a firm of caterers who built three massive hotels in London – the Regent Palace, Strand Palace and Cumberland – in the first forty years of the twentieth century. Each had from 750 to over a thousand bedrooms, and they offered accommodation at very reasonable prices. This was totally novel; it paved the way for today's monster caravanserai and made it feasible for the more modestly endowed public to stay in hotels.

Lyons was the result of the inventiveness of the Salmon and Gluckstein families. They came to Britain in the 1840s and were originally cigarette and cigar makers. Cigar and cigarette manufacturing were in their infancy in the nineteenth century, and many Jewish companies emerged. Among them was Godfrey Phillips, which was noted for the introduction of cigarette cards. In the 1870s, however, the Salmons and Glucksteins recognized the potential catering opportunities offered by the major commercial exhibitions, which were starting to take place in major cities.

An old Jewish friend, Joseph Lyons (1847–1917), had worked with exhibition contractors, and Isidore Gluckstein (1857–1920) asked him to join them in creating a new company. In case the new venture was unsuccessful, however, which could have adversely affected the reputation of the tobacco business, they borrowed his name for the venture, and the company became known as J. Lyons.

Under successive members of the families – almost all the directors were Salmons and Glucksteins – the company also developed a chain of teashops, which were immensely popular, and where the waitresses were nationally known as 'Nippies'. The engine room of the company for many years was Sir Isidore Salmon (1876–1941), who served as a director and managing director from 1903 to 1941. Salmon was also the Conservative MP for Harrow from 1924 to 1941 and a powerful figure in the United Synagogue.[1]

He was one of the first to recognize the need for technical colleges to train hotel staff if the industry was to grow and, in 1903, founded the first, the Westminster Technical College. At the time, the concept of a hotel school was totally foreign to the British tradition. Practical training, rather than an academic course, had always been the rule. Following Salmon's lead, however, for many years after the Second World War, Britain had more hotel-training schools than were to be found in Europe. The country's ability to sustain its position as the sixth-largest tourist nation is based, among other attributes, not only on its hotel capacity but also on the number of hotel-school graduates it produced over the years. The hotel-training schools also played their part in transforming the image of British haute cuisine by educating a large number of youngsters in the intricacies of high-quality cooking.

When the Second World War loomed, Neville Chamberlain, the prime minister, asked Salmon to take responsibility for feeding the armed forces. As a result Salmon created the Royal Army Catering Corps. In their time, Lyons was a household name, famous for its ice cream and a host of groceries. It became the largest food-producing company in Europe, but eventually the two families ran out of offspring of commercial brilliance and, as a consequence, unwise financing in the 1970s led to its demise.

Powerful as Lyons was, its catering operations took precedence over its hotels. Good British hotels at the turn of the century were small in number, and mostly catered for the well-to-do; boarding houses catered for the masses, and seaside landladies were the butt of any number of jokes. As was British food, which was often considered a laughing stock; cabbage and Brown Windsor Soup were particularly popular topics with comedians in the music halls. The combination of a nationally poor product and an increasing demand for travel after the Second World War made the profit potential very favourable, if the right entrepreneur seized the opportunity. Assuming that the money could be raised to build new hotels and modernize the existing stock.

It was in the profits from luxury hotels that Britain suffered from one of its rare errors in the treatment of its Jews. When Major Frank Goldsmith MP (1878–1967) was attacked for his German origins during the First World War, he enlisted in the army and served with distinction. Disgusted by the accusations, however, he left Britain after his demobilization to settle in France. There he built up a chain of forty-eight luxury hotels, including the Hôtel de Paris in Monte Carlo, the Carlton in Cannes and the Lotti in Paris. He was also one of the founders of the King David in Jerusalem. The profits of his company, however, went to the French Treasury rather than the British.

After the Second World War, banks disliked lending to hotel companies because of the bad experiences they had suffered during the Slump. The hotels themselves had also not been able to redecorate during the war years. Even worse, the British did not have hotel keeping in their culture, unlike the French, Italians and Swiss. So trained staff were hard to find, and employment in hotels was not considered a high-status occupation. In addition, outside London, the beaches near the seaside hotels had been mined during the war, and the only major national company which could offer real quality was British Transport Hotels. This was a division of the railways, created by the government in 1948, after their nationalization. It was significant, though, that BTH rarely announced their profits;

perhaps there weren't any. What was badly needed, therefore, was a belief that good provincial hotels could prosper. From such an unpromising base, one of the companies that took up the challenge was De Vere Hotels.

De Vere was the creation of Leopold Muller (1902–86), a Czech refugee from a family of butchers. Muller arrived in London from Brno in 1938. Catastrophically, while he was settling down, before sending for his wife and two daughters, his homeland was invaded and he lost them all in the Holocaust. He never married again.

From a single restaurant, Muller built up a chain of hotels. They included such famous names as the Royal Bath in Bournemouth and the Grand in Brighton, and they were run as luxury hotels from the beginning. His right-hand man was his financial director, Lazarus Javonici (1916–2011) who was from Rumanian-Jewish stock. Javonici wanted to be an accountant but, with that name, couldn't find a practice which would take him on. This was the experience of many Jewish youngsters at the time. So he changed his name to Leslie Jackson and that solved the problem.

Muller would have liked to have London hotels as well, but there he usually found himself in competition with Max Joseph (1910–82) who was building up his own Grand Metropolitan Hotels. As Jackson said, 'We were always beaten by MJ. And every time we said he's paid too much for the hotel this time. And he never had.'[2]

De Vere went public in 1964 and, as Muller got older, his company became the target for a takeover. Muller always resisted until, in 1984, the financial director of a brewery, Greenall Whitley, arrived at his office with a cheque for £41 million. Muller took the money and ran. He died in 1988 and left £15 million in trust to charity. By 2008, with interest, the trust had given away £30 million. Among the beneficiaries were the creation of the Leopold Muller Lecture Theatre at the Imperial War Museum, and the Leopold Muller Memorial Library at the Oxford Centre for Hebrew and Jewish Studies.

The first Jewish FTSE-100 company that began from the hotel business was Grand Metropolitan, which would grow in thirty years from one small hotel in London's Marylebone to be the tenth-largest company in the UK. It is worth examining in greater than usual detail, because it was an astonishing achievement and helped, more than any other company, to lay the foundations for the tourist industry we have in Britain today.

Max Joseph was an estate agent before the war. He was based in the Home Counties when he joined up and he turned his attention to buying and selling small hotels when he was off duty. He had got into debt when the housing market collapsed before the war, and this was the only way he could see of paying off his creditors. When one hotel, the Mandeville, near Selfridges, didn't find a buyer, Joseph went into the hotel business.

He was not a success and it was always said that Joseph couldn't run a milk bar. He was far too concerned with the relatively unprofitable food-and-drink side of the industry. He was, however, an exceptional judge of the value of property. He was fortunate to meet a Jewish Czech architect who was prepared to take on half the debts of the hotels he owned in return for half the shares. Fred Kobler (born Bedrich Kobler, 1899–1985), had fled Europe just ahead of the German army, and served as a private in the Czech army in Britain during the war. Having nowhere to live afterwards, he took a job as manager of a small boarding house in Marylebone. It was Kobler who was to prove the hotel genius. He moved in as managing director, after agreeing with Joseph that there would be no interference with the way he wanted to run the hotels.

On a busy day, Kobler might read half the *Financial Times*. The rest of the time he spent looking out of his office window and thinking. Recognizing the importance of this major aspect of a managing director's job, it struck him that the profits in the business were all coming from selling bedrooms, but the industry traditionally concentrated almost entirely on selling food and drink – Joseph's problem. Thereafter, nobody talked about food and drink in Kobler's presence without risking his very public and lachrymose rage. He then also realized that the business in future was far more likely to come from America than either the shattered Continent or the declining British Commonwealth. His experiences in Europe hadn't endeared the Continentals to him anyway.

So Kobler went out for American business and paid travel agents commission for it. This latter move was unheard of at the time. He also set up the first sales department in the modern industry, following in the footsteps of the Americans. He went on to insist that every bedroom should be altered, if necessary, to add a private bathroom, which was again very unusual. In 1945, there were practically no hotel bedrooms with private bathrooms – in Wales!

It was Grand Metropolitan which pioneered Short Break Holidays, taking advantage of the introduction of the five-day working week. Where the industry as a whole viewed the shorter working hours as a disaster, because businessmen wouldn't need accommodation on Friday night, the alternative viewpoint was that the public could now enjoy a two-night weekend holiday. It was a very Jewish way of looking at a problem. At the time, 25 per cent occupancy of the bedrooms over winter weekends was pretty standard. The Grandmet marketing budget for the first year was £1,000. It produced 325 people. Six years later it was £1 million (£11 million today), and 150,000 people were transforming Grandmet's occupancy. The campaign also proved the positive value of advertising for hotels, and Grandmet was the first hotel company to advertise on television.

The development of the British hotel industry was a major part of the creation of a viable tourism product and, where the Salmons and Gluck-steins, Max Joseph, Fred Kobler and Leopold Muller pioneered, the rest of the industry followed suit. Grand Metropolitan did have one non-Jewish director originally; otherwise the board was 100 per cent Jewish, including Joseph's cousin, Victor Mishcon, a lawyer who became Lord Mishcon and advised Princess Diana in legal matters.

The Jewish ability to view situations internationally was particularly useful in the hotel industry, and Kobler's antipathy towards a concentration on food sales was essential to the company's success. Joseph was very unusual in one respect, going totally counter to accepted Jewish commercial traditions; he always said that if he couldn't do his job in four or five hours a day, then he wasn't doing it right. Long hours and Max Joseph were total strangers.

Grand Metropolitan led the way in changing one other tradition in the British hotel industry. If you visited the British Airways terminal in the late 1960s, you would find a full typewritten list of London hotels at the desk. By each hotel was a mark in pencil which read either C or NC. Over 90 per cent of the hotels had NC beside them – No Coloureds! Whenever

Grand Metropolitan took over a hotel, they threw out the colour bar. Kobler had lost family in the Holocaust. He was not into discrimination, or turning away respectable customers. He retired in 1964 and Joseph reassumed control.

In economic terms, the building of great companies proceeds in accordance with well-defined rules. There can be vertical integration, where a company has the ability to both manufacture and retail its products. There are carefully designed five-year plans for growth, and the possibilities of economies of scale are evaluated – 'if we bought that company, we would have two accounts departments and could save a lot of money by getting rid of one of them' sort of thinking. There are also well-developed plans for how additional finance and personnel will be available when the need arises.

There are, however, some companies which downgrade the importance of such rules and pay even less attention to them. The *Economist* in the 1960s, commenting on Grand Metropolitan, said that the thing that had to be understood about its strategic plan was that it didn't have one! Indeed Joseph's purchase of the then massive Express Dairy Company was a typical instance. A friend of Joseph knew that the controlling 'A' shareholders of Express wanted to sell out; Express had A and B voting shares. The votes of the A shares vastly outranked the B shares – though the B shares were the majority. So, over a weekend, Grand Metropolitan was able to buy the company.

The financial media tried to make sense of the diversification from hotels and catering – Grand Metropolitan's core business – by pointing to the small hotel chain which Express owned as a tiny part of its whole. The overwhelming majority of the company's activities, however, had been moving milk from country to town since the invention of the railway and its emblem was still a Victorian train. In fact, the commercial rationale for the deal was that the milk came through the Milk Marketing Board, which paid for it every twenty-eight days. For the other twenty-seven days, you could have the use of the money. Joseph recognized that the cash-flow advantages were enormous, and the Express hotels were all sold, except one.

One of the Express Dairy directors, at a subsequent meeting with his opposite number, offered to exchange the internal-structure diagrams of the two companies. He produced an enormous and detailed breakdown of the various Express Dairy divisions. The Grand Metropolitan director felt in his inside pocket for an envelope, on the back of which he wrote out the company structure with room to spare!

If the deal was good enough, Max Joseph would do it without a thought. Sometimes, in the early days of the company, he made commitments without any idea of how he'd pay for them. An opportunity came up in 1957 to buy a large block of flats at Marble Arch in London, which had been turned into a hotel. It was called the Mount Royal, it would cost just over a £1 million and the deal was done, which would double the number of hotel beds Joseph's company operated in London.

The only problem was that the company didn't have a million pounds, and none of the banks wanted to lend that sort of money to a small, private outfit, in what happened to be difficult economic times. Eventually, about forty-eight hours before the completion date, Joseph went to what the Jewish business community knew as 'the Bank of Last Resort'. That was how insiders described Sir Isaac Wolfson, the head of Great Universal Stores. Wolfson came up with the million – at 12.5 per cent interest! The bank rate at the time was about 5 per cent.

Joseph ran Grand Metropolitan as a fiefdom. He brooked no opposition to his decisions and was seldom questioned by his senior colleagues. One exception arose when the company was in severe financial difficulties during the slump of 1974–77. It almost became necessary to produce a detailed strategy for the financial directors if a department wanted to buy a filing cabinet! In the middle of the Stock Exchange mayhem, with his own shares a tenth of their former value, Joseph agreed to pay £500,000 for a packet of Savoy Hotel stock. The Savoy Group were paying a 1.5 per cent dividend, while the bank rate, if a bank would lend £500,000, was 15 per cent!

The Grandmet managing director, infuriated that the board had not been asked for their agreement to the purchase, raised the subject at the next board meeting: he asked Joseph why the board hadn't been consulted. The reaction was like Oliver Twist asking for more. There was a shocked silence, a pregnant pause, and then Joseph gave what he thought was a totally adequate explanation. He said, 'Well, I think I know more about this subject than anybody else. Next business!' Nobody said a word, and six months later Joseph sold the shares to an Arab investor for 50 per cent more than he'd paid for them. The managing director did become chairman after Joseph's retirement, but didn't last long.

When it came to catering, Grand Metropolitan bought two small industrial-catering companies which it grew and then sold off. That company is now Compass. Grand Metropolitan itself merged with Guinness and that company is now called Diageo. Both Compass and Diageo are in the FTSE 100. An examination of the current lists of directors does not immediately suggest that any Jews remain, but it seems churlish to ask for confirmation.

Of course, companies produce new divisions after the founder has died, and these grow the economy as well. For example, from Compass came a subsidiary, SSP, which was later hived off. Today it provides catering at airports, railways stations, motorway service areas and shopping centres in thirty countries. It is the twenty-second largest private company in the country, with sales of £1.5 billion a year. So Max Joseph begat Grand Metropolitan which begat Compass which begat SSP.

Grand Metropolitan sold its hotel division at the end of the 1970s, and Max Joseph died in 1982. Short Break Holidays, however, became a national habit. The significant point is that the money that pays for them comes from the public's disposable income. It is money that won't be spent on imported cameras or hi-fi equipment. There is no imported element in a Short Break Holiday. So the money spent in the hotels reduces the country's import bill and helps the balance of payments.

Grand Metropolitan's CEO in the beginning was Henry Edwards (born Henry Eisenschmidt, 1923–2007), a Jewish refugee who had reached Britain as a child before the war. Edwards left Grand Metropolitan in 1964 and, over the next forty years, created three chains of hotels: Cranston, which became Centre; Comfort Hotels; and Friendly Hotels, which became Choice Hotels Europe. To his annoyance, he got offers for Centre and Comfort that he couldn't refuse on behalf of the shareholders, and had to sell out and start again each time. Nobody, before or since, has started three hotel chains from scratch.

Like so many other industry leaders, considerable numbers of future senior executives got their start with Edwards. He was famous throughout the British hotel world for his infinitely detailed cost controls. It was said of Edwards that his ideal Sunday would be to drive from London to his hotel in Hull, in order to count the paper clips! He retired from Choice when he was over 80, and the company went into administration a few years later.

It would have been logical for the British hotel industry to be created by the brewers, but they were late coming in, because they always concentrated on the turnover of beer sales. Their boards included a considerable number of senior ex-service officers, and if the Brewery Queen's Regulations said concentrate on beer sales, that was what they did. When Grand Metropolitan bought Trumans Brewery, they found the pubs valued according to their beer sales. Joseph, the ex-estate agent, valued them logically, according to their worth as properties. But then, in marked contrast to the senior brewing-company executives, when he was in the army, Joseph had never risen in rank beyond lance corporal. It's another example of being bound by tradition.

Where British hotels hardly figured in the world of international chains, the situation changed in the 1970s and 1980s, as the success of Grand Metropolitan showed the possibilities. Grandmet bought Intercontinental from Pan American, Ladbrokes bought Hilton International from TWA and even a considerable number of the finest French hotels finished up in British hands. One Jewish hotel director from Grand Metropolitan, Eric Bernard (1932–89), who had survived in France during the war, was even recruited to be the CEO of the American company, Holiday Inn Hotels. Bernard had all the attributes of a fine French hotelier, but after seeing the indifference with which so many French people had viewed the fate of their Jewish fellow citizens during the Nazi occupation, he would never work in France again.

The largest privately owned hotel group in Britain is Britannia Hotels, the creation of Alex Langsam (1939–). Langsam's parents fled the Nazis from Vienna before the war, and Langsam was brought up to be suitably grateful. Recalling his father, Langsam said, 'Britain saved his life and gave him a living and he instilled that in me. I am grateful for what this country has given me.'[3]

Langsam started with one hotel in 1976 in Manchester, and now has thirty-six, and Pontins Holiday Parks as well. Langsam is an opportunist, seeing the possibilities of business developments that more staid hotel companies reject. For example, in 1982 he transformed Watts Warehouse, a derelict 1856 Manchester carpet store into a hotel. It now has 363 bedrooms. He also bought the Adelphi in Liverpool, an iconic landmark, but fallen on hard times, like the city itself. The Adelphi was originally a railway hotel designed to help with Liverpool's tourism. Unfortunately it was completed in March 1914 and, by the August of that year, there was no tourism to help after the outbreak of the First World War.

Langsam employs 4,000 people, but is a strict taskmaster. The company has a lovely hotel at Canary Wharf in London but there were several false starts before a manager, suitable for Langsam, was identified. When, in 1997, the BBC did a 'fly-on-the-wall' documentary series about the Adelphi, all the crises inherent in running a hotel were put on public display. Only from the assumption that all publicity is good publicity could permission have been given for the filming. The industry winced, not because of the shortcomings, which were nothing unusual, but because they had been revealed. What Langsam has shown, however, is that with sufficient determination, almost any hotel can be made profitable.

Apart from a number of good restaurants in London, before the Second World War there was not much in the way of a restaurant industry in Britain. There were teashops and there were pubs and there was Soho, but Michelin inspectors had little to exercise their minds. There were, however, a lot of pubs that served food and, while this is common today, it wasn't in the nineteenth century; pubs were commonly known as Gin Palaces and Holbein's *Gin Alley* reflected the ravages of alcohol over the centuries.

One Jewish salesman in the East End, Isaac Levy, decided to become a bookmaker, and while plying that trade he 'noticed that so many punters who backed horses and had money to spare were, in fact, publicans'.[4] So he managed to buy the Pitts Head pub in the City and, a couple of years later, the Bell in Shoreditch.

Jews are ambivalent about alcohol. On the one hand, wine is used sacramentally every Friday night to welcome in the Sabbath. On the other, mobs attacking Jews have very often had their antagonism fuelled by drink. Speaking generally, Jews tend to enjoy eating more than drinking, and it was not surprising that this element of the culture came out in Isaac Levy's marketing. He decided to sell food in his pubs. It was a practice that, as his business grew, was copied by most other publicans, but Isaac Levy could lay claim to have created the pub restaurant we know so well today. His son, Dick, and his son-in-law Harry Franks, formed a company in 1911, Levy & Franks, and the business was a great success.

It was seemly that a descendent, Manny Franks (1921–2010), was one of the founders of the Restaurant Association of Great Britain, which did much good work to get the opening hours of pubs liberalized in the latter part of the twentieth century. Levy & Franks' brand name was Chef & Brewer, which is today part of Punch Taverns.

In the growth of the restaurant industry, *Caterer*, the trade paper, has labelled Phillip Kaye (Kropifko) (1932–) as the godfather of casual dining in Britain, not realizing the contribution of Lyons or Levy and Franks. With his brother, Reggie (1930–92), the Kayes came from a Jewish family in East London and started with a concept called Golden Egg in the 1960s. They went on to run Angus Steak Houses, a chain of steak restaurants and then, in 1979, to found Garfunkels. Restaurants suffer the problem of fashion; a brand can be popular for many years and then lose its appeal. The Kayes overcame this by selling each chain at its peak and then starting another. Golden Egg no longer exists, but Garfunkels is still with us, though the Kayes sold that as well.

On this occasion, the apple didn't fall far from the bough. Philip's sons, Adam (1968–) and Sam (1972–), were sent by their father to Westminster Hotel School, and came out wanting to start their own restaurant company. This they called Ask Pizza, after their initials; the idea was to improve the image of pizza as a food and to sell 'posh pizzas'. The Kayes have always had an excellent understanding of what the eating-out public want. 'Look what the boys did with Ask, which was similar to Pizza Express. But they had a more varied menu and it had nicer decor, with white tablecloths on the tables. That made it more appealing to Middle England.'[5]

Ask's first pizza restaurant was opened in 1993, and in 1995 they floated their nine-strong chain. The shares were priced at 52p and rose to 85.5p on the first day of trading. The power of the Kaye name in the restaurant world was apparent. In 2004, just eleven years after they started, they sold the company to Pizza Express and made £30 million. By that time there were 112 Asks and another sixty-eight Zizzi Restaurants, which were designed to set the pizza standards even higher. After which the Kayes started again and are still powers in the restaurant land.

Restaurants are good news for the chancellor of the Exchequer. Like hotels, they soak up disposable income without a major additional import content. The restaurant industry is severely traditional, though, with its practices firmly cemented in nineteenth-century procedures, while the best of the restaurateurs come from countries which have it as part of their heritage. Lord Forte, the great caterer, was once asked why the British couldn't run restaurants as well as the Italians. 'Well, it's part of the Italian culture', he said. 'In Britain – we garden.'[6] Which the British do better than any other country in the world.

What is missing in the restaurant industry is new marketing thinking, but for nearly twenty years there was a gale of fresh air in the world of British haute cuisine. It emanated from Bob Payton (1944–94). Payton was 'a working-class Jewish kid from Miami'.[7] He went into advertising in America and was sent to the London office of J. Walter Thompson, one of the biggest and best. He was a very senior executive, but he decided he'd rather start a restaurant and, in 1977, he opened the Chicago Pizza Pie Factory in London's Hanover Square. He died in a road accident in 1994, the same year his company was floated on the Stock Exchange for £33 million.

The restaurants he opened introduced such dishes as deep-pan pizza and onion loaves. They were very informal and the staff were trained to sell as if they were marketing an advertised product. Patrons wouldn't be asked if they wanted a dessert, like every other restaurant. The waiter would say, 'We have some wonderful desserts this evening. We have … ' and then describe each one in mouth-watering detail. Payton hated the formal approach taught in all hotel schools; he said he'd never take a graduate for that reason. He got the results that he knew would come from better marketing.

He had one young lady barrister, working as a waitress, who was wildly over-qualified for the job. So he offered her a management position, which she turned down. She said she couldn't afford to switch, as she made £250 in tips on Saturday nights alone! Payton's genius lay in the business rather than the catering skills of his profession. Therefore he was sensible to get on board probably the best catering man of his generation, the Jewish Peter Webber (1940–), who was also ex-Grand Metropolitan. The combination of marketing flair and sound management ensured success.

Payton was a jolly 6' 4" giant, very American and determinedly Jewish. He put a *mezuzah* on the door of his restaurants, as instructed in Deuteronomy 6, and closed on Yom Kippur. He opened on Jewish festivals, but sent the profits from those days to charity. Then, when he had opened other restaurants and bars equally successfully – the Chicago Rib Shack, Henry J. Beans – he bought a stately home in Leicestershire called Stapleford Park and turned it into a hotel.

For this new venture he also brought in new innovations. He got major companies, like Wedgwood, Evelyn & Crabtree and Turnbull & Asser, to design the rooms. At the bottom of the page, his hotel notepaper always invited the guests to *Come to Sunny Leicestershire*. He recognized fully – when so many still don't – one of the great truths about the hotel industry: that the guests are staying for fun. As an industry, most hotel management would prefer to think of themselves as part of the Arts Council; it adds status.

At Stapleford Park, Payton found a plaque on the wall of the original mansion which read 'William, Lord Sherard, Baron of Letrym, repayred this building, Anno Domini 1633.' He added to it, 'And Bob Payton did his bit. Anno Domini 1988'. It was akin to his strapline which he used from 1978 – 'Chicago Pizza Pie Factory. Famous since 1977'. If Payton hadn't died so young, his influence might have changed the way the hotel and restaurant industries approached the modernization of their products. Like so many other Jewish entrepreneurs, he wasn't committed to other people's cultures and traditions, so he could look at them with fresh eyes. He wasn't betraying his heritage because it wasn't his heritage. As it is, he will be remembered as a maverick who saw the future before most other people.

Another who saw the shape of things to come very clearly was Robert

Earl (1951–), whose father started life as Montague Levy. He changed his name when he became a successful pop singer and his son took the same name when he went into business. Robert Earl Jr went to the best Hotel School in Britain at Surrey University. He got an early taste of running his own business when a family friend asked him to take on the catering at a rock festival. Earl recruited 400 Surrey students and looked after 250,000 visitors over three days.

When he graduated, he started President Entertainments at the age of 26 in 1977. What Earl spotted was the potential attraction of properly themed restaurants. This was a time when a large number of pubs had gone in for themes, but the decor was very limited. Earl started the Beefeater, a dinner and cabaret show, and then Shakespeare's Tavern and the Cockney Club with a similar format. Unlike his competition, the target market was the tourists in London for, as he recalled later, 'the thought of 50 Americans pulling up in a coach repulsed the average English restaurateur'.[8]

In 1983, Earl moved to America but he still has strong roots in Britain: he now owns 23 per cent of Everton FC. Looking at Everton's financial position in 2011, this shows a good deal of patriotism. In 1987, Earl sold out President Entertainments for £67 million, but he was only just getting started. In 1991 he persuaded four mega film stars, Sylvester Stallone, Bruce Willis, Demi Moore and Arnold Schwarzenegger, to join with him in the creation of Planet Hollywood. The idea was to use Hollywood as the theme for the restaurants and the concept caught on in a very big way.

The restaurants today are full of Hollywood memorabilia and merchandise sales account for one third of the annual turnover. It isn't just gimmicks though. As Earl told the *American Nation's Restaurant News*, 'People don't eat themes. No concept in the world can succeed for long unless it also delivers great food at the right price.'[9] That's the Surrey Hotel School man talking. Today, the Planet Hollywood organization includes the Italian restaurant chain, Bula di Bieppo, the Earl of Sandwich restaurants and Planet Dailies, which is a 24/7 coffee shop concept. Salomon Brothers in the City call Earl, 'The grandfather of the theme restaurant business'.

Of course, tourism goes both ways, and Britons spend far more abroad than foreigners do in this country. It was no fault of the government after the Second World War. For years they fixed the amount of foreign currency which could be taken abroad at £50, and even reduced it to £25 at one time. Package holidays were unheard of, and it wasn't until 1971 that a travel agent could sell a package for less than the normal return airfare. The pioneer who, in breaking the mould, 'played a profound role in shaping the UK Travel Industry', was Vladimir Raitz (1922–2010).[10] Raitz's dentist mother fled Russia in 1927 with her parents; Raitz never saw his doctor father again. In 1936, the family arrived in Britain, via Berlin and Warsaw. Raitz, at 14, went to Mill Hill School. He was fluent in Russian, German, Polish and French, but had no English. By the end of his first term he was top of the English class.

He went on to the London School of Economics and worked as a translator for news agencies until 1949, when he found himself in Corsica on holiday. Encouraged to build up tourism there, he started Horizon Holidays with a legacy of £3,000 from his grandmother. He chartered a government surplus DC3 aircraft and sold two-week package holidays for £32.50 when the return flight to Nice nearby cost £70. He was only allowed to sell the packages to teachers and students at the beginning, and British European Airways tried to stop his activities, on the grounds that they were a 'material divergence of traffic'. This argument was advanced, even though BEA didn't fly to the island. Eventually Raitz overcame the opposition and could fly anybody.

For £32.50, the package included the flight, fourteen nights under canvas on the beach, and a guarantee of one meat meal a day. Meat was still rationed in Britain at the time, so this was a particularly relevant selling point. The tourists could also drink all the local wine they could stomach. Airport transfers were somewhat primitive: 'we had to shelter from the sun under the wings of the plane while we waited for the bus to pick us up'.

Raitz overcame all the obstacles put in his path. He was 'unfailingly urbane and mordantly witty',[11] with a penchant for large cigars. Horizon became one of the biggest UK tour operators and he chaired the company from 1949 to 1974. In 1970, he also invented Club 18–30. There then followed a price war and the effects of the Yom Kippur War; Horizon, in trouble, was bought by another company, which went bankrupt in its turn.

Raitz didn't die for a further thirty-five years, but his later travel ventures met with limited success, including even the Cigar Tours to Cuba in the 1990s. He was elected, though, to the British Travel Industry's Hall of Fame, which was a signal honour, and died at the grand age of 88.

Contributions to the economy come in many different ways. The efforts to bring visitors to towns and cities throughout the country have become ever more important as the British manufacturing industry declined at the back end of the twentieth century. Many of the cities have needed considerable promotion, and one of the most successful early ideas after the war was to create an arts festival in August, in Edinburgh.

The resulting Edinburgh Festival has promoted the Scottish capital throughout the world ever since its inception and it has grown colossally. The Fringe, an important part of the festival today, sold 1.8 million tickets in 2009. These were for 34,000 performances of 2,100 shows in 265 venues over twenty-five days. There were 19,000 performers from sixty countries. In 2011 there were 2,542 shows in all, at 258 venues over the three weeks.

The Festival was the brainchild of Rudolf Bing (1902–97). Bing came from an Austrian–Jewish family and was the general manager of the Berlin Opera when Hitler came to power. In 1934, he came to Britain and helped found the Glyndebourne Opera. He looked at many towns for a major annual cultural event before choosing Edinburgh, where the first Festival opened in 1947. Bing later went on to be the general manager of the Metropolitan Opera in New York from 1950 to 1972, and was knighted in 1971.[12]

Festivals, great gardens, museums and stately homes are all part of tourism. Irrespective of whether it is the British or overseas visitors who spend money on such attractions, there is a particular advantage for the economy from this form of expenditure; like hotels, it doesn't involve imports. The balance of trade does not worsen when people spend their disposable income marvelling at the flowers at Stourhead, Wisley or Sissinghurst. There is little additional import cost for the economy in running a stately home or a theme park.

The problem remains of how to provide the public with new attractions. There is a limit to the numbers who can visit the Tower of London or watch the Changing of the Guard. When the year 2000 was approaching, the government tried to add to London's attraction by the creation of the Millennium Dome. Initially, it was a damp squib. What was enormously successful – and remains so to this day – was the London Eye, the brainchild of a Jewish architect, David Marks (1952–) and his wife, Julia Barfield (1952–). As young architects, they spent a number of years in the prestigious practice of Richard Rogers, but, in 1989, they struck out on their own. The early years were difficult, but their lives were transformed when, in 1993, they entered a competition run by the *Sunday Times* to find a suitable structure to commemorate the Millennium. Their idea was for a giant Ferris wheel, but the concept was turned down by the judges.

The construction of a Ferris wheel was not a new idea. There had been a very large one created for a Victorian Exhibition at Earl's Court, which was only dismantled by George Cohen's 600 Group in 1907. This may well have been forgotten nearly a century later. Being a determined character, though, rejection only strengthened the Marks' determination to see the project come to life. It took them two years to get planning permission and a further two years to raise the finance. British Airways and Madame Tussauds became the funders and, in 1998, construction started.

In October 1999 the largest structure ever to be raised from the horizontal to the vertical arose on London's South Bank. The cost was well over £30 million and the final towering edifice was 135 metres high, by far the tallest Ferris wheel in Europe at that time. On a clear day, from the top of the wheel, it is possible to enjoy panoramic views of London and to see parts of seven counties. The income to the economy came from the 50 million people who took the opportunity to do just that. The concept also spawned associated attractions in the area. Since the Eye opened for business in March 2000, there have been changes of ownership, arguments over the lease – it was settled at 25 years in 2006 – and Marks and Barfield have sold their interest, but the Eye is firmly established as a major tourist attraction for the capital. It seems very likely that, in the future, there will be further imaginative concepts emerging from Marks and Barfield.

Finally, in a review of the Jewish contribution to the leisure industry, a luggage manufacturer doesn't fit easily into any sector of the economy. If there had been no Constellation luggage, the balance of payments would not have been materially affected. On the other hand, generations of inhabitants of Chadderton near Manchester would have had to look elsewhere for jobs, and it would be more difficult to get the day-to-day problems everybody faces into perspective.

Jack Aizenberg (1928–) was born in Poland in 1928, and when the war broke out his father told him, 'Jack, if we go together, we may all die together'.[13] The family split up and Jack never saw his parents and his siblings again; they died in Belzec concentration camp. Aizenberg was captured by the Nazis and sent on a 200-mile death march to Buchenwald. Hundreds died from exhaustion, cold and disease on the road. From Buchenwald he was sent to Theresienstadt concentration camp and from there, still miraculously alive, to Colditz, where he was liberated in May 1945.

A compassionate British government agreed to allow 1,000 Jewish orphans to leave the camps and be flown to Windermere, where Aizenberg recovered his physical strength. What was astonishing about him was that he recovered his mental strength as well. It is hardly surprising that many of the survivors never got over the appalling experiences they had suffered, and the horrendous sights they had seen in the camps.

With two other Holocaust survivors, Aizenberg started a company called Japinda, named after Aizenberg and his two friends, Pinkie and David. They made luggage and, over the next forty years, they built Constellation into a highly successful company. It still operates today, though it imports its products and the factory site is being redeveloped. Aizenberg continues to lecture to schools and other organizations on his wartime experiences, so that the lessons of the Holocaust are not forgotten. When his grandson was Bar Mitzvah, he recalled his 9-year-old brother, who had died in a gas chamber. He considered his grandson's Bar Mitzvah the replacement for the one his brother never enjoyed.

NOTES

1. Peter Bird, *The First Food Empire: A History of J. Lyons & Co* (Stroud: Phillimore, 2000).
2. In discussion with the author.
3. *Jewish Chronicle*, 8 June 2011.
4. Harold Pollins, *Economic History of the Jews in England* (London and Toronto: Fairleigh Dickinson University Press, 1982).
5. *Sunday Times*, 1 October 2006.
6. In conversation with the author.
7. *Independent*, 15 July 1994.
8. http://encyclopedia.jrank.org/articles/pages/6193/Earl-Robert.html.
9. Ibid.
10. *Travel Weekly*, 14 September 2010.
11. Roger Bray, *Guardian*, 9 September 2010.
12. *Independent*, 17 February 1997.
13. http://news.bbc.co.uk/1/hi/uk/8597635.stm.

Chapter ten

Chicken Soup Plus

Perhaps the first new food product for which a Jewish entrepreneur was responsible was Virol, which is still taken as a health supplement. It was the creation of Bertram Strauss (1867–1933) and its contents were bone marrow, malt extract, eggs, lime and lemon juice. Its main attribute was said to be its ability to ensure a progressive increase in the actions of white blood cells. It was also said to kill germs. In a world where life remained a lottery – diphtheria, tuberculosis and typhoid were just a few of the major killers – such miracle products were very popular and, in fairness, Virol certainly did you no harm and is still marketed.

The company was set up in 1900, and substantial financial backing came from the Lawson Johnston family, who owned Bovril. The brand was heavily promoted. In 1901, the advertising budget was £9,000 and the annual profit a somewhat smaller £2,000. Whether a child liked Virol or not, innumerable parents added it to their diets, and the company made very substantial returns; dividends averaged 8 per cent for the first twenty-five years. Strauss served as the chairman of the company for more than thirty years and, even during the Slump, it paid a dividend of 10 per cent in 1932.

In 1906, Strauss was elected MP for Mile End, having lost on the three previous occasions. Rather unluckily, he lost it again by four votes in 1910. While he was in the House, he was given the responsibility for guiding through Parliament the bill which established speed limits for cars. He also acted as vice consul for the Netherlands in Manchester and was a founder of B'nai B'rith, the Jewish charity. In 1926, he was the treasurer of the Board of Deputies.

Another early Jewish food company emerged from far-off New Zealand. Joseph Edward Nathan (1835–1912) was the sixth child of a struggling London tailor. He started work as a jobbing tailor at the age of 12, and took night classes at the Bishopsgate Institute. When that experience failed to create a fortune, he went to Australia in 1853 to try to benefit from the gold rush. His small store failed, however, and so he went on to New Zealand. There he started another store, importing goods from England and selling the local wool and butter.

Nathan married, had thirteen children and held services for the local Jews in his house in Wellington. When the first synagogue was built, he became its president from its opening in 1870 until 1874. In 1881, he also became president of the Wellington Chamber of Commerce. By this time his business was sufficiently successful to justify starting an office in London. Nathan moved back there in 1887, leaving the business in New Zealand to be run by his sons. In 1899, he formed a limited company in England, with a capital of £127,000 (today £10 million).

New developments in food production were available to the entrepreneur prepared to gamble and, from 1901 to 1903, Nathan negotiated for the rights to sell a New Zealand dried-milk product. When he had the agreement, he launched it in Britain but couldn't settle on an appropriate name. The original choice was Lacto, but the association with Lactose made it indistinguishable in the public mind from other similar products. So he changed the name to Glaxo. Sales still lagged until, in 1908, the company produced the Glaxo Baby Book, an initiative by the public-relations inspired Glaxo Mothers' Help Bureau! The book was something mothers really wanted and, among the advice they received, of course, was to give their babies plenty of Glaxo. The slogan was, 'Builds Bonnie Babies'. In 1915, the *Advertising Age* magazine called the whole campaign 'the most successful form of advertising of the present day'.

When Nathan died, his sons stayed in the business and another major success for the company was the introduction of Vitamin D from fish oil. In 1995, Glaxo joined with Wellcome to become Glaxo Wellcome, and in 2000 amalgamated with Smith, Kline & French to become Glaxo Smith Kline.

One of the reasons for deflation in Britain between 1837 and 1900 was the availability of cheap food imports and, by the early twentieth century, Britain was known for good plain food, but not for haute-cuisine delicacies. If there was one exception, it was smoked salmon, and this remains a favourite luxury today. Salmon is smoked to preserve it; the fish is buried in salt in Scandinavia for the same reason – *Gravilax* is *gravi* (buried) plus *lax* (salmon). British salmon used to be imported from Scandinavia before the quality of the supply available from Scotland was fully appreciated. Aaron (Harry) Forman (1876–1959) migrated from Odessa and started smoking salmon in about 1905 in the East End. There were many Jewish smoked-salmon curers at the time, using oak indoor bonfires with the salmon hanging above. Barnett's of Frying Pan Alley was one of the most highly regarded and, in the latter half of the twentieth century, its sales director, Joe Barnett, would become one of the best-loved and most popular figures in the British hotel and catering world. The Scots smoked other fish too, and smoked them more pungently, in the way that kippers are still prepared from herring today.

The East End curers recognized that the Scottish salmon would arrive in London long before the Scandinavian, and that it would be fresher. So they started getting their supplies from the north. The quality of the fish they produced was good enough for Forman's to win the Fortnum & Mason contract in the 1920s, and Selfridges in the 1930s. Harry's son Louis (1903–35) came into the business, and then came his grandson, Marcel (1934–); today, it's Lance (1962–): four generations of the family, though Lance is also an accountant. Marcel was, in fact, Marcel Anisfeld, and married Louis' daughter. He was Polish and spent the war in a Siberian prison camp, reaching England through the Kindertransport after 1945. He wasn't even a teenager by that time, and his survival was a small miracle.

In the 1970s, with the coming of salmon farms in Scotland, the super-markets emerged as customers for smoked salmon, but the quality suffered. To increase shelf life and to avoid losing weight in the curing, short cuts were introduced. The result still looked pretty much the same, but the standard was poorer. The reduction in price, however, forced many of the original curers out of business, until only Forman's remains, still using the traditional methods. As a result, you can find Forman's smoked salmon at stores such as Fortnum's and Harrods, and at the best hotels: quality products can still survive in the most competitive of circumstances.

When the Jews arrived from Eastern Europe they brought their own cuisine, and companies were started to provide them with the raw materials for cooking the delicacies. One of their needs was to obtain the curd they used to make cheese cake, and Raines Dairy in the East End was set up to provide it. While Jewish cuisine didn't catch on with the general public, as did Chinese, Indian and Italian cooking, there were a few foods, such as bagels and cheesecake, which are now widely enjoyed outside Jewish circles.

After it began in 1910, Raines went from strength to strength, led for many years by the second generation, Israel (Tubby) Raines (1916–93). It developed into a major provider of yoghurt, cream, cottage cheese and chilled desserts. Raines later seized the opportunity to offer supermarkets their own brands, and became a major supplier. The company also specialized in producing bulk packs for specialist manufacturers. After Tubby died, Raines was sold, in 1998, for £66 million.

Supermarkets are so much a part of everyday life that it is easy to forget that the first of them was created not much more than seventy-five years ago. In Vance Packard's seminal work, *The Hidden Persuaders*, he describes the doubts that the grocery industry had about their viability. The public, which had been accustomed to the personal service of the corner shop, could easily have found the larger stores intimidating and impersonal. To discover what housewives actually thought of the new concept, the marketeers fixed up cameras to film the ladies' eye-blink rate when they first entered the store. Why the eye-blink rate? When people are nervous this rate increases. When they're mesmerized, it stops. The ladies were near-mesmerized by the far larger displays than were feasible in a small shop. The marketeers now knew that all was well.

There was, of course, the strongest of competition for market leadership. Sainsbury's was a very early entry in the field, and John Lewis would have Waitrose as its own brand. The Jewish company that would eventually lead the rest was Tesco. The company was founded by Jakob Kohen (1898–1979), the son of yet another Polish tailor. Kohen left school at 14 and served in the First World War. With his £30 demobilization gratuity, he decided to buy some surplus stores for which the government's NAAFI had no further use. Kohen initially sold them in Hackney market, but went on to operate other stalls in different markets during the rest of the week. In 1931, he joined forces with his tea supplier, T.E. Stockwell, to open shops in Becontree and Burnt Oak, which they called Tesco. By now Kohen had become John

Cohen, as his Hackney bank manager said he had too many Jakobs on his books. By 1939, there were 100 Tescos in London and the Home Counties.

After the war, Cohen went to America and observed the move to self-service and paying at check-out counters. He adopted these ideas and, by 1959, he had 185 stores and was making £1 million profit a year. It is also to Cohen, among others, that we owe the eventual abolition of Retail Price Maintenance. This was a system by which manufacturers set the minimum prices retailers could offer, when selling their products. The practice boosted the profits of manufacturers, but diminished competition and kept prices artificially high. Cohen, by contrast, was known to believe in the market-stall concept of 'Pile 'em high and sell 'em cheap'. The resistance to abolishing Retail Price Maintenance was extensive, long-lasting and determined, but eventually it vanished, much to the satisfaction of the public.

In 1963, another incentive for shoppers was introduced – Green Shield Stamps. Now, when you paid your bill in Tesco, you were given stamps that you could exchange for items in a catalogue. Sainsbury's were very much against this innovation, believing quite correctly that the stamps didn't increase the total size of the grocery market, but the stamps proved very popular for many years.

When Cohen died in 1979, he was buried in the Jewish cemetery in Willesden. The family put up a very large coloured marble column, which dominates its surroundings. The showman in Jack Cohen would have approved the dedication which reads, 'In their humility lay their greatness'. Since Cohen's death, the company has continued to expand both in Britain and internationally. It is widely admired as a very well run organization and contributes handsomely to Britain's balance of trade.

From very much the same background came Percy Dalton (1909–83). He also left school at 14 to sell fruit and vegetables from a barrow in the East End of London, and did well enough to take a pitch in Spitalfields market. As his business became more profitable, he was able to buy an old ware-house and start to sell wholesale as well as retail. What made his fortune was his experiments with peanuts, or monkey nuts, as they were called at the time. Dalton devised a way of roasting them that improved the flavour without drying them out. The same cooking oils that he used are sold in many supermarkets to this day and, when he retired in 1975, Dalton had become the largest independent dealer in nut kernels. In 2009, the company became part of Intersnacks.

One of the staple products sold in supermarkets is bread and, today, it is assumed that it will always be available and relatively inexpensive. The key ingredient, of course, is the milled flour and, up to 1878, all the grinding of cereals was carried out between millstones. The entrepreneur who changed this in Britain was Henry Simon (1835–99). Simon was born to a Jewish family in Germany and obtained an Engineering degree at Zurich University, where the curriculum was strongly biased towards the creation of new machinery. At the time of the 1848 revolutions in Europe, his uncle, Heinrich Simon, was a prominent liberal politician. The Frankfurt parliament, initially granted by the Prussian crown, was eventually put down by force, and Heinrich thought it prudent to seek refuge in Switzerland. Some of the family, including Henry, followed him and, in 1860, Henry migrated to Manchester. He acted as a consultant to many companies on technical engineering problems and soon realized that the country's millers were finding their procedures cumbersome, slow and costly.

In Switzerland, however, there was a company called Daverio, Seissardt and Geisler, and they had invented a rolling mill to replace the use of millstones. So in 1878, in partnership with Daverio, Simon created an updated roller flour mill for the premier miller, McDougall's. It revolutionized the industry and reduced the price of bread, which was a staple for the diets of poorer families. By 1892, there were over 400 mills in operation around the world working on the Simon principle, and the company was floated in 1897.

Inflation has been part of modern life for so long that the idea of deflation is very strange to modern ears. The fact is, however, that if the Retail Price Index was 100 in 1837, when Victoria came to the throne, it was only 74 in 1900 at the end of her reign. One reason was the availability of cheap American food imports, but another was the reduction in cost made possible by mass production; the ability to mill flour so much more cheaply had its effect.

In 1881, Simon added to his development of the rolling mill with the first coke-oven plant. It was produced by a company he formed called Simon Carves. Coke was needed for iron and steel production, but the waste products had always been thrown away and they caused severe pollution. With the invention of the coke-oven plant, those by-products could be usefully employed, and a healthier atmosphere was brought a little nearer. Simon also endowed the Chair of German Literature at Manchester University and, when he died, the business went to his son, Ernest, who had a distinguished career with the company and helped the youthful Labour Party a great deal. Unhappily, three of Simon's sons were killed in action during the First World War.

Henry Simon died in 1899. He was one of those German immigrants who was not, technically, Jewish because, though his father was Jewish, his mother was Christian and he practised Unitarianism. Like a small number of other prominent immigrants from similar backgrounds, however, he was widely regarded as Jewish, suffered petty discrimination as a result, and is recalled as Jewish even many years later.[1]

Refugees from the Nazis brought their own food-manufacturing skills with them. One was Richard Mattes (1897–1970), who came from a family of Rhineland sausage makers. He arrived penniless in England in the 1930s, and it took him until 1947 to start Mattessons, making German sausages. This wasn't easy with food rationing continuing after the war, as the recipe for German sausages required a high percentage of meat. It was easier, however, when meat rationing finally ended in 1954.

Mattessons grew to be a large company with the catchy slogan, 'Just try saying Mattessons without saying Mmm!' In 1970, they produced the first pre-packed sliced meat and, in 1971, the first British pâté. Unilever bought out the company in the early 1980s and the products are still popular throughout the country.

It was a jeweller, however, who created one of the most famous Jewish food companies: Lithuanian refugee, Lloyd Rakusen (1881–1944). It was quite common for Orthodox families to bake their own matzos for Passover. This unleavened bread is an essential part of the festival, and before there were companies making matzos, it was a home-based activity. The religious rules for their production are extensive and the process is a lengthy one. As Rakusen got an increasing number of requests for the matzos he made in his kitchen, he suggested to a baker friend in Leeds, Calman Shreiber, that they set up a company.

Shreiber was not the most skilled of businessmen and opined that there would be no money to be made in such a venture. Rakusen went ahead anyway, and the business did well enough to justify the building of a factory in the early 1930s and has managed, albeit with occasional difficulties, to still be in existence today. The Shreiber family, however, found another niche market. Calman's son changed his name to Sol Scriven (1900–79), became an optician and, in 1938, started his own business. He recognized the potential of hearing aids at an early stage, and Scrivens now has over 100 branches and 400 partner opticians and hearing centres throughout the country.

Of course, grocers sold a wide range of products, one of which was cigarettes. Many Jewish companies made cigars, including the original Salmon & Gluckstein Company, the families who founded Lyons. In their time, they were also the largest retail tobacconists in Britain, with 140 shops.

In the early nineteenth century, those who smoked either lit up pipes or cigars. Henry Mayhew in his study of London in 1851 noted that the manufacture of cheap cigars was almost entirely a Jewish preserve. Then, in 1883, James Bonsack invented a cigarette-making machine and, instead of a manual production of about 1,500 cigarettes a day, the machines could turn out 200 cigarettes a minute. W.D. & H.O. Wills bought the British rights to the machine and nobody else could use it.

A large number of the smaller Jewish tobacco companies continued to compete with Wills, but the market was transformed by Bernhard Baron (1850–1929). This Jewish refugee from Russia had been brought to New York at the age of 16, and he invented a machine that was as good or better than the Bonsack. He came to London to make his fortune with it and found plenty of manufacturers who were glad to get hold of his new creation. There was, for example, Godfrey Phillips who, in 1904, was one of the first to produce cigarette cards featuring anonymous pin-up girls.

Other Jewish companies were Abdullah, Marcovitch, J. Wix, Ardath, Balkan Sobranie and Rothmans. Baron's great opportunity came in 1903 when he was able to buy Carreras. In 1910, by the time he was 60, he was a multimillionaire.[2] The activity for which Baron should be remembered, however, was his tremendous contribution to various charities. He was estimated to have given away more than £2 million in his lifetime, with

75 per cent going to non-Jewish charities and 25 per cent to Jewish philan-thropy. He refused a knighthood from Ramsay Macdonald, the Labour leader, and lived a modest life. He was described as a 'simple, gently-spoken, pious, generous man'.[3] It was certainly one of the great rags-to-riches stories, and his name lives on in the Charitable Trust itself, the Bernhard Baron Cottage Homes and the Bernhard Baron Pathological Institute at the London Hospital.

Now that the major smoking market in the twentieth century was cigarettes, one of the essential ingredients became the filter tip. This was invented in 1925 by a Hungarian called Boris Aivaz, but it was first manu-factured commercially by Bunzl & Biach. This was originally a Jewish haberdashery firm in Bratislava, which moved to Vienna in 1883. Moritz Bunzl left the business to his sons and they built up a large paper company.

In 1938 there was 'political upheaval in Central Europe', according to the current Bunzl company website, a somewhat delicate description of the Anschluss and the Nazi takeover of Austria. The Bunzls realized they had to get out quickly, and obtained visas for England. This was always easier at the time, as has already been seen, if the refugee was prepared to set up a business that would reduce unemployment. It was particularly helpful if the immigrant agreed to do so in an area with a major unemployment problem. It took time, but Bunzl set up in Jarrow in the North East of England, an iconic place in the history of the effects of the Slump after the Jarrow March by the unemployed.

The Bunzls started again, with a £5,000 bank loan, as Tissue Papers Ltd. Moritz's son, Hugo (1884–1961), led the company until his death, when his son, George (1915–81), took over. The company was given its Austrian busi-ness back after the war and, where profits in 1940 had been £179, by 1957 they were over £1 million. They still made vast number of filter tips, but diversified into other fields and spread into many overseas countries as well. George died in harness, well known for his 'kindliness, efficiency and ebul-lience'. At the same time, the obituarist had to admit, 'he did not suffer fools gladly and expressed his views emphatically, but he had a special charm'.[4] George Bunzl was the chairman of fund-raising for the Royal Marsden Hospital and treasurer of the Jewish Youth Aliyah. He did much good work for the British Institute of Management and was very popular.

The significance of Bunzl to Lord Roll, writing of his friend after his death, was that the company was 'yet another example of the benefit which the British economy, and indeed British life in general, has derived over the centuries from having in its midst immigrants, forced to leave their home due to political or racial persecution'.[5] After George's death the company went downhill, but re-entered the FTSE 100 in 2008, with half its business being done in the United States and a turnover of £3.6 billion. There are, however, no longer any Bunzls on the board. When assessing the British economy, the contribution of companies like Bunzl are often overlooked.

A key element in the administration of any shop is the need to control sales' records. For this an effective cash register is needed, and this was the case in the 1930s when the Gross family bought a tobacco shop. Irritatingly, the previous owner had taken the cash register with him, and so young Henry Gross (1914–2009) settled down to produce his own. As he said, 'I had an enormous urge to carry on experiments which would ultimately result in the production of a cash register'.[6] It was an odd obsession, which Henry had first acquired in childhood. 'I was intrigued that a machine as well as a man could add up.'[7]

It took many years but, in 1946, with £2,000 raised from his family and friends, Henry and his brother, Sam, started to produce Gross Cash Registers. The back parlour of their home in North London was the factory, and the front parlour was the showroom. In the first year they made fifty, almost by hand, and sold them for £75 each. As they cost them £150 to produce, this was not the kind of progress they needed, but their bank manager came up with £5,000 more capital and, in 1949, they managed a surplus of £29,000. In 1965, they went public and, by 1970, they were making over £2 million profit. From an initial labour force of twelve they had moved to a major factory in Brighton in the 1950s, which would employ 2,000.

The golden age for the company came with the introduction of decimalization. Henry invented a machine that could switch conversions from the old currency to the new. They sold like wildfire and more than 60,000 were produced in a single year. Henry moved on to inventing an electronic desktop calculator, which was the first to be manufactured in Britain. The company was eventually sold to Chubb.

Supermarkets need basic-food suppliers, and one of the most important commodity traders in the second half of the twentieth century in Britain was Ephraim Margulies (1925–97). His family came to England from Poland when he was 3, and his ancestors were a dynasty of Chassidic rabbis. His father started a small synagogue in the East End of London and, during the war, Margulies served on minesweepers in the navy. When he was demobilized, his father's supporters financed him in buying J.H. Rayner, a small cocoa-broking company. This flourished sufficiently for a major commodity trading company, S. & W. Berisford, to buy it in 1969; Margulies got 17 per cent of the new company. He soon became chairman and then proceeded to run the organization almost as a one-man-band.

There were two sides to Margulies. In business this 'small, portly and ebullient' man was 'quick, perceptive, resourceful and tireless'.[8] He was 'brisk, hectoring, barking out orders'.[9] He used language he might well have picked up in the navy, and was considered a genius trader. In his private life, however, he was extremely Orthodox, 'calm, benign and beatific'.[10] He spent many hours studying the Torah, lived quietly in the Orthodox homeland of North London and supported any number of charities. He was known in Orthodox circles as Reb (Rabbi) Zelman.

As the chairman of Berisfords, he soon set out to buy one of the biggest trading companies, British Sugar. He was relentless in his pursuit of it. The BSC chairman went on record as saying, 'The next time he comes round here, we will switch off the lifts so that the b … has a heart attack climbing the stairs'.[11] Margulies eventually did take over British Sugar and he then 'totally dominated the soft commodity market through his expertise and force of character'.[12] The company became one of the world's major trading groups.

Although he had arrived in England as a little boy, Margulies had a thick European accent. He never left behind the culture of his forebears, nor would he have wanted to do so. When he was asked the secret of his success, he said, 'We buy a little, we sell a little, and with God's help, we make a little'.[13] When it was needed, though, he was a great deal more switched on than that. During a slump in commodity prices, he was advised to buy futures by his colleagues. As he reminded them, 'Always remember, boys, every bottom's got a hole in it'.[14] Margulies had many years of great success and, in the 1980s, the company's sales exceeded £2 billion. Where, in 1969

Berisford had been capitalized at £4 million, in 1989, it was worth £500 million.

For reasons that seemed sound at the time, Margulies then made a major mistake in deciding to invest in property in New York, which proved disastrous. He nearly brought the company down, and it had to be sold to Associated British Foods in 1990 for £880 million. The board voted Margulies out and he retired. When he died in 1997, however, he was still highly regarded in his own community and left a wife and eleven children, as well as a large fortune.

The ability to build a major food company from scratch might seem difficult in the modern competitive market; a large number of massive firms are so well entrenched. One entrepreneur who managed it, however, was Harry Solomon (1937–), a solicitor who, in 1976, started a company called Hillsdown Holdings, with a non-Jewish partner called David Thompson, who was a butcher. Their wives had met at an antenatal class and the relationship grew from there. In 1993, when Solomon retired, he left one of the largest food businesses in Britain.

The key to Solomon's success was to buy poorly performing companies and revitalize them. He did this on an enormous scale. The firm was launched on the Stock Exchange in 1985 and, in a twenty-month period, bought forty-two companies. Solomon bought Smedley's canning business for £1, Henry Telfer's meat-pie business for another £1 and FMC (The Fatstock Marketing Corporation) for a knockdown £4.9 million. In 1987, the company made another fifty purchases and in 1988, slowed down to only buying thirty-one. In all, more than £50 million was laid out to buy new companies, and Hillsdown became the largest producer in the country of eggs, poultry, meat and canned foods. By 1991, it was the fourth-largest food manufacturer in Britain, with sales of over £1 billion.

One innovation which proved particularly helpful to Hillsdown was the development by supermarkets of their own brands: products which mirrored those branded by manufacturers, but which could be sold more cheaply, because the prices didn't have to include the manufacturer's heavy marketing and advertising expenses. Hillsdown produced a large number of them.

In 1991, Solomon was knighted for services to the food industry, and the firm grew even larger after his departure, building on the foundations he had laid. It was very much a one-man band at the top in his time, as there were no non-executive directors, and Solomon was always firmly in control. His main contribution to the food industry had been the revitalizing of any number of food manufacturers who had not kept up with the times. Wedded to old traditional practices, a surprising number had needed the input of newcomers who were not. That is what Solomon provided. In retirement, he has spent a lot of time, money and energy trying to improve the relations between the Arab and Israeli communities in Israel.

Not all immigrants arrive in Britain looking for a better life. Manfred Gorvy (1938–) comes from a well-to-do Jewish family in South Africa and studied accountancy at Wits University in Johannesburg. In 1961, he became a chartered accountant and went to work for the Shlesinger Organization, which had vast interests in South African property, citrus farms, insurance and banking. In 1973, he was asked to take over the London office, which he did with some reluctance, as he was perfectly happy in his own country.

In a large company, however, to turn down an overseas posting is seldom an option, and so Gorvy moved. A year later, Shlesinger sold everything except their citrus farms and UK operation, leaving Gorvy pretty well high and dry. What was worse, 1974 was the middle of a very nasty slump in Britain. Gorvy grasped the nettle, and arranged management buyouts with Schlesinger. He then started Hanover Acceptances, of which he has now been chairman for nearly forty years. The business has grown like Topsy, and the products of the citrus farms were the basis, from which emerged the largest growing and processing manufacturer of citrus in Southern Africa. It is also Europe's largest juice-drink manufacturer, besides branching out into property investment and venture capitalism.

With sales of well over £500 million a year and Dr Sean Gorvy (1963–), the chairman's son, as CEO, the organization is now one of the largest private companies in Britain. Benefiting from its success has been the Old Vic, the National Theatre and the Victoria and Albert Museum, all of whom have received a great deal of financial help from the family.

Of course, eating well is a mixed blessing. The public has become more knowledgeable and more concerned over the years about cholesterol levels, obesity, diabetes and binge eating. As we've seen earlier in the chapter, some firms have been in the health food business for over 100 years, addressing these concerns. Today, for example, the huge conglomerate, Glaxo Smith Kline, produce Horlicks, which was invented in 1873 and first produced in Britain at a factory in Slough in 1906. It should be remembered that Joe Nathan's Glaxo was from the same era. Glaxo Smith Kline also manufacture long-established brands like Lucozade which started in 1927 and Ribena, which began life in 1936. It is fair to assume that it couldn't have come as a surprise to the company that health foods can be a profitable market.

What does seem odd, therefore, is that, in 2010, it became advisable for the company to pay Zef Eisenberg (1974–) £162 million for his sports-nutrition company, Maximuscle. Admittedly it was the largest organization in its field with a turnover of £85 million a year, the only British one, and it held 43 per cent of the market, but Maximuscle was the brainchild of a 22-year-old who had just £3,000 in 1996 with which to start up.

Eisenberg was always going to go into business. At his prep school at the age of 8 he was said to be selling sweets and stationary to his fellow pupils.[15] He left school to go to work in a small health shop and, when he was 20, he self-published a book discussing which health-related products worked and which didn't. The first run of 24,000 sold out, and that was where the £3,000 came from.

Eisenberg accepted the old sales adage that there's always a market for quality products:

> I got the best food technologists, the best protein houses and doctors. I told them exactly what I wanted and what I wanted was very expensive. This was the first time they'd met someone who asked for something that worked, tasted and looked good, as opposed to cost, cost, cost. We are known as a premium brand and the point is that, if people enjoy the taste, they'll use it again and again.[16]

From this philosophy of a man in his 20s came products like Maximuscle Cyclone, a jar of which, lasting twenty days, costs about £45. This includes a daily dose of sixty grams of protein, ten grams of creatine monohydrate and ten grams of glutamine for muscle repairs, plus beta-ecdysterone.

There were difficult times. As the drive for athletic success became increasingly intense, athletes were found to be testing positive for banned substances. Some blamed Maximuscle products, but Eisenberg spent 'around £200,000 a year putting all of its products through a stringent WADA (World Anti-Doping Agency)-approved Drugs screening lab'.[17] When athletes who failed tests blamed his products, Eisenberg gathered all the national press into his factory and gave them the facts about the care used to ensure that the products were safe; the resulting news stories gave the company millions of pounds of free publicity. As Eisenberg has said, 'It was always my goal from day one to build the company and have an exit, origi-nally to one of the big food boys'. Which is what can still happen if the hole in the market is correctly identified.

If you're going to eat, you need cutlery. So when the Viener family came to Sheffield in 1901, they set up as small silversmiths and then decided to see what they could achieve by making knives, forks and spoons, and anglicizing the company's name to Viners. Adolphe Viener had migrated from Germany, and he and his family joined a Jewish community in Sheffield which consisted almost entirely of foreigners. When a Westminster MP at the time accused immigrants of being responsible for a disproportionate amount of the nation's crime, the Sheffield Jews appealed to the chief constable to speak up for them. In the *Jewish Chronicle* on 27 February 1903, he was reported as saying that only five Jews had been accused of felonies in Sheffield in the last three years, and none of drunkenness. Only three were on parochial relief (in the workhouse). The Sheffield Jews rested their case.

Viners was a family business until it became a public company in 1934. Sheffield cutlery had been known since the fourteenth century, but there was a lot of unemployment in the industry in the 1920s and 1930s. Viners survived very well; Adolphe, Emile, Mark, Ruben and Lionel ran it. Adolphe (1885–1955) was the chairman, and Emile and Mark were joint managing directors. As a public company in the difficult pre-war and wartime years, they did very well for their new shareholders. Dividends were 12.5 per cent from 1935 to 1938, 20 per cent from 1939 to 1941, 30 per cent in 1942 and 1943, and 45 per cent in 1946. During the war, they made bay-onets in vast quantities. After the war they became the largest cutlery firm in Sheffield.

Adolphe died in 1955 and Emile took over as chairman, while Ruben be-came managing director. He had left school at 16 to join the firm in 1924, so it had been a long apprenticeship; he succeeded Emile in 1966. The firm made silver cutlery and the cheaper Sheffield plate. This is the process of fusing a sheet of silver to the top and bottom of a sheet of base metal. Viners also created rustless nickel silver before stainless steel came on the market.

Ruben did a great deal for the Sheffield cutlery industry as president of the Cutlery Manufacturers Association, though he was never made the Master Cutler, head of the ancient guild which had first started in 1624. He was a city councillor and he did sterling work for his own community, and for the Jewish Board of Guardians in all its senior offices. In 1980 he retired and the firm went bankrupt in 1985. Cheap competition from the Far East was the explanation, though the firm was eventually bought by the largest American cutlery company and is part of it to this day. In 1975, there had been 900 employed at Viners but, in 1982, it was down to 150.

NOTES

1. The author, in discussion with a current director of Simon engineering.
2. Gerry Black, Presidential Address, Jewish Historical Society of England, 1998.
3. Ibid.
4. Lord Roll of Ipson, *The Times*, 14 February 1981.
5. Ibid.
6. *Jewish Chronicle*, 1 October 1971.
7. Ibid.
8. Chaim Bermant, *Jewish Chronicle*, 5 September 1997.
9. Ibid.
10. Ibid.
11. Andrew Wilson, *Herald Scotland*, 4 September 1997.
12. Ibid.
13. Jeremy Warner, *Independent*, 30 August 1997.
14. *Evening Standard*, 22 September 1998.
15. Candice Krieger, *Daily Mail*, 26 January 2011.
16. Ian Wallis, *Growing Business*, 1 October 2006.
17. Ibid.

Chapter eleven

The Motor Age

Shells were used for decoration in the Stone Age. They were popular among the well-to-do in England during the seventeenth century and were widely fashioned into trinkets and boxes in the nineteenth century. So, in 1833, a Whitechapel Jew, Marcus Samuel, started a shell shop and his son, also Marcus (1853–1927), joined him when he grew up. As some of the finest shells were to be found in Japan, now emerging from its self-imposed isolation after many centuries, in 1876 young Marcus took himself off to Yokohama and formed the business of Samuel & Samuel.

He was only 23, and he widened his scope to deal in rice, feathers and pepper, as well as shells. It was enough to earn him a reasonable living, but he wasn't satisfied. Samuel was sure the road to success would have to involve finding a first-class niche market. The question was, what did the Japanese need that they hadn't got? He decided that one crucial answer was oil. Now, when most people think of oil, they think of the Middle East. In 1900, though, half the world's oil production came from Russia and, even in 1944, less than 5 per cent came from the Middle East; only in 1906 was oil first discovered in that part of the world, in Iran. The Middle East wasn't in the frame.

If oil was found, there were then the problems of extracting, purifying, distributing and selling it. At the beginning of the twentieth century, the largest single firm in the oil industry was the American Standard Oil Company, founded in 1870 and controlled by John D. Rockefeller. American oil was first discovered in 1859 in Pennsylvania, and would be found in Texas and Oklahoma in 1901. Because of its sheer size, Standard Oil was able to undercut competitors, not only at home but in many countries overseas as well. For Samuel the problem was to work out how a small

Jewish company, that wasn't even in the oil business, could successfully take on the giant Standard Oil.

Not fazed, in 1890, Samuel went to Russia to see what the possibilities were. He had the vision at the time to recognize the commercial potential inherent in a number of comparatively new factors; in 1878, the first oil tanker had been launched on the Caspian Sea by Ludwig Nobel, so cargo capacity was being addressed. Then, again, the Suez Canal was now under British control, so the journey time to Asia was substantially reduced. Best of all, as far as he had seen on his travels, Standard Oil hadn't taken much interest in the Far East.

Samuel put all the elements together. He conceived the idea of buying the oil in Russia, transporting it on new, specially built tankers through the Suez Canal, and selling it in the Far East. This breadth of vision mirrored the Jewish involvement in the eighteenth-century Indian diamond market. In 1892, Samuel got permission to send the tankers through the Canal and, in 1897, he floated the company, which would grow to be one of the major powers in the oil industry. Out of nostalgia, he called it Shell. Today, in spotting their future markets, Shell still look to recruit those who have the attribute Samuel showed: the 'helicopter' quality, able to see how disparate pieces fit into the jigsaw puzzle.

The business flourished. Another competitor to Standard Oil, however, was the Royal Dutch Petroleum Company. Like the British, the Dutch had been heavily involved in South East Asian trade for centuries. In 1903, Shell and Royal Dutch merged their Far Eastern marketing. At which point Samuel made a major mistake. He agreed a deal with a Texas petroleum company. He bought a fleet of tankers to transport their oil across the Atlantic. Unfortunately, the Texas well then ran dry. The vessels had to be converted into cattle ships, Shell lost a fortune and, by 1907, the company had to be fully merged with Royal Dutch, with the Dutch holding 60 per cent of the company stock.

The profits of Royal Dutch Shell helped the British balance of trade, as they still do, but Samuel had started to make an even greater contribution to the welfare of his country. He had seen that it was possible to transport oil from Borneo in tankers, using only oil for propulsion, rather than coal. He brought this to the attention of Admiral Fisher, the First Sea Lord, who was trying to create a British navy that would be larger, faster and more heavily armed than that of any other nation in case of war.

The key to success, Fisher and Samuel recognized, was to use oil to fuel the engines, rather than the traditional, but less efficient, coal. It took Fisher a number of years to convince the government of the sense of the argument but, by 1912, the change was agreed. In Fisher's memoirs he pays tribute to Samuel, 'for services of the utmost importance to the fighting forces'. Samuel was also one of those who ensured Britain had sufficient supplies of oil during the war.

Marcus Samuel still had a fair share of the 40 per cent that was the British part of Shell, so he was a very wealthy man. The Dutch, though, under Henri Deterding, were now increasingly running the company. Samuel had by now reached his mid 50s; he had started a bank, M. Samuel, and he had already become a very charitable benefactor to both Jewish and non-Jewish charities. In 1902, he had been elected Lord Mayor of London. As a proud Jew, he felt for his persecuted brethren and so, at his Lord Mayor's Banquet, there was no invitation for the Romanian ambassador, because of his country's treatment of its Jewish community.

The main persecution, however, was occurring, as was normal for the period, in Russia. In 1903, there was another outrage in the Ukraine in Kishinev. A pogrom, instigated by the minister of the interior, saw forty-nine Jews killed, 500 injured and 2,000 left homeless. The world shrugged. Like so many other pogroms, there seemed little that could be done about it, except voice complaints. After all, Russia's appalling treatment of its Jewish citizens had been going on for centuries. There was a joke prayer at the time in the community that, 'the Lord should help keep and preserve the Czar – well away from me!'

Back in Japan at this time, relations with Russia were at an all-time low. Indeed, Japan wanted to go to war with Russia over disputes in Manchuria and Korea. The problem was that the four comparatively small islands which made up the country didn't have the money to do so. What was more, the likelihood of a newly developed nation defeating a great empire was very remote. Nobody was keen to back an almost certain loser to the necessarily massive financial extent which would be involved.

As a consequence, when Japan tried to sell what were recognized to be, effectively, war bonds, there were no buyers in New York. Moving on to London, the Japanese minister appointed to try to raise the funds, Baron Korekiyo Takahishi, contacted Samuel because of the Samuel & Samuel connection.[1] Coincidentally, Samuel would have known that Jacob Schiff, of the New York bankers Kuhn Loeb, was in town. Schiff's ancestors had been distinguished rabbis in Germany since the fourteenth century and one of them, David Tevele Schiff, had been chief rabbi in England from 1765 to 1791.

Samuel could arrange a meeting if you wanted to network: being an ex-Lord Mayor of London opened all doors. When Schiff was informed that the Japanese wanted to go to war with Russia, he recognized the opportunity for a reckoning with the Czar: revenge at last. Nothing would fully make up for all those Russian Jews who had been forced into the army for an inordinate number of years, who had died in innumerable pogroms, been confined to the Pale, exiled from their home towns by the infamous May Laws and discriminated against in a whole range of everyday activities. Assisting Japan could, however, be a major step in the right direction. Schiff agreed with Takahishi to help raise nearly $200 million to enable them to go to war.

Schiff sold the bonds and with this financial wherewithal, the Japanese won the Russo-Japanese War. It was a serious blow for the Czar. The almost universal acceptance of his dictatorial power hitherto was shattered. In Japan, the status of Samuel & Samuel rose even higher. For Samuel had not only helped with Schiff; he had negotiated to get them the support of the Rothschilds as well.

The alleged power of Jewish bankers is often exaggerated, and the plight of persecuted Jewish minorities is often overlooked. Here, the co-religionists of the Russian–Jewish victims were given the opportunity to fight back against their oppressors, and they took it. The American and British Jewish bankers had seen the effects of maltreatment by the Russian government in the teeming masses of refugees who flooded through Ellis Island in New York and the East End of London. Appealing to the better instincts of the Czar had proved useless; helping to destroy him was the only alternative left.

When the First World War finally began, however, Britain and Russia were allies. All that mattered then was to defeat the enemy, and Samuel went to work for the government again. There was now a great need for effective explosives, and one of the vital ingredients was toluene, used in the manufacture of TNT. It was said that Samuel built a refinery to produce toluene in a few weeks, and Lord Birkenhead wrote in his memoirs, 'Lord Bearsted [Samuel was made a peer in 1921] is entitled to be regarded as one of the deliverers of his country'. For all this help, the Samuel family would have said they were only doing their patriotic duty. Like millions of other families, though, they were heartbroken at giving up their younger son, who was killed in the conflict.

Samuel was knighted when two of his Shell tugs salvaged HMS Victorious in 1898, after the warship went aground at Port Said. He was made a baronet when he stepped down as Lord Mayor, and he enjoyed his peerage for six years before he died in 1927, a few hours after his wife, to whom he was married for forty-six years. He left £4 million (£178 million now, using the retail price index.) Today, Shell Petroleum is a monument to his enterprise, but his contribution to the survival of his country is only a footnote in the history books.

Apart from Shell, there were no British oil companies founded by Jews, in those early heady years. There were, however, three companies constructing engine-driven ships that had Jewish founders: Samuda Brothers, Harland & Wolff and Yarrow & Co. Samuda Brothers did not build ships on the Clyde or on Tyneside. They had a massive shipyard on the Isle of Dogs in London where the Samuda Housing Estate is today. In 1832, Joseph d'Aguilar Samuda (1813–85) set up as a marine engineer with his brother, Jacob, and in 1843, they started to build ships. Jacob invented the 'atmospheric railway' that used air pressure to provide propulsion for trains which, by 1845, could reach speeds of 70 mph. He was, unfortunately, killed in a shipping accident, and Joseph ran the company after that, building everything from iron and steel warships and steam packets to royal yachts.

By 1863, Samuda was building twice the output of all the other London shipyards, and had overseas contracts with Russia, Germany and Japan. One Japanese employee, who joined them for work experience, was Togo Heihachiro, who finished up an admiral and was known as the

Japanese Nelson. It was under his command that the Japanese navy successfully fought the Russian fleet in the Russo-Japanese war.

In addition to his work in the shipyard, in 1865 Joseph Samuda became the MP for Tavistock and then represented the Tower Hamlets constituency from 1868 to 1880. In 1860, he helped establish the Institute of Naval Architects but, when he died in 1885, there were no buyers for the yard. It closed in 1890.

Harland & Wolff, the great Belfast shipyard, starts with the story of a German–Jewish banking family, the Schwabes. After the end of the Napoleonic Wars, much of Germany went back to its old anti-Semitic ways. Napoleon might have given the Jews emancipation, but Napoleon had been defeated. Many of the 300 small German states had, as an excuse for persecution, the argument that the promise of emancipation might have made the Jews favour Napoleon. There were pogroms, Jews lost the rights of citizenship they had been awarded by the French emperor, they had to pay special taxes again, were driven from their homes and forbidden to practise occupations such as teaching in schools and universities

Only twelve Jewish weddings a year were permitted in Frankfurt, and great pressure was put on the community to become Christians. The Schwabes and their relatives, the Wolffs, were forced to convert to Lutheranism. From the Jewish point of view, this did not affect their religious status at all. There have been far too many forcible conversions in Jewish history and, therefore, none of them have been acknowledged as legitimate in Jewish eyes. If a man has a Jewish mother, he is able to claim he is a Jew, even if he converts half a dozen times to six different religions. If a woman has a Jewish mother and is forcibly converted, not only is she still accepted as a Jew, but her children are recognized as Jewish as well.

If the nineteenth century was the peak of British power, Germany's rulers were stupid enough to make its contribution to that hegemony. It drove some of the best German commercial brains out of the country, and Gustavus Schwabe was one who migrated to Liverpool. In 1849 his 14-year-old nephew, Gustav Wolff (1834–1913), followed Gustavus, who effectively adopted the boy, and the lad became a draughtsman. Another apprentice was Edward Harland, whose family was friendly with

Schwabe. The banker helped him get a job, and Harland eventually went off to Belfast to work in a small shipyard. In 1857, Schwabe persuaded Harland to take on Gustav Wolff as his personal assistant and a year later, when the shipyard owner got into financial difficulties, Schwabe helped Harland to buy the firm on the condition that Wolff became his partner. The two worked very well together. Wolff managed the yard and Harland came up with the innovations that would make their ships attractive to buyers. He put in iron upper decks instead of wooden ones, and he flattened the bottoms of the ships and squared the sections to make more space for cargo.

In 1860, Harland did a deal with a Liverpool contact, John Bibby, who had started the Bibby Line. Bibby had looked to Harland for technical advice before he went to Belfast and, now that he had a shipyard, he was happy to place orders with him. Of the first twenty-one ships built by Harland & Wolff, eighteen were for Bibby.

Wolff might officially be a Lutheran but he kept his Jewish links. His co-religionists were well aware of the difficulty of resisting the pressure to convert, which had been so severe in Germany. Converted Jews at the time were often regarded all their lives by society as still Jewish. This attitude hindered both Disraeli and Hambro; Wolff, however, used common ancestry to cement a relationship and do a profitable deal with Albert Ballin of the Hamburg America Line.

The real making of the yard came about in 1867, when the White Star Line went bankrupt. Thomas Ismay bought it, with the help of Gustavus Schwabe. This did not involve teams of merchant bankers, massive amounts of paper work and impressive levels of fees to professional advisers. The banker agreed to finance the line over a game of billiards, so long as Harland & Wolff were contracted to build the ships that the White Star Line needed. Ismay did the deal on the condition that Harland & Wolff didn't build ships for anyone else, and in the years to come, the Belfast shipyard built seventy ships for White Star, including the *Titanic*. The yard developed the largest dry dock in the world and, by 1900, was the biggest employer in Belfast. It held that position for many years thereafter and, from the harbour, it is still possible to see how far the works stretched at their peak.

Gustav Wolff seems to have acted very much in the role of deputy chairman, charged with keeping everything moving smoothly. As he once said, 'Sir Edward builds the ships, Mr Pirrie [the managing director] makes the speeches and, as for me, I smoke the cigars.'[2]

As this didn't take up all his time, in 1880, he supervised the building of the engine works and also founded the Belfast Ropeworks Company; this became one of the largest ropemakers in the world. Both Harland and Wolff were knighted and sat in Parliament for Belfast North and Belfast East respectively, Wolff for eighteen years. They were known in the House of Commons as 'Majestic' and 'Teutonic', after two ships they built. Harland died in 1895, and when Wolff died in 1913 the Belfast council hung the Union flag at half-mast. They had both done a very great deal for the economy of the province, but the story might have been very different if the Germans had left the Jews in peace after the Napoleonic Wars.

Yarrow & Co. was the creation of Alfred Yarrow (1842–1932), who was particularly close to his Sephardi mother. He was a brilliant marine engineer and started, in 1868, to build steam launches on the Isle of Dogs when he was only 26. He went on to build submarines and torpedo boats, both of which were new kinds of naval vessels. In 1906, he made the move to the Clyde, abandoning the old London shipyard. During the First World War, the company built twenty-four destroyers. Yarrow also personally organized the building of gunboats for action in the Middle East. The intricacies of naval building are complicated; for example, Yarrow solved the problem of the excessive vibration of engines by creating the Yarrow-Schlick-Tweedy system. Known as an enlightened and patriarchal employer, in 1916 he was knighted. The firm today is part of BAE Systems Marine.

As the turnpike roads gave way to the railways and steam succeeded sail, there was a need for improved communications throughout the country. One innovation was the Mersey Tunnel, which was created by Samuel Isaac (1812–86). Isaac was the son of a Jewish Dorset furniture broker, and had started his business life as an army contractor. The firm of Isaac, Campbell & Co. became the largest European firm supporting the Confederacy in the American Civil War, and were famous as blockade runners. Military equipment was sent to the South and cotton came back. Unfortunately for the company (but fortunately for American civil rights) the Confederacy lost and, as their currency became worthless, the firm went bankrupt.

By 1881, Isaac had recovered and was asked by the Mersey Railway Company to help create a tunnel under the river. Without any previous experience of what was involved, he undertook the task, his major contribution being to arrange the finance. He agreed to complete the work and pay all the legal, parliamentary and other expenses, until the tunnel was completed and certificated. He supervised the boring of the tunnel until its opening in 1884. He also built Birkenhead station. When he died in 1886 he left £200,000 (£16 million today).

The Jews played their part in the development of the railways, with Lewis Gompertz inventing the expanding chuck as early as 1814. Abraham Cohen improved railway couplings, Abraham Lindo created a third rail to prevent derailment, Solomon Solomon invented better axle-boxes and Emanuel Myers a superior method of preventing engines and carriages running off the rails.[3] Major growth in railway development occurred before the influx of Jews from Europe following the 1848 revolutions. Indeed 1848 signalled the end of the Railway Mania and the collapse of railway shares, in a major stock-market slump.

Another new form of transport later in the century was the London underground railway, and this was largely created by Sir Edgar Speyer (1862–1932). Speyer was an American Jew, related to a German banking house, which specialized in railway projects. In 1892, he became a British subject and from 1906 to 1915 was the chairman of the Underground Electric Railway Company of London. During his time, the company opened three lines, electrified a fourth, and took over two more. The Northern, Bakerloo and Piccadilly lines were, basically, his creation. It wasn't easy to make the Underground financially viable and the company struggled for many years. In 1912, however, it bought the London General Omnibus Company and was then able to use the profits from the buses to bolster the losses on the new railway system.

Speyer was a great music lover. The Promenade Concerts had been founded in 1895 and, in the early days, from 1902 to 1914, Speyer financed them. He also acted as honorary treasurer for Captain Scott's last, ill-fated expedition to Antarctica. A friend of Prime Minister Asquith, he was knighted in 1906 and made a privy councillor in 1909. It would prove unfortunate that, because of his German banking connections, in 1911 he was also given the Order of Crown, 2nd Class, by the Kaiser.

For Speyer, everything fell apart when the Great War broke out. The responsibility for identifying German spies rested with Captain Vernon Kell, who had been recruited to set up what is now known as MI5 in 1909.[4] Prior to 1914, only a small number of prosecutions for espionage came to court.

Anti-German feeling in Britain was obviously extensive. Even the royal family would change its name to Windsor. As a consequence, many German–Jewish immigrants who had contributed substantially to the economic welfare of the country were suspected and even denounced as potential traitors. Of those convicted, only one was a Jew: Wilhelm Klauer tried to buy a secret report on torpedo trials and, when he was caught, was sentenced to five years in prison.

The main defence against the German spy network was the completion of a registry of all German aliens in Britain, largely based on the 1911 census. This resulted, in 1914, in the arrest of twenty-two German spies and the almost total destruction of the ring. There had been over 1,000 intercepts of letters over the years, so that Kell had every opportunity to identify potential Jewish German spies, if they had existed. In fact, they didn't, and Berlin was told how difficult it was to recruit migrants, who would have nothing to do with activities which would harm the interests of the country that had taken them in. It didn't prevent spy mania, however, and the assistant commissioner at Scotland Yard said that it 'assumed a virulent epidemic force, accompanied by delusions which defied treatment'.[5]

Speyer was attacked for his German connections, his family was ostracized, his children asked to leave their schools, and he was viciously attacked in the press. He offered to resign both his baronetcy and his privy councillorship, but Asquith wrote to him, 'I have known you long, and well enough to estimate at their true value these baseless and malignant imputations upon your loyalty to the British crown. The King is not prepared to take any such steps as you suggest.'

Even so, Speyer and his family returned to America. After the war there were investigations into those British citizens who were accused of having traded with the enemy. The case was found proven against Speyer, who was crossed off the privy council list and lost his British nationality. The grounds on which he was found guilty were that he had written during the war to his German brother-in-law. He had also traded with a Dutch company which, being neutral, had perfectly legitimately also decided to trade with Germany. Finally, he had a friend who was the conductor of the Boston Symphony Orchestra, who was suspected of being a German agent. The war had, however, so poisoned the atmosphere that these very minor allegations of misconduct were considered sufficiently venal crimes to lead to the guilty verdict. Speyer died in America in 1932.

There was a time when there were any number of British car firms. Alas, today, there are some excellent Japanese, French and German companies, but very few British ones remain. Car manufacturers, however, assemble vehicles from parts provided by all kinds of companies, and one of the most important in Britain, until a few years ago, was Clayton Aniline.

The origins of the company go back to 1876 and Dr Charles Dreyfus (1848–1935). He was a distant relative of Alfred Dreyfus, the French-Jewish military officer wrongly accused of treason. Charles Dreyfus had a Chemistry degree from Strasbourg University and, in 1869, he came to Manchester from Alsace to take a job as a chemist to a printing company. In 1876, when he was 28 years old, he started Clayton Aniline. The city was at the centre of the British textile trade, and Dreyfus soon learned that the local calico printers needed artificial aniline oil and aniline salts. Dreyfus 'introduced valuable secrets of Germany's dye industry to England fifty-five years ago [1880]'.[6]

The business flourished, though the working conditions were hardly ideal: 'We worked there in a noxious atmosphere of fumes, and in indescribable mud and filth [no paved roadways]. More unhealthy, dismal and repulsive surroundings it is difficult to conceive.'[7] By 1900, however, Clayton Aniline was selling its dyestuffs throughout Europe and America; it also had the sales concession for CIBA in Switzerland and, in 1911, CIBA took it over.

Dreyfus retired in 1913 but the firm produced vast quantities of uniforms in Switzerland for the British forces during the First World War. It continued to make dyed cloth in Manchester thereafter and, at one time, its annual production was in excess of 350,000 metric tonnes. More than one half of the cars manufactured in Britain at the end of the twentieth century had their internal fabrics manufactured in Manchester. Unfortunately, however, the competition from Asia became so intense that, in 2007, the factory had to close.

Dreyfus had a distinguished record of working to help the infant Zionist movement survive. In 1901, he was introduced to Chaim Weizman at the Fifth Zionist Conference, and employed the future president of Israel as a chemist in his company. Weizman first met Arthur Balfour, who was the local MP, at Dreyfus's suggestion. Weizman valued Dreyfus very highly, telling one of his colleagues, 'Contact Dreyfus and use him to establish relations with Balfour. Dreyfus is in favour of Palestine ... Dreyfus must be promoted. He wields enormous influence.'[8] By 1901, Dreyfus was president of the Manchester Zionist Society and a leading figure in the East Manchester Conservative Association. In 1906 he managed Prime Minister Balfour's election campaign, though the Liberals won the country with an enormous majority. In 1904, Dreyfus had also become a founder member of the Victoria Memorial Children's Hospital in the city.

Another innovator was Siegfried Bettman (1863–1952), who came to Britain at the same time as the host of Jewish refugees fleeing persecution in Eastern Europe, though he wasn't one of them. He came from Nuremburg in Germany and, in 1884 when he was 21, became the British representative of the White Sewing Machine Company. Sewing machines were part of the new technology but so, Bettman recognized, were the new possibilities created by the developments in bicycles. In 1887, he borrowed £500 from his family and founded the Triumph Company in Coventry: 'I gave it the name Triumph which would be understood in all European languages.'[9]

Bettman was interested in engineering, but very like Alan Sugar nearly 100 years later, his greatest skill lay in marketing and merchandizing new products. Bettman had arranged financial support from Dunlop Rubber and set out to take advantage of every new piece of cycle technology he could find. In 1894, the Coventry factory produced its first motorcycles (designed by Hildebrand and Wolfmuller), but then created the first all-British motorcycle at the turn of the century. In 1885, Daimler in Germany had produced the first motorbike. Triumph's first tricycle was produced in 1903 and, in 1905, Bettman was the first to use ball main bearings in an engine.

To make motorcycles fashionable, in 1907 the first competitive races were held in the Isle of Man, and a Triumph came second. By the same year, the Coventry factory was producing 1,000 machines a year and, in 1909, this increased to 3,000. The excitement of the TT races and the glamour of the machines were akin to Formula One racing in Britain today. In 1911 came the first Triumph with a clutch. In 1914, the outbreak of the First World War made the company even more famous, as it produced 30,000 Type H machines during the next four years for the use of the troops.

After the war, in 1923, Bettman turned to making cars. In 1925, the company produced the cheapest 500cc motorbike ever sold, for just under £43. In that year, the factory employed 3,000 people and, in 1929, it produced 30,000 motorcycles. The Slump, however, was a disaster, and Bettman was moved to the honorary role of chairman. In 1937, the company revived with the 500cc Special Twin, which sold for £77.75 and was in production for thirty years. The Triumph sports cars were also very popular, but after Bettman died in 1952, the long decline led to the Japanese dominating the market and the Triumph is now manufactured there.

It isn't often that the products of a company become antiques in a lifetime; one exception is the Red-Ashay car mascots, which were produced by Hermann Ascher (1889–1943) between the wars. Ascher was a Czech Jew, who was educated at the Reichenberg Technical High School as a chemist. He came to London just before the outbreak of the First World War, choosing the winning side at a very early stage of the conflict. After five months in an internment camp on the Isle of Man – just as during the Second World War – he was released and decided to settle down in Wakefield.

After the war, he re-established contact with his friends in the glass industry in Czechoslovakia. The Czechs had a distinguished history of glass production and were instrumental in creating the Irish glass industry. Ascher decided to import glass car mascots, a field in which the Frenchman, René Lalique, was the master. Car mascots were very popular, and Ascher's range of thirty Red-Ashay car mascots, imported from Czechoslovakia, often to his own designs, sold very well. They were not only stunningly attractive, but they had the special attraction that they could be lit from within, by a bulb attached to the car's electrical system. What was more, the lights could be changed to different colours. Today, a Red-Ashay car mascot in perfect condition can easily sell at auction for several thousand pounds. Many of Ascher's family died in the Holocaust, but he himself died peacefully in 1943. The firm continued for a few years, but was dissolved in 1952.

Another refugee who had a big influence on the British car industry was Max (Mac) Goldsmith (Goldshmidt) (1902–83). He was born in Frankfurt, and by the age of 23 had his own company producing car components. He was a friend of Porsche, Daimler and Benz, when the German car manufacturers were in their prime and at the cutting edge of technology. Goldsmith also made a number of visits to Detroit to learn from the Americans, and brought their ideas and methods back to Europe.

When Hitler came to power, Goldsmith was threatened with a concentration camp if he didn't give up his patents and, in 1937, he fled to Britain. He went on to be instrumental in producing thermostats, single- and twin-disc clutches, and finding a substitute for scarce copper tubing in cars. Although he was interned for six months at the beginning of the war, he was soon back with his company, helping to improve tanks, naval vessels and aircraft. Of particular help was his importation of the American method of bonding rubber with metal, which was the basis of shock absorbers. His major invention, though, was the single-disc clutch.

Goldsmith set up in Leicester, and started with fifteen staff. At its peak, his company employed 1,000 people until it was sold to Dunlop. In 1970, Goldsmith retired and he devoted his later years to the interests of the town and his own community. He endowed a coronary unit in a Leicester Hospital, gave the town a vast record library and worked hard to improve the employment prospects of the blind and disabled. Goldsmith came from a very Orthodox family and was a major donor to Charedi projects.

Arthur Ney (1902–97) was another German–Jewish refugee who made a real difference in the Second World War. He had hoped to have a banking and accountancy career, but he saw the necessity to get out of Germany and, in 1936, he came to Britain and set up a firm called Londex. It specialized in electrical automatic-control apparatus. Nowadays, most people take it for granted that street lights will go on when it becomes dusk, but it is, of course, the control apparatus that enables this to happen. Londex also supplied control systems, so that seaplanes could see what they were doing when they landed on water at night. The company also provided lighting-control systems for lighthouses and harbour beacons. In later years, they produced photoelectric switches and time switches.

In 1962, Elliott Automation bought the company for £840,000 and Ney went on to sort out the problems of the Clark Clutch company, which produced electromagnetic clutches and brakes, and a cost-effective tension-control system. He was successful in this effort as well, and both brands continue to this day.

Cars have parts made all over the world. One of the best British post-war, car-part manufacturing companies was Tudor Accessories, the brainchild of another German–Jewish refugee, Fred Worms (1921–2012). Worms came from Frankfurt in 1937, was briefly interned during the war and eventually became a chartered accountant.

One day, his local garage man commented on how difficult it was to get wing mirrors for cars, and Worms determined to start his own company manufacturing car accessories. 'I was a know-all and wanted to do things my way.'[10] With a loan of £5,000 from his mother, and a staff of two in Hayes, Middlesex, Worms built up an organization which, by 1970, had a £2 million turnover. He produced windscreen washers, locking petrol caps, mud flaps and up to 200 accessories which cars and other industries needed.

In 1970, he moved to a new factory in a depressed part of Wales, which cost £500,000 and employed 400 people. James Callaghan, the local MP, who would become prime minister, spoke at the opening: 'We are very grateful to you for coming among us.' It was typical of Worms' philosophy that he chose to help a depressed area, even though there was no longer any incentive to do so coming from the government. The pre-war efforts to attract industry no longer applied in Wales.

Worms was, however, always a considerate man. In 1973, he sold out and devoted himself to a wide variety of good causes within the Jewish community. He was a power in the land of the charitable B'nai B'rith organization, the sporting Maccabi World Union and the student-oriented Hillel foundation. In 1998, he was awarded the OBE.

Car manufacturers created a world where, today, the roads in Britain are packed with cars. Yet, seventy years ago, after the Second World War, there were very few cars around and, therefore, very little in the way of traffic problems. Those were the halcyon days of no traffic wardens and no parking meters, when cars could be left almost anywhere, for almost as long as the driver liked. What might have been foreseen by any businessman was that people would want to own cars, and that car ownership would grow to previously undreamed of numbers, as the standard of living improved. Moreover, that this would produce an urgent need to control the inevitable resulting traffic congestion. As a result, the associated markets were likely to become vast and, if an entrepreneur was in at the beginning, there were fortunes to be made.

One man who recognized this potential was Rosser Chinn (1906–2000). Born in Wales of Lithuanian-Jewish parents, he left school at 14 and became an engineering apprentice. He abandoned his taste for that occupation when he lost a finger in an accident, and he spent some years thereafter as a tallyman in the Welsh valleys. Moving to London, he grew a moustache and added ten years to his age for an interview to get a job as assistant manager of a furniture shop. His recent experience, running a stall in the Caledonian market, stood him in good stead and, within a few years, he was able to buy his own furniture store.

It wasn't until 1946, however, when he was already 40 years old, that the opportunity occurred which was to make his fortune. A car park with 1,000 spaces in Soho couldn't pay for its tiling. The tilers took shares in the company in settlement and then sold them for the cash. Rosser and his brother bought them and, over the next twenty-seven years, they expanded into car dealership and vehicle leasing.

Rosser Chinn became very well known in the motor industry. He was gregarious and good at thinking outside the box. The problem was how to break into the magic circle of selling cars en masse? As the well-established and entrenched distributor companies were chasing deals with manufacturers like Ford and Vauxhall, it was with the small Swedish car industry that Chinn got involved. For thirty-four years, Lex, his company, imported Volvo cars. The car was solid, highly respectable and well made, even if it lacked romance and glitter. One of the markets, where it became almost a status symbol, was very Orthodox Jewish communities.

Later, when the government created a committee to try to ease traffic congestion, it was Rosser Chinn who came up with the idea of the multi-story car park. In 1973, when he retired to concentrate on raising funds for many Jewish charities – he was aggressive in his approach and extremely successful – there was a worthy successor. His son, Trevor (now Sir Trevor), took over the company and built it up to a far greater prominence. When, at the turn of this century, profits reached £65 million, it was a very long way from the small shop in Wales with which his grandfather had started.[11]

As the world of masters and servants faded in the memory, the public became accustomed to helping themselves in supermarkets, self-service breakfasts in hotels and using cash machines. One other innovation came from Gerald Ronson (1939–), whose company, Heron, had a number of petrol stations. It was Ronson who popularized the self-service petrol station. Everybody learned how to fill up their own car.

As traffic became an ever-greater problem in the country, a 1935 American invention, parking meters, came into operation. The difficulty here was to obtain a reliable supplier at a reasonable price, and Geoffrey Bloom's small company stepped into the breach. Bloom's main attraction was that he could be trusted to do what he promised – another Jewish business trait. Efficiency and trustworthiness may not seem to be difficult customer benefits to supply, but such companies are not so easy to find.

Max Joseph was once talking to the largest buyer of hotel rooms in the country, American Express. He was told quite bluntly, 'We've never used your hotels because they were particularly good, but because they have always been so easy to buy!'[12] The personal touch, the ability to talk to a human being, and the total absence of answering machines; they may not constitute rocket science, but these are some of the secrets of commercial success.

Manufacturing cars is one thing. Selling them is quite another, and it is the distributors who keep the wheels of the factories turning. Before the Second World War, in South Africa, Israel Jaffe imported cars, and his son, Abe (1929–2009), took on the business. In 1975, he bought a car dealership in Britain and, in 1978, changed its name to Currie Motors. It was Israel who coined the company slogan, 'Nice people to do business with', and Jaffe sold Ford cars on that basis for the next seventeen years. A problem developed when he wanted to sell other cars, but was prevented from doing so by the Ford agreement. In 1992, he therefore took a major risk, and gave up his twenty Ford dealerships.

This could have led to disaster, but the new Japanese manufacturers in Britain also needed good dealers, and Currie signed up with Toyota and Lexus. Jaffe also expanded into America, and set up a number of dealerships in the Chicago area. The third generation, Joe Jaffe (1955–), joined the board and, when his father died in 2009, he took over the running of the still privately owned family company. Israel Jaffe's wife, Annie, died in the same year a month before, also in South Africa, at the incredible age of 107. Today, Currie Motors has a turnover of about £150 million a year with its dealerships in South East England, but the margins in the industry are very tight and profits hover around the £3 million mark.

Car parking, car garaging and car sales; what would be the next business opportunity in the motor trade? As tourism grew throughout the world, a market emerged for car rentals but, initially, it wasn't taken very seriously. Travel agents didn't bother to sell car rental to clients, partially at least because their commission for doing so could come in months afterwards. The public, trying to hire a car at a competitive price in foreign locations when they arrived, weren't all that happy with the existing offers either.

The man who spotted this hole in the market was Clive Jacobs (1961–), but he would have seemed an unlikely candidate. Jacobs was born into a Jewish family in North London and left school at 15. He got jobs on building sites and in Selfridge's fish department, moving on to be a messenger in a travel agency. He was then employed to sell cheap air tickets and, at 21, he started his own company, European Airtours. As is so often the case, this only involved an office and a lot of hard work. Jacobs merged European Airtours with another small operator, but in 1986, the company collapsed. In 1987, looking for what to do then, at the age of 27, the possibilities inherent in car rentals occurred to him, and so he started Holiday Autos.

His product was simple; he offered the public the opportunity to rent a car in advance, at a guaranteed price, and payable in sterling. He also gave the travel agents immediate commission when they booked the cars. That was also the way Grand Metropolitan first got agencies to sell short break holidays. Travel agencies are far more interested in products where they can see definite financial benefits, preferably arriving instantaneously.

Holiday Autos grew to be the largest leisure car-rental broker in the world. In the course of the next fifteen years it achieved a turnover of £200 million, out of branches and franchises in thirty countries. From 1995 to 2003, it won no less than sixty-eight awards in eight countries for service and innovation. In 1999, Jacobs also introduced the first website, where you could book a car in the same way. In 1997, it was not surprising that Holiday Autos won the World Travel Market Global Award for its contribution to British Tourism.

Jacobs fits the entrepreneurial pattern. As the company expanded, he said, 'I'm a workaholic. I work 14–16 hours a day and even when I'm on holiday I keep abreast of what's happening.' It certainly wasn't easy in the beginning: 'In the early years when I was building my first company, I worked through the night as a minicab driver to earn a living. But my motto has always been that if you want something badly enough, you can get it – and I'm living proof of that.'[13] In 2003, Holiday Autos was bought for £43 million and, today, Jacobs is chairman of the TW Group, which publishes *Travel Weekly*, the industry's trade magazine.

NOTES

1. Richard Smethurst, *Korekiyo Takahishi, the Rothschilds and the Russo-Japanese War 1904–1907*. http://www.rothschildarchive.org/ib/articles/AR2006Japan.pdf.
2. John Cannon (ed.), *Oxford Companion to British History* (Oxford: Oxford University Press, 2002), from www.encyclopedia.com/topic/gustav_wilhelm_wolff.ASPX.
3. Michael Jolles, *Jews and Transport*, http://www.jtrails.org.uk/trails/Miscellaneous/articles/c-245/jews-and-transport/.
4. Christopher Andrew, *The Defence of the Realm* (Harmondsworth: Penguin, 2009).
5. Ibid.
6. *Jewish Chronicle*, 13 December 1935.
7. Obituary of Julius Berend Cohen by G.T. Morgan, 1935. www.rsc.org/delivery/.
8. Weizman to Ussishkin, 1905, Jeremy Schonfeld Archive.
9. Bill Cawthon, *A Visit to Oddball's Autos*, *Promotex* online, 1 January 2003.
10. *Jewish Chronicle*, 26 June 1993.
11. Rosser Chinn, *Jewish Chronicle*, 14 April 2000.
12. Author present at conversation.
13. Clive Jacobs official website.

Chapter twelve

There's no Business like ...

Jews had only played a small part in the initial development of show business in Britain. In 1742, Solomon Rietti had created the Ranelagh Pleasure Gardens in London, and an early pub theatre, the Brown Bear, was run by Ikey Solomons. A number of the music halls were run by Jews but, overall, when they arrived in Britain in reasonable numbers at the back end of the nineteenth century, the theatre was well established without them. Where, as with the music halls, a business had a strong connection with drinking, a lot of Jews kept their distance anyway; they always associated serious drinking with drunken mobs and pogroms. Pubs were definitely not their scene. Indeed, one of the complaints against the Jews coming to live in numbers in the East End at the end of the nineteenth century was that they ruined the trade of the local publicans by staying away, as had their multicultural predecessors.

As far as the legitimate theatre was concerned, there was also a language problem. The Ashkenazi Jews spoke Yiddish rather than English and their own theatrical performances were in the ancient language. A promising Yiddish theatre did develop in the East End of London, complete with its own stars, music and plays. The tradition continued until fifty years later, when the next generation of Jews began to forget their old tongue, and plays like *The Dybbuk* ceased to impinge on the native culture.

There was an additional problem with a career on the English stage: the performances on Friday nights and Saturday afternoons, which made the proper observance of the Sabbath impossible. Orthodox Jews didn't choose the profession for that reason. One evening, at the Palladium after the war, the Jewish American comedian, Danny Kaye, was topping the bill. It was on the eve of the Sabbath and he made a Jewish joke which was applauded. Kaye rounded on the audience and said, 'I have to be here on a Friday night, but why aren't you at home?'

Many Jews became theatrical agents and performers, but the only Jewish theatre-company developer of note at the end of the twentieth century was Sam Wanamaker (1919–93). He worked tirelessly to get the Globe Theatre reconstructed at Southwark, as it had been in the time of the first Queen Elizabeth.

If the community was too late to get into the well-established world of the Strand and Shaftesbury Avenue, it was in good time to take advantage of the invention of film. The wonders of the flickering screen proved a tremendous attraction to the general public, and cinemas started to spring up all over the country. They were primitive to begin with, but they would come to be called 'the Palaces of the People'.

In these days of small, multi-screen, single-feature cinemas with over-priced confectionary and often dull and utilitarian decor, it is difficult to recapture the glamour of going to a Picture Palace, like the State in London's Kilburn at the back end of the 1930s. The Hyams brothers had built a massive, 3½-acre extravaganza in a rundown London suburb, and it was the largest cinema in the world. Phil Hyams (1895–1997) was the oldest, then Sid and then Mick. Their father, Hyam Hyams, was an immigrant from Russia and, at the turn of the twentieth century, he owned a cinema called the Popular in Stepney. Before the First World War, Phil went to work for him to learn the business, and over the years the family built up a small chain.[1]

The brothers sold the circuit, H. & G. Kinemas (Hyams & Gale), to Gaumont British in 1928 and then set out to create monster cinemas with the proceeds. Cinemas like the Elephant and Castle Trocadero in London, which could seat 3,500. From there, in 1937 they opened the State. Within its vast auditorium you would see a programme of a main feature film, a second feature and a newsreel. From the bowels of the cinema would then rise a tremendous Wurlitzer organ, manufactured in Illinois, and costing the Hyams an astounding £28,000 (about £800,000 today). The organist was Sidney Torch, who was paid £250 a week when the national average wage was about £3. He would play the top tunes of the day and then there would be a stage show as well. The whole programme could easily last well in excess of three hours. The cinema was open for seven days a week, though performances didn't start until four o'clock on Sunday. The Lord's Day Observance Society was quick to clamp down on any infringements of the current Sabbath laws.

The State sat 4,000, and behind the circle seats there was standing room for another 4,000! There were continuous performances from early afternoon till late at night. There was also the opportunity to have a meal in the cinema restaurant, when restaurants in Britain were hard to find. The staff were dressed either in Ruritanian costumes or near-evening dress.

Admittedly, you could only enjoy the Italian Renaissance decor of the main lobby if you paid 7½p for your ticket. There was plenty of room at 4p, but then you had to go in through a side entrance to your seat. Dominating the lobby were two vast chandeliers, modelled on those in Buckingham Palace. But, where the State's had 125 lamps, Buckingham Palace's only had eighty. The State's chandeliers also had 8,000 pieces of crystal. Having boggled at the beauty of the chandeliers, you could go on to mount the Italian marble double staircase to the Round Lounge, but male patrons had to wear at least a bow tie with their shirt and coat. The tower was forty metres high, and 'A gold-green dome tops the incredibly large auditorium'.[2]

Not surprisingly, the Hyams brothers ran out of money before they could finish the State, but Gaumont British took a share and, in December 1937, the opening show included Henry Hall and his Orchestra, Gracie Fields, George Formby, Vic Oliver and a row of dancing fountains to further enliven the entertainment. That was a top-class variety bill for its day. Until the war, the cinemas were coining money, and the Hyams' policy, 'If you give 'em value for money, they'll come', proved absolutely correct.

The Hyams eventually sold out to Gaumont British in 1944, when a V1 or a rocket could still have knocked down almost any building. They went into film redistribution, but television spelt the end of the great British cinema-going habit. Phil was the last of the brothers to die, in 1997 at the age of 102. The obituary in the *Independent* labelled him, 'The last of the great showmen'.[3] What Phil Hyams and his brothers had done was illustrate how far you could extend the boundaries of the cinema industry.

As films grew ever more popular, there inevitably developed a number of chains of cinemas, one of the first of which was Essoldo. This was founded by Solomon Sheckman (1893–1963). The family came from Plock in Poland and started in business in North Shields, selling clothing to visiting seamen. Solomon Sheckman stayed in North Shields all his life. If it didn't have quite the glamour of Wardour Street and the West End of London, it was still home. He left school at 14 and bought a cinema fleapit, a ramshackle building, when he was 15. From this humble beginning he slowly created a company owning nearly 200 cinemas and halls. It was to be the third-largest chain in the country, and acquired its name from the first letters of his wife, Esther, his own name and those of his daughter, Dorothy – Es-Sol-Do.

Although a very dynamic personality, Sheckman always avoided publicity. He was very charitable and totally devoted to the world of the cinema. The peak period between the wars saw some 8,000 cinemas created in Britain. The boom lasted Sheckman's lifetime until he died in 1963, but the attempt after his death to change the halls over to Bingo was not a success.

The first Essoldo opened in 1930, just two years after the first Odeon was opened in Brierley Hill in the Black Country of the Midlands. This chain was the brainchild of Oscar Deutsch (1893–1941), its name an adaptation of Nickelodeon, as the first cinemas were called. Where Sheckman had bought and converted many old theatres into cinemas, Deutsch built his own. He adored Art Deco and to visit an Odeon in the 1930s was to be transported into a massive wonderland of ultramodern architecture. The expansion of the chain was meteoric and, by 1937, there were 250 Odeons in the country, but Deutsch died in 1941 when he was only 48.

Gaumont British was founded by Isidore Ostrer (1889–1945) and at its peak had 343 cinemas and 16,000 employees. Ostrer had been born in the East End where his father was a jewellery salesman, originally from the Ukraine via Paris. His daughter, Pamela, married the famous British film star, James Mason, who said of the Ostrer family, 'The five brothers had one opinion and one brain between them'. Everybody agreed that Isidore was brilliant and, after a stint as a stockbroker's clerk, in 1919 he started the grandiosely titled Lothbury Investment Corporation. His brothers, Maurice and Mark, joined him. They saw the potential of cinemas and, in 1927, floated Gaumont British. Isidore was chairman, Mark, vice chairman and Maurice, joint managing director.

The Ostrers moved into film production as well and, at Lime Grove in Shepherd's Bush, London, they made the Jewish Michael Balcon (1896–1977) their production chief. Balcon had started Gainsborough Pictures in 1924 and made many good films during the 1930s, including musicals starring the most popular British star, Jessie Matthews, who was also Jewish. He really got into his stride, however, when he became director and production chief of Ealing Studios, which produced some of the finest comedies ever to epitomize the quirks of British life: *The Titchfield Thunderbolt*, *The Ladykillers*, *The Lavender Hill Mob* and *Kind Hearts and Coronets* were brilliant examples.

There is a plaque at Elstree which Balcon had put up; it reads, 'Here during a quarter of a century many films were made projecting Britain and the British character.' It is a modest enough memorial to a company which gave filmgoers enormous pleasure. Altogether, between 1938 and 1957, Ealing produced ninety-five feature films and dramas such as *The Cruel Sea*, *The Blue Lamp* and *Scott of the Antarctic*, which were all great successes.

The only comparable British producer between the wars was Sir Alexander Korda (1893–1956). Korda was a Hungarian Jew (Sandor Kellner), who eschewed small productions and took on Hollywood at its own game. He arrived in Britain in 1931 and persuaded the Prudential to finance the building of Denham Studios for him. There he was responsible for the most successful British film up to that time, when he made *The Private Life of Henry VIII*. His London Studios Company was also responsible for such fine films as *Rembrandt*, H.G. Wells' *Things to Come*, *The Scarlet Pimpernel* and *The Thief of Baghdad*. With his brother, Vincent Korda, designing the most elaborate sets, Korda set standards which no other British director could approach, though, after the war, a considerable number of fine films were also made by the Jewish Boulting Brothers, Roy and John. Mention should also be made of Emeric Pressburger who, with the non-

Jewish Michael Powell, produced such great films as *The Life and Death of Colonel Blimp*, *A Matter of Life and Death* and *A Canterbury Tale*.

In addition to the massive cinema groups, there were other Jewish entrepreneurs who made a difference, like Elsie Cohen (1895–1972) who, in 1931, opened the Academy Cinema in London, to show major foreign films. This was the first art-house cinema in the country and, although the venue was closed by bombing in 1941, Elsie Cohen had shown by that time that such a cinema could be a viable financial proposition.

Of all the British Jews in show business since the war, the most successful in making Hollywood films, and the highest profile today, is probably Michael Winner (1935–). A flamboyant character with a fine, self-deprecating sense of humour, he made a number of successful films, and his food-critic column in the *Sunday Times* has been very popular for years.

There was another invention in the nineteenth century which was to transform the entertainment world, and for which profitable development opportunities were available to Jews, who had the courage, foresight and intelligence to exploit them. In 1877, Thomas Edison worked out how to reproduce sound, and so invented the phonograph. Naturally, there were teething troubles and it took some years for the quality of the sound reproduction to be perfected. It was the cylinders on which the sound was recorded that could be improved most easily. In 1888, an American Jew, Emile Berliner, created the round disc on which the record was played from side to side, instead of up and down. As Britain was the greatest trading nation, Berliner decided to form a British organization for this burgeoning industry and, in 1898, he launched the Gramophone Company.

Making gramophones was one thing. Selling them was another and, naturally, firms which were already selling musical instruments should have recognized the possibilities straight away. The most successful of those that did was Barnett Samuel & Co. The original Barnett Samuel (Boruch ben Shmuel Loblinski, 1819–82) was born in Gniezno in Poland and migrated to Sheffield. There, as a young man, he joined with two partners to create a company that would sell musical instruments, as well as tortoiseshell doorknobs, knife handles and combs.[4]

Samuel was a religious man and a founder, in 1863, of the orthodox Bayswater Synagogue in London. In 1869, his third son, Nelson (1853–1920), joined the firm and, when Barnett died in 1882, he took it over. He served as a warden of the Bayswater Synagogue and he was a strong supporter of the Jewish Stepney Schools. When he died in 1920, he was sadly missed in both the musical and Jewish worlds.

In 1878, Barnett Samuel & Co. had opened its first harmonica factory and by 1901, 'the firm was one of the largest musical instrument wholesalers in the country and had its own piano factory in North London'.[5] By 1914, they were also one of the largest record wholesalers, and they had just patented the first portable gramophone, the Decca Dulcephone, with the strapline, 'She shall have music wherever she goes'. Nobody could foresee one of the next mass markets for these portables: they were to become extremely popular in the trenches during the First World War, where the monotony of waiting for orders to advance could be allayed a little by listening to records. After the war, Frank Samuel (1887–1954) became the moving spirit of the company and, by 1927, 22 per cent of the gramophones exported from Britain came from Decca.[6] The sales of records was seven times the level pre-war; when the company floated in 1928, the issue was oversubscribed twenty times. At which point Samuel decided he had had enough and departed.

Samuel had maintained the growth of one major company. He was now invited by an old school friend, Sir Robert Waley Cohen, to take over an ailing part of the Unilever business, the United Africa Company. He was instrumental in turning it round from loss making to a £14 million profit, but from 1946 to 1951, it was responsible for the Tanganyika (Tanzania) Groundnut Scheme, which failed somewhat disastrously. A man with a strong sense of justice and an ability to concentrate fiercely, Samuel was not just a Jewish businessman always in the office. Before he died, he was also president of the Orthodox United Synagogue organization.

One of the steps on the road from record cylinders to stereophonic sound and DVDs was the invention, in America in 1925, of the Westrex Electric recording system. This improved the quality of the sound reproduction enormously and its manufacture in Britain was the work of another Jewish entrepreneur, Sir Louis Sterling (1879–1958).

Sterling was born in Russia and taken to New York when he was 3 years old. He left school at 12, sold newspapers and, in 1903, came to England on a cattle boat. He celebrated his arrival rather too well and was put in jail overnight. When he was knighted by George VI in 1937, the king asked him how he had spent his first night in Britain. 'I was a guest of your grandfather, Sir', said Sterling.

In a couple of years he started his own Sterling Record Company, sold out to the pre-eminent American Columbia company in 1909, and became their sales manager in Britain. The British subsidiary grew famously but the American parent fell on hard times. In 1922, Sterling raised the money to buy the British subsidiary and when, in 1925, Columbia in America went bankrupt, he found the finance to buy it for $2.5 million.[7] Columbia was now a British company and, with a licence for the Westrex recording system, it flourished. The shares, which had only a nominal value before, increased in price by 100 times from a very low base. That licence cost Sterling $50,000; his gambling instincts were well tuned.

In 1931, when the Slump was destroying record sales – they plummeted 80 per cent in the 1930s – Sterling put the Columbia, HMV and Parlophone record companies together as EMI, and became managing director of the new company until 1939. During the difficult years of the 1930s, he opened the legendary Abbey Road studios in 1937. Of rather more importance were the products of the EMI laboratories. There, under the supervision of Sir Isaac Shoenberg (1880–1963), Alan Blumlein produced the first TV transmitter for the BBC, enabling the corporation to start the first television service in the world.

By 1939 Sterling was 60, and when the EMI board decided to appoint a managing director for the Gramophone Company division without his approval, he resigned. An immensely charitable man, when he died in 1958, *Gramophone Magazine* said of him, 'Few men have been as well loved as Louis Sterling and one may speculate whether any businessman has ever been as much loved as that remarkable little man.' Sterling estimated that he had given away about two-thirds of all the money he had earned.

Dance tunes sold a large proportion of the gramophone records before the war and bands who could play that kind of music became very popular. The influence of American jazz, and more intimate forms of dancing, created the need for something more than the sedate Palm Court Orchestra. Among the great line-ups of the Dance Band era in the 1930s and 1940s were the Jewish Benjamin (Bert Baruch) Ambrose (1896–1971), Gerald Bright (Geraldo 1904–74), Harry Roy (Harry Lipman, 1900–71), Nat (Nathan) Temple (1914–2008) and Joe Loss (1909–90).

There have been Jews involved in football-club management and cricket county presidents, helping to run British athletics and playing in many sports. The one who made the biggest impact on the public was Jack Solomons (1900–79). He started promoting boxing and boxers in the 1930s, and when he retired in the 1960s, he had set up twenty-six world title fights.

Solomons once said, 'I was born in Petticoat Lane and that makes me a Cockney and British as well as being a Jew. And I'm proud of being all of them.'[8] He started his business life as a fishmonger in the Petticoat Lane market, and fought three times as a featherweight under the name of Kid Mears. He then tried putting on small boxing shows in the East End at a venue called the Devonshire Club, which was a converted church in Hackney. He eventually attracted crowds of up to 1,500. At the time, the licensing of boxing shows was the responsibility of the British Boxing Board of Control but, in 1939, Solomons resigned from the organization to put on his own shows without interference. His bill in that year, featuring Eric Boon, was the first fight to be shown on television.

After the war, he started to stage really important contests, like the American Gus Lesnevitch versus Freddie Mills for the world light-heavyweight championship. The two fights for which he will be most remembered were, in 1951, when Randolph Turpin beat Sugar Ray Robinson, a great American fighter and, in 1963, when Muhammad Ali defeated Henry Cooper. Solomons came to dominate British boxing: 'To see Jack Solomons at the ringside was to understand why he was called King Solomons. His face beamed with satisfaction, his outsize cigar belched smoke, his hands fell on appreciative shoulders in warm greeting. It was as fine a performance as any given by the brilliant boxers in the ring.'[9] In 1978, Solomons was awarded the OBE for his work for charities, which included a campaign that raised £60,000 for the Bud Flanagan Leukaemia Fund for the Royal Marsden Hospital.

Thanks to EMI, television sets could be found in many well-to-do homes before the Second World War, but the development of their manufacture and the mass ownership of sets was delayed for the duration of the conflict. When services were restarted after 1945, television remained a BBC monopoly until sustained lobbying led to agreement to allow commercial channels to be set up. The right to broadcast was then divided into sections of the country, and two Jewish companies came into the market. These were Granada, which gained the Manchester–Liverpool franchise, and Associated Television, which was granted London.

Granada TV was the brainchild of Sidney Bernstein (1899–1993). His family left Latvia in the 1890s, and his father, Alexander (1870–1922), was a shoemaker. He had a contract to supply boots to the Boers, but this disappeared when the Boer War started in 1899. As a result he went bankrupt. He got started again by buying land in Edmonton, which at the time was way out on the outskirts of London. To entice buyers to take up the land, Alex Bernstein decided he needed an attraction.

So he put up the Edmonton Empire Theatre and ran it initially as a music hall. When he died in 1922 he owned twenty cinemas. Many had been built in cooperation with the construction firm, Bovis, which had been bought in 1909 by Samuel Joseph (1888–1944) when he was 21 years old. In 1942, Joseph would be elected Lord Mayor of London and knighted. His son, Sir Keith Joseph, had a major influence on the political thinking of Margaret Thatcher. The further expansion of Bovis would also owe much to a Czech refugee, Sir Frank Lampl (1927–2011), who chaired the company from 1985 to 1999.

Bernstein invested heavily in the new art form, and the building company shared the risk. Bernstein and Joseph put up cinemas, like the Granada in Tooting, designed by the Romanian Jew, Theodore Komisarjevsky, whose original training was at the Imperial Institute of Architecture in St Petersburg. For suburban Tooting to have a building conceived from a pre-revolutionary Russian background and with a heady confection of Moorish, renaissance and classical architecture, was something of a culture shock, but it proved immensely popular.

Alexander Bernstein had been one of the founders of the East Ham and Manor Park Synagogue, which he later served as warden and treasurer.

Sidney Bernstein, his son, took over the company on the death of his father, and became film adviser to the government during the Second World War. This was against the advice of MI5, who did not trust the scion of an immigrant family with such a crucial role. Bernstein proved a good choice, though, and ended the war, from 1944, as head of the film section of the psychology and warfare division at the Supreme Headquarters of the Allied Powers in Europe (SHAPE).

After the war, Bernstein formed the Transatlantic Picture Company and tried his luck in Hollywood. He had one great hit with Alfred Hitchcock's *Rope*, but then dissolved the company and, in 1954, wrote to the Independent Television Authority for permission to produce television in Manchester and Liverpool. He had started the campaign in 1948 but didn't get his way until 1957.

The tone of Granada's productions was epitomized by Bernstein's reaction to a thorough professional he tried to recruit. Philip Mackie wrote to him, 'I see you are offering me the post of Head of Drama'. Bernstein replied, 'No, I'm asking you to be in charge of plays'. One such production was 'Coronation Street', which has been a popular soap opera for longer than half the country has been alive.

In Bernstein's time, as head of Granada, there was a very tight circle controlling the company. It consisted of his brother, Cecil, who was an accountant and a director for business matters. The position of primus inter pares has seldom had much attraction for the founders of Jewish businesses, and Bernstein was no exception in his intention to run the show without undue interference. His hero was not, however, David Garrick or D.W. Griffith. Instead, he gave instructions that every office in Granada should have on a wall a framed picture of P.T. Barnum, the great American showman: 'There is a sucker born every minute' was his contribution to human understanding. Granada, nevertheless, soon won a well-deserved reputation for the quality of its programmes.

The other main television franchise to go to a Jewish company was Lew Grade's Associated Television, which kept viewers glued to their sets with everything from *Robin Hood* and *Sunday Night at the London Palladium* to *The Saint* and *The Prisoner*. Originally Louis Winogradsky (1906–98), he was born in Russia and the family fled the country in 1912. At his school

90 per cent of the children spoke Yiddish. His entry into show business came about in 1926 after he won a Charleston dance competition. He decided to become a professional dancer, but in 1934, gave that up to become a booking agent with the Jewish Joe Collins, the father of Jackie and Joan. The popularity of the iconic Quintet of the Hot Club of France (Stéphane Grappelli and Django Reinhardt were the famous names) was one of their successes.

After the war, Grade spent time in America and loved the Hollywood-mogul image. He looked exactly like the boss of a major studio, smoked a number of very fine, very big cigars every day and was a much-larger-than-life character. He was exceptionally good at selling his British television programmes in America, which helped the balance of trade considerably. His greatest success in this field was his decision to produce Jim Henson's *Muppet* series in 1976. The innumerable lovers of *The Muppets* are indebted to his ability to spot potential winners, and could have seen the award of his life peerage in the same year as a suitable 'thank you'.

Unfortunately, it is almost impossible to always make the right decision and, in 1980, when Grade decided to make *Raise the Titanic*, he committed one of his rare mistakes. As he contemplated the vast losses which ensued, he mused, 'It would have been cheaper to lower the Atlantic'! There was a feeling after *Raise the Titanic* that Grade was past his sell-by date, though he made fine films like *On Golden Pond* thereafter. Always influential, Grade remained a guru in the industry until his death in 1998. In the family, his nephew, Michael (now Lord) Grade (1943–), was also to be a major player.

Although Brian Epstein (1934–67) could not claim to have founded a massive manufacturing or retailing empire, he did put Britain firmly on the modern record map, when he became the manager of the Beatles. Epstein's Jewish family came from Lithuania at the back end of the nineteenth century, and they finished up with the North East Music Stores in Liverpool. Epstein was not the ideal child. He was expelled from two schools in Southport for laziness and poor performance, and went into the family business after army service and dropping out of RADA.

He met the Beatles at Liverpool's Cavern Club, when they were struggling and, in 1962, agreed a contract to be their manager. Looking back on their amazing success, it is surprising that Epstein was unable initially to get any record company to produce their work until, at last, he got a contract from Parlophone, a small EMI label. From then on the Beatles went from strength to strength, and Sir Paul McCartney said, 'If anyone was the fifth Beatle, it was Brian'.

With his management company, NEMS, Epstein also looked after Cilla Black and Gerry and the Pacemakers, transforming the image of British rock music and making the Beatles a worldwide phenomenon. Sadly, in 1967, he died from an accidental overdose of drugs.

Michael Green (1947–) was still at school when Sidney Bernstein was trying to get an agreement for commercial television. He had won a scholarship to Haberdashers, but left at 17 with four O-levels, which would seem to indicate a dislike for the books, rather than an inability to master them. His grandparents were refugees from Eastern Europe, but his father had done well with Tern drip-dry shirts. Green and his brother, David, had the clever idea of producing a direct-mail service for estate agents, and did so well with mail-order catalogues that they were millionaires by the time he was 21.

When, in 1972, Green married Sir Isaac Wolfson's daughter, he became part of one of the most important families in the Jewish community. His entry into the world of television was as a supplier of technical equipment, through a company called Carlton Communications. When it was floated in 1983, it had a turnover of £13.4 million and had made a profit of £2.7 million. Less than twenty years later its turnover was over a billion and its profits £118 million.

The key to Green's success was in persuading the prime minister, Margaret Thatcher, to change the criteria by which commercial television franchises were awarded. Where originally the quality of the programmes likely to be made was considered of great importance, now the major consideration would be the amount paid for the licence. Over the years, Green made higher offers than the competition. The most notable example was when he outbid Thames Television for the London contract, paying £43 million. In addition, he bought one of the great Hollywood icons, Technicolor, for $780 million in 1988. Green didn't make programmes; he bought them all in, and with substantial share stakes in Central, GMTV, ITN and West Country TV, he had a commanding position in the industry.

There were two sides to Green's personality. His good friend, Lord Young, a member of Margaret Thatcher's cabinet, said, 'The great thing about Michael is that everybody likes him, he really is immensely likeable, probably the most pleasant successful individual I know.' He could also show great sensitivity. Gerald Ratner, another friend, remembered, 'he let me win at tennis once when I had a problem'.[10] On the other hand, Jeff Randall, the business editor of the BBC, said that when things went sour, there was 'A backlash from investors who for years had to endure his volcanic temper and a preference for confrontation rather than conciliation'.[11]

The bridge too far for Green came in 1997, when he joined a consortium to bid for the national digital terrestrial TV licence. Originally Sky was part of the group, but in the end it was not included in the winning team. Which was just as well for them because, in 2002, the company, ITV Digital, collapsed and by 2003, it had lost £1.2 billion on the venture. In that year, Carlton and Granada merged, and it was confidently expected that Green would be the new CEO. To everybody's surprise, a good third of the shareholders demanded his resignation and he had to stand down. A meteoric rise and fall.

Show business is built on first-class public relations. The glamour is hyped, the best actors are called stars and a great deal of spurious publicity attempts to keep the pot boiling. Behind all the flimflam, though, there is the necessity to provide the technical back up which will enable the public to enjoy the programmes. In Britain, in the world of television, for many years the viewers were indebted for that to Jules Thorn (1899–1980).

Born in Austria in 1899, Thorn was Jewish but not a refugee. After service in the Austrian army during the First World War, in 1920 he came to Britain as the representative of an Austrian electrical company. When the firm ran into financial difficulties, he started his own firm as the Electric Lamp Service Company and started to rent out radio sets. Nowadays, when everybody expects to have their own radio and TV, it is difficult to imagine a time when they were such luxuries that large swathes of the population hired them. In 1936, Thorn bought Ferguson Radio and floated his company in the same year, when its share offering was thirty-six times oversubscribed. During the first year of trading, the company made £42,000 profit. Forty years later, in Thorn's last year as chairman, the company would make £956 million profit.

Thorn was comfortable with new technology. He spotted the commercial possibilities quickly and his firm, Thorn Electrical, was early into tape recorders, record players and TV rentals. When TV resumed service after the war, Thorn only had one rental shop. By 1968, under the name of DER, it had 397. Those rental shops had over a million customers that year. Thorn also made TV sets, and one advantage of the rental business was that it could take surplus sets, manufactured in the summer, but not selling in the quiet period.

Thorn showed many typical Jewish characteristics: in business, he ran the show. He was managing director from 1937 to 1969 and chairman from 1937 to 1976. He wasn't a large man and he gave the impression of gentleness when you first met him. If that was the whole story though, he wouldn't have finished up second only to Phillips in lighting manufacturing. Nor was it easy to become the largest maker of TV sets in Britain, which he achieved in 1964. Thorn could be as tough as he needed to be. He was always prepared to gamble on new developments and even on the potential of horses. His colt, High Top, won the 2,000 Guineas in 1972.

As the years went by, the burden began to tell on him. The company 'lost momentum as Thorn aged'.[12] He retired in 1976 and, just before he died, the business merged with another giant, Louis Sterling's EMI creation, which managed to lose a billion pounds in 2010.

Thorn was knighted in 1964, the same year that he set up the Sir Jules Thorn Charitable Trust. Over the years – and it is still doing tremendous work – the Trust has given the best part of £100 million pounds to medical research, establishing nursing homes for the disadvantaged and a host of other good causes.[13]

One entrepreneur who was into and then out of the music business in just fifteen years was Michael Levy (1945–). Born into a very poor Orthodox family in the East End, Levy lived in the family's one room till he was 9. By dint of hard work, he set himself up as an accountant and in

1973 started Magnet Records, which he sold to Warner Brothers in 1988 for approximately £10 million. 'What Michael does is he picks people, trains them, then he backs them. He is the greatest salesman I have ever met in my life.'[14] One of those he nurtured for five years was Chris Rea, who eventually sold 30 million albums worldwide by 2009. Rea said that Levy was, 'One of the hardest bastards I have ever met, but I would leave him with my children rather than anyone else'. Levy's record company at one time sold 10 per cent of all the records in the pop charts.

When he left the music business, Levy devoted his life to charity work and to supporting the Labour Party. He financed Tony Blair's private office and was well known as the prime minister's tennis partner. In 1997, he was made a peer and acted as treasurer for the Party. It was estimated that he raised £70 million for Jewish charities and £40 million for Labour in ten years. He has always been a controversial character, but his intelligence, tenacity and ambition have stood him in good stead.

There is one other aspect of show business which fascinates Jews, and that is gambling. There have been numerous countries where, for many centuries, it was considered common and vulgar to be 'in trade'. Bookmaking would certainly come under that heading. If, however, a Jew was trying to survive in a highly competitive environment, the indulgence of deciding what would enhance his social status, and what was beneath his notice, was not a luxury he could afford. While it is perfectly true that gambling is the Jewish disease, there were a number of Jews who sensibly realized that the profits in gambling were more likely to be made by the bookmakers and casino owners than by the punters.

Bookmaking had begun at the end of the eighteenth century when Harry Ogden was the first man to offer to take bets on races at Newmarket. The wagers were, primarily, made by the gentry, and the phrase, 'the sport of kings', set down a marker that this was a form of entertainment where ordinary citizens were not expected to participate. Betting on horses spread to the London clubs and officers' messes but remained, primarily, an upper-class pursuit. The Gaming Act of 1845 made the wagers unenforceable in law and the Betting Act of 1853 restricted gambling to the racecourse. Bets made in a shop were strictly illegal, and many who tried to take bets in this way, or on the street, were prosecuted.

The ambience of horse racing was, however, foreign to most immigrant Jews. They were intimidated by royal patronage, stewards from the peerage, events such as Ladies Day at Ascot and the immense amounts of money at risk. It was alright if you were a Rothschild or a Sassoon, but Jews were almost all out of their depth in the more expensive enclosures at Newmarket or Epsom.

At just the right time, there came a new form of racing. In 1926, in Manchester, greyhound racing began. The impressively named Greyhound Racing Association was founded and, in 1927, a new track was set up on the site of the 1906 Olympic Games stadium, the White City at Hammersmith in London. This was far more manageable. No royalty, no peers, only six runners in a race, a far more urban crowd of punters, and on the doorstep. It was well worth a try.

Among those who dipped their toes in the water was a Polish immigrant called Joseph Kagalitzky (1904–96), who had been born in Warsaw and, in 1912, came to Britain with his mother. Right at the beginning of the new greyhound-racing fad, he decided to take a pitch and he progressed to establishing speedway and greyhound tracks, including Haringey, with his partner, Tom Bradbury-Pratt.

Kagalitzky changed his name to Joe Coral and, as a senior citizen, he recalled his beginnings as a fledgling bookmaker: 'In my early days I used to drive about with a big cigar, in a big flashy American car, like all the rest of them. I had to create an air of confidence and prosperity – it's all part of the showmanship. Otherwise the punters won't bring you their business.'[15]

It was perfectly true, but the image of the flashy Jew with a camel-hair coat and a big cigar was one which aroused derision in the upper classes and jealousy in the have-nots. Coral didn't worry about belonging; he didn't even try to get naturalized until 1952, when he was nearly turned down because he had thirty-nine driving offences and a conviction for perjury in his naturalization application. It was eventually decided to approve his application as an official remarked, 'For a bookmaker in Stoke Newington, he is not a bad fellow'.[16]

It was the Betting and Gaming Act, 1961 that transformed the fortunes of the bookmaking industry. Off-course gambling was legalized and by the 1970s there were four major companies: William Hill, who was not Jewish, and Coral, Ladbrokes and Stanley Leisure who were. In 1962, there were 13,340 bookmakers' offices, and Coral had twenty-three of them. By 1977, there were 13,254 and he had 589.

The company had been floated in 1964, when the profits were £248,000. It is never easy to forecast profits in the world of bookmaking, because it depends very much on which horse or dog wins. Well-backed winning favourites are not good for bookmakers' profits. Coral still forecast a 50 per cent dividend on the 5p shares and suggested that this would be covered a respectable 2.15 times. Coral diversified into social clubs, casinos, holiday camps and hotels, but by 1981 he had had enough. He sold the business to Bass, remaining life president. He was a popular figure, slightly built, now quietly dressed, softly spoken and driving a Rolls Royce Silver Shadow. He died in 1996.

Another giant company, emerging originally from the pre-war dog tracks, was the creation of Mark Stein, who set up as a small bookie after he, too, emigrated from Russia. He decided that an English name would look better on his board at the track, and so he traded as Max Parker. He also provided jobs and an apprenticeship for members of his family, one of whom was his nephew and successor, Cyril Stein (1928–2011).

One of the prominent Victorian stables was Ladbroke Hall and, in 1886, Messrs Schwind and Pennington started a company to take bets on the horses trained there. In 1902, the company name was changed to Ladbrokes and, for the next fifty years it continued to be a bookmaker for the gentry. In 1956, however, having fallen on hard times, it was bought by Max Stein and his nephew Cyril. The younger Stein had been weaned on bookmaking and was absolutely ready for the Betting and Gaming Act, 1961, which made betting shops legal too.

Stein was a very Orthodox Jew and inherited the tradition of being a great innovator. He took advantage of every empty niche in the market. He introduced 'No Limit' and 'ante-post' betting and extended the opening hours of the organization to take into account the needs of punters at evening greyhound meetings. He introduced fixed odds for betting on football matches, he was the first bookmaker to sponsor a race – at Newmarket – and the first to take bets on general elections.

Such an opportunity suited Max Joseph of Grand Metropolitan very well. He put £50,000 on Labour, to win £37,500 in the 1964 election. In today's money that's a £1.6 million bet to win £1.2m. Labour won and Max Joseph collected his £37,500 winnings. He then pointed out that, if the Conservatives had triumphed, he expected his shares on the stock market to go up by as much as the bet; a somewhat novel form of insurance.

When the government legalized casinos in Britain, Joseph plunged in straight away. His first casino was in the main ballroom of his May Fair hotel. Admittedly, there were some 200 bookings to use the ballroom, but Joseph closed it immediately and left it to his sales director to sort out the cancellations. Grand Metropolitan became the country's largest casino operator for some years. The sales director gave up the hotel business and became an MP. Stein would take bets on anything. In 1974, he opened a book on who would become the next archbishop of Canterbury, and offered long odds on the chief rabbi being the successful candidate!

In 1962, Stein opened his first betting shop and went on to open thirty-five every week for a long time. In 1967, he floated the company very successfully. Certainly, there were glitches as the company expanded. For example, he opened casinos, but an unwise attempt to gain more members by poaching them from competitors led to the company losing its casino gaming licences. Not all the property developments were successful either, but when Stein decided to go into the hotel business, it proved a masterstroke.

He started in 1972 with three newly built hotels and, when Max Joseph died in 1982, there was plenty of room for another major player. In 1987, when the airline TWA was in terrible trouble, Stein bought its Hilton International hotel-chain division for £1 billion. When Ladbrokes was floated in 1967, its value was £1 million. When Stein retired in 1993 its value was £2 billion.

Bookmaking still didn't have an upmarket image in Britain after the war, but this didn't concern Leonard Steinberg (1936–2009), the founder of Stanley Leisure, one of the future major players in the industry. Steinberg was tough-minded. His parents were refugees from Russia who settled in Northern Ireland. His father, Isaac, took the name of Stanley for his business dealings and started three companies: manufacturing optics, running a milk bar and operating an illegal betting shop. His son started as a bookmaker in 1954, when his school friends asked him to put bets on the Derby for them. When the winner came in at 33–1, Steinberg made £1 and decided this was easy money.

When he died in 1954, Isaac Steinberg was only 47 and, within a couple of years, the optical and milk bar sides of the family fortunes had foundered under Leonard's management. All that was left was the illegal betting shop, but the situation changed when the government legalized them. Leonard started Stanley Leisure, named after his father. The business expanded satisfactorily because the Irish love a bet, but when the Troubles began, the sectarian violence was accompanied by the development of all kinds of protection rackets. Steinberg stood his ground and refused to pay. Some of his betting offices were burnt down, his staff were threatened and, in 1977, he was shot twice in the legs on the doorstep of his home.[17]

When he recovered, he left Ireland. He moved to the North West of England and set out to prove the leading firms in the industry wrong. London was their magnet for gambling, so Steinberg didn't develop in London for many years. He went into towns which the major companies considered had insufficient profit potential. He took on what others didn't want. If he had but known it, Steinberg was the latest in a line of Jews that went back in England to at least Carl Hambro, supporting Cavour in Italy 100 years before. Steinberg was determined to prove his olders, if not betters, wrong about the availability of punters.

Which was exactly what happened. He built up a massive company, eventually did move into London and even bought Crockford's, the venerable eighteenth-century gambling house. Stanley Leisure became the largest casino operator in the country and, in 2003, opened the largest single unit in Britain, the Star Casino in Birmingham. With forty gaming tables, 200 slot machines and eighty games, there were almost unlimited ways for customers to lose their money. Before he died in 2009, he had sold his 600 bookmaking shops for £504 million, his forty-plus casinos for £639 million and amassed a personal fortune of over £100 million.

His last battle was with the government over betting duty. Many of the major firms had decided to set up offices overseas, to enable the punters to avoid tax by, effectively, betting outside the country. This threatened employment in the industry in Britain and its likely destruction. Steinberg, now as a member of the House of Lords since 2004, was influential in the eventual compromise. It was agreed to eliminate the 9 per cent betting tax on the winnings of punters, in exchange for a 15 per cent tax on the gross profits of the companies.

What made Steinberg so successful was his persistence and his determination. In his soft Irish lilt he once said, 'I don't want put on my gravestone "he was a nice guy". I'd like to have "he always spoke his mind". I've known a lot of nice guys who have never done a thing with their lives.'[18] Apart from becoming one of the most respected leaders in his industry, Steinberg packed a great deal into his own life. He supported the Conservative Party and was elected president of the Lancashire Cricket Club, which he considered one of his proudest moments. He set up the Stanley Family Charitable Trust, was the first chair of the Northern Ireland Friends of Israel and also amassed a fabulous art collection and a fine stamp collection.

The traditional world of bookmaking was that of pitches on the courses, betting shops and telephones to back your fancy from your home. Where was the niche market for the small newcomer? The answer was the potential provided by on-line gambling, the opportunity to use the Internet. The bookmaker who was fastest away from the start was Victor Chandler (1951–).

Chandler's grandfather started the business in 1946, and did well enough for his grandson to be educated at Millfield. The lad didn't intend to go into the family business, but when, in 1973, his father died at the early age of 50, there was a family which needed supporting. Chandler took over and, in 2006, the *Racing Post* called him 'arguably the most famous bookmaker in the world. He is the Indiana Jones of bookmaking, the fearless, swashbuckling layer who lit up Britain's racecourses for two decades.' *The Daily Mail* added in 2007 that he was 'about as far as you could get from the traditional image of a bookmaker. Charming, modest and a gracious host, he has the air of an archetypal, middle-aged English company chairman; not a trilby in sight.'

Gambling is a major worldwide industry, often associated with malpractices of various kinds. It is to the credit of both the British industry and successive governments that there has been comparatively little in the way of scandal to hold back its progress as part of the UK economy. Chandler has played a large part in extending the international market, often only after extensive court cases with governments who wanted to stop him developing his promotion of games like poker. Overseas gamblers now use his services extensively, but to make his product as attractive as possible, in 1999 he moved the company to Gibraltar where it is now the biggest employer.

The *Daily Mail* may have failed to spot a trilby, but Chandler possesses almost all the great Jewish entrepreneurial skills. Obviously, he is a gambler. He began in a domestic industry, but recognized its possibilities for international development. He, too, was not blinded by traditional methods, but saw the opportunities thrown up by the modern developments in IT. He saw the gap in the market before others, and was prepared to argue his case internationally with other governments. If there are no trilbies, the ghost of a yarmulke hangs in the air.

Another Jewish bookmaker made a very different impact in the racing world. In the 1960s, Michael Tabor (1941–) borrowed the money to buy two betting shops in High Wycombe. From that small base he built up a chain named Arthur Prince, which he sold to Corals in 1995 for £28 million. At the same time he had developed a passion for owning race-horses, and in that same year, 1995, he saw his Thunder Gulch win the Kentucky Derby at 25–1. He followed this up with Desert King, who won the Irish Derby in 1997 and, with Irish partners, won the Epsom Derby with Galileo in 2001 and High Chaparral in 2002. Not surprisingly, Tabor features in the *Sunday Times* Rich List.

The latest gambling product is on-line poker, and the popularity of the Texas 'Hold'em' variety has made many fortunes for those good enough and lucky enough to win. Among these has been Tony Bloom (1970–), who comes from a comfortable Brighton family and was educated at Lancing and Manchester University, where he gained a Mathematics degree. Bloom spent his pocket money as a child on one-arm bandits, and gambling became his great love. After a couple of years in an accountants' firm following college, he gave it up to become a professional gambler.

This was successful, but when the bookmakers, Victor Chandler, wanted somebody to develop the Asian handicapping market, they made Bloom an offer, and he spent three years at their office in Gibraltar. Asian handicapping is betting on the results of football matches, but with a difference. The teams are handicapped, with the poorer side given an advantage over the better one. So if you wanted to back Accrington Stanley to beat Manchester United away, you might be given a two-goal advantage to begin with. Only if the result was that Manchester won 3–0, would you lose.

Bloom mastered all this and, in 2002, started his own business, Premierbet. In poker circles he became known as Tony (the Lizard) Bloom because a friend said he had alligator blood. He specialized in Asian handicapping, but in his spare time he also won poker tournaments. By 2009, he had won over $2 million. Bloom sold Premierbet, started Tribeca Tables, sold that for $75 million and then started and sold St Miniver, a company which specialized in on-line bingo. He has also raised the necessary money for Brighton and Hove Albion's new stadium, the club to which his family have been devoted fans for many years.

It may seem strange for the British balance of payments to be supported by the profits companies make from international gambling, but that has been the effect of the Internet. Naturally, if you're a professional gambler, the future is always uncertain, but Bloom has certainly made the grade in a big way so far.

NOTES

1. Juliette Soester, Willesden Local History Society, www.london-northwest.com/sites/wlhs/books.htm.
2. Ibid.
3. *Independent on Sunday*, 20 October 2003.
4. Grace's Guide, *The Best of British Engineering, 1750–1960s*. www.gracesguide.co.uk.
5. Ibid.
6. Decca Prospectus, *The Times*, 24 September 1928.
7. 'Frankly Speaking', BBC, 1957.
8. *Jewish Chronicle*, 28 December 1979.
9. *Independent*, 17 February 1997.
10. Geoffrey Foster, *Management Today*, 1 May 1996.

11. David Richings, Thorn Trust.
12. Paul Vallely, *Independent*, 18 March 2006.
13. *Jewish Chronicle*, 24 April 1970.
14. *Daily Telegraph*, 1 November 2005.
15. The author in conversation with Lady Steinberg.
16. *Liverpool News*, 2 November 2009.
17. *Daily Mail*, 22 April 2007.
18. Andy Naylor, *The Argus*, 22 May 2009.

Chapter thirteen

Someone has to be a Developer

Although there were many fine mansions built by rich Jews in the nineteenth century, there were very few property developers. Sir Isaac Lyon Goldsmid developed Palmeira Square in Hove, and added hundreds of houses to Brunswick Town. Emanuel Lousada is credited with some Regency houses in Sidmouth in Devon, but Jews were seldom landowners and built little other than their own homes and offices. There was one notable exception: in 1885, Nathaniel Mayer Rothschild formed the Four Per Cent Industrial Dwellings Company. He recognized the deplorable housing conditions in the East End of London and was determined to try to alleviate the situation by encouraging like-minded philanthropists to do something about it.

The funds for the housing were raised by offering a return on investment of 4 per cent a year, where the dividend on Consols, government gilt-edged stock, was 3½ per cent. £50,000 was raised (£26 million today, using average earnings as the criteria). The idea was to provide poor people 'with excellent accommodation consisting of two rooms, a small scullery and WC which could be supplied at a weekly rent of five shillings [25p]'.[1] By 1905, 1,500 flats had been built and there was a waiting list of 1,000 for new ones. One of the rules from the beginning was, of course, that tenants should not be restricted to Jews. In 1952, the company was renamed the Industrial Dwellings Society (1885), and it is a Registered Housing Association today.

Although 1,500 flats would only make a dent in the demand for better housing, the real significance of the Four Per Cent Industrial Dwellings Co. was that it was the predecessor of council housing. What the Jewish philanthropists had started, local councils would eventually pick up and improve upon.

One of the necessary attributes for the survival of the Jews was the determination to be upwardly mobile. Time and again, over the centuries, they had struggled to achieve a reasonable standard of living in one country or another, and then had been expelled or taxed into penury again. The Jews who came to Britain as a result of the pogroms in Eastern Europe, from 1880 to 1914, were no different. They knew that one important measurement of wealth in the wider community was the ownership of land, and in many countries they hadn't been allowed that option. If most of them had to start again in menial jobs, they wanted their children to own land and, particularly, to do better than they had.

The professions were the ultimate objective. Hence the jokes about every Jewish mother wanting her son to be a doctor. A solicitor or an accountant would also do – but what if the lad didn't have the mental ability to aim so high? Then one answer was the occupation of estate agent. The studies were less rigorous, the competition was less entrenched and they could be involved in property.

Between the wars, a lot of young Jews left school to become estate agents. In London, a number joined a firm in Mayfair called Dudley Samuel & Harrison. Dudley Samuel was the doyen of Jewish estate agents. The biggest task in his time was to find shop premises for the growing number of multiple stores which were expanding and, of course, to sell houses. Jackie Phillips was another major player, who obtained the site for the BBC's building in Portland Place.

When, however, the war could be seen to be approaching, there was a disastrous slump in property values. The bombing of towns, like Guernica during the Spanish Civil War, had shown that you didn't have to be in the front line to have your house destroyed. So the question arose, if the Germans bombed British cities, what would happen to the value of the properties destroyed? What compensation would the government provide to repair them, if any? And when? Worse, if the war was lost, there would definitely be no compensation.

Consequently, property prices slumped, especially because vast numbers of people were evacuated from the major towns at the beginning of the war. The banks could have foreclosed on any number of developers at the time. Alec Colman would have one of the most prosperous property companies after the war, but his firm was saved by a moratorium on debts. This, the lenders – the banks, building societies and insurance companies – applied very widely. As Colman recalled, 'But for the moratorium on building society loans, I would have been bust. No question of it.'[2] Max Joseph was a successful pre-war estate agent too, buying and selling property on his own account, but he was also caught by the drop in prices. He owed his cousin, Victor Mishcon (later Lord Mishcon), £500 for seven or eight years.[3] Jackie Phillips's company did go into receivership and, in 1939, he died bankrupt on Christmas Day.

Where Jewish property owners suffered like everybody else, a considerable number of their brightest entrepreneurs, particularly the young, decided to take a pragmatic view about the future. They knew that, if the Nazis won, they were going to finish up in gas chambers anyway. If the Nazis lost, the value of property was going to recover. That led to the logical conclusion that now was the time to gamble and buy property – and many did.

The Blitz on London wasn't as bad as the Great Fire in 1666. That destroyed 437 acres of the capital, where the Blitz only accounted for 225 acres. Reconstruction took a long time. When the war was over there was still, naturally, a tremendous shortage of building material, as the war effort had swallowed all the available supplies. To even replace the offices the government needed, it was necessary to set strict priorities. If your plans didn't involve the government, there was a long queue to get planning permission to do anything about repairing the damage.

The situation only slowly improved. The Conservatives regained power in 1951 and, in 1954, the minister of works announced in the Commons that, 'Licences are now issued freely in nearly all areas, and neither the cost nor the inconvenience caused to architects and contractors can any longer be justified.'[4] The floodgates were opened for repairs and new constructions. A large number of Jewish entrepreneurs took the opportunity to become involved in the mammoth task of replacing the country's bombed offices, shops and houses, and improving old office blocks and buildings. The necessary basic ingredients were very simple:

a company, a site, a design and the money to build it. There was no need for a large office, a substantial number of employees or machinery. Max Joseph worked from a tiny office with a telephone and a secretary. In 1958, from that base, he bought Dolphin Square, a very large block of flats, for £2.375 million (£42 million today). This was not at all unusual.

The aim of the owners of property, bombed or otherwise, was to maximize their income. When income tax could be as high as 90p in the pound, this was an uphill struggle, but there was no capital gains tax if the income came from selling property. Because of this, Joseph was also able to buy the freehold of the St Ermin's Hotel in Westminster for only £500,000. The owner had been paying almost all the hotel's profits out in tax, but the money gained, if he sold, was not subject to the same level of taxation.

Joseph then borrowed a leaf out of Joe Littman's book. That ex-furrier had a company called Aldford House, and had spent some of his spare time between the wars buying up pieces of London's Kilburn High Street. He financed many of these purchases by selling the freeholds and then taking a long lease from the new owner. Sale and leaseback was soon recognized as a good manoeuvre within the profession. It enabled Joseph to get £625,000 for the property from the Church Commissioners, when he sold them the St Ermin's freehold. He then took back a forty-year lease at a rent which was paid by the office block which abutted the hotel and came with the deal. It was a fantastic coup.

The aim of the property developer was to keep as much of his profit as he could legally achieve. Land which received planning permission for redevelopment obviously had an enhanced value. This was not taxed until July 1948, when a 100-per-cent development tax on the increased value was imposed. It only applied to the increased value of the land, though, and it was abolished in 1952 by the Conservative government. Even when it was in operation, it didn't apply to the restoration of blitzed buildings. If even a few bricks were still standing, the whole building could be reconstructed without the development tax applying.

The problems facing the authorities in restoring London to its former condition were immense. It wasn't just that so much of the capital had been bombed. It was also that no resources had been available for refurbishment during the six years of the war. To make matters worse,

London had also grown shabby during the Slump, as so often the necessary money to keep up the infrastructure was not available. It was recognized in the City that it was essential for a major world financial centre to look the part, but there was an immense amount of work to do if this objective was to be achieved.

To make matters even worse, there was the fact that so much of the land was in the ownership of organizations which had not kept up with the times. In 1948, the Church Commissioners was formed by a merger of the £70 million of the Queen Anne's Bounty and the £40 million of the Ecclesiastical Commissioners. So far, so good, but the core problem was to convert the resulting organization from being simply a landlord, to an organization which would maximize the return from its enormous assets. The salaries and pensions of a lot of vicars depended on the Commissioners getting it right.

The property developer whose advice was to prove crucial was Max Rayne (1918–2003). He had been recommended to the Church Commissioners because of the work he had done for the Portman Estate, one of the old, established families that owned so much of the capital. The Portman Estate, at the end of the war, owned 258 acres of London, most of which it had held since 1533. Max Rayne was the grandson of a synagogue minister and the son of a Polish tailor, Philip Rayne, who had migrated to Britain before the First World War. Max had joined his father after his service in the Second World War, and realized that the building they owned for their company was far larger than they needed. So he leased off the surplus and found himself in the property business.[5]

Rayne's first major coup was a £2 million deal with the Portman Estate for an office development near Selfridges. He went on to advise the Church Commissioners to redevelop the swathe of land they owned in Bayswater, between Paddington to the north and Hyde Park to the south – the Paddington Estate. This dilapidated area was to become one of the most expensive housing projects in the district. In addition, a set of office buildings was put up opposite Paddington station which cost £1.75 million and, by 1996, made a profit of £5.8 million. This was achieved by setting up a joint company consisting of the Church Commissioners and Rayne's London Merchant Securities.

The Church Commissioners financed the whole operation and the profits were split 50/50. Rayne's share was £2.9 million and his initial investment in the company was £1,000. This successful cooperation led the Church Commissioners to work with many other developers in future years, but it was Rayne who pointed them in the right direction. Many other ancient estates like the Bedford, Eton College, the City Livery Companies and Howard de Walden took notice.

Max Rayne's contribution to the country broadened when, in 1962, he set up the Rayne Foundation. For the rest of his life, he was a major player in the work of any number of charitable organizations. He was asked to serve on the boards of most of the London teaching hospitals and became vice chairman of Jewish Care. He gave the London Library the endowment it needed to stay afloat and, from 1971 to 1988, was chairman of the National Theatre.

Always immaculate, as befitted the son of a tailor, 'his real monument lies in the vitality of the countless organisations that he brought into being or enabled to achieve new success'.[6] In 1976, he was made a peer. The only criticism was that, 'He worked others, as well as himself, far too hard'.[7] Rayne handed over to his son, Robert (1949–), who remained chairman until 2002. The Rayne Foundation still dispenses £400,000 a year to charities, and London Merchant Securities has gone from strength to strength.

Of course, an estate-agent background provided a great deal of professional knowledge of the market, but the Jewish entrepreneurs came from every kind of background. Sidney Block (Hallmark Securities) was a solicitor, Bob Harris (Harris & Co.) was a furrier, Cecil Fox (Stem Properties) was a tailor, Barnett Shine (Central & District Properties) was a skirt manufacturer and Harold Wingate (Chesterfield Properties) was a chemist. You could also name thirty former estate agents, including such future luminaries in the industry as Jack Cotton (City Centre Properties), Harold Samuel (Land Securities) and Harry Hyams (Oldham Estates).

Initially, in the world of property, most of the Jewish companies were minnows. They couldn't in any way compare with the major insurance companies, merchant banks, old established estates and building societies.

That so many of them were able to enter the marketplace and do so well says something about the executives of those companies who could have been their competition, but stayed away. It was another example of the individual founder versus the grey-flannel-suit man; the entrepreneurial boss against the paid – often highly paid, but still paid – employee.

For the senior member of staff of a major company, a large error could have a disastrous effect on his career. Post-war property development was potentially a commercial minefield. If, on the other hand, the company director followed the normal company line, stuck to well-tried formulas and didn't put his head very far above the parapet, his salary, company car, share options and pension were as safe as he could reasonably expect them to be.

For the Jewish entrepreneur none of this mattered. There was just the ambition to make a fortune for himself; nothing really to do with a company, when the staff roster was one chief and a secretary. He knew the risks he was taking: the building might not find a tenant; there could be industrial strikes and delays in the delivery of vital components; the market could become saturated and space rentals collapse. It was enough to discourage a very large percentage of the grey-flannel-suit men. Which left so much of the field open to the men whose ancestors had gambled against the odds time and again. A lot of Jewish companies did fail, but a high percentage of the successful ones were Jews as well.

Naturally, those who had remained in London during the war had a head start. Two wartime firemen, the sons of a bookmaker, were David (1905–52) and Joe (1906–90) Levy. Their company redeveloped the north side of Euston Road in London, between Regents Park and Tottenham Court Road. It was a massive site, involving 315 individual plots. Part of the project was to enable the council to widen the roads and Joe Levy gave them £2 million worth of land for that purpose. This donation was often a quid pro quo for getting planning permission, but it was the only way the councils could legally obtain the land they wanted at a price they could afford. They were restricted, by law, to only offering pre-war prices.

Like the Levys, most of the most famous Jewish property developers of the time had left school without qualifications. One exception was

Harold Samuel (1912–87) who did pass the exams of the Royal Institution of Chartered Surveyors at the College of Estate Management. In 1944, he started Land Securities. The assets were then about £30,000 but, by 1952, they were over £11 million and by 1967, £193 million. It looked inevitable that competition to redevelop London was going to be fierce in the future. Louis Freedman (1917–98) therefore decided to try his luck in the provinces. With Harold Samuel's support, he formed Ravenseft Properties, which did a tremendous amount of rebuilding in town centres like Bristol, Coventry and Plymouth.

Louis Freedman's uncle was Joe Freedman, who started his business life as a pedlar in the Welsh valleys but ended owning, with Sir Julien Cahn, the Jays & Campbell chain of furniture shops. Louis finished up as deputy chairman of the Jockey Club and the owner of a Derby winner. As the family had always had its fair share of wild gamblers, Louis recounted that as he led the horse into the winners' enclosure he thought of the relatives in heaven saying, 'At last we made it'![8]

Another experienced developer was Jack Cotton (1903–64), who had owned his own business in Birmingham since 1924 when he was 21. It was his City Centre Properties which developed the Big Top site at the junction of New Street and High Street in the city. It was the first major shopping centre development, and created a sensation when it opened. Today, its architecture is not much admired, but somebody had to be first.

Even small towns could be enhanced by good property men. Gabriel Harrison (1926–75) redeveloped a swathe of Lytham St Annes in Lancashire. The town had been created from the sand dunes by a small group of Victorian businessmen in the late nineteenth century and, in 1962, Harrison's Amalgamated Investment & Property Company bought it, 'lock, stock and pier'.[9] Here was the opportunity to improve the town, and thereby increase the value of the land which Amalgamated had bought for £240,000. Through a series of other shrewd deals Harrison built up Amalgamated to be the eighth-largest property company in the country. A generous man, when times were good he donated the Seething Lane Gardens to the City of London and gave £100,000 to the North Kensington Amenity Trust.

During the halcyon years, it wasn't necessary to be brought up in the property business to make a fortune. Lew Hammerson (1916–58), whose share from the sale of the family clothing company was £15,000, started his property company in 1942 after being invalided out of the army. He died young, but Hammersons went on to become the third largest property company in the country and, in 2007, entered the FTSE 100. Perhaps his most remarkable building was completed just after his death: Castrol House in Marylebone Road in London was entirely faced with very colourful green-glass panels, a long way from the traditional Victorian brick. His company in later years would develop the Brent Cross shopping centre in North London. In his memory, his wife Sue paid for the Lewis W. Hammerson Memorial Hospital in Barnet.

In the early post-war years, the accepted practice for a large number of the companies was to find the site, borrow the money from the banks at a low rate of interest, and then build offices, for which there was a tremendous demand as the City of London started to grow again. The building would then be mortgaged to a building society or insurance company at a fixed rate of interest and for a long period of years, without rent revisions. This happy state of affairs for the developers was due to the fact that high inflation was simply not the norm. If the Retail Price Index is taken as 100 in 1837, in 1937 it was only 135. The figure nearly doubled by the end of the war, but this was considered an anomaly.

Many of the developers made enormous profits, and the whole property world became extremely unpopular in a Britain with strong socialist leanings at the time. In a country coming out of a period of stringent austerity after the war, it seemed unfair that a few people could make fortunes out of repairing the destruction which had cost so many lives. Ten per cent of the offices in London had been destroyed in the war, but by 1966 there was 72 per cent more office space than there had been in 1939.

The fact was, however, that somebody had to do it, that the property developers had no responsibility for the Blitz, and they broke no laws in developing their companies. They might be subject to jealousy and envy, but they were simply able and courageous businessmen. It was easy to see how successful they were in retrospect; it was a far more hairy prospect in advance. They didn't have the advantages of the nineteenth-century

Prince Regent, who arranged to have a considerable area of the West End cleared and much of Regent Street, Great Portland Street and Regents Park built on the sites.

If the government had wanted to stop businessmen profiting from speculation, they made some major blunders in their efforts. Take one of the largest new office blocks, Centre Point, at the junction of Oxford Street and Tottenham Court Road in London. The council wanted to ease traffic congestion by building a roundabout. They could only buy the land at pre-war prices, which were unrealistic in post-war conditions. So Harry Hyams (1928–), who had created Oldham Estates, offered to buy the land for them, in exchange for an unofficial agreement that he'd get planning permission to build the office block on the rest of the site.

It had happened many times before. It was perfectly legal. As Joe Levy was to negotiate with his site further up the road, Hyams paid out £1.5 million for the land that he gave free to the council but in return, in 1959, the council leased him the land for the 385ft-high skyscraper for £18,500 a year – for 150 years! There were no rent revisions. It was a gold mine for Hyams – and then the council decided to make Tottenham Court Road one-way, so that the roundabout was hardly necessary!

Another regulation which aided property developers was the law that you could get planning permission for a site you didn't own. This was changed in 1959 by a provision in the Town and Country Planning Act, but it had meant that developers could buy a property, knowing that they could build on it. There was nothing to stop the owner finding out that planning permission had been given, but many institutions, and those who were naive, didn't bother.

Developers were also helped by the fact that council planning authorities were often not very good at negotiation. The planners were hampered by regulations, which could be used for purposes for which they had not been originally intended. Many old Victorian houses and office blocks had high ceilings. If they were knocked down, the new buildings might have far more letting space, even though the buildings were no larger overall than before.

Publicly quoted companies grew rapidly. If 25 per cent of the shares in a company were owned by the general public, there was no capital gains tax until 1962. Family companies floated in profusion. Where, in 1958, property-company shares were worth £103 million, in 1962 they were valued at £800 million. When the bad publicity against property speculation had grown to a crescendo, Harold Wilson's government thought it would be popular to stop any future office building in London. This would end the problem, as they saw it. George Brown guided a law through Parliament to this effect, banning all new office building in the capital. As a result, however, with no further supply coming onto the market, the growing demand was bound to result in higher rents. The property companies made another fortune.

When it came to illegal practices, there was one notable exception to the generally scrupulously honest conduct of the industry. A minor government minister was discovered to have taken petty bribes, something like a box of cigars, for obtaining permits for businessmen for various kinds of scarce materials. By comparison with the scale of corruption in overseas countries it was minuscule, but Britain rightly sets very high standards.

The man who bribed the junior minister was the Jewish Sidney Stanley (1899–1969), born Solomon Wulkan, and alias Stanley Koszyski and Stanley Rechtand. In 1948, the unsavoury details emerged in an official government enquiry, called the Lynsky Tribunal (after the judge). Because it was investigating government corruption, anybody called to give evidence was obliged to do so. As long as he told the truth, however, he could not be prosecuted afterwards for the offences which he had admitted. You can't be forced to incriminate yourself.

One or two prominent Jewish businessmen were peripherally involved. Isaac Wolfson gave evidence. The tribunal lasted three weeks. At the beginning Wolfson had black hair. At the end it was white. It took a number of years and an immense amount of charity – Wolfson College, Cambridge and Wolfson College, Oxford being just two major beneficiaries – before the slate was apparently considered to have been wiped clean, and Wolfson received a knighthood. Yet, at no time had he, in legal terms, any stain on his character.

Not all the stories of the property boom had happy endings. Two of the most prominent property men to come to the fore were Charles

Clore (1904–79) of City & Central and Jack Cotton, of City Centre. In 1960, they decided they could work in harmony and merged their companies. The result was one of the largest property groups in the world, and Cotton's ambition to be chairman of such an enterprise led to him offering far too much for the shares in City & Central. It was considered unlikely that Clore would accept second billing on the board, but when the subject was broached to him, he said, 'For 70 shillings (£3.50) a share, I'll be the office boy'.[10]

The problem for a lot of the entrepreneurs, however, often emerged when they had to move from being, effectively, a one-man band, to running a major organization. Cotton was accustomed to having all the information in his head about the various deals in which he was engaged. To run a massive property company that way was a terrific strain. Cotton was a heavy drinker as well. As early as June 1963, the other directors of the organization produced a memorandum itemizing the things of which they disapproved in Cotton's management. There was a meeting and Cotton resigned on the grounds of ill health. In November 1963, he sold his shares in the company to Isaac Wolfson for £8.5 million. In March 1964, he died of a heart attack at 51.

One of the smaller property companies was Eldonwall, which was founded by David Young (1932–). Young became one of a number of Jewish ministers in Margaret Thatcher's governments. He was the son of a coat manufacturer and became a solicitor. When he found this unattractive, he set out on a business career, and was fortunate to have some excellent gurus to provide him with the necessary training. From 1956, he was Isaac Wolfson's assistant and there was no better mentor. He obtained funding for Eldonwall from the Gestetner Family Settlements and went into industrial property, together with construction and plant hire. In 1970, he sold out to Barry East's Town & City and went on to help Jeffrey Sterling create the modern P&O. His career was transformed, however, when he joined the Centre for Policy Studies, as an adviser to Sir Keith Joseph (1918–94) on privatization. Joseph was, in his turn, a guru for Thatcher.

Young later accepted the role of chairman of the British Organization for Rehabilitation by Training. This body achieved good results in teaching people how to adapt to new jobs and, in 1981, he became chairman of the Manpower Services Commission. Unemployment was very high at the time and Young was brought into government as a minister without port-folio in the House of Lords. Mrs Thatcher went on record as saying that ministers always brought her problems, but Young brought her solutions.

Young had a distinguished career in the cabinet, but retired from politics in 1989 and later chaired Cable & Wireless. In the Jewish world, he was the first president of Jewish Care from 1990 to 1997, the umbrella organization for efforts to coordinate Jewish voluntary aid for the weaker members of the community.

Some property men just found the going too tough. Others failed to foresee that the good times don't go on for ever. When a property crash came in 1973, Gabriel Harrison's Amalgamated Investments, for one, was very exposed. In 1975, Harrison died bankrupt and, in 1976, Amal-gamated went into liquidation.

On the other hand the cleverest developers walked away unscathed. One such was 'Black Jack' Dellal (1923–), his nickname deriving from his passion for gambling. Born in Manchester of a Persian Sephardi family, in 1972 he sold his bank, Dalton Barton, for £58 million, to Keyser Ullmann. He became deputy chairman of Keyser Ullmann, but it had to be rescued by the Bank of England in later years. When he was 64, he bought Bush House in the Strand in London. He sold it six months later to a Japanese company for £74 million more than he paid for it. In 2008, at 85, he showed a profit of £150 million after selling the Shell Mex building in the Strand, which included the Edwardian, 1,000 bedroom Cecil Hotel.[11] Not surprisingly, the *Sunday Times* called him 'one of the most amazing money making machines to pass through the City since the war'.[12]

If it's easier to avoid disaster in a boom period rather than a slump, it's also true that slumps don't bring down the canniest practitioners. British Land was founded in 1856, but in 1971 its assets were only £37 million when it was owned by Jim Slater. He was a non-Jewish business meteor whose fringe bank, Slater Walker, exploded in and out of prominence before being brought down in the 1970s in the secondary banking crisis. Sir John Ritblat (1935–) bought the wreckage and built British Land up to assets of £1.6 billion in 1990. Today it has a portfolio of £20 billion.

The property companies were also on the lookout for under-utilized assets. If they could buy a company which wasn't trading to the best advantage, it could be transformed if it was taken over. Such attempts were not always conducted in a gentlemanly manner. Harold Samuel and Charles Clore recognized that the Berkeley Hotel in Piccadilly owned by the Savoy Hotel Company would make a fortune if it was knocked down and rebuilt as an office block. They made a bid for the whole Savoy Company in 1953 and, according to Samuel's partner, Louis Freedman, the result was the most anti-Semitic defence he ever came across in his career.[13]

The power in the Savoy company at the time was Sir Hugh Wontner, who would be elected Lord Mayor of London twenty years later, and was alleged to have marshalled a defence using such questionable tactics. In Parliament, one Conservative MP voiced the popular feelings of the time: 'Is it not in the national interest that our best hotels should be preserved as such, and would it not have been a tragedy if the group in question had been bought by speculators?'[14] Well, not for the shareholders of the Savoy Company, it wouldn't. In the end the Savoy bought up the shares Samuel and Clore had amassed in the company and the two entrepreneurs retired from the battlefield, defeated in their objective, but considerably richer.

When businessmen try to get a better return for the company's assets, they are often condemned as asset strippers. The criticism makes no sense. Directors have a legal responsibility to act in the best interests of their shareholders; not those of the government, or of the unions or of the heritage. If the value of a company asset can be improved, it must be, or the directors are negligent. That is commercial reality. Ignoring the facts, however, gets a warm round of applause at many political party conferences.

Of course, many of the property companies needed estate agents on their teams and, in its heyday, one of the top three was a Jewish Yorkshireman, Edward Erdman (1906–2003). Erdman started his business in 1934 with a £1,500 loan and trained many future leaders of the profession, including Sir John Ritblat. In 1974, Erdman retired, the firm declined and, in 1995, went into receivership.

Many of the Jewish property men created charitable trusts and worked for charities. Joe Levy was chairman of the Cystic Fibrosis Trust for twenty years and in 2000, the Edward L. Erdman Environmental Library was opened at Fitzwilliam College, Cambridge. John Ritblat financed the Sir John Ritblat Gallery at the British Museum to house its treasures, and Harold Samuel bequeathed to the Corporation of London his collection of Dutch Old Master paintings when he died in 1987; the director of the Victoria and Albert Museum estimated its value at £100 million Maurice Wohl (1923–2007), of United Real Property, donated a Virus Research Centre at University College, London, a General Dental Practices Centre at King's, a laboratory for the Institute of Liver Studies and a Research Fellowship to the Royal College of Surgeons in Edinburgh.

When George Brown stopped new office building in London, a considerable number of the Jewish developers called it a day and enjoyed a comfortable retirement. Slowly over the years, however, a new generation stepped into their shoes, though they had to survive the property slump of the 1970s. Among them were British Land, the Canadian Reichman brothers who built Canary Wharf in the redevelopment of London's Docklands, and Elliott Bernard (1945–) of Chelsfield. Bernard bought 90 per cent of the failing Merry Hill Shopping Centre business in the West Midlands from the receiver for £35 million, and turned it into a £2 billion operation. Gerald Ronson (1939–) of Heron is another major player.

The efforts of the present generation have helped to enable Britain to modernize much of its property infrastructure, and often the size of the developments dwarfs the efforts of most of the post-war developers. The golden age, however, was that brief ten years, between 1954 and 1964, when the ravages of the war had to be repaired. A representative list of Jewish property companies is in Appendix B; it is estimated that about 70 per cent of the property companies at the peak of redevelopment were Jewish.

When it comes to landlords, as against property developers, the biggest success story was Osias Freshwater (1897–1976). A penniless refugee from Galicia, he managed to reach England three days before the outbreak of the Second World War. His wife and three children were stranded in Poland and died in the Holocaust. Slowly but surely, over the next thirty years, Freshwater built up his company until, when he died, he was London's biggest private landlord with over 20,000 tenants. The company is now run by his son from his second marriage, Benzion (1948–).

The importance of landlords to the economy is that they are a vital cog in the infrastructure of a city. If there aren't enough decent homes, the city can't house the workers who are needed to keep everything going, from transport systems to hospitals, and from local councils to the hospitality industry and tourism.

There is always a suspicion, when it comes to landlords, that there will be one or two villains among them. One Jewish property owner was the – originally Polish – Peter Rachman (1919–62), who treated his tenants so badly that the government finally took notice, and passed the 1965 Rent Act to give tenants additional protection. Rachman was a pleasant personality and had fought in the Second World War after a period in a Siberian labour camp. It is more significant, however, that the Oxford English Dictionary now has the word 'rachmanism' in it to denote any 'greedy, unscrupulous landlord'. Rachman was popular, however, with the newly arrived black immigrants to whom he was always willing to rent property. At the time, blacks were often discriminated against and refused accommodation.

The more acceptable face of being a landlord is the Pears family who grew their property portfolio for sixty years from 1952, under grandfather William, son Clive, his wife, Clarice, and three grandsons, Mark, Trevor and David. They formed the Pears Trust and now give about £6 million a year to Jewish and non-Jewish charities. Another major landlord is David Pearl (1945–), who built his company, Structadene, from the humblest beginnings. His father worked in a hat factory, and life in Stamford Hill in North London was very hard. Pearl left school at 15 with no qualifications, and became a packer in a clothing factory and a part-time croupier. In 1965, at the age of 20, he decided to start a property-management and letting agency called Pearl & Coutts, with his own contribution being £75. The first property had a mortgage of £7 a week and Pearl rented it out for £10 a week. His third property could only be bought by his mother guaranteeing the cost, with the collateral of the family house.

It was a long haul for Pearl; ten years in his office in Hackney, buying houses at auctions and trying to find the capital he needed to expand. It wasn't until 1978, when he had changed the name of the company to Structadene, that he was able to take on his first employee. His big break came in 1980 when he was backed to buy the Jesus Bethnal Green Hospital Estate of 350 houses for £1.2 million. By 2007, his company had 1,500 commercial and residential holdings, and Pearl's fortune was estimated at £230 million.

As his predecessors in the property boom after the war had discovered, there were plenty of opportunities. Pearl is the kind of entrepreneur who achieves a great deal by understatement. He is said to be permanently dressed down and famously scruffy. Relationships are casual: 'I have 27 joint venture partners and I don't have [legal] joint venture agreements with any of them. We buy properties together. We shake hands, do a deal and that's the way it is.'[15] In recent years the state of the economy has not made life any easier, but Structadene is still one of the biggest companies in the industry; its net profit in 2010 was £22 million.

Other newcomers from the next generation included Eddie (1951–) and Sol (1953–) Zakay, two Israelis, headquartered in London, who started their Topland property company in the 1980s and ranked twenty-ninth in the *Sunday Times* Rich List in 2011, with a fortune of around £2 billion. There are also Vincent (1956–) and Robert (1960–) Tchenguiz who have been involved in both the property and trading sectors almost since the family first arrived from Iran in 1979.

The Jewish community in Iran was well treated by the Shah and thrived. The Tchenguiz grandfather had owned most of the cinemas in Iraq and, when he had to flee to Iran, his son ran the Iranian mint. When the Shah was overthrown, a great many of the resident Jewish community didn't fancy their chances in a state now controlled by an Ayatollah. They left in droves and many countries welcomed them, including Britain. They were Sephardim and their generosity benefited the Sephardi community in particular.

The Tchenguiz brothers created a company called Rotch Property and it traded on a vast scale. It was said to have borrowed £3.5 billion and bought £4 billion worth of property. In 2007, Vincent Tchenguiz said he was trading £750 million a day in currencies. A great deal of the money was borrowed from banks in Iceland and, indeed, Tchenguiz was said to be their biggest debtor. The whole exercise ended in tears when the banks failed and the creditors wanted their money back. 'Robert famously lost £1 billion in 24 hours in a scramble to raise cash.'[16] In 2007, the brothers had been in the *Sunday Times* Rich list in 78th place with a fortune of £850 million.

Another of the new generation is Laurence Kirschel (1943–), who started Consolidated Developments in 1983 with £5,000. The company now has over £200 million in assets and is deeply involved in property in the Soho and Tin Pan Alley districts of London. Other majors still with us include Heinrich Feldman's (1935–) Inremco, Dr David Gabbay's (1944–) O&H Holdings, Leo Noe's (1956–) F&C Reit, Cyril Dennis' (1949–) Rumford Investments, with Manny Davidson's (1931–) ASDA Property Holdings, now part of British Land.

For London to remain a major financial centre, there has to be sufficient office space to house the vast number of firms who want to have a presence in the capital. So there has to be a constant increase in the number of new buildings. Among those who have contributed to that increase are Sir David Garrard (1939–) and Andrew Rosenfeld (1962–). Garrard was the son of a Stamford Hill Jewish upholsterer and left school at 16 to go into an estate agency. Rosenfeld got his BSc in Estate Management at the South Bank University, and passed his surveying exams as well. They both finished up at a property company called Land Investors and, when it was sold, in 1988 they started Minerva, a classic property developer, with Garrard as chairman and Rosenfeld as CEO.

The original capital was £70,000. In 1996, they went public and when they stood down before the property bubble exploded, the company was worth £600 million. In the twenty years, they built such new City landmarks as the Walbrook and St Botolph's House, which added a million square feet to the office space available. Another million came from their new Minerva building.

Rosenfeld's greatest contribution to the country, however, was his leadership in a campaign to raise money for the National Society for the Prevention of Cruelty to Children. Called Full Stop, it raised £268 million, the largest total ever for a charitable effort. He also served as chairman of Fund-Raising and Appeals for UNICEF.

Last, but certainly not least, there is Favermead, the property company of Dr Nasser David Khalili (1945–). Khalili was born in Iran to a dynasty of antique dealers and he completed a degree in Computer Science at New York University, and a DPhil in Art History from London University. He was always fascinated by Arabic art and started collecting it at an early age. In 1978, however, it was becoming obvious that the Shah's days were numbered, and Khalili came to London with the large exodus of Jews from Iran. He set up Favermead, which developed shopping centres and office buildings in the City. After thirty years of trading and collecting, the Khalili figures are astronomical; the art collection has 20,000 pieces and is valued in billions of pounds.

There is now a Nasser David Khalili Chair of Islamic Art at the School of Oriental and African Studies at the University of London, and a research fellowship in Islamic Art at Oxford. His Maimonides Foundation exists to promote interfaith dialogue between Moslems and Jews. There have been thirty-five international exhibitions of parts of the Khalili collection. Khalili is known as 'the Cultural Ambassador of Islam' and has been given honours by two popes. In a world where so many Islamic countries have a stated wish to destroy Israel, it is remarkable that the best collection of Arabic art has been carefully accumulated by a Jew.

NOTES

1. *Jewish Chronicle*, 13 March 1885.
2. Oliver Marriott, *The Property Boom* (London: Hamish Hamilton, 1967).
3. The late Lord Mishcon in conversation with the author.
4. Hansard.
5. Nicholas Baker, *Independent*, 13 October 2003.
6. Ibid.
7. Ibid.

8. In conversation with the author.
9. Rossendale Lancashire Family History and Heraldry Society, Newsletter, February 2005.
10. Marriott, *The Property Boom*.
11. *Money Week*, 16 June 2008.
12. Ibid.
13. The late Louis Freedman in conversation with the author.
14. Lt. Col. Bromley Davenport, MP, 3 June 1954, Hansard.
15. Emma Vere-Jones, *The Lawyer*, February 2003.
16. Ian King, *The Times*, 10 March 2011.

Chapter fourteen

The New Clo' Man

The modern fashion world is not the sole prerogative of the upper classes, as it was when the old clo' men started knocking on doors. It now covers all sections of society and has spawned supermodels, a raft of glossy magazines, annual changes in styles and colours and a glamour image, with role models and icons. In the Jewish community, though, it is still known as the 'shmutter' business. That's Yiddish for a ripped article of clothing, from the Polish *szrata*.

Many of the earlier Jewish entrepreneurs had the difficult task of deciding who would succeed them when they left the scene. Nepotism was always a possibility and Raymond Burton (1917–2011) was well into his 30s when his father, Montagu Burton, died. Nevertheless, the founder of the business did not think him capable of taking over such a major concern, even though he had been appointed a director with his two brothers.

Young Burton set out to prove his father wrong and, in 1964, he launched Topshop, within the company's Peter Robinson store in Oxford Street. The idea of launching a youth-oriented brand was in contrast to his father's formal suit product, but Topshops went into twenty countries. In 1981, Burton retired as joint chairman and president of the Burton Group, with a major achievement his father would have been proud to acknowledge.

In retirement, Burton became chairman and president of the Jewish Museum in London and oversaw its development from a small room into a major attraction. He also financed the Raymond Burton Library for Humanities Research at the University of York, though it's more common for Jews to name such buildings after their parents.

Another Jewish refugee from Poland in the 1880s was Sam Lyons (1885–1959), who went to Leeds and started a clothing factory and a few retail shops under the name of Alexandre. Here, it was his two sons, Bernard (1912–2008) and Jack (1916–2008), who really grew the business, which merged with United Draperies in 1954. By a series of further takeovers and the creation of a good export trade, they became the third-largest retailers in the country in the 1960s. Bernard became chairman of UDS and Jack, deputy chairman.

Bernard looked after the manufacturing and Jack the retail side. At their peak they had 1,300 shops and in 1967 stocked 1.1 million suits. The conglomerate included such well-known names as Richard Shops, John Collier and Fifty Shilling Tailors. It was United Draperies who were the first to open duty-free shops in the airports. Eventually, in 1983, the business was sold and broken up when the brothers approached retirement, but it had been a power in the land in its day.

Both the Lyons brothers were very charitable and Leeds and York Universities, as well as the Royal School of Music and many Jewish charities, received substantial donations. Jack saved the Leeds Music Festival from bankruptcy, and the theatre of the Royal Academy of Music is named after him. He was, however, also involved in the Guinness scandal which concerned a takeover bid in the 1980s. In 1990, he would have gone to prison if the court hadn't taken into consideration the fact that he had been diagnosed with cancer. In 2008, when he eventually died, he had the satisfaction of knowing that, in 2001, the European Court of Human Rights declared that the original trial had not been fairly conducted. Nobody came out well from the Guinness scandal.

For Britain, the Second World War was enormously expensive. From the time the Americans came in on the side of the Allies, Britain could buy whatever was needed on credit, but there would come a day when arrangements would have to be made to pay it all back. At the time – and for years afterwards – Britain hadn't even paid the Americans what was owed for the First World War! When Franklin Roosevelt, the US president, asked Congress for financial support for Britain, he assured them that the United Kingdom had no money left, having sold its overseas assets to pay for the war; all the British investments in overseas railways, for example, had had to be liquidated to buy war material and food. It was only on that basis that Congress agreed that Britain could have as much credit as it needed.

When the war was won, the Americans turned the tap off. In Britain, as a consequence, some foods started to be rationed which hadn't even been rationed during the war: bread, for example. There just weren't the dollars available to pay for it. What became an essential plank in any government's economic policy for the next forty years was to implore the public to 'Buy British'. Marks & Spencer took up the challenge and Simon Marks advertised that 90 per cent of their products were manufactured in the United Kingdom. Among the companies which benefited from this policy was the Nottingham Manufacturing Co., which would supply Marks & Spencer for nearly seventy years. Behind this quintessentially British name was the Djanogly family.

The Djanoglys had been based in Germany at Chemnitz, which was the textile capital of the country between the wars. When they realized that the time had come for Jews to get out after Hitler came to power, they decamped to Nottingham. The Djanoglys set up shop there, prospered and were duly grateful. Today, Nottingham boasts the academically excellent Djanogly City Academy School. It was Tony Blair's idea to set up city academies to replace failing schools; Sir Harry Djanogly (1942–) gave £2 million to establish the college. There is also the Djanogly Library at the City University and the Djanogly Art Gallery; Djanogly has the largest collection of Lowrys in the world.

About the same time as the Djanoglys reached Nottingham, Jakob Spreiregen (1893–1974) arrived from Paris. He wasn't a refugee from the country, but an agent for a French beret company. He had been born to a Jewish family in Poland, and served in the Royal Army Medical Corps during the First World War. Spreiregen decided to start a factory in Cleator Moor, Cumberland to make his own berets. It would be called K (for silk) ANG (for angora) and OL (for wool) – Kangol.

It was an expensive business buying beret-making machines and Jacques Spreiregen, as he was now called, made large annual losses until 1942. In that year, though, General Montgomery adopted the beret instead of the peaked army cap and made it really famous, as well as patriotic. A Montgomery beret became the equivalent of an Arsenal or Manchester United shirt today. Kangol made hundreds of thousands of caps for the forces and, after the war, were making the right product at the right time.

The British working classes had worn flat caps for years, where the middle classes had chosen bowlers, homburgs and trilbies. Now, in a less class-conscious, post-war world, there was a market for a less formal hat, but one which still had style. It took some years, but Spreiregen was very willing to go for other new markets while he waited; the increasing consciousness of the need for more safety on the roads led to the introduction of seat belts, and the Kangol Magnet seat belt became very popular. The next turning point for the company, however, was the arrival of 'Swinging Britain' with Harold Wilson's Labour government.

All of a sudden the beret became 'cool'. Mary Quant and Pierre Cardin started to design them and, by 1968, there were sales for Kangol of £28 million, though profits remained at only £200,000. The good times rolled for many years, and Jacques Spreiregen only retired as chairman in 1973. In 2006, the company was sold to Sportsworld and the factory was moved overseas but, for well over fifty years, it had been a godsend for employment in Cleator Moor.

Not all the Jewish retail-clothing shops came from refugee families whose ancestors had been old clothes men. One at least emerged from a reluctance to get up in the small hours of the day to buy fruit and vegetables from Covent Garden market. David Lewis (1924–2011) was born David Pokrasse and came from a greengrocer's family in the Holloway Road in North London. He lived above the shop and was left in charge on occasions by his father when he was only 9 or 10. After war service in the RAF, in 1946 he opened a greengrocer's on a bombsite, built of old timber and corrugated iron. The winter of 1947 was particularly harsh, and Lewis gave up green-grocering and opened a shop called Lewis Separates in 1948.

Sixty years later he was still in charge of the family business. It now had nearly 300 outlets, and since 1988 has been called River Island. Before that it was called Chelsea Girl, but Lewis had the sense to rebrand his shops when their appeal started to get out of kilter with modern taste. Sir Philip Green, a man who should know, said of Lewis, 'he is an old style dyed-in-the-wool retailer, which they don't manufacture any more'.[1]

If there has been a sea change in retailing in past years, it has been the way in which the retailers have become the innovators, rather than just leaving it to the manufacturers. Lewis recognized this very early, and his design room employed more than seventy people. As he said, 'The retail industry in this country is innovative, socially conscious and responsible, and a credit to the country.'[2] The Lewis family had built their business without any form of government subsidy, the mainstay of so many failed British industries. Lewis again, this time on the government: 'Sometimes I think that the best thing they can do is stay in bed all day and leave us all alone.'[3] Certainly, for many years after the war, the successful growth of the British hotel industry owed much to its neglect by the trade unions and successive governments.

The family also expanded overseas and developed into other markets, including more than twenty hotels. The core business makes profits in excess of £150 million a year and the *Sunday Times* values the family's assets at £1.6 billion. The Bernard Lewis Family Charitable Trust concentrates on helping medical, child-care and educational charities, with substantial gifts to cancer research, the treatment of head injuries and birth defects, rehabilitation and education. Lewis was awarded the OBE for his charity work, but died in 2011 at 87. Almost in his spare time, he effectively created the Israeli resort of Eilat, which now attracts vast numbers of tourists with its guaranteed, year-round fine weather.

At about the same time that Lewis started, Norman Freed (1930–2011) found another niche in the market. He recognized that young women wanted to be in fashion, even if they couldn't afford the latest Paris creations. So in 1952, he opened a shop in Wood Green, London offering 'sexy and affordable adaptations of catwalk trends'.[4] He called it Jane Norman, combining the first names of his mother and himself. Slowly but surely the business grew, and eventually could boast the highest sales per square foot in the fashion high street. Young women found that, for almost the first time, somebody was concentrating on their specific needs. If the clothing didn't always stand the test of time, it didn't need to, because there would be a more current fashion emerging within a year or two.

Freed grew by opening stand-alone shops and by taking concessions in department stores, notably Debenhams. He did no marketing, nor did he bother with a PR department. The essential ingredient of his success was that the goods on offer were always up-to-date with the latest trends. In 1994 Freed retired and, in 2003, sold the company for £70 million. When he died in 2011, he had a high reputation for his charitable work and also for his sense of humour; he strongly believed shopping ought to be fun. The company, however, ran into serious financial difficulties in the same year and the banks took it over.

You still hear a well-known Jewish saying that to get on in life you need *mazel*, which is luck with a tinge of Divine-authorization. On the other hand, you can make your own luck and, as Gary Player, the great golfer said, 'the harder I practise, the luckier I get'. Stephen Marks (1947–) benefited from both kinds of luck. He was born the son of a hard-working Jewish hairdresser in Harrow. Marks recalls him rising at 6.30 in the morning and not getting home till nine in the evening. It was a good example. Marks didn't excel at school but he was a very good tennis player, winning the Plate at Junior Wimbledon in 1964. He couldn't, however, see himself making a fortune at tennis.

So he got a job with a coat manufacturer and learned the business. In 1969, with a £17,000 loan, he started his own firm, Stephen Marks Ltd. He didn't hang around. He went to a Paris fashion show and saw that a manufacturer was making hot pants. He copied them and sold 100 pairs to Miss Selfridge; they went in a day. That led to an order for 2,000 pairs, and Marks found he was already beginning to make an impression.

In 1972 he met Nicole Farhi (1946–), a young French-Jewish fashion designer with a Turkish background. Marks changed the company's name to French Connection and Farhi became the chief designer for the next ten years, before branching out on her own very successfully. Marks was always a driven man: 'If a person has to ask how long a working day is with us, they've come to the wrong place.'[5] He was also impatient. As an *Independent* journalist reported, 'He is a fully paid up member of the Not Suffering Fools Gladly Club'.[6]

In 1996, the fortunes of Marks' company really changed as a result of an inter-company message. It was signed as having come from 'French Connection United Kingdom.' Only it was abbreviated to FCUK. When Marks saw it, the advertising possibilities were suddenly obvious, and Marks didn't hesitate to exploit the opportunity. The subsequent advertising cost money, but the publicity which erupted, as 100,000 T-shirts with FCUK on them flooded onto the market, was free.

In another age or with another product, the concept could have been disastrous. In a copyright court case on the use of the phrase, Mr Justice Rattie called it 'a tasteless and obnoxious campaign'. French Connection's counsel said, 'Your Lordship may find it offensive. I might find it offensive. But young people who buy clothes do not find it offensive. They find it amusing.' Marks defended his decision 'to be cheeky. To put a smile on people's faces.'[7] 'Cool as FCUK' was just one of the variations. But then, as Marks said, 'If it's not controversial, who's going to be interested?' It may be a sad reflection on the world as it is today, but Marks can hardly be held responsible for that.

The Advertising Standards Authority eventually insisted that all French Connection posters be submitted to them before they were used. The American Family Association wanted the public to boycott the products. It didn't happen. French Connection have had good years and bad years since they adopted the slogan but, in 2010, their turnover was £205 million, their profit £7.3 million and their products were sold in thirty countries all over the world.

The aftermath of the Israeli War of Independence in 1948 saw the Jewish communities in Arab countries in great peril. The Middle East Arabs were smarting from their defeat, the Jews were considered akin to the Israelis, and were readily available to take revenge on. Over the next few years a large number of Jews fled to more hospitable shores. These included many from Iran, although the Shah's regime had been more tolerant towards its Jews when he came to power in 1953. One migrant was David Alliance (1932–) who was 19 in 1951 when he migrated to Manchester; he had previously sold laces to shoemakers in his native Kashan.

Manchester had been the capital of the British textile trade. Nathaniel Rothschild started as a textile merchant there, when he left the family in Frankfurt in the early part of the nineteenth century. Many Sephardi Jews had been agents for Lancashire companies in their export trade to the British Empire, particularly to India. So there was plenty of precedent for Jewish immigrants to settle down in Cottonopolis, as Manchester had been appropriately nicknamed.

In 1969, Alliance became fascinated by the possibilities of the mail-order industry. He sold his existing company and bought a small mailing house. Under the name N. Brown, this developed until it had about a quarter of the market. In 1985, Alliance agreed a merger with the Djanogly family's Nottingham Manufacturing Co., and in 1986, they bought Coats Patons, which became Coats Viyella, a £2 billion business.

The British textile industry eventually could not compete with the lower costs of labour in Asia, and Alliance retired. Djanogly took over, but the decline continued until Coats Viyella moved its manufacturing to Asia, and the rest of the company was broken up. Alliance and Djanogly had put up a good fight to keep the British textile industry alive, but this was one battle that they lost. Alliance went on to become a Liberal peer and a major philanthropist.

The community in Iraq was as old as that in Iran. When the Jews were conquered by Nebuchadnezzar, as told in the Bible, they were taken to Babylon. Eventually many returned to Jerusalem, but some stayed behind and still constituted a Jewish community, 2,000 years later in the twentieth century. Among the most prominent were the Zilkha family, who had branches of their bank in many parts of the Middle East. Khadouri Zilkha (1884–1956), with great regret, saw little future in staying in the country and, in 1930, migrated to the United States. One of his sons, Selim (1927–), was brought up in America and served in the United States forces.

After the 1948 Arab–Israeli War, the Zilkha banks were nationalized in Iraq, Syria and Egypt, without compensation. Unfortunately, not all the members of the family saw the writing on the wall and, in 1969, after a show trial, Saddam Hussein had nine Jews publicly hanged for spying for Israel, including a Zilkha cousin, Ezra Nasi Zilkha (1909–69). The crowd bayed their approval, and protests from around the world had no effect.

After the war, it took some years for Selim to discover he didn't enjoy banking in America, but that decision brought him to Britain in the late 1950s. He decided to buy a group of stores and specialize in providing for the needs of young mothers. In two years he managed to lose £180,000, in what was described as 'a complete fiasco'. So he sold out and, instead, bought W.J. Harris, a group of fifty stores. In partnership, initially with Jimmy Goldsmith, he changed the name to Mothercare and, in 1972, was able to take the company public.

One of the significant aspects of Mothercare was Zilkha's readiness to open stores on the Continent, in Scandinavia and Northern Europe. By 1981, there were over 400 stores in the organization and profits had reached more than £22 million. At which point Zilkha seemed to have lost interest in the company, and soon sold out for £48 million. He left behind, however, a sector of the market which was better focused than it had ever been before, and one which made a useful contribution to the economy. In 1982, he went on to invest $22 million in an oil company and, in 1998 sold that for $1 billion. His most notable charitable donation was $20 million to complete a Neurogenetic Institute in Los Angeles for research to alleviate the symptoms of Alzheimer's disease.

The world of textiles and fashion is particularly cut throat; you can have a successful business for twenty years and one bad season can ruin you: six months when your new winter overcoats prove to be unsellable in an unusually warm period, and it can be all over. That, however, is bad luck rather than doing anything criminal. Lord Kagan (1915–95), on the other hand, was a crook. He got ten months for tax evasion and, in 1980, was fined £375,000 (nearly £2 million today).

These are the bald facts, but Kagan was as damaged by his upbringing as any child suffering from abuse. Joseph Kagan was born Juozapas Kaganas in Lithuania and, after studying Textiles at Leeds University, he went home and was unable to leave when the war broke out. He then spent three of the war years in the Kovno ghetto, but that wasn't safe either. The Lithuanians had a dreadful record for helping the Nazis kill the Jewish community and, in 1944, Kagan and his family finally took shelter in the attic of a factory they owned. They were there for nine months, relying on a Christian friend to keep them alive.[8]

In those circumstances, laws come to mean very little. With almost every man's hand against you, it's long odds against even surviving. Kagan made it though, and in 1946, finished up in Huddersfield. The Kagans were survivors par excellence; Ben Kagan, his father, managed to arrive in 1940 and now owned a textile mill in Yorkshire. When he died at 109, he was the second-oldest man in Britain, having given up work at 102.

There is another scar, however, that affects a lot of refugees; this is a very natural tendency towards taking care in spending money. The thought is always there that it could happen again. How can they be ready for it? Many feel the best insurance is to have hard cash readily available to get them out of trouble. A lot of refugees managed to buy their way out of Germany before the war, but often at ruinous cost. Hoarding money wasn't a question of meanness; it was a precaution against execution. Tax evasion might be rationalized as coming under the same heading.

Kagan took a job as a blanket weaver and, in 1951, he invented a new kind of fabric called Gannex. It involved bonding a woollen lining to a waterproof nylon outer layer. It became very popular and presented the perfect image for a future Labour prime minister; Harold Wilson's home town was Huddersfield, and Wilson and Kagan became friends. In 1956, Wilson wore a Gannex coat on a world tour. Other world leaders who eventually wore them included the Chinese premier, Mao Tse-tung, American president Lyndon Johnson and Russian premier Nikita Khruschev. The fabric was used when climbing in the Himalayas and exploring the Arctic and the Antarctic. It was popular with the police and the army. As a publicity stunt, Kagan even made coats for the Queen's corgis. He became a multimillionaire.

When Harold Wilson lost office in 1970, there was a need for supporters to finance his private office. Kagan was one of those who contributed, as was Sir Eric Miller (1927–77), of Peachey Properties, who committed suicide while being investigated by the fraud squad. In 1970, Kagan was knighted when Wilson lost office, and was made a peer when the prime minister finally resigned in 1976.

If you're a multimillionaire, you really don't need to get involved in tax evasion. Kagan did, however, and fled to Israel, which threw him out. So he fled again to Spain where there was no extradition treaty, but he unwisely holidayed in Paris, was betrayed there by a former mistress, arrested and extradited. When he went to prison he lost his knighthood, but it takes an Act of Parliament to deprive a man of his peerage and the government didn't bother.

On his release from prison, Kagan went back to the House of Lords and spoke on prison reform. He was quite incorrigible and said he had no feelings of guilt at all. The reputation of his business suffered, however. He died in 1994 and the factory was due for demolition by 2002.

In 2010, part of the site was approved for development into ninety two-bedroom flats.

Among the very successful Jewish fashion retailers were Ralph (1939–) and David Gold (1940–), who overcame a disastrous start in the East End in abject poverty, and a father with a police record. Both left school early with only one GCE between them, and joined their father on his stall in the local market. They found a growing demand for soft-porn magazines, and were able to branch out into shops in Soho selling such products. Although their future success would label them 'porn barons', the truth was that they really started making money when they sold two shops in 1967 while they were still in their 20s; they had bought the shops for £20,000, and sold them for £3 million. Even so, their core business was another example of a newly developing market being exploited by entre-preneurs who recognized the opportunity. The 'Swinging Sixties' had introduced a far less restrictive attitude to sex, the demand was there, and the Golds took advantage of it.

In 1972, they bought Ann Summers, a company selling sex products, and now have 140 shops throughout the country. Like Tupperware, they sell Ann Summers products through 4,000 parties a week in people's homes, and have 7,500 party organizers on their books. With a turnover of over £100 million, they have reached the *Sunday Times* Rich List, and own West Ham FC after a long connection with Birmingham FC.

One problem they have carefully addressed is the succession to the empire. So many Jewish businesses didn't survive the departure of the founder, and as David Gold said, 'When you read statistics showing that 71 per cent of second generation businesses don't succeed, it makes you think'.[9] The result of the thinking is that two daughters now run the business.

One of the major innovations in retailing since the war has been the shop-within-a-shop, the idea of renting floor space in a department store to a company which will sell its own products. The pioneer of this development was Raymond Zelker (1915–2011), who was the sixth child of Polish immigrants who became market traders in the East End. Zelker started on his own in about 1935, manufacturing women's fashions.

During the war he made gas-mask cases, and then the business took off when he recognized the possibilities of the shop-within-a-shop. The first was in Harrods, but eventually there were 120 of them, called Polly Peck. The business was bought in 1979 and its new owner fled to Cyprus in 1993 when the company collapsed. The notoriety of this rather tended to take the spotlight off Zelker, who should have received the credit for the original concept.

One of the most successful Jewish manufacturers in Britain today is David Reiss (1943–). His great uncle, Samuel (1903–95), came over from Poland and started a clothing shop in Bishopsgate, in the City. This came down through the family to David, who took it over in 1971. It was always his intention to build up an international fashion brand, and the hole in the market he perceived was 'affordable luxury'. Clothes for the aspirational, or those who were trading down in hard times. He describes his clothes as 'elegant, clean, sexy, refined and edgy'. The objective was to keep the price in check, while offering superior quality.

Over the years he opened sixty-five stores, and ventured into the United States, Ireland, the UAE, China and Malaysia, among other overseas markets. There are a lot of franchises as well. He has twenty designers scouring the world for new ideas and 45 per cent of his turnover is spent on salaries, as he has 1,200 staff in the UK. Reiss is a man of firm opinions. The company isn't listed. 'Being private means I can back my own beliefs. If I want to expand or take a risk, I can go for it.' And this is important to him, because 'the minute anyone says you can't do something to me, that's when I set out to prove them wrong'.[10]

Reiss could sell out; in 2006, he turned down an offer from Liz Claiborne of £150 million, but he still gets a buzz from the business. Never more so than when the Duchess of Cambridge wore a Reiss dress for her official engagement photographs with Prince William. The resulting publicity for the company was monumental. Reiss's ambition is to have over 250 stores all over the world, and all the profits of the company help the economy in the UK. Reiss has no intention of departing overseas, though his manufacturing has been forced to relocate. At the moment, Britain's manufacturing costs in producing clothing cannot compete with, in Reiss's case, Romania.

Another very successful clothing manufacturer came from a family who made their fortune in taking wedding photographs. Boris Bennett (1900–85) was born Boris Sochaczewska in Ozokoff in Poland. At the end of the First World War he went off to Paris where he joined a camera company. In 1922, they sent him to London and in 1927, he branched out for himself by opening a studio in the East End. This was sufficiently successful for him to have five studios before the Second World War broke out, including one in Oxford Street. A charitable man and a strong Zionist, in 1945 he financed the Freshwater Hostel in London for refugee boys who had survived the Nazi concentration camps.

After the war, Bennett opened camera shops, but in 1964 he sold out to Stanley Kalms of Dixons. His two sons, Maurice (1930–) and Michael (1932–), decided to go into the fashion business and, in 1976, opened a store called Warehouse. The concept was for a British, own-brand, design-based fashion retailer. The remarkable success of the Bennetts was that, although they were already well into their 40s when they began, and during a slump as well, by 2006, they were receiving the Lifetime Achievement Award at the Drapers' Gala Dinner.

In just thirty years they had built up and sold the Warehouse, Oasis and Coast chains, and were hard at work on Phase Eight and Kookai UK. Those who had backed them had received substantial returns on their investments and the companies they sold continued to flourish on their sound foundations. It's hard enough to build up one successful chain in a lifetime; to build up a number of them is a very substantial achievement.

While it is quite true that the apple often falls not so much far from the tree as out of the county, there are exceptions. Isaac Wolfson's son, Lord Leonard Wolfson (1927–2010) built Great Universal Stores to even greater heights when, in 1981, he took over from his father. When he retired in 1996 he handed over to his cousin, Lord David Wolfson (1935–), who had been Margaret Thatcher's chief of staff at 10 Downing Street from 1979 to 1985. Leonard Wolfson also headed the Wolfson Trust, which by 2010, had made charitable donations in excess of £1 billion. Its funds today are in the region of £750 million.

A major hole in the market that Leonard Wolfson spotted was a corollary to the vast expansion in business paid for with credit cards: he recognized that everybody would want to know more about the creditworthiness of the cardholders. From this came the development of a data company called Experian, which is now independent of GUS and one of the FTSE 100.

The Wolfson family continued to produce very able businessmen in the third generation. In 1991, David Wolfson's son, Simon (1967–), joined Next as a sales consultant, after studying at Cambridge. Next was founded in 1982 to offer the younger market modern clothes sold in boutique-type shops. David Wolfson had become the chairman of the company in 1990 and by 2001, Simon was the youngest chief executive officer of a FTSE 100 company. If there were accusations of nepotism at the time, the progress of Next under his leadership was the best possible refutation. In 2010, Simon Wolfson was made a peer and Next has led the way in the changing world of buying clothes.

The company has produced far glossier brochures than were the norm for catalogues, and has taken advantage of the possibilities of on-line purchasing. The majority of their products are sold on-line and they recognized the importance of dealing with the great bugbear for direct-mail customers – slow delivery. If you buy from Next, you are almost certain to get the goods the next day.

Finding holes in the fashion market is never easy, but Harold Tillman (1946–) has been more successful than most. His father, Jack, was originally a tailor with Montagu Burton, and he sent his son to the London College of Fashion to learn the business properly. When Harold Tillman qualified, he became an apprentice with the Savile Row tailors, Lincroft Kilgour, and was made their managing director three years later at the age of 22. Two years after that, he launched the firm on the Stock Exchange and sold out at the age of 30, already a multimillionaire.

There were many innovations. 'He made a mint supplying Carnaby Street with hipsters in the late '60s'.[11] Before footballers became the style icons they are today, he signed up George Best, the peerless winger of Manchester United, to endorse a range of kids' clothing. He also whole-saled the T-shirt.

In those years, however, Tillman was more a 'global concept' than a 'detail' man. He bought a company called Honorbilt, left it in the hands of an incompetent team, and found it had to be put into liquidation. 'I was virtually wiped out financially. I kept my house by my fingertips. But it taught me a valuable lesson. Now I keep in close touch with everything I do and if I buy anything I always do due diligence.'[12] It is true that the best team in business is a partnership between a detail man and a visionary. Both need each other.

Tillman was banned by the Department of Trade and Industry from being a director for three years after Honorbilt, but bounced back. He still takes risks. 'A long elegant man with courteous manners', Tillman has not lost his passion for a challenge.[13] He has used part of his new fortune to sponsor ten MAs at the London College of Fashion at a cost of £1 million, and he became the chairman of the British Fashion Council. He was awarded the CBE in 2010.

As Britain lost much of its export revenues from coal, shipbuilding, steel and machine tools, the overwhelming necessity for the economy was to replace these traditional industries. Was it becoming too late to create new export earnings from scratch? One great success has been a designer label called Ted Baker. This was the creation of Ray Kelvin (1955–), born in North London and educated at the Jewish Free School. His grandfather was a refugee from Eastern Europe and had a tailor's shop in Edmonton. When Kelvin left school at 18, he went into the business and learned all the minutiae. He then ran a firm providing clothing to high-street retailers for ten years, but sold it and decided to start again.

It was while he was quietly fishing that he came up with the idea of selling top-quality men's shirts, and he opened a shop in Glasgow with that in mind. Ted Baker was the name he chose and, from the beginning, Kelvin was determined to be quirky. If you bought a shirt from the shop you also got free laundering for it thrown in. Later, at Christmas, he would give away Paxo stuffing for the turkeys and, at Easter, cans of chocolate-bunny hotpot. As he couldn't afford advertising, he relied on word-of-mouth and continued that policy for many years.

Kelvin was always extremely reticent about obtaining personal publicity because he recognized that everything depended on the image of Ted Baker, who was portrayed as the last word in male elegance. There were no pictures of Kelvin and no interviews. In 1990, when he opened a shop in Covent Garden, his mother, Trudie, would work there on a Saturday, wearing a badge that read, 'Ted's Mother'.

The fundamentals of the brand were quintessential English touches, great attention to detail, quality and flair. As the business grew, their head office was opened in St Pancras in a block named 'The Ugly Brown Building'. The strapline for the company was 'No ordinary designer label'. In 1995 he was able to launch a women's range, then Teddy Boy for children, and on to perfumes, sunglasses, homeware and even Baker's Butler, which was a concierge service that provided you with a butler to do all the chores. Whatever the range, the humour and the quirky designs were trademarks. Ted Baker shops are now to be found worldwide, from the USA to Hong Kong and from Dubai to Australia. The company's profits in 2011 were over £24 million. Overseas earnings help the economy and Kelvin was awarded the CBE in 2011 for services to the fashion industry.

In the fashion world there have been any number of Jewish companies. It is a hard business and the firms have waxed and waned; two comparative newcomers have been Marilyn Anselm's (1944–) 1981 creation of Hobbs and Peter Simon's 1973 Monsoon. Simon started by selling shaggy woollen coats on the Portabello Road and in 2005, featured in the *Sunday Times* Rich List as worth £400 million. The names could go on for a long time – the older generation of clothing retailers, for instance, included Lou Harris's Harella and Jack Steinberg's Alexon.

As the Jewish community left the workshop, the great tradition of fine tailoring was taken on by new waves of immigrants, such as the Cypriots and the Indians. The caricature of the rotund, avuncular Jewish tailor with his tape measure around his neck and his Victorian shears almost vanished. It reappeared, in 2011, for the wedding of Prince William and Catherine Middleton. The most important uniforms were produced by the Queen's Warrant Holder, Kashket & Co.

Alfred Kashket (1914–77) became a Savile Row tailor when he grew up, and developed into a very fine practitioner. In 1961, he set up his own company with his wife, Debbie, and decided to specialize in military uniforms. By 1963, 90 per cent of the uniforms of the Brigade of Guards were made by Kashket, and he was employing 150 workers at his factory in Hackney, the traditional East End home of the Jewish tailoring trade in years gone by. The family followed him and his son, Bernard, came into the firm after national service with the Scots Guards. In time, the third generation, Russell, arrived and runs the company today. Talking of Prince William's uniform on TV on the day after the wedding, only a change of dress for Russell would have been necessary to have the same face and figure talking about Victoria's Prince Albert.

The oldest tailoring firm in the country was Firmin & Sons, which had been established in 1655 and also specialized in military uniforms. When they went into administration in 2010, Kashket bought the company and now has six royal warrants. The company has produced clothing for the royal family for over twenty years now, and has eight other monarchs among its clientele. The family were also founder members of the Loughton, Chigwell and District Federation Synagogue.

Where an industry has been in existence for a very long time, there can be considerable difficulty in breaking into the magic circle. In something as basic as shoes, it would seem likely that companies like Clore's British Shoe Company and Ziff's Stylo Shoes would comfortably resist newcomers. There are exceptions, though, and Harvey Jacobson (1956–) provided one of them.

Jacobson's grandfather was a Jewish immigrant from Russia, and his father started a shoe shop after he left the army at the end of the Second World War. Harvey Jacobson was precocious. He first went into the Manchester shop at the age of 6, sold five pairs of shoes during the day and earned himself commission of 6p. He left school at 15 and went to work for his father but, in 1978, he branched out on his own, with two stalls in Stafford Market and Manchester's indoor market.

With his brother, in 1981 he opened a Cash and Carry for shoes and was one of the first people to examine the potential of importing from China. 'We paid far too much for the stuff but we didn't half learn quick.'[14] Jacobson's business became largely one of selling to shoe retailers and, by the early 1990s, he had a turnover in excess of £15 million. 'Above all I'm a trader.'[15] The best deal came in 1996 when he bought Gola. This was a company founded in 1905, but coasting. It had iconic products like the Gola bag and very popular trainers and tracksuits. 'When we bought Gola we thought we'd bought silver when, in fact, we'd bought gold … having realised we'd bought gold, it turned out to be platinum.'[16]

Although the company has suffered through the recession and made a loss in 2008 and 2009, it relishes its record of being the largest importer and distributor of footwear in the UK. It distributes seventy-five different shoe and clothing brands, and sells 10 million pairs of shoes a year to retailers; everything from £1.99 slippers to £300 boots. Jacobson put £2 million of his own money into the company to support the balance sheet, and the family still own 89 per cent of the stock. Overall, the old clothes men would have been pleased to see what had emerged from the traditions they initiated.

NOTES

1. *Retail Weekly*, 23 January 2009.
2. Ibid.
3. Ibid.
4. Jane Norman website.
5. Beverley D'Silva, *Independent*, 8 August 1998.
6. Ibid.
7. Ibid.
8. http://everything2.com/user/aneurin/writeups/Joseph+Kagan.
9. Alistair Osborne, *Daily Telegraph*, 14 April 2009.
10. *Independent*, 4 May 2008.
11. Andrew Davidson, *Sunday Times*, 18 January 2004.
12. Ibid.
13. Ibid.
14. Laura Weir, *Drapers*, 1 September 2008.
15. Ibid.
16. *Jewish Chronicle*, 20 May 2011.

Chapter fifteen

The New World of Information Technology

The great Jewish comedian, Jackie Mason, has a very funny routine in which he discusses the difficulties Jews have with even the simplest aspects of any new technology, from changing a tyre to replacing a bulb. As with all generalizations, there is a good deal of truth to this, but there have been some major exceptions over the years.

The benefits of new technology come from, first, inventing it and, second, finding the right ways to use it. For example, in Victorian times, there was a large gap between producing a document and printing a book. If you wanted a lot of copies of a document, you had to write each of them by hand, and then check carefully that you had rewritten every one of them accurately. What was desperately needed in the burgeoning world of commercial administration was a method of copying documents that was quick, accurate and available in whatever numbers were needed.

The solution was invented by the very Orthodox David Gestetner (1854–1939), who left school at 13, and Hungary – where Jews were very much second-class citizens – at 19. Gestetner went first to America, but returned to Europe to become involved in a company that made equipment for copying documents using a gelatine plate. It wasn't very effective, and Gestetner moved on to London. There he became an assistant to a printer in the City, but worked on the copying problem in his spare time. In 1881, he finally found the solution and took out a patent for a new method of copying, based on a waxed paper similar to that used to make kites, which he had once sold in Chicago.

The principle was that a stylus would cut into the wax surface, and then ink would be forced through the deep indentation onto a sheet of white paper, making a perfect copy. It was called an automatic cyclostyle machine, but it became so famous that, for years, it achieved the ultimate commercial accolade – it became a generic term. Just as 'to Hoover' would become the expression for vacuum cleaning, and 'a Guinness' the word for a stout, so 'to Gestetner' became the term for copying documents.

As a result, Gestetner could justly claim to be the founder of world-wide office copying and duplicating machinery. He built his company, Gestetner Cyclograph, for the next fifty years, never retiring, and eventually exporting to over 150 countries, from his factory in Tottenham, North London. He went to his laboratory in the factory every weekday, except for Jewish festivals.

When he grew old, Gestetner did take time off to holiday on the Riviera. There, in 1939, he died at the plush Hotel Ruhl in Nice, at the age of 85, a long way away from his obscure origins in Hungary. A devoted family man, Gestetner's only interest outside business was the very Orthodox Adath congregation in North London, where he was a financial pillar of strength. He left the business to his sons, and the company was later amalgamated with other copier manufacturers to become NRG, which created the first digital copier.

At the end of the eighteenth century, a Polish Jew called Moshe ben Avraham arrived in Liverpool, married Hannah Wolf and had a son called Sampson (1838–91). Sampson decided he needed an English surname, rather like Calmer Levy Hambro. So he called himself after his business and, as he was a jeweller, he became Sam Goldstone. Goldstone had a son, Meyer Hart Goldstone (1874–1943), who was captivated by the inventions of the modern world around him. He became an electrical engineer, through practical experience, and went to work for English Electric. He then complained when he didn't get a bonus to which he was entitled, and was fired. His boss, Henry Ward, felt his staff member had been treated badly and so he complained. He was fired as well. The two men then decided to start their own business, which they called Ward & Goldstone. It was one of the best things that ever happened to Salford, which abuts Manchester.

At the beginning, Ward & Goldstone were wholesalers, selling all kinds of electrical goods. They soon moved into manufacturing in Salford, and made products which they had patented themselves. The credit for this should probably go to Meyer's brother, Albert (1880–1953), who had been educated at Manchester Grammar School and had gone on to Manchester University to read Engineering. Their inventions were often unusual. In 1916, they patented a razor with a light attached, so that you could see what you were doing if you were shaving. In 1918, they patented an incandescent electric lamp holder and, in 1934, improved electric torches. Indeed, in the lifetime of the firm, they took out around 150 patents for every sort of electrical improvement.

Meyer Goldstone was not just creative. He was also fast on his feet. When Ford imported a cargo of cars in the 1920s, they forgot to fit them out with the necessary wiring. So they asked Goldstone if he could supply what they needed. He agreed to do so immediately and, when their representatives were gone, asked his staff whether they knew what Ford were talking about![1] The company provided Ford with vehicle harnesses for years after: a vehicle harness wraps all the car cables in easily installed and protected packaging.

Goldstone built a big business, and was also the lay leader of the Orthodox synagogue in Southport. When he died in 1943, his only son, Sam (1907–89), took over the business and devoted almost all his adult life to it. Ward & Goldstone grew to have fifteen factories in the 1970s, employing over 7,000 staff and was the largest industrial employer in Salford. Profits grew to £2.7 million on a turnover of over £35 million. In 1979, single-cable car wiring was introduced, and the company was selling everything from electric blankets to hair dryers.

The 1970s, however, also brought inflation, slump and increased foreign competition. Sam Goldstone was getting on and he was devoted to his long-serving and loyal staff. What the firm needed was a trimming of excess manpower and a faster turnover of stock. Neither happened until Sam's son, Michael (1946-), took over as managing director; his father resented the changes and refused to accept them. Eventually, in 1982, Sam gave up his position as chairman, forced out by the rest of the board. Loyal to his father, Michael wouldn't stop the old man continuing to interfere, and was fired in his turn. The company is now Volex and doing very well, but the manufacturing is no longer in Salford. Sales in 2010 were over £200 million, but no Goldstones remain connected with it.

The twentieth century would see changes in technology on a monumental scale. Creating and developing a major company was a tremendous challenge for those who wanted to undertake it. Louis Newmark (1870–1924) was a watch importer before 1900. In 1922, he brought his son, Herbert, into the business and, after his death, another son, Geoffrey, joined the company in 1930. They obtained inexpensive watches from Switzerland but, in 1948, decided to branch out into making their own. So, during the 1950s, the company started manufacturing watches at a plant in Croydon. It also dipped its toes very successfully into the electronic and electro-mechanical markets.

The firm had the expertise to produce finely tuned instruments and, among its products, would be flight path controls for helicopters, automatic pilots and heading systems, which enabled the pilot to know where he was. The difficult decision was whether to jettison the watch business and concentrate entirely on electronics, because the demands for capital were too great for both divisions. It was decided to give up making watches and import them again.

In 1961, the company went public with the family still firmly in charge and, by 1982, Louis Newmark & Co. made £1.5 million profit on a £22 million turnover. They also had orders worth more than £5 million from the Ministry of Defence. Geoffrey Newmark was still active, even though he had been with the firm for over fifty years. Eventually, however, economic conditions, the need for ever more capital for product development and some unwise diversification, brought the company down. It was liquidated in 1995.

Today, we take the existence of hearing aids for granted, but they were very much part of the progress in twentieth-century technology. The Poliakoffs were an important part of the story. The overthrow of the czar didn't end the Russian persecution of the Jews. 250,000 died in the civil war which followed the revolution and, when Lenin attained full power, he started to confiscate private businesses, which would adversely affect the community as well. One of the firms taken over was the creation of the Poliakoff family, who had worked with Marconi on the development of the wireless, and was one of the first companies to record sound on film. Bit by bit they had their company taken away from them and so, in 1924,

Joseph Poliakoff (1874–1960) came to Britain with his son, Alexander (1910–86).

Poliakoff *père* was a radio and telephone engineer and an inventor. His first job in London was working for a Russian company, which was exposed as a communist spy centre. So, in 1931, he took the wise step of starting his own business, the Multitone Electric Co. in Islington in London. Poliakoff *fils* graduated from University College, London and joined him. In 1933, Joseph Poliakoff took out a patent for the first wireless for the deaf; it was a tremendous boon for those who had thought they would never be able to enjoy the radio. The company also made hearing aids and, in 1937, Poliakoff took out a patent for an induction-loop hearing assistance system. Now it was possible for hearing aids to be worn, rather than remain on a desk. In 1938, Joseph Poliakoff retired and Alexander took over as chairman. He was also very technologically minded and, during the war, he invented a bomb-clock detector, which the air force disposal squads used.

One of the company's illustrious clients for hearing aids was Winston Churchill, and Alexander Poliakoff would go to Downing Street in the Blitz to see that the machinery was working correctly. The Poliakoffs were impeccably patriotic, but Joseph Poliakoff had that Russian spy-centre note on his CV. So, eventually, MI6 warned Churchill that it could be dangerous to allow Alexander Poliakoff into the building and he was banned thereafter. The advice came from Sir Roger Hollis, the head of MI6 who, it has often been suggested, was a Russian mole, though nothing has ever been proved.

The company's development was materially helped by the recruitment of a Polish refugee, Ian Karten (1921–2011), when he was demobbed from the Polish air force. Poliakoff and Karten worked well together over the years and eventually Karten owned half of the greatly enhanced company. He used the money to set up a charitable trust, which has made many important grants, including a £300,000 endowment of a Fellowship in Jewish and non-Jewish Relations at Southampton University.

The success of Multitone was made even greater by their invention of paging systems. One of the first organizations to benefit was St Thomas' Hospital in 1956 and, by 1970, the company had really effective systems of electronic bleepers. Before mobile phones, the bleeper transformed communications between company personnel who were finally able to contact each other, even if they were not at their desks. All British lifeboats came to be fitted with Multitone equipment and fire and rescue services were made far more efficient as well. The systems were exported all over the world.[2] Poliakoff remained chairman for forty years and, when he retired, the business was eventually sold to Champion Technology, a Hong Kong company.

As the world of technology has changed out of all recognition over the last fifty years, from the British point of view the key priority has been to remain at the cutting edge of developments. After the Second World War, the major change in production methods has continued to be from hand processes to more advanced automation. The initial resistance to automation was, however, considerable. The problem was that automation would often make craftsmen redundant, demand changes in working practices and be more intellectually challenging for management. A lot of Luddites were still alive and well and living in factories.

To make the changes, you needed men of vision, and few saw quicker, further and earlier than Sir Leon Bagrit (1902–79). He was born in Kiev and his parents went to Belgium where, in 1914, they lost all they had when the Germans invaded. They escaped to England and Bagrit went to Birkbeck College. He was always an inventive youngster and a good enough violinist to help support himself by playing occasionally with the London Philharmonic.

After college he went to work for Avery, the scales company, but in 1935, he set up his own firm, B. & P. Swift, to take advantage of his own patents. The firm did well with war work and, in 1946, was bought by Elliott Bros, an old-established firm of instrument makers. Bagrit became joint managing director and then managing director. The question was, with war work coming to an end, what products were going to be needed in the future?

Bagrit was a deep thinker, and he had been particularly impressed by the fact that only automation had enabled the possibilities of nuclear power to be utilized. The argument went, if nuclear power then why not everything else? Bagrit became a crusader for automation and started to produce control systems for nuclear, aeronautical and industrial purposes. This was in the very early days of computers, when whole rooms would be needed to house just one of them.

For years Elliott-Automation, as it became in 1957, advised companies on how to introduce automation. Bagrit pioneered computers in industry and, eventually, became the largest manufacturer of industrial computers outside the United States. By the early 1960s, the company had 16,000 staff, including 2,000 in research establishments, and was making over a million pounds profit a year. As *The Times* said in his obituary, 'Behind his operations as a business man lay much deep thinking about the needs of British industry in the second half of the 20th century.'[3] In 1962, Bagrit was knighted and, as chairman of Elliott from 1963 to 1973, he earned the title of 'Father of Automation in Britain' and gave the BBC Reith Lectures on the subject in 1964 in 'The Age of Automation'. In them he said:

> It is now possible to envisage personal computers small enough to be taken around in one's car, or even one's pocket. They could be plugged into a national computer grid to provide individual enquiries with almost unlimited information. Perhaps the most far-reaching use of the new generation of computers will be in the retention and communication of information of all sorts within a national, possibly worldwide, information system.[4]

It was only 1964, but he could already see personal computers and the Internet on the horizon. This brilliant forecasting of the future was matched by a keen interest in the arts; *The Times* suggested that Bagrit was 'of a type not often encountered in the business world'.[5]

Bagrit used his experience to help Israel with its own technological problems and he established the Friends of Covent Garden. He also set up the Bagrit Trust and, after his death, this paid for the Bioengineering Department at Imperial College, London, which was named after him in 1991. In his private life he was also the president of British Technion, which helped the Israel University of Science and Technology, and was a governor of the Hebrew University in Jerusalem. In 1967, Elliott-Automation was taken over by English Electric, but Bagrit remained chairman till he retired at 70 in 1973.

Another budding engineer was Jack Dickman (1916–82). Son of a

Latvian Jewish father, he grew up in the Shoreditch Buildings in the East End. He was not encouraged in his youthful interest in engineering because the profession was considered downmarket at the time, and viewed as not much more than a grimy job where you got your hands covered in oil. It was only when he served in the Royal Electrical and Mechanical Engineers during the war that he was allowed to follow his hobby, as he was put into the team developing radar.

In 1946, when Dickman was demobilized, he used his £250 gratuity, plus £100 he borrowed from his mother, to start making radios in a back street, and then selling them to shops in the Edgware Road, a less than upmarket shopping area in the West End of London. He was the first to agree in later life that it was a sellers' market, as the manufacture of consumer goods had been practically halted during the war, so that everything could be concentrated on making war material.

Dickman called his company Fidelity, and it went on to manufacture not just radios, but radiograms, record players, tapes and stereos. Dickman described the growth of the company as 'one long slog' but, in 1973, the company grew to a manufacturing facility of 65,000 square feet and, thereafter, went on to build a 171,000 square-foot factory in West London.

By 1972, the company had gone public and the shares, which were launched at 70p, were 230p only a year later. £2.5 million profit was made on a £14 million turnover and Fidelity became the largest manufacturer of radios in the UK, with 55 per cent of the market.[6] They also produced one third of the stereos and quickly entered the new hi-fi market. Dickman was highly successful but continued to live a quiet life in Ealing, though he did buy himself a yacht, which he seldom had time to use. As he grew older, he brought his children into the business but he died in 1982, and by 1989 the business had been sold to Amstrad.

The most prominent amalgamator of major companies in the electrical industry during modern times was Arnold Weinstock (1924–2002), but few Jewish entrepreneurs could have risen from such unpromising beginnings. His mother was 46 when he was born in Dalston in London, where his father was a master cutter. The family had emigrated from Poland in 1904 and joined the Poets Road Synagogue with other Polish refugees; young Arnold sang in the choir.

Unhappily, his father died when he was 5, and his mother when he was 11. For some years he was brought up by his older brother. By dint of hard work he got into the London School of Economics and did his national service in the navy. He then took a job with a property developer, but his life changed when his friend, another property man, Max Joseph, sold him a ticket for a charity ball. Joseph sat him next to Netta Sobell, the daughter of Michael Sobell (1892–1993), who had a large electrical business. When Weinstock married her in 1949, he went to work for his father-in-law, who was also born in Dalston and came from a very similar background.

Sobell had gone into radios in 1920 when the medium first emerged and manufactured them successfully. In 1954, he sold the business but started a new one making television sets, again at the beginning of a market which was to boom. Sobell and Weinstock made Radio & Allied Industries one of the most efficient companies in the field and, when, in 1961, the giant General Electrical Company got into financial difficulties, the City financiers persuaded Sobell to merge with GEC. What they wanted was Sobell's management and, after the merger, which was really a reverse take-over, Radio & Allied were the largest shareholders in the new company.

In 1972, Sobell became Sir Michael, retired and left the running of the business to his son-in-law. From a £100 million turnover in 1960, the new company was to do £11 billion worth of business in 1996, the year Weinstock himself retired as managing director. The conglomerate that Weinstock built included the purchase of two other major British companies, Amalgamated Electrical Industries in 1967, and English Electric in 1968. He also took over Plessey, Ferranti and Avery Scales. Even in his last year in charge, he bought VSEC, the last seagoing-platform builder in Jarrow.

The *Guardian* is not the paper of choice for capitalists, but their obituary of Weinstock in 2002, when he died, was fulsome. He was lauded as, 'One of the nation's greatest and most successful industrial entrepreneurs in a period when manufacturing was steadily declining. The fact that Britain is still a major player in the global power industry and has a world-class, re-search-based, defence industry, can largely be attributed to his precocious skills.' The paper summed him up as, 'Britain's premier post-second-world-war industrialist'.[7]

The list of major activities undertaken by GEC in Weinstock's time was astounding. It manufactured all British naval vessels, radar systems and advanced avionics. It controlled the British nuclear-power programme until Weinstock fell out with Tony Benn, the Labour minister, just before Margaret Thatcher gained power. Benn was prepared to support some failing British companies, but Weinstock closed uneconomic factories without a second thought. He would take on the unions, too, when they were at the peak of their power. He earned the soubriquet of 'Britain's largest unemployer' from Hugh Scanlon, leader of the TUC.[8] When he moved in at GEC, Weinstock cut the headquarters' staff from 2,000 to 200.

There was another viewpoint, however. Professor William Gosling, first UK president of the European Society of Electrical Engineering, said in 1978, 'without Sir Arnold and his company, Britain's balance of trade would be unmanageable'.[9] Even in the slump of 1990/92, GEC turned in profits of £1 billion a year. Weinstock was knighted in 1970 and made a peer in 1980. He was still a Jew, though, and was blackballed for membership of Brooks's Club. In fairness, at about the same time, the pre-eminent Athenaeum Club accepted the application of a former Jewish Sergeant Major without demur. This was Moshe Davis, Chief Rabbi Jakobovits' secretary, whose list of supporters for membership on the notice board included the Archbishop of Canterbury and the Cardinal Archbishop of Westminster. Weinstock loved racing and won the 1979 Derby with Troy. He created a record when the horse was sold to stud for £7.2 million. Of course, he had his business failures too, notably the high-speed train and the Nimrod surveillance aircraft in the 1980s.

How did Weinstock achieve such remarkable success? By being single-minded, intellectually rigorous, exercising rigid cost control and applying thorough management. He abolished committees because he considered them a waste of time. In a lot of major companies this policy could be adopted with advantage; it is well said that a camel is a horse created by a committee. He was considered a forbidding figure when examining the divisions of the company, but among his intimates he was fair, witty and even sentimental. He was obsessed with his health and always wanted the best medical attention for his employees. He was also philanthropic on a massive scale with his Weinstock Fund, and in this he mirrored Sir Michael Sobell's charitable work.

It had to count, though, that he wasn't part of the Establishment. He wasn't running a collection of long-established British companies because he had the right parents, the right education, the right connections or was brought up in the same traditions. It must have made it easier to adapt to change, to seek the better way, to abandon old shibboleths and tear up the old rulebook. Brooks's Club was a long way from the Poets Road Synagogue, and perhaps it was as well for the country that he was never accepted as a member of the former and never forgot the latter.

In 1996, Weinstock was 72 and it was felt that his day was over. The company was worth £10 billion, its shares stood at £12.50 and the organization had amassed a cash mountain of £3 billion. It was agreed that he should stand down. It then only took his successors six years to ruin the firm. They invested heavily in far too many of the wrong things and lost a massive fortune in the dot-com crash. The shares were down to 4p in 2002, the year Weinstock died; he was much admired for never publicly criticizing the performance of those who came after him. At the same time, he might well have agreed with the comment of the great American investor, Warren Buffett, who said that one of his criteria for buying shares was, 'Could this company be run by an idiot?'

There is very little to be said about the early years of Sir Maurice Hatter (1930–). His parents were Orthodox Jews and he was demobilized in 1951 from the Royal Signals, where he had served as a radio mechanic. He had £100. In 1972, he founded IMO Precision Controls and he and his family still own the shares. It specializes in electrical components and started as a distributing company. Now it manufactures its own products and services customers who need factory automation and controls. It has subsidiaries in France, America and Italy and is very successful. Its sales in 2007/08 totalled over £13 million.

Hatter used his money in 1987 to create the Maurice Hatter Foundation and, in 1999, he was knighted. Among many other donations, in 1990, the Foundation financed the creation of the Hatter Institute for Cardiovascular Studies at University College Hospital in London and, in 1997, gave £1 million to help solve the problems of illiteracy in Britain. He also paid for the Hatter Student Building at Haifa University in Israel, and the fund has £6 million from which to finance its largesse. Much of the family money comes from dividends paid by the company, of which the most noteworthy, was one of £145 a share in 1991. As the family owned all the shares, the total of £14 million paid a lot of charitable bills.[10]

A strong supporter of Labour, between 2001 and 2009 Hatter donated £176,000 to the Party. He has also served as president of the Jewish charity, ORT, and is the honorary life president of Charlton Athletic. Highly regarded for both his business and charitable work, Hatter remains a very private man, as he is fully entitled to do. Certainly, IMO has helped keep Britain in the worldwide electronics business.

In 1952, the American post-war occupation of Japan came to an end. In 1949, the Americans had encouraged the creation of the Japanese Ministry of International Trade and Industry (MITI), which was one of the prime factors in Japan's astonishing growth as a manufacturing nation. The MITI decided that one method of improving the performance of Japanese industry was to go and study what Western nations were doing. In the 1950s, Britain played host to many Japanese groups, which came to look over factories to see what they could learn. They were taught well and learned what not to do, as well as what was beneficial. When they got home, with the help of their government they built factories and started to go into competition with the West in a wide variety of areas, such as cars and electronics. While their success was at the cost of many British manufacturers, it can be considered that the company with a long lead over its competitors is usually poorly run if it is overtaken by them.

There were, of course, British manufacturers who competed with the newcomers. One of the most successful was Amstrad. If Britain was to match exports with imports, this was absolutely vital. Amstrad is Alan Sugar (1947–), and the name comes from Alan Michael Sugar TRADing. Sugar was the son of an East End tailor, Nathan Sugar (1907–87), and left school at 16 to work as a clerk. This did not appeal for long and, by the time he was 17, he was selling car aerials and electrical goods from the back of a van he bought with a £100 loan. It was a modern form of the tallyman, and Sugar's principle, like Jack Cohen's at Tesco, was 'Pile 'em high and sell 'em cheap'.

As (the now Lord) Sugar said one evening in 2009 at Brunel University, there were, in his opinion, three requisites for success in business. You had to have knowledge of the industry, you had to have something special – what salesman call 'a hook' – and you had to work hard. Sugar's knowledge of electronics and, indeed, manufacturing were obviously limited but, as he is often quoted as saying, 'once you decide to work for yourself, you never go back to work for somebody else'.

In 1968, he started Amstrad and his first breakthrough was making hi-fi turntable covers and audio-amplifiers that could undersell the market leaders. By 1980, it was possible to float Amstrad on the Stock Exchange and the profits doubled every twelve months for years after. This was the time of the first tentative moves to bring computers into private homes. Sir Clive Sinclair was a pioneer and Sugar recruited a number of bright graduates who were happy to experiment to try to come up with a competing machine. William Poel, who had a Jewish grandmother, had been in electronics for over ten years and, in 1982, was made general manager of computer products. Before he left in 1985, Amstrad was launching computers. The year 1984 saw the first mass-market home-computer package. When the CPC 464 was launched, it was one of the most successful computers in Europe. It was said that two million were sold.

Sugar was a good manager, and if he was sometimes considered in the press as 'volcanic and irritable', it befitted the man whose TV programme, *The Apprentice*, would give the same impression many years later; publicly, he invariably appeared with a twinkle in his eye. In 1985, Amstrad went on to produce the first mass-market word processor and, in 1986, the first IBM-compatible PC, at a quarter the price of the market leaders. Within six months of its launch it had 25 per cent of the personal computer market. In 1989, Amstrad produced the first Sky satellite receivers and the first combined fax, telephone and answering machine. The company achieved 52 per cent of the personal fax market. In 1996, they launched mobile phones and in 1999, were voted the makers of the best Sky receiver. It all helped the economy.

There are, however, many ways of doing that. The 1990s was not a very happy period for John Major's government, particularly when sterling was forced out of the European Exchange Rate Mechanism. There was a run on the pound and the currency was under threat. To rebuild a currency, it helps if local businessmen can arrange for large sums of other currencies to be diverted into sterling in future years. In 1993, Sugar had come across a Danish company going bankrupt. He bought it and invested a total of £16 million in its mobile-phone production and technology. In 1997, he sold the company to Bosch, a German company, for £95 million. The difference of £80 million bolstered sterling and took a fraction of the pressure off the new Labour government's balance-of-payments problems.

It was, however, being chairman of Tottenham Hotspur that really brought Sugar into the public eye, but the job of football-club chairman is often a thankless task. Sugar said of his ten-year tenure that it was 'a waste of my life'. He would have been prouder of completing a task he agreed to perform for the Jewish Educational Development Trust, which was headed by a major customer of his, Stanley Kalms of Dixons. Chief Rabbi, Lord Jakobovits had enlisted Kalms to help build more Jewish faith schools, and Sugar agreed to take responsibility for creating one in Redbridge in Essex. King Solomon High School was opened in 1993. In addition, among many other charitable donations, Sugar gave £350,000 for the local Sugar Home for the Elderly and £200,000 to the Sinclair House Youth and Community Centre. He has acted in the best traditions of Jewish charity workers.

Inevitably, when you're at the frontiers of science, there are going to be failures. For Sugar, the most serious problem was a hard-drive controller he obtained from America that simply didn't work very well, and adversely affected the company's reputation in the 1990s. Clive Sinclair, though, had other problems and, in 1986, had been bought by Amstrad. In 2007 Amstrad itself was bought by BSkyB and in 2008, Sugar stood down as chairman. He was 61.

Away from Amstrad, Sugar achieved national recognition for *The Apprentice* TV shows, testing which young contestant was the most promising, in commercial terms. In 2009, he was given a peerage and became 'Enterprise Champion' for the government, an apparently rather meaningless appointment. What cannot be taken away from Lord Sugar is that, in 2009, he came fifty-ninth on the *Sunday Times* Rich List, with an estimated fortune of £830 million. Not bad for forty-six years' hard work, after starting from the back of a van.

Sugar made a fortune from recognizing new opportunities. Paul Eisler

(1907–92) invented the opportunities, but didn't have Sugar's ability to turn them into the sort of fortune his ability merited. For it was Eisler who invented the printed circuit board, which is a crucial part of any number of electrical products, from planes to computers, dishwashers to escalators. Eisler was reported to have been persuaded, in return for a job as head of a company's instrument division, to give up his patents for £1. He did receive recognition for his invention from France, Italy and Britain, but it was a poor return. Many claimed credit for inventing the printed circuit board, but Lord Herrman said in the Court of Appeal, 'There had been many attempts to do something of the sort before and none of them had ever proved useful or got on the workshop floor before Dr Eisler hit on his idea.'

The creation of modern information technology obviously involved highly sophisticated scientific innovation. To be valuable, however, it needed to be used by small organizations worldwide. Lyons was the first company to use computers in a big way to simplify and control its administration. This was many years before the owner of a small printing company in Newcastle stumbled across the possibilities of the new Amstrad 8256 computer.

David Goldman (1937–99) was a Sunderland man from an Orthodox family, who left school at 16 without any qualifications. He started a small printing company and ran it for twenty-five years, before he employed a young student, Graham Wylie, who believed that small businesses could benefit from the capabilities of the new Amstrad computers. Goldman saw the possibilities of Wylie's idea. It was an opportune time to make a sea change in his working life as the print unions were giving him a lot of trouble. So he packed in the printing and, in 1981, formed a new company, the Sage Group. In 1984 they produced a software programme for the Amstrad PCW word processor. It filled an enormous gap in the market and in 1989, the company was launched on the Stock Exchange. In 1999, it reached the FTSE 100.

David Goldman reminisced on his success one day, and said,

> We all started out because we needed to make money and, for most people, that's where it ends. We've obviously gone further and I have

to say that, when you float, it's rather like winning the pools. I'd always thought that I'd buy two cars and three yachts but when we did float, I discovered it wasn't to do with that – it was to do with security and peace of mind.

'Security and peace of mind': those who had persecuted the Jews over the centuries had created that overwhelming mindset. Goldman died in 1999, but the business went from strength to strength. Today, it is the third-largest supplier of enterprise resource-planning software in the world, and the largest supplier to small businesses. It operates in twenty-four countries and had a turnover in 2010 of £1.4 billion.

Goldman's insight and entrepreneurial flair built the company, but he was known as a relaxed and level-headed character. To create a company the size of Sage in such a small number of years was an astonishing achievement, and its location in Newcastle, which had been through very hard economic times, was a particularly happy coincidence. The company was eventually patron for the magnificent Sage Music auditorium on the Tyne quayside in Gateshead, and Goldman also contributed anonymously to any number of charities. As is the wish of many Orthodox Jews, he is buried in Jerusalem.

When the Japanese started to make first-rate televisions, hi-fis and transistor radios, they realized that they would have to have outlets in overseas countries in which to sell them. So did Stanley Kalms (1931–). Kalms is very typically Jewish. His parents were immigrants from Russia, and his father ran a company selling space on the London Underground before the war. Charles Kalms (1898–1978) then went into portrait photography in Southend with a friend, calling the company Dixons because there was only space for six letters on the shop front. Everybody wanted a picture of their loved ones during the war, and the business flourished as long as hostilities lasted. The company opened more branches, but were back to one in Edgware in 1947 when son, Stanley, joined the firm at the age of 16. His had been a comfortable middle-class upbringing, so the incentive to escape from poverty was not a consideration.

If portrait photography was off the boil, selling cameras might be a good substitute, and Kalms became a first-class salesman. He also built up a mail-order business which, by 1958, had 60,000 customers on its database. The big move, however, was when he spotted the possibilities of importing from Japan. Here again we see a Jewish entrepreneur seizing a new market before others climb on the band wagon. The key to his success was the drive and energy he brought to the business. He pushed his staff hard and became famous for the shouting and impatience with which he tackled problems. As his successor, John Clare, recalled, the atmosphere in the business was always 'competitive'.

With the standards that Kalms set, however, those who learned from working with him did very well. At one point it was said that no other company in the FTSE 100 has trained so many financial directors. His senior people were also given a good example in business morality: Kalms realized that a Jewish entrepreneur was always likely to be attacked if he put a foot wrong. 'Never let yourself be criticised for unethical behaviour', was his core belief.[11] By 1969, Dixons had over 100 shops.

Whatever was new in electrical retailing was going to be investigated by Kalms. He was quickly into the sale of video recorders, home computers and digital watches. He made a lot of good decisions, like buying Bennetts, and in 1984, he paid £248 million for his major competitor, Currys, in what he called 'the deal of the century'. He also made some very bad ones when he diversified into America, failed to buy Woolworths, and wished he had been unable to purchase Silo Inc. This adventure, in particular, led to massive losses – in 1994, Dixons lost £165 million – but his success with the core electrical shops pulled him through. Later ventures, like the creation of Freeserve, made Dixons the largest Internet service provider in the country by 1999, and PC World has been a very successful operation as well.

In his private life, Kalms did not set out to have the trappings of a typical tycoon. He lived in the same house in Stanmore for many years and his only real luxury was a thirty-metre boat parked on the Riviera. He got away from his office in Mayfair on many occasions to play bridge at a small club near Selfridges. One day, he was being told off by his bridge partner. When the criticism was over, Kalms said, 'If I'm so bad, how is it I'm running a large company and you're a minicab driver?'[12]

Outside business, he became treasurer of the Conservative Party from

2001 to 2003 and, in 2004, was awarded a peerage. He also created the Stanley Kalms Foundation, and has made very substantial contributions to a wide variety of charities. One of the secrets of Kalms' success was always his attention to detail. John Clare says, 'He could walk into any store and find ten different ways to improve business, however successful it was.' Kalms had endless enthusiasm and verve and an enormous amount of restless energy. He was also a great plagiarist. As he once recounted, 'My wife will tell you that going out with me in the first ten years of our marriage was agony. I had to stop at every competitor, get out of the car, and look at their windows.'

The downside to this style of management, of course, is that it is far more difficult to have a hands-on approach when the business is thousands of miles away, as with America. The ability of the founder to turn up in any store in the UK and keep the staff on their toes – for which Kalms was famous – often just doesn't work at long distances. If you can find the right staff to whom to delegate, overseas investments can be very profitable, but the wrong management can have a disastrous effect, which is far less easy to correct. The use of family members brought up with the same outlook by, say, the Rothschilds, is one solution, but the sheer scale of major companies today makes this solution practically impossible to adopt. The Rothschilds are the exception which proves the rule, though many of their top executives too are, of course, not family members.

Ranges of cameras and major photographic studios may get the head-lines, but not much is normally known about the small photo booths which are to be found in profusion on railway stations, in shopping centres and airports. If, however, a company owns 27,000 of them it is very big business indeed. Photo-Me was not the creation of Dan David (1929– 2011), but it grew to be an international world leader through his efforts. David was born to a well-off family in Romania and survived the war in Bucharest. 'We were lucky … my father lost his job, we were taken out of the flat where we lived, and I was thrown out of school ... we were not de-livered to the Germans.'[13]

After the war, in 1947, he helped Hanoir Hatzioni, a Zionist youth movement, to send 15,000 Romanian Jews to Palestine. He wanted to join them, but somebody had to stay behind to keep the organization in being.

He got married and his wife did get an exit visa to the new State of Israel. David was refused one and eventually they had to divorce.

In the 1950s, David formed a photographic cooperative in Romania and learned a lot about the industry. He was finally permitted to leave the country in 1960, and found his way to a small factory in Hersham in Surrey which made photo booths. They weren't very good but he got the right to set them up in Israel. In 1968, he joined the board and went to work to develop a process which would enable customers to get their photographs in colour. As this had to function all over the world and in different climatic conditions, the technology was complicated, but in 1972 he managed it. The company had moved to Walton-on-Thames and from then on it grew massively. In 1992, David became chairman and the company now has outlets worldwide.

In 2001, he was able to set up the Dan David prizes with a $100 million endowment. The objective is to reward outstanding achievement in scientific, technological, cultural or social areas. There is also an essay prize for British students, administered by the Royal Institution. David didn't sit back, though. In 2007, the company won the best innovator prize for its Photobook Pro, in 2008 the Best Dry Mini-Lab prize for its DKS 910 and in 2009 the Best Photo Kiosk TIPA Award for its Photobook Maker. David died in 2011 at 82.

Competition from cheap labour in Asia was always going to be a problem for British manufacturing. So was bad union–management relations. As the mills closed, the mines shut and the shipbuilding yards ran out of orders, the urgent need was for the country to take advantage of the newly developing hi-tech industries to replace what was being lost. The computer age opened up all kinds of opportunities, and tycoons like Alan Sugar and Stanley Kalms successfully stepped up to the plate.

It will, however, come as no surprise to the older generation that a lot of credit for Britain's success in this new IT world went to an under-21 year old. Grandchildren today so often know more about computers than the grown-ups. Indeed Jez (Jeremy) San (1966–) got his first computer from his parents as a Bar Mitzvah present. He was educated at JFS (the Jews' Free School), which he left at 16 for a course at Southgate Technical College. What really counted for San, however, was the work he did in his bedroom in Mill Hill, North London. He was deeply into computer software; the question for San was always, what else could you do with a computer?

Precociously, San wanted to get consulting jobs from large companies, but they were hardly likely to employ a 16 year old. So he set up Argonaut Software and was retained by British Telecom and Acorn to help improve their security systems. He went on to create the Super FX chip for the Super NES. He also took the time to write a book on quantum theory about the Sinclair QL. If this is getting a little technical, we can turn to what really fascinated San, which was the chance to produce games to play on the different computers which were now being manufactured. In 1986, he produced *Starglider* for the Atari ST and the Commodore Amiga. It was one of the first popular 3D computer games and it sold in the hundreds of thousands. San got £2 for each copy. Its success enabled him, at the age of 20, to start hiring people.

San's *X* was then published by Nintendo as the first Game Boy game, and he helped develop the first 3D graphic accelerator, which made his *Star Fox* game possible on the Super NES. *Star Fox* was one of the best-selling computer games of all time. The business flourished, even producing games for Disney and Harry Potter and, in 2000, still only 34, San went public. The shares he sold produced £24 million. As far as computer games were concerned, he had become a highly regarded professional. So much so that, at only 34, in 2002, he was awarded the OBE for services to the computer-game industry.

Argonaut produced well over forty games between 1984 and 2004, but then ran into serious cash-flow problems. These led to the collapse of the company, but by then a whole industry had been established in Britain. San had been a pioneer and he went on to get involved in Online Poker and in producing software for the iPhone and Blackberry, which is where he is today.

Argonaut wasn't the only company to hit choppy commercial water. The reputation of Scottish banks plunged during the debt crisis, but their support for Scottish enterprise was a vital component of the Scottish economy for very many years. One of the beneficiaries was Richard Emanuel (1968–) who came from a Jewish family in Glasgow, where his father was a chemistry lecturer at Glasgow University and his mother a teacher. Coming from an academic family, Richard was encouraged to study, but it really wasn't his scene. With no hard feelings, a lot of sons would rather strike out on their own than follow in their father's footsteps.

So he foreswore university and looked for what was new in business. Initially he thought the future might lie in health clubs and he got a job in one as a trainee sales manager. He was the top salesman in selling vitamins to the members, but he found the banks wouldn't lend a 19 year old the money to start his own health club. Then the club discovered he was trying to set up on his own and fired him. He had noted, however, how many of the members needed someone to look after their mobile phones. Changing tack, he thought maybe that was the future. He became a trainee sales manager for a small telecom firm and, in 1991, at the age of 23, he had £1,300 in savings, and Bank of Scotland gave him an overdraft of £3,000 to start his own business.

Full of enthusiasm and prepared to work extremely hard, Emanuel was in the right place at the right time; the demand for mobile phones was enormous. He set out to sell them door-to-door and he was so good at it that, in 1993, he was able to open his first shop in Glasgow, even if it was only 200 square feet. Over the next few years he opened a shop about every three weeks. By 1999, he had 150. His turnover increased, year on year, by over 150 per cent. He became the fastest-growing retailer in Scotland and, in 1999, he was awarded the Entrepreneur of the Year prize. In that year, BT Cellnet made him an offer of £42 million for his company, DX, and Emanuel decided to take it. He also got an MBE for services to the telecommunications industry.[14]

At which point he switched to Holland and started Interactive Telecom Solutions, which is active in many areas of the electronics and telecommunications fields. In eight years, he moved the annual turnover from €5 million to €500 million and his personal fortune to over £200 million. How is all this done? Energy and detailed application, eighteen-hour days, and, in Emanuel's case, an ability to merit loyalty. In the early days, he would phone any manager who had done well and congratulate him, and this kind of positive head-office involvement makes a difference. He did not want to get a reputation as a ruthless boss. Emanuel has his own philosophy: 'The most important thing in a goal is not what you achieve but what you become in the achievement … if you set a goal to become a successful person, but become a horrible person in the process, that's not good.'[15]

It had always been shipbuilding on the Clyde, but when that collapsed, it certainly helped the local economy when Emanuel started one of the largest mobile repair and servicing companies in his home town. Emanuel is only one modern Jewish entrepreneur who reassures the community that the supply of able businessmen is not drying up.

NOTES

1. Goldstone family folklore.
2. Joanne Vronskaya, *Independent*, 31 July 1996.
3. *The Times*, 30 April 1979.
4. Ibid.
5. Ibid.
6. *Jewish Chronicle*, 20 July 1973.
7. Alex Brummer, *Guardian*, 24 July 2002.
8. Ibid.
9. Ibid.
10. *Management Today*, 1 September 1992.
11. Often quoted.
12. The author was playing at the same table.
13. Jenni Frazer, *Jewish Chronicle*, 4 April 2005.
14. Michael Greenwood, *Independent*, 26 February 1998.
15. *Fife Today*, 11 July 2011.

Chapter sixteen

The Will to Survive

The problem for any developed nation is to remain in that fortunate position: the forces which may bring about its decline are many. One of the most important is the ability of poorer nations to undercut the costs of manufacturing by the use, by Western standards, of underpaid labour. Where industries are labour intensive, competing with the poorer nations is extremely difficult. The decline of the clothing sector of British manufacturing is an example of this. Britain has also seen the elimination or major decline in its economy of shipbuilding, coal mining, steel production and china and pottery.

To deal with these problems, developed nations turn to economic areas where they can still lead. Among these are those industries that emerge from technological improvements which they have themselves created. One study in the latter part of the twentieth century suggested that as many as 40 per cent of the new inventions in those 100 years had emerged from Britain. Everything from television and the jet engine to the hovercraft and the computer. Unfortunately, the British are better at inventions than they are at marketing.

In the attempt to keep the balance of payments in some kind of equilibrium, there is also, of course, the section of trade called 'invisibles'. The City of London plays a very important role in international finance, and the earnings it produces are very substantial under this heading. Overall, there is the constant need to adjust to a changing world, to adopt new technology, to reduce overmanning – made possible by that technology – and to provide the world with better-quality products.

All of this involves change – and change is often uncomfortable. It takes fresh thinking, it often involves gambling and it means giving up traditional methods. As we've seen, in tackling the problems of change, the Jews had a number of advantages. Because they were wedded to the traditions of their religion, they were often not accepted into normal mainstream organizations. They were not allowed to join guilds during the middle ages, as these were Christian fraternities. For centuries they were not allowed to be members of government, so they felt no responsibility for the status quo; they would abide by it, but it wasn't theirs. When the opportunity for change occurred, they were often more willing to make the effort to move with the times than those who felt they had played a part in creating the traditional approach.

The Jewish community in Britain today is concentrated in a few major cities: London, Manchester and Leeds are the largest. This contraction is due to the greater business opportunities they offer, but it is a change from the situation in the eighteenth and nineteenth centuries. In those days the geographical expansion of the community was due to poor emigrants, and the settled congregations wanting their new poverty-stricken brethren to go somewhere else, if humanly possible. So they would give them some money to get started as pedlars, and they would head for the new towns being created by the industrial revolution.

This process went on for a long time and, as we've seen, it also applied before the Second World War, when the government wanted new business development in the areas worst hit by unemployment. So we find that a considerable number of provincial towns and cities benefited from Jewish entrepreneurs. The list is remarkable:

Aberbargoed	Sterilin
Banbury	S. Samuelson
Basingstoke	Lansing Bagnall
Belfast	Belfast Ropemakers
	Harland and Wolff
	Jaffe Spinning Mills
	Stanley Leisure
Biggleswade	Kayser Bondor
Birmingham	Foseco
Blackburn	Arthur Hubert

Blackley	Blackley Dyeworks
Bradford	S.L. Behrman
Brighton	Alliance Building Society
	Gross Cash Registers
Cambridge	Warmex
Cardiff	Tudor Accessories
Chadderton	Japinda
Cleetor Moor	Kangol
Cleveland	S. Samuelson
Coventry	Coventry Machinist
	Triumph
Derby	British Cellulose
Edinburgh	Edinburgh Festival
Gateshead	Sigmund Pumps
Glasgow	Yarrow
Glemsford	Cannon Avent
Huddersfield	Gannex
Hull.	M. Samuelson
Huntingdon	Horatio Myer
Leeds	Alexandre
	Berwin & Berwin
	Montague Burton
	Rakusens
	Stylo
Leicester	Hart & Levy
	Metalastik
	Nailsworth Colliery
Liverpool	Lewis's
	Mersey Tunnel Co.

Luton	Marida
Manchester	Clayton Aniline
	Coats Viyella
	Granada
	Jerrold Holdings
	Marks & Spencer
	Simon Engineering
Newcastle	Jackson the Tailor
Northampton	Mettoy
	The Sage Group
North Shields	Essoldo
Norwich	Soman
Nottingham	Hyman & Alexander
	Nottingham Manufacturing
	Simon May & Co.
Plymouth	Ravenseft
Salford	Ward & Goldstone
Sheffield	Viners
Shrewsbury	Corset Silhouette
Stalybridge	Stering Group
Stansted	Neotronics
Sunderland	Usworth Colliery
Swansea	Mettoy
Walton on Thames	Photo Me
Whitehaven	Marchon

Of course, the Jews seldom dominated an industry. The property companies, who took advantage of the post-Second World War demand for reconstruction, were an exception. What the Jews did, time and again, was spark new thinking and set better standards for others to follow: 'As good as Marks & Spencer' when it came to looking after staff; 'Not a gin

palace – a Chef & Brewer' for selling food in pubs; not settling for
wounded ex-servicemen making only wicker baskets at Remploy. It had
always been part of the survival system of the Jews to be better than their
oppressors. They weren't strong enough to overcome them, they were
only a tiny minority and they had no power. The only options left were the
ability to work harder, to think more cleverly and to look at the problems
positively. If there were obstacles, they were there to be overcome.

There are a number of ways of contributing to a country's economy.
There is the invention of new products, helping those who create them
to develop them, and leading by example. A large number of products
which Jews actually invented have been chronicled. Companies have
been detailed, which would have been likely to fail without the ability of
their Jewish leader to point them, and keep them going, in the right direction. And there have been the examples so many of them have shown
to the industries in which they were working. If they were the biggest,
the most innovative, or the highest regarded, their influences would be
great, even if they were only primus inter pares, the first among equals
in their field.

Very often, the Jews were to be found leading the industry, appointed
as chairman or president of the association, sitting on the council and
serving in public office. For those who were anti-Semitic, it smacked of
conspiracy and overweening ambition. The truth was that the Jews were
invariably chosen for the posts because, like the far greater number of
non-Jewish incumbents, they were considered the most likely to carry
them out well.

This didn't mean that they would, necessarily, be given the posts with
the most prestige; the Viener cutlery family in Sheffield may have served
as president of the Cutlery Manufacturers Association, but they were
never chosen to be Master Cutler. Lord Weinstock was blackballed at
Brooks's. Those who looked down on Jews as newcomers, interlopers
and foreigners often had the power to deny them the positions they
deserved, and used it. These are exceptional cases though, and exceptional cases make bad law. For the most part, the candidates won through
on merit and were given the prizes.

Over a period of 350 years, any commercial group of people is going to have some bad apples, and the Jewish community is no exception. It might have been standard practice for a general fighting a Continental campaign to take bribes from battlefield suppliers in the eighteenth century, but that didn't help Solomon de Medina when Marlborough fell out with Queen Anne. With the general in disgrace, Medina only had his knighthood for comfort when he tried to get paid for the bread and wagons he had provided for the allied armies. As far as the £63,000 of bribes was concerned, it was money very badly invested.

In modern times, a number of scandals involving Jewish entrepreneurs have made lurid headlines, and sent the community into paroxysms of despair. For the Jewish community, six peerages, five high offices of state, four Fellows of the Royal Society, three Nobel Prize winners, and two Lord Justices do not equal one Lord Kagan or Robert Maxwell. Few of the scandals were criminal, though a handful of miscreants did finish up in jail. The black sheep, however, are only specks in the law-abiding flock.

In idle moments, one might mull over again the loss other countries suffered by forcing their Jews to migrate to Britain. Berlin might have had the Edinburgh Festival if they had kept Rudolf Bing; Hungary might have had the duplicator industry if they hadn't made life so difficult for the Gestetners; the Russians could have pioneered fork-lift trucks, if they had avoided losing Sir Leon Bagrit. Romania could have had photo booths if it had kept Dan David. Instead the talents of these men were placed – and with gratitude – at the disposal of the British economy. Obviously, the democratic environment and the equal opportunities Britain offered were major factors in the success of the Jewish entrepreneurs, but the human raw material for creating valuable companies was provided by other countries.

Many of the organizations the Jews created are still in good economic health, though a lot more have disappeared over the decades. Where the companies still ply their trade, the number of Jewish directors on their main boards are usually few and far between. It's difficult to generalize as to why this is so. A lot of Jews would put it down to anti-Semitism, because the centuries of discrimination from which their ancestors suffered have left deep scars. Many have a tendency to see anti-Semites under the bed. Another truth, however, is that Jews have another centuries-old tradition; that they only survive by being prepared to look after themselves. It is only, if all else fails, that they fall back onto 'God will provide'.

In the 1980s Chief Rabbi Jakobovits was asked to join with the Church leaders in the country in condemning the insufficient effort they considered the government was making to look after the poor. The Chief Rabbi regretted he couldn't give his clerical friends that support. He pointed out that the Jewish approach was to give the poor some money to start up in business in a small way. The money did not carry interest, and could be paid back when something had been sold. That was the task and responsibility of the community. A lot of Jews still remain uneasy about relying on others to look after them. They protect their own synagogues and have their own charities to look after those who are disadvantaged. They feel safer looking after themselves. That means running their own businesses and not being at the mercy of anybody – in the boardroom or anywhere else.

It was the same with education. For centuries free schools were not a state benefit. Most people couldn't read or write. For Jews, it was part of the culture to learn from reading books. The learning was self-imposed, not education by the state. It applied to every family as a desirable objective. Sergey Brin, co-founder of Google, once said that he came 'from one of those Russian–Jewish families where they expected even the plumber to have a PhD'.[1]

At the end of the day, we are left with the words of the poet Shelley. When the traveller reaches the ruin in the desert, he sees an inscription, which is still legible among all the rubble. On it are the words, 'My name is Ozymandias, king of kings: Look on my works, ye Mighty, and despair!' For, in a couple of generations, who will remember the colossi who in their day were Isaac Wolfson, Jack Cohen, Marcus Samuel, Alfred Mond, Sidney Bernstein or Max Joseph? We come full circle to Chris Patten on the first page of the book: 'How do we pass over the extraordinary Jewish contribution – out of all proportion to their beleaguered numbers – to what we call European civilization?'

When the Jewish community considers the success of its former members in the economic world, there is always a thought that perhaps the process will come to an end. Perhaps the next generation will be unable to emulate their ancestors. That they will lack the goad of original poverty to encourage them to try harder. That they will desert commerce for the higher-status worlds of medicine, the law and accountancy.

When, however, you look at the present crop of Jewish businessmen in this country, a lot of them are still working to the same principles that motivated their ancestors; they are still looking for the holes in the market, the gaps that need filling. They are still prepared to gamble, still uncommitted to traditional methodology. From the great retailer, Sir Philip Green, to the creator of the largest foreign-currency company, Lloyd Dorfman, to massive property companies like Sir John Ritblat's British Land, they keep looking for opportunities, and it is only with such an outlook that Britain can flourish in the years to come.

Does all the credit for the economic contributions belong to the Jewish entrepreneurs? Not for a moment. Many had partners, all had members of their staff who made major contributions, they had large workforces who were loyal to the companies. Where they deserve credit is for providing the leadership, without which the companies would not have been successful, and would often have never seen the light of day. They often needed luck, but when you consider the problems they had to overcome, the backgrounds they came from, and the narrow escapes so many had from death by one dictatorship or another, they also followed an old English saying, 'you have to make your own luck'.

Just as vital a point, though, is the sheer grit of the Jewish families from which sprang the entrepreneurs. All they ever had to do to avoid the discrimination and persecution from which they suffered was to adopt the national religion. The later generations had seen six million of their co-religionists murdered, just for being Jews. The temptation to give up had been attractive to millions of Jews over the centuries, and they had given up what they considered to be an unequal struggle. Those who became modern Jewish entrepreneurs were from families which hadn't given up; their offspring might do so, but they had to have come from generations who had stuck it out, who would – and, quite literally, millions did over the centuries – die for it. This inner strength was built into them.

For many Jews, there now comes an embarrassing moment. Religious belief is so unfashionable today that many of the entrepreneurs would deny that they owed much to the faith of their ancestors. Many also converted during their lifetimes. The fact remains, though, that in their success, they showed the attributes which emerged from the experiences of their forebears. Unfashionable or not, Judaism deserves the credit.

In Britain today, there is the serious challenge of what can be done to help the underclass. Those who have no strong family backgrounds, no decent education, no jobs and feel they have no prospects. Most of the Jewish community came from exactly the same background of poverty, no prospects and a lack of formal education. They often couldn't even speak English. What they did have were two advantages which are often derided today: their religion and their families. Perhaps it is time to re-evaluate these old-fashioned concepts to see whether they have been discarded unwisely.

Of course, a lot of Jews who are not mentioned in the book could lay claim to being unfairly excluded. I plead guilty and apologize to their memories, or to their present-day contributions. There may well be sufficient candidates for a second book, so prolific has been the community in turning out exactly the sort of businessmen who were needed, and when they were needed. Equally, I can foresee criticism that more space should have been devoted to one or other of the more than 300 founders identified.

Any author writing history hates to hand over the manuscript. There are always ways of improving it, details which might benefit from even deeper research, and the question of whether each interpretation is 100-per-cent fair and objective. The flip side of the coin is that the reader has the same opportunity to decide whether they agree with the conclusions.

At the 250th anniversary dinner of the Jewish Board of Deputies in July 2011, Prince Charles said, 'the talents and contributions of our Jewish community are not sufficiently well known by the public at large, and not sufficiently celebrated'.[2] So, at a very, very distant remove, it could be held that this book is by Royal Command.

Everybody would like to be immortal but, as positive contributors to the economy of Britain, all the Jewish entrepreneurs would take pleasure in having made a contribution to the country which is known in very Orthodox Jewish circles as 'The Land of Mercy'. Britain has shown great tolerance towards its Jewish population for 350 years. That continual kindness was morally and ethically correct, but it was also one of the best financial investments the country ever made.

NOTES

1. Chief Rabbi, Lord Sacks, *The Times*, 24 September 2011.
2. *Jewish Chronicle*, 20 July 2011.

Appendix A

Jews who Contributed to the British Economy

Aizenberg, Jack	Japinda
Alliance, Lord David	Coats Viyella
Anselm, Marilyn	Hobbs
Arbib, Sir Martyn	Perpetual Fund Management Co.
Ascher, Hermann	Red-Ashay
Atkin, Edward and Celia	Cannon Avent
Austin, Frank	Austin Furniture
Bagrit, Sir Leon	Elliott-Automation
Balcon, Michael	Ealing Films
Baron, Bernhard	Carreras
Behrens, Sir Jacob	Sir Jacob Behrens & Sons
Behrens, Solomon Levi	S.L. Behrens & Co.
Benjamin, Susan	Halcyon Days
Bennett, Maurice and Michael	Warehouse, Oasis
Bernard, Elliott	Chelsfield Partners
Bernstein, Lord Sidney	Granada
Bernstein, William	Fortress Property
Berwin, Barnett	Berwin & Berwin
Bettmann, Siegfried	Triumph Motorcycles
Bing, Sir Rudolf	Edinburgh Festival

Bischoffsheim, Henri Louis	Bischoffsheim & Goldschmidt
Blausten, Cyril	Simo Properties
Blausten, Leonard	Simo Properties
Bloch, Sidney	Hallmark Securities
Blond, Anthony	Anthony Blond
Bloom, John	Colston Dishwashers
Bloom, Patsy	Pet Plan
Bloom, Tony	Premierbet
Bloomfield, Instone	Oddeninos Properties
Blumenau, Hans	Corset Silhouette
Bourne, Sir Clive	Seabourne Express Couriers
Bradman, Godfrey	European Land
Bruh, Max	Frank Usher
Brunel-Cohen, Sir Jack	Remploy
Bunzl, Hugo	Bunzls
Burton, Sir Montagu (Moshe Osinsky)	Burtons the Tailors
Burton, Raymond	Topshop
Byng, Gustav (Gustav Binswanger)	General Electric
Cahn, Albert	Nottingham Furnishing Co.
Cahn, Sir Julien	Jays & Campbell
Carrizos, Joseph	
Chandler, Victor	Victor Chandler
Chinn, Rosser and Sir Trevor	Lex
Clore, Sir Charles	City & Centre Properties
	British Shoe Corporation
Cohen, Elsie	Academy Cinema
Cohen, George	George Cohen 600 Group
Cohen, Sir Jack (Jakob Kohen)	Tesco
Cohen, John	Rodwell Group

Cohen, Levy Emmanuel	*Brighton Guardian*
Cohen, Lord Lewis	Alliance Building Society
Cohen, Sir Ronald	Apax Partners
Colman, Alec	E. Alec Colman Investments
Conrad, Neville	Conrad Ritblat
Coral, Joe (Joseph Kagalitzky)	Corals
Corob, Sidney	Corob Holdings
Cotton, Jack	City Centre Properties
Cowan, Sidney	Samuel Properties
Cussins, Manny (Manessah)	Cussins Group
da Costa, Anthony	
Davidson, Manny	Asda Property Holdings
Dalton, Percy	Percy Dalton Group
David, Dan	Photo Me
Davis, Mick	X Strata
de Medina, Sir Solomon	
Dellal, Jack	Dalton Barton
Dennis, Felix	Dennis Publishing, Microware
Desmond, Richard	Northern & Shell, *OK Magazine*
Deutsch, André	André Deutsch
Deutsch, Oscar	Odeon
Dickman, Jack	Fidelity Radio
Djanogly, Sir Harry	Nottingham Manufacturing
Dorfman, Lloyd	Travelex
Dormido, Solomon	Cargo Insurance
Drage, Benjamin	Drages
Dreyfus, Charles	Clayton Aniline
Dreyfus, Henry	British Cellulose
Duveen, Lord Joseph	Duveen Brothers

Earl, Robert	Planet Hollywood
East, Barry	Town & City Properties
Edwards, Henry (Henry Eisenschmidt)	Friendly Hotels
Ehrman, Ralph	Airfix
Eisenberg, Zef	Maximuscle
Elias, Lord Julian	Odhams
Ellis, Joseph Joel	Ellistone Colliery
Elek, Paul	Granada Publishing
Emanuel, Richard	DX
Epstein, Brian	NEMS
Erdman, Edward	Edward Erdman
Feldman, Lord Basil	Dunbee-Combex
Feldman, Heinrich	Inremco
Fenston, Felix	Metropolitan & Provincial Properties
Fink, Lord Stanley	The Man Group
Finniston, Sir Monty	British Engineering
Fiszman, Leon and Danny	Star Diamonds
Forman, Harry	Forman Smoked Salmon
Fox, Cecil	Stem Properties
Fox, Victor	Medopharma
Freed, Norman	Jane Norman
Freedman, Joseph	Jays & Campbell
Freedman, Louis	Ravenseft
Freshwater, Osias	Freshwater Group
Friedlander, Ernest and Julius	Singer & Friedlander
Gabbay, David	O & H Holdings
Galley, Carol	Mercury Asset Management

Gavron, Lord Robert	St Ives Group
Gerstenberg, Isidor	Council of Foreign Bond Holders
Gestetner, David	Gestetners
Gideon, Rehuel & Samson	
Gliksten, Jacob	J. Gliksten & Son
Gold, David and Ralph	Ann Summers
Gold, Joe	Centrovincial Estates
Goldberg, Samson J.	Smart Brothers
Goldman, David	Sage Group
Goldschlager, Laurent	Thames Estates
Goldschmidt, Louis	B.A. Goldschmidt
Goldschmidt, Louis	Pantherella
Goldsmid, Benjamin and Abraham	B. & A. Goldsmid
Goldsmith, Mac (Max Goldschmidt)	Metalastik
Goldstein, Arthur	Warmex
Goldstein, Ronald and Peter	Superdrug
Goldstone, Meyer	Ward & Goldstone
Gollancz, Sir Victor	Victor Gollancz
Goodenday, Jacob Nathan (John)	Kayser Bondor
Gorvy, Manfred	Hanover Acceptances
Gotley, Andrea	Alphasense
Gotley, Paul	Neotronics
Grade, Lew (Louis Winogradsky)	Associated Television
Graff, Laurance	Graff Diamonds
Grant, Albert (Abraham Rotheimer)	Leicester Square
Green, Michael	Carlton Communications
Green, Lionel	Windsmoor
Green, Sir Philip	BHS

Hambro, Carl Joachim	Hambros
Hamlyn, Lord Paul (Paul Hamburger)	Octopus
Hammerson, Lew	Hammerson Properties
Harris, Bob and Harry	Harris & Co.
Harris, Lou	Harella
Harris, Lord Philip	Carpetright
Harrison, Gabriel	Amalgamated Investments
Hart, Sir Israel	Hart & Levy
Hatter, Sir Maurice	IMO
Hecht, Ernest	Souvenir Press
Herbert, Arthur	Tom Martin
Heymann, Lewis	Heymann & Alexander
Heymann, Lutz	Marida Hats
Hille, Salaman	Hille
Hirst, Lord Hugo (Hugo Hirsch)	General Electric
Horwitz, Bela	Phaidon
Howard, Alan	Brevan Howard
Hulse, R.J.	Medo Chemicals
Hyams, Harry	Oldham Estate
Hyams, Joe	Viyella
Hyams, Phillip and Sidney	H. & G. Kinemas
Isaac, Samuel	Mersey Tunnel
Jacobs, Clive	Holiday Autos
Jacobs, John	Times Furnishing
Jacobson, Harvey	The Jacobson Group
Jacobson, Lionel	Jacksons the Tailors
Jaffe, Abe	Currie Motors
Jaffe, David	David Jaffe & Co.

Jonassohn, David	Ulsworth Colliery
Joseph, Sir Maxwell	Grand Metropolitan and Compass
Joseph, Samuel	Bovis
Kagan, Lord Joseph (Juozapas Kaganas)	Gannex
Kalms, Lord Stanley	Dixons, Freeserve, PC World
Kaye, Sir Emmanuel	Lansing Bagnall
Kaye, Phillip and Reggie (Krapifko)	Garfunkels
Kaye, Sam and Adam	Ask Pizzas
Kelvin, Ray	Ted Baker
Khalili, Nasser David	Flavermead
Kirschel, Laurence	Consolidated Developments
Kissin, Lord Harry	Guinness Peat
Kobler, Fred (Bedrich Kobler)	Grand Metropolitan
Korda, Sir Alexander (Sandor Kellner)	London Films
Kove, Nicholas (Miklos Klein)	Airfix
Lampl, Sir Frank	Bovis
Langsam, Alex	Britannia Hotels
Leaver, Marcus	Allied Land
Lebus, Louis	Harris Lebus
Lee, Arnold	Imry Properties
Leigh, Kennedy	Kennedy Leigh
Levene, Lord Peter	United Scientific Holdings
Levine, Peter	Imperial Energy
Levinstein, Herbert	British Dyestuffs Corporation
Levinstein, Ivan	Blackley Dyestuffs
Levy, Isaac	Levy & Franks
Levy, Joe	Stock Conversion

Levy, Joseph	*The Daily Telegraph*
Levy, Lewis (Turnpike)	
Levy, Lord Michael	Magnet Records
Lewis, Bernard and Jack	United Draperies
Lewis, Cecil	Burlington Estates
Lewis, David (Pokrasse)	River Island
Lewis, David	Lewis Stores
Lewis, Philip	Lambert, Smith, Hampton
Lewis, Samuel	Samuel Lewis
Lipton, Stuart	Chelsfield Partners
Littman, Joe	Aldford House
Lobbenberg, Hans	Corset Silhouette
Loewe, Siegmund	Vickers
Lopez, Menassah	
Lottenberg, Jacob	Lynton Holdings
Luck, Laurence	Charterbridge Corporation
Lyons, Sam	Alexandre
Manousso, Luke	Maybrook Properties
Margulies, Ephraim	S. & W. Berisford
Marks, David and Julia	Marks & Belfield
Marks, Harry	*Financial News, Evening News*
Marks, Sir Simon	Marks & Spencer
Marks, Stephen	French Connection
Mattes, Richard	Mattessons
Maxwell, Robert (Jan Ludwik Hoch)	Pergamon Press
Mayer, Sir Robert	Robert Mayer Concerts for Children
Messer, Sam	Mansion House
Miller, Sir Eric	Peachey

Mintz, Lou	Selincourt
Mocatta, Moses	Mocatta & Goldsmid
Mond, Lord Alfred	ICI
Mond, Ludwig	Brunner Mond
Montagu, Samuel (Lord Swaythling)	Samuel Montagu & A. Keyser
Morrison, Jack	Amalgamated Securities
Moser, Henry	The Jerrold Group
Moses, Elias	E. Moses & Co.
Moses, Moses	Moss Bros
Muller, Leopold	De Vere Hotels
Myer, Horatio	Horatio Myer
Myers, Bernard	Rodwell Group
Myers, Sefton	Rodwell Group
Nathan, Barnett	B. & I. Nathan
Nathan, Joseph Edward	Glaxo
Nathanson, Hilton	Marble Bar
Neurath, Walter	Thames & Hudson
Newmark, Louis	Louis Newmark
Ney, Arthur	Londex
Oppenheim, Henry	City Wall Properties
Oppenheim, Meyer	Argyle Securities
Oppenheimer, Hans	Coutinho, Caro
Oppenheimer, Ralph	Stemcor
Ostrer, Isidore	Gaumont British
Oved, Moshe	Cameo Corner
Payton, Bob	Chicago Pizza Pie Factory
Pearlberg, Beatrice	Ve-ri-best Man

Pearl, David	Structadene
Pears, Bernard	William Pears Group
Phillips, Jackie	Jackie Phillips
Phillips, Samuel Levi	Haverfordwest Bank and Milford Bank
Plurendon, Lord Rudy (Rudy Sternberg)	The Sterling Group
Poliakoff, Joseph	Multitone
Potel, Robert	Star (Greater London)
Raines, Israel	Raines Dairy
Raitz, Vladimir	Horizon Holidays
Rakusen, Lloyd	Rakusens
Ratner, Gerald	Ratners
Rayne, Lord Max	London Merchant Securities
Reiss, David	Reiss
Reuben, David and Simon	Transworld Metals
Reuter ,Paul	Reuters
Ritblat, Sir John	British Land
Roden, Stuart	Lansdowne Partners
Ronson, Gerald	Heron Holdings
Rose, Jack and Philip	Land Investors
Rosenfeld, Andrew	Minerva
Rothschild, Lord Jacob	RIT Capital Partners
Rothschild, Nat	Atticus Fund
Rothschild, Nathan Meyer	Rothschilds
Rothschild, Lord Nathan Meyer	Rothschilds, Four Per Cent Industrial Dwelling Society
Rubens, John	Central & District Properties
Rubin, Berko	Liverpool Shoe Co.

Rubin, Stephen	Pentland
Saatchi, Lord Maurice and Charles	Saatchi & Saatchi
Salmon, Sir Isidore	Lyons
Salomans, Sir David	London & Westminster Bank
Salomon, Myer and Nathan	Salomons
Salvador, Francis Joseph	
Samada, Joseph	Samada Brothers
Samuel, Barnett (Boruch Lieblinski)	Barnett Samuel
Samuel, Basil	Great Portland Estates
Samuel, Dudley	Dudley, Samuel & Harrison
Samuel, Frank	Decca, United Africa
Samuel, Harold	Land Securities
Samuel, Harriet	H. Samuel
Samuel, Howard	Great Portland Estates
Samuel, Lord Marcus	Shell, M. Samuel & Co.
Samuelson, Sir Bernhard	Sir Bernhard Samuelson & Co.
Samuelson, Martin	Martin Samuelson & Co.
San, Jeremy (Jez)	Argonaut Software
Sassoon, Vidal	Vidal Sassoon
Scheckman, Solomon	Essoldo
Schon, Lord Frank	Marchon
Schreiber, Chaim	Schreibers
Schuster, Sir Felix	National Provincial Bank
Scriven, Sol	Scrivens
Sebba, Sam	Warnford Investments
Seligman, Richard	APV
Sherman, Archie	Metrovincial Properties
Shine, Archie	Archie Shine
Shine, Barnett	Central & District Properties

Sigmund, Miroslav	Sigmund Pumps
Simon, Henry	Simon Engineering
Simon, Peter	Manson
Singer, Julius	Singer & Friedlander
Sobell, Sir Michael	Radio & Allied
Solomon, Sir Harry	Hillsdown Holdings
Solomons, Jack	Jack Solomons Boxing
Somerfeld, John (Kurt Joachim)	Somerfeld Track
Somlo, Paul	Somportex
Soros, George (Soros György)	The Soros Fund
Sorrell, Sir Martin	WPP Group
Speyer, Sir Edgar	London Underground
Spiro, Moss	Fly Over Investments
Spreiregen, Jacob	Kangol
Sputz, Otto	Parway Land
Steigenberger, Louis	Berger Paints
Stein, Mark	Ladbrokes
Steinberg, Jack	Alexon
Steinberg, Lord Leonard	Stanley Leisure
Steinkopff, Edward	Apolinnaris, *St James's Gazette*
Sterling, Sir Louis	EMI
Stern, David and Hermann	Stern Brothers
Stern, William	The Stern Group of Companies
Sternberg, Rudy	Stirling Group
Sternberg, Sir Sigmund	CRU
Strauss, Bertram	Virol
Sugar, Lord Alan	Amstrad
Tabaznik, Anthony	Arrow Generics
Tabor, Michael	Arthur Prince

Tait, Richard and Thomas	Sterilin
Tchenguiz, Robert and Vincent	Rotch Property
Tell, Wernher	Tell
Thorn, Sir Jules	Thorn Electrical, DER
Tillman, Harold	Honorbilt
Tobin, Leonard	Lintang
Tuck, Raphael	Raphael Tuck
Ullmann, Philip	Corgis
Viener, Adolphe	Viners
Walton, Issy	Scottish Metropolitan Properties
Wanamaker, Sam	The Globe Theatre
Warburg, Siegmund	Warburgs
Weidenfeld, Lord George	Weidenfeld & Nicholson
Weinberg, Jacob	Simon May & Co.
Weinstock, Lord Arnold	GEC
Weiss, Sir Eric	Foseco
Wilson, Geoffrey	Amalgamated Investment Properties
Wingate, Harold	Chesterfield Properties
Wingate, Maurice	Wingate Investments
Wohl, Maurice	United Real Properties
Wolff, Gustaf	Harland & Wolff
	Belfast Ropemakers
Wolfson, Lord David	Experian
Wolfson, Sir Isaac	GUS
Wolfson, Lord Leonard	GUS
Wolfson, Lord Simon	Next
Worms, Fred	Tudor Accessories

Yablon, Ralph	Town & Commercial
Yarrow, Alfred	Yarrow & Co.
Young, Lord David	Eldonwall
Zakay, Eddie and Sol	Topland Group
Zelker, Raymond	Polly Peck
Ziff, Arnold	Town Centre Securities
Ziff, Fanny	Stylo
Zilkha, Selim	Mothercare

Appendix B

Jewish Property Companies

Chairman		Former Occupation	Company
Bernard	Elliott		Chelsfield Partners
Bernstein	William	Furrier	Fortress Property
Blausten	Cyril	Estate agent	Simo Properties
Blausten	Leonard	Estate agent	Simo Properties
Bloch	Sidney	Solicitor	Hallmark Securities
Bloomfield	Instone	Property dealer	Oddeninos Properties
Bradman	Godfrey	Accountant	European Land
Clore	Charles	General dealer	City & Centre Properties
Cohen	John		Rodwell Group
Cohen	Lord	Estate agent	Atlas Homes
Colman	Alec	Estate agent	E. Alec Colman Investments
Conrad	Neville	Estate agent	Conrad Ritblat
Corob	Sidney		Corob Holdings
Cotton	Jack	Estate agent	City Centre Properties
Cowan	Sidney	Housebuilder	Samuel Properties
Davidson	Manny		Asda Property Holdings
Dellal	Jack	Banker	Allied Commercial
East	Barry	Estate agent	Town & City Properties
Erdman	Edward	Estate agent	Edward Erdman
Feldman	Heinrich		Inremco
Fenston	Felix	Estate agent	Metropolitan & Provincial Properties

Fox	Cecil	Tailor	Stem Properties
Freedman	Louis	Estate agent	Ravenseft
Freshwater	Osias	Estate agent	Freshwater Group
Gabbay	David		O & H Holdings
Garrard	Sir David	Estate agent	Minerva
Gold	Joe	Estate agent	Centrovincial Estates
Goldschlager	Laurent	Banker	Thames Estates
Hammerson	Lew	Mackintosh maker	Hammerson Properties
Harris	Bob	Furrier	Harris & Co.
Harris	Harry	Furrier	Harris & Co.
Harrison	Gabriel	Housebuilder	Amalgamated Investments
Hyams	Harry	Estate agent	Oldham Estate
Hyams	Phillip	Cinema owner	
Hyams	Sidney	Cinema owner	
Joseph	Maxwell	Estate agent	Union Property
Kirschel	Laurence		Consolidated Developments
Khalili	Nasser	Antique dealer	Flavermead
Leaver	Marcus	Estate agent	Allied Land
Lee	Arnold	Solicitor	Imry Properties
Leigh	Kennedy	Merchant	Kennedy Leigh
Levy	Joe	Estate agent	Stock Conversion
Lewis	Cecil	Estate agent	Burlington Estates
Lewis	Philip	Surveyor	Lambert, Smith, Hampton
Lipton	Stuart	Estate agent	Chelsfield Partners
Littman	Joe	Furrier	Aldford House
Lottenberg	Jacob	Silk merchant	Lynton Holdings
Luck	Laurence	Estate agent	Charterbridge Corporation

Manousso	Luke	Estate agent	Maybrook Properties
Messer	Sam	Estate agent	Mansion House Ch.
Miller	Eric	Estate agent	Peachey
Morrison	Jack	Retailer	Amalgamated Securities
Myers	Bernard	Tailor	Rodwell Group
Myers	Sefton	Estate agent	Rodwell Group
Oppenheim	Henry	Property owner	City Wall Properties
Oppenheim	Meyer	Furniture manufacturer	Argyle Securities
Pearl	David		Structadene
Pearlberg	Beatrice	Dentist	Ve-ri-best Man
Pears	Bernard		William Pears Group
Potel	Robert	Solicitor	Star (Greater London)
Rayne	Max	Coat manufacturer	London Merchant Securities
Ritblat	John		British Land
Ronson	Gerald	Furniture maker	Heron Holdings
Rose	Jack	Estate agent	Land Investors
Rose	Philip	Estate agent	Land Investors
Rosenfeld	Andrew	Estate agent	Minerva
Rubens	John	Accountant	Central & District Properties
Samuel	Basil	Estate agent	Great Portland Estate
Samuel	Dudley	Estate agent	Dudley, Samuel & Harrison
Samuel	Harold	Estate agent	Land Securities
Samuel	Howard	Estate agent	Great Portland Estates
Sebba	Sam	Solicitor	Warnford Investments
Sherman	Archie	Estate agent	Metrovincial Properties
Shine	Barnett	Skirt manufacturer	Central & District Properties
Spiro	Moss	Solicitor	Fly Over Investments

Sputz	Otto	Engineer	Parway Land
Stern	William		Stern Group of Companies
Tchenguiz	Robert and Vincent		Rotch Property
Tobin	Leonard	Solicitor	Lintang
Walton	Issy	Property dealer	Scottish Metropolitan Properties
Wilson	Geoffrey		Amalgamated Investment Properties
Wimbourne	Ivor	Solicitor	Somerlee
Wingate	Harold	Chemist	Chesterfield Properties
Wingate	Maurice	Property dealer	Wingate Investments
Wohl	Maurice	Property owner	United Real Properties
Yablon	Ralph	Solicitor	Town & Commercial
Young	David	Solicitor	Eldonwall
Zakay	Eddie and Sol		Topland
Ziff	Arnold	Shoe shops	Town Centre Securities

Thirty-two estate agents; nine solicitors; five property dealers; four clothes manufacturers; three furriers and retailers; two accountants, bankers, builders and tailors; one chemist, cinema owner, dentist, engineer, general dealer, furniture manufacturer, merchant and surveyor.

Primary source: Oliver Marriott, *The Property Boom* (London: Hamish Hamilton, 1967).

Bibliography

Andrew, Christopher, *The Defence of the Realm* (Harmondsworth: Penguin, 2009).

Aris, Stephen, *The Jews in Business* (Harmondsworth: Pelican, 1970).

Bird, Peter, *The First Food Empire: A History of J. Lyons & Co.* (Chichester: Phillimore, 2000).

Bookbinder, Paul, *Simon Marks, Retail Revolutionary* (London: Weidenfeld and Nicholson, 1993).

Cannon, John (ed.), *The Oxford Companion to British History* (Oxford: Oxford University Press, 2002).

Clapham, Sir John, *History of the Bank of England* (Cambridge: Cambridge University Press, 1944).

Elzas, Rabbi Dr Barnett, 'Joseph Salvador', *Boston News and Courier*, 1903.

Faber, Eli, *Jews, Slaves and the Slave Trade* (New York: New York University Press, 1998).

Falk, Bernard, *Bouquets for Fleet Street* (London: Hutchinson, 1951).

Ferguson, Niall, *The World's Banker: The House of Rothschild* (London: Weidenfeld and Nicolson, 1998).

Ferguson, Niall, *High Financier: The Lives and Time of Siegmund Warburg* (Harmondsworth: Allen Lane, 2010).

Horner, Arthur, *Incorrigible Rebel* (London: McGibbon and Kee, 1960).

Jamilly, Edward, *Patrons, Clients, Designers and Developers: The Jewish Contribution to Secular Building in England*, Proceedings of the Jewish Historical Society of England, 38 (September 2003).

Levenson, Thomas, *Newton and the Counterfeiter* (London: Faber and Faber, 2009).

Loebel, Herbert, 'Refugees from the Third Reich and Industry in the Depressed Areas of Britain', in *Second Chance. Two Centuries of*

Geman-speaking Jews in the United Kingdom, ed. Werner Mosse (Tübingen: J.C.B. Mohr, 1991).

Marriott, Oliver, *The Property Boom* (London: Hamish Hamilton, 1967).

Patten, Chris, *Not Quite the Diplomat. Home Truths about World Affairs* (Harmondsworth: Penguin, 2005).

Peck, Helen, Moira Clark, Adrian Payne and Martin Christopher, *Relationship Marketing: Strategy and Implementation* (Oxford: Butterworth-Heinemann, 1999).

Pollins, Harold, *Economic History of the Jews of England* (London and Toronto: Fairleigh Dickinson University Press, 1982).

Samuel, Edgar, *At the End of the Earth: Essays on the History of the Jews of England and Portugal* (London: Jewish Historical Society of England, 2004).

Scott, Peter, 'Mr Drage, Mr Everyman, and the Creation of a Mass Market for Domestic Furniture in Interwar Britain', *The Economic History Review*, 62, No.4 (November 2009), pp.802–27.

Selbourne, David, *Moral Evasion* (London: Centre for Policy Studies, 1998).

Simpson, John, *Unreliable Sources: How the Twentieth Century Was Reported* (Basingstoke: Macmillan, 2010).

Soester, Juliette, 'The Gaumont State Cinema' (London: Willesden Local History Society, September 2000).

Stein, Sarah Abreyava, *Plumes: Ostrich Feathers, Jews and a Lost World of Global Commerce* (New Haven, CT: Yale University Press, 2008).

Sutherland, Lucy Stuart, 'Samson Gideon; 18th Century Jewish Financier', *Jewish Historical Society of England*, 17 (1951/52).

Swann, June, *Shoemaking*, Shire Album.

Taylor, Derek, *British Chief Rabbis: 1664–2006* (London and Portland, OR: Vallentine Mitchell, 2007).

Taylor, Derek, *Don Pacifico: The Acceptable Face of Gunboat Diplomacy* (London and Portland, OR: Vallentine Mitchell, 2008).

Wechsberg, Joseph, *The Merchant Bankers* (London: Weidenfeld and Nicolson, (1966)

Index